In the Land of Invisible Women

A Female Doctor's Journey in the Saudi Kingdom

Qanta A. Ahmed, MD

SOURCEBOOKS, INC.
NAPERVILLE, ILLINOIS

Published by Sourcebooks, Inc.
P.O. Box 4410, Naperville, Illinois 60567-4410
(630) 961-3900
Fax: (630) 961-2168
www.sourcebooks.com

Library of Congress Cataloging-in-Publication Data

Ahmed, Qanta.
  In the land of invisible women : a female doctor's journey in the Saudi Kingdom /
Qanta A. Ahmed.
      p. cm.
  Includes bibliographical references.
  1. Ahmed, Qanta. 2. Women physicians—Islamic countries—Biography. 3. Women
in medicine—Islamic countries—Biography. 4. Muslim physicians—Islamic coun-
tries—Biography. I. Title.
  R692.A346 2008
  610.82092—dc22
  [B]

                              2008009548

          Printed and bound in the United States of America.
                          VP 19 18

For my parents, who gave me my Islam and my love of words.
And for Joan Kirschenbaum Cohn, who shows me how to live,
as a better woman, as a better Muslim.

CONTENTS

THE BEDOUIN BEDSIDE

SEEKING RESPITE FROM THE INTENSITY of medicine, I trained my eye on the world without. Already, the midmorning heat rippled with fury, as sprinklers scattered wet jewels onto sunburned grass. Fluttering petals waved in the Shamaal wind, strongest this time of day.

In a pool of shade cast by a hedge, a laborer sought shelter from the sun. An awkward bundle of desiccated limbs, the Bengali lunched from a tiffin. His shemagh cloth was piled into a sodden turban, meager relief from the high heat. Beyond, a hundred-thousand-dollar Benz growled, tearing up a dust storm in its steely wake. Behind my mask, I smiled at my reflection. Suspended between plate glass, a woman in a white coat gazed back. Externally, I was unchanged from the doctor I had been in New York City, yet now everything was different.

I returned to Khalaa al-Otaibi, my first patient in the Kingdom. She was a Bedouin Saudi well into her seventies, though no one could be sure of her age (female births were not certified in Saudi Arabia when she had been born). She was on a respirator for a pneumonia which had been slow to resolve. Comatose, she was oblivious to my studying gaze. A colleague prepared her for the placement of a central line (a major intravenous line into a deep vein).

Her torso was uncovered in preparation. Another physician sterilized the berry-brown skin with swathes of iodine. A mundane procedure I had performed countless times, in Saudi Arabia it made for a startling scene. I looked up from the sterilized field which was quickly submerging the Bedouin body under a disposable sea of blue. Her face remained enshrouded in a black scarf, as if she was out in a market scurrying through a crowd of loitering men. I was astounded.

The scraggy veil concealed her every feature. From the midst of a black nylon well sinking into an edentulous mouth, plastic tubes snaked up and away from her purdah (the Islamic custom of concealing female beauty). One tube connected her ventilator securely into her lungs, and the other delivered feed to her belly. Now and again, the veil-and-tubing ensemble shuddered, sometimes with a sigh, sometimes with a cough. Each rasp reminded me that underneath this mask was a critically ill patient. Through the black nylon I could just discern protective eye patches placed over her closed eyelids. Gently, the nurse lifted the corner of the veil to allow the physician to finish cleansing. In my fascination, I had forgotten all about the procedure.

From the depths of this black nylon limpness, a larger corrugated plastic tube emerged, the main ventilator circuit. It snaked her breaths away, swishing, swinging, with each machine-made respiration. Without a face at the end of the airway, the tubing disappeared into a void, as though ventilating a veil and not a woman. Even when critically ill, I learned, hiding her face was of paramount importance. I watched, entranced at the clash of technology and religion, my religion, *some version* of my religion. I heard an agitated rustling from close by.

Behind the curtain, a family member hovered, the dutiful son. Intermittently, he peered in at us. He was obviously worrying, I decided, as I watched his slim brown fingers rapidly manipulating a rosary. He was probably concerned about the insertion of the central line, I thought, just like any other caring relative.

Every now and again, he burst into vigorous rapid Arabic, instructing the nurse. I wondered what he was asking about. Everything was going smoothly; in fact, soon the jugular would be cannulated. We were almost finished. What could be troubling him?

Through my dullness, eventually, I noticed a clue. Each time the physician's sleeve touched the patient's veil, and the veil slipped, the son burst out in a flurry of anxiety. Perhaps all of nineteen, the son was demanding the nurse cover the patient's face, all the while painfully averting his uninitiated gaze away from his mother's fully exposed torso, revealing possibly the first breasts he may have seen.

Each staccato command was accompanied by the soggy mumblings of Arabic emerging from behind the physician's mask, asking the nurse to follow suit and fix the veil. The physician sounded unconcerned, yet the son was suspended in an agonizing web of discomfort. He paced in anxiety about his mother's health, anxiety about her dignity, and anxiety about her responsibilities to God. The critically ill, veiled face and her bared breasts, pendulous with age, posed an incredible sight. I was as bewildered as the Saudi son.

I gazed at the patient, completely exposed, except for her veiled face, and her fragile son supervising (why not a daughter, I thought). The veiling, even when her face slept, deeply comatose from sedation, was disturbing. Surely God would not require such extreme lengths to conceal her features from her doctors who needed to inspect her body? Did an unconscious sickly Muslim have the same responsibilities as a conscious, able-bodied one? Although a Muslim woman myself, I had never faced such questions before. My debate was internal and solitary; those around me were quite clear of their obligations. The patient was a woman and needed to be veiled. The physician was instructing the Filipina nurse throughout to comply with the son's concerns. The Filipina was obviously inured to the whole spectacle. The son knew his duties to his mother. Only I remained locked in confusion.

I studied her more closely, trying to understand more. Thin arms lay flaccid at the side of her supine body, palms upwards, pools of lax flesh puddling under feeble triceps. She seemed very short, perhaps four and a half feet tall at most. On each palm, in the center, I could see bluish stigmata. These were the dark, circular marks of tribal tattoos. The nurse removed the veil to attend to the airway, suctioning out the frothing saliva which had collected in the last half hour.

Now that the limp black nylon was lifted, I could finally see Mrs. al-Otaibi. Her weathered, leathery face was in pain. Congealed tears streaked from under the taped eyelids. I called to the nurse for some pain relief, following the silent tears as they wound to her receding jaw. They pooled into deep wells in a face made ancient by sun-lashed desert winds. Proud cheek bones climbed high above hollows where her teeth should have been. Her chin met in a defiant point, conferring a determined, dour look. I wondered what she was like when awake.

Her facial markings belied a woman of status. Now I could see complicated blue tattoos in cross-like formation. They centered on the exact middle of her cheeks, much like marks delineating fields of radiation in a cancer patient, but bigger. She had similar marks on her brow, centrally placed above her balding eyebrows, perfectly symmetrical. All this painful decoration only to remain concealed behind a veil? Wondering what the marks could mean, I asked my Arab colleagues. She turned out to be a senior elder in her tribe, the tattoos on her face defining her rank, they explained, already bored by my curiosity. Obviously, they had seen many such tattooed Bedouin women. To them there was nothing remarkable about Mrs. al-Otaibi.

Small brown hands were clenched in a sleeping fist. I unpeeled them and looked at the stubby, anemic, orange-tipped nails. This color I knew to be henna. I looked at my own hands grasping hers, my glossy, noired nails contrasting against her orange manicure. Mine were Western, hers Eastern, so different but both seeking the same folly: to change the color of our nails.

I smiled in silence at the first similarity I could draw between us. Saudi Bedouin women would wear this cosmetic coloring often, placing a viscid blob of the dark green henna in the palm of their hand and then holding it tight in a fist, burying the tips of their nails into the pool of thick dye. The women would often sleep like this, securing their hands with string, to wake later with orange-tipped fingernails. This is what Mrs. al-Otaibi must have done, some weeks earlier, when she had been well. I looked up at her straggly, sweaty hair and saw the streaks of henna there too, slowly losing the battle against a burgeoning mass of white roots.

On her rotund belly, several inexplicable scars, small, puckered, and paler than the surrounding skin, peppered the surface. They were evenly distributed over the right upper quadrant of her abdomen. They were in the wrong place for laparoscopic surgery but I knew of no other tool that left such marks. I looked up at my colleague, puzzled.

"She went to the shaman, the Bedou healer. They all do that. We often see these marks on our liver patients." He went on, "The shaman uses a branding iron to treat pain which the patient probably had months ago."

Later I would observe that many patients carried these same marks, often seeking relief from the pain of enlarging, inflamed livers. Hepatitis is common in Saudi Arabia and indeed my new workplace, the King Fahad National Guard Hospital in Riyadh, was a center of excellence for treating liver disease. There we saw hundreds of patients with liver failure. The poorer patients had avoided the many public health centers in the Kingdom, instead choosing traditional healers; by the time they came to us, their diseases were often too advanced.

So, in the midst of the familiar, shiny, high-tech intensive care environment in which I was so at home, I encountered the unfamiliar. I was deeply perplexed by the active ancient practices which this woman's body disclosed. Even more disturbing, what role did shaman and other pagan healers have in a world which subscribed to Islam, a religion which enshrines the advancement of knowledge?

I wondered about the lengths to which the son continued to veil his mother, even when she was gravely ill. Couldn't he see it was the least important thing for her now at this time, when her life could ebb away at any point? Didn't he know God was merciful, tolerant, and understanding, and would never quibble over the wearing of a veil in such circumstances or, I doubted, any circumstances?

Somehow I assumed the veil was mandated by the son, but perhaps I was wrong about that too. Already, I was finding myself wildly ignorant in this country. Perhaps the patient herself would be furious if her modesty was unveiled when she was powerless to resist. Nothing was clear to me other than veiling was essential, inescapable, even for a dying woman. This was the way of the new world in which I was now confined. For now, and the next two years, I would see many things I couldn't understand. Even though I was a Muslim, here I found myself a stranger in the Kingdom.

Chapter
Two

A Time to Leave America

I RECALLED THE COLD NIGHT of my departure only a few weeks earlier. Black rain glistened on liquid streets. Squinting between raindrops, I peered into the red river of brake lights. A blurred boa of traffic oozed ahead. I motored onto the Belt for a final time. A grim weight bore downward upon me, grinding me deeper into the creaking leather seat. Would I ever again call this country home? My flight to Riyadh, the capital of Saudi Arabia, would depart Kennedy at nine. My recent past rushed by in the rearview mirror of a migrant's regret. It was time to leave America.

Denied visa renewal, the magic spell of my U.S. immigration was at an end. After a final appeal to revert my status had failed, I had decided to take my medical credentials to the Middle East where U.S. medicine was widely practiced. It had been a spur of the moment decision and with it I became once more an outcast in motion.

During my years in New York City, I had completed a residency and fellowship, gaining certifications in internal medicine, pulmonary disease, and critical care medicine. I had also finished a fellowship in sleep disorders medicine in which I would also soon be certified. My short years here had been productive, and within a few weeks of learning I could not stay in the U.S. any longer, I had been head hunted by a hospital in Saudi Arabia. After allaying my initial hesitations, I had accepted the job, lured by free accommodation and a fat salary. As a Muslim woman, I believed myself well-acquainted with the ways of an Islamic Kingdom, feeling no apprehension about life in Saudi Arabia. I dismissed the cautions of concerned friends at my sudden decision and thought no more of it.

Accelerating the silent Lexus, wipers beat metronomically to my sorrow. I wondered when I would next be at the wheel of a car. I knew already that it is illegal for a woman to drive in Saudi Arabia. In Riyadh, I would be licensed to operate procedures on critically ill patients, yet never to drive a motor vehicle. Only men could enjoy that privilege.

I felt the car purring under me as I drove myself to the airport. I already missed the primal thrill of pedal and power, the visceral surge uniting me with machine. Soon my car keys would be gone. Atlantic winds ruffled my thick hair, caressing ripples of my femininity. Soon my hair would be covered, banishing such playful breezes. Legislation would stipulate my head be veiled in the Kingdom. Everything would be different.

I return in my memory to the rainy surroundings. Arriving at Kennedy, the airport was empty. These were the halcyon, forever-lost days before 9/11. Check-in was completed in minutes. The contents of my apartment were to remain in storage in New York, a casual decision. My car was to be retrieved by a friend who would keep it for me until my return. Intuitively, I knew I was embarking on a stage of transience.

"What's a year?" I remembered thinking to myself, as I had signed the contract recklessly, flicking through pages, ignoring bold capitals announcing the death penalty. In a thoughtless flourish I found myself now subject to the laws of Saudi Arabia, decapitation included.

I waited alone at the gate, making calls on a dying cell phone. I kept up a banter fueled on bravado, while I studied the passengers gathering for my flight.

My prior sightings of Saudis had been rare, clusters of them at the Cleveland Clinic awaiting consultation, a sprinkling of Saudi figures bustling at the Dior counter in Harrods, and the odd exotic Saudi traveler connecting at Heathrow. Tonight there were dozens of them. Everywhere I looked, Saudi men and women were seated apart, cordoned by invisible barriers. I caught some murmuring Arabic. A knot of Saudis caught my eye. I watched.

Squadrons of Saudis condensed around symmetrical lines in a precise, invisible geometry known only to them. They aligned themselves in sharp rows towards the tarmac, facing the nighttime Atlantic. It was time for Isha prayers, the final evening prayer which Muslims observe after sunset. Watching them pray made me uncomfortable, reminding me of the many prayers I failed to observe myself, but still I found myself entranced by the scene. Around me, in the airport lounge, a veritable Masjid (mosque) was in session. The Saudis prayed for twenty minutes. I couldn't stop watching them, though no one else seemed remotely interested.

As they prostrated to God, I wondered how the men's head-dresses stayed put as they touched foreheads to the ground. Each time, I waited to see if the checkered red and white coverings would fall. What could be securing the cloth underneath? The women were blending into one another. Against plate-glassed night, they were a mass of black bundles, their silhouettes invisible. I paid barely any attention to these Saudi women. I had already forgotten that in a few hours, I would be joining their ranks. For now, my eye was drawn to the elegantly robed men.

I was puzzled. This was no scene from my New York City life. Until now, these robed and veiled worshippers had been concealed from me here. I had been at airports countless times in this city, yet until now these Saudis had been invisible. Feeling exposed by their conspicuous piety, I glanced nervously at my own attire for the journey. I hoped I was properly dressed to enter the Kingdom. Saudi Arabia is an Islamic Kingdom, governed by Islamic Sharia law (The Holy Law of God).[1] Saudi Arabia is also a revered holy land for all Muslims, and most notably, guardian and home to Mecca, the spiritual and historical epicenter of Islam. As a Muslim woman myself, I wanted to respect the ways of the Kingdom. I certainly didn't want to offend.

The flight was announced. Shuffling and rambling, the Saudis rolled towards the gate. I was one of a handful of Westerners on the flight. Very few passengers were like me, single, female, "non-Saudi"—a phrase which would define me from now on. Glancing at the heavy veils surrounding me, I doubted any other women on the flight were Westernized, moderate Muslims like me.

I downed the cold remains of a final Starbucks, spellbound, watching black bundles of women tumbling down the gangway. I switched off the cell phone. I was now completely disconnected. America was hurtling into my nascent past.

At the gate, a Saudi stewardess beckoned me eastward. A hybrid hat with attached veil covered some hair while revealing most of

---

[1] Sharia Law was originally derived from multiple schools of legal thought interpreting Divine Law originally codified in the Quran. In the first few centuries of Islam over thirty schools of legal thought existed and originally the Sharia was diverse and pluralistic. Some of this rich diversity has been lost over time, particularly in the modern era of resurging orthodoxy. Sharia literally means "The Way" and refers to the body of Islamic Law codified by the Quran and teachings referred to as hadith and sunna which recount the Prophet's sayings and actions respectively. Reference: *The Great Theft*, by Professor Khaled Abou El Fadl. In, "Introduction: Islam Torn Between Extremism and Moderation," page 23.

her creamy, unlined neck. I could hear her speaking to passengers in rugged, near-Germanic tones of what I was soon to learn to be Saudi Arabic. Every clipped, guttural sound came from deep within a bottomless, muscular pharynx.

"Good evening madam," she enunciated precisely. "Boarding for Riyadh tonight?" I nodded an ambivalent yes.

"This way to the Saudia flight, madam. Enjoy your journey." She waved elegantly toward the gangway. Fellow travelers scurried by, hurrying on board with their children, packages, and carry-ons all in tow. Gathering up my fast-dissipating courage, I began to follow the others.

My journey had begun.

I settled back into the seat, girding the seat belt a little tighter. We waited to taxi away from America when a disembodied voice began to pray.

"Bismillah Walhmadu lillah, subhan'al-lathee sakh hara lana hadha wama kunna lahu muqrineen wainn a ila rabbina lamunqal-iboon..."

"In the Name of Allah and all Praise is for Allah! How perfect is He, the One who has placed this transport at our service and we ourselves would not be capable of that and to our Lord is our final destiny."

The pilot was reciting the special Muslim prayer dedicated for travelers about to embark on a journey. The amplified, melodious tones of classical Arabic startled me. I stared stupidly at the PA speakers. Soon, I sank into the calligraphic cocoon they were broadcasting. Invisible verses from the Quran wove a soft gauze of security around me. I found myself relaxing. This was already a different journey. Until now, these had been prayers that I had only heard uttered by my father. Islam was growing in dimensions; what had been limited to the privacy of my small family was becoming very public indeed.

I was constantly reminded of my religion during that first journey to Arabia. By climbing into this plane, I had tumbled head-first into the whale-belly of Islam. In the center of the cabin there was a big screen, normally for showing in-flight movies. Instead, it showed a motionless plane-shaped silhouette impaled on a white arrow. The image never changed. The arrow pointed to the direction of Mecca, the spiritual anchor for all Muslims. Muslims call this direction the *Qibla*. I found myself staring at it. I felt drawn.

Sleep deserted me. To relieve monotony, I watched other travelers. The gangway bustled with busy passengers even at thirty-five thousand feet. On board, numerous clearings had been established by the removal of rows of seats. Appearing every ten rows or so, even in the economy section, private alcoves allowed passengers to pray during the flight. I saw only men seeking out these semi-public sections to observe prayer, their wives preferring to remain semi-prostrate in their seats performing abbreviated travelers' prayers.[2] Throughout the night, Saudi men walked up and down the aisle, hands dripping fresh water from their ablutions (required before prayer), velvet prayer mats casually tossed over their tall, surprisingly broad shoulders, as they made their way to the alcoves. From my aisle seat I could anticipate their passages; breezing by, each man trailed the sharp but pleasing fragrance of the Saudia flight cologne freshly applied from their preparations in the restroom. (Aware that fragrance is recommended for men in Islam, the airline had thoughtfully provided ample supplies for liberal use.) In their right hands, rosaries revolved in time with silent prayer. I watched them for a long time, unable to sleep and unwilling to pray.

From time to time, I pulled out the copy of *Fortune* I had grabbed minutes before boarding. The cover that month portrayed

---

[2] In Islam, travel is regarded as a hardship for Muslims and therefore the five daily mandatory prayers are ascribed shorter duration to ease the difficulties borne by the traveling Muslim.

a Saudi billionaire, appropriate reading for my journey, I thought. I began to learn about Prince al-Waleed Bin Talal.[3] He was photographed in his Saudi robes, and when I looked up, distracted by wafts of cologne which followed the Saudi men rustling by, I could see no difference between the prince and these passengers. This ancient dress seemed to contain a message of equality. I devoured the article and tried hard to remember the prince's name. I was hungry for any knowledge about the country I was now making home.

Silent apprehension took firm root. I was worried about everything, most acutely about my appearance. Only hours away from arrival, I considered my outfit: loose-fitting, beige slacks, a turtleneck, and a gray, long-sleeved cardigan, complete with hood. In my desire not to draw attention to myself, I had already donned the camouflage of desert colors. I sought reassurance from the stewardess.

"How do I look? Am I dressed properly? I am worried because I don't have an abbayah[4] for when I land. I know all women in the Kingdom have to wear one. Will I have any problems in the airport?" I sounded as though I was babbling.

"You are dressed perfectly," she said warmly. She had to be lying, I decided. My cardigan seemed short to me. I should know; I was a dues-paying Muslim. I knew my hips were showing, noisily announcing my sex. I wished I had something to engulf my debilitating gender. I almost wished I was a man.

---

[3] A nephew of the current monarch King Abdullah of Saudi Arabia and grandson to the original founder of Saudi Arabia, King Abdul Aziz al-Saud, Prince al-Waleed, often known colloquially as "Waleed," is renowned as a progressive agent of reform, most notably promoting women's rights throughout the Kingdom.

[4] Abbayah means veil. Every woman, western or non-western, Muslim or not, is required by law to wear an abbayah over her clothing whenever in public. These garments are full length and include a head scarf to cover all hair. In Saudi Arabia they are almost always black in color.

"The King Khalid Airport is an international area," she went on. She seemed to be addressing everyone within earshot, oblivious to my mounting anxieties. "You won't need an abbayah in there. When you arrive at your destination, ladies will help you find one." She silenced me with a final, firm smile.

An hour after crossing into Saudi airspace, we had landed in Riyadh. I looked out of the porthole. For a long time I stared through the window while the rest of the plane stirred into action. Outside in the late night an oceanic panorama of starlit sand stretched for miles. "Nevada!" was my first conscious thought. For miles in every direction the barren landscape was desolate, utterly flat. I felt the sudden tug of quiet intrigue. This was going to be an adventure.

Deplaning through the covered gangway, I stepped beyond the vanishing point of twelve hours earlier. The heat of the night seeped under my cuffs, sinking its lazy weight under my clothing. Even though this was two a.m. in late November, I was already too warm in light woolens. At the mouth of the dim gangway, disheveled passengers spilled out into the blazing lights of a world made glossy with black gold.

Trembling with a mixture of fear and fascination, like the quivering bride of an arranged marriage, I stole a virginal view of Saudi Arabia. Blinking in the harsh lights, I glanced overhead. A giant Raymond Weil clock marked time. I could first hear and then later see the tinkling cascades of marble fountains, spilling precious water, here more costly per liter than petroleum. My eyes, gritty with fatigue, rested gratefully on interior gardens. Underfoot, my shoes resonated on marble floors gleaming with geometric designs. Travertine parquetry rippled away from each footstep in soft shades of gray and white, beige and sand. Chrome and glass divided the massive, marble space into wide stairways, giant atria, and immigration control. The marble scene was refreshing. No unsmiling, visored limo drivers, with hand-held signs and curlicue ear pieces, no Haitian cabbies touting for rides here. I was a world away from the pent fury of Kennedy. I felt suddenly remote.

Argumentative Arabic wrenched me from the scene. I coiled with tension. For a moment, Saudi soldiers, armed and red-bereted, flanked me. I stood right next to them, close enough to see their ripe stubble pushing through on chiseled jaws, but they seemed not to see me. They were dark-eyed and handsome. Their voices rose to a crescendo of purpose and strain, but I understood nothing. They searched for a face. Finally, a cry of recognition, a flurry of melodramatic salaams, and they had moved ahead. They were the security detail for a dignitary, apparently aboard the same plane. Whisking the influential bundle of red and white cloth away, they took their animated aura of accents with them.

I descended stairs toward passport control. Ahead to both the left and the right were huge lines of impoverished Bengali men arriving to take up menial laboring jobs. They stared at all women. Being the lone, unveiled, nonwhite face at the airport, they stared at me unflinchingly. Already I was maddened by the scrutiny. I covered my head with the hood of my sweater. The spear-like focus of the staring men, enclosing me with their collective gaze, was deflected. Like a child, if I couldn't see them, they couldn't see me. I felt better inside my "veil."

Other lines were made entirely of women. The segregation had begun. I noticed Filipina women, maids or nannies arriving for their Saudi employers. They looked poor, none wearing jewelry or makeup, so unlike the designer-clad, Gucci-brandishing Filipinas in New York City. I selected the least intimidating lane: the one with the most Western women in it.

I could see I wasn't the only one concealing myself. Others were already wearing their crumpled up abbayahs, hurriedly yanked out of carry-on luggage, scruffy Nikes peeping out from under askew hems. They had obviously been to the Kingdom before, probably returning home after a vacation away. Not only Westerners rushed to dress themselves before disembarking, but Saudi women, too, veiled more fully. One Saudi woman, caught unprepared, waited patiently in line under the airplane blanket that she had draped, chadhur-like, over her expensively colored hair and her sleeping, cherubic prize, a Saudi son.

I studied the Western women in my queue. Many were nurses at neighboring hospitals, Irish, English, white South African women. Not the least perturbed by the staring, they reassured me with the smug luxury of the veteran. I envied their confidence and huddled a little closer.

At last, my turn. An impeccably coiffed Saudi soldier scrutinized my passport. I glanced around to see if anyone from my hospital had appeared. I also knew that as an unmarried female employee in Saudi Arabia, I could not enter the country without my "sponsor" (a representative from my employer) receiving me and handling my papers through passport control. If no one arrived, I would be held at the airport.

As I wondered who would be sent to meet me, I looked on at hundreds of Malaysian Muslim women quietly squatting on the marble floor by a silenced baggage carousel. All were fully veiled. Even buried in material, each emanated resignation, defeat. They huddled, eyes downcast, silently awaiting their employers. I heard no laughter, no muted chit-chat. Piled like the uncollected baggage around them, they were silent and inanimate. Yet their inertia was much more than just the pounding fatigue of jet lag; these were women stripped of hope.

Even the security of my medical skills could not change the fact that doctor or domestic, Muslim or not, an unmarried woman cannot enter Saudi Arabia alone. Without a sponsor, without husband or father, without son or brother, I would wait as a maid would wait, *with* cargo, *like* cargo, until collected. Women cannot function as independent entities in the Kingdom. My autonomy had already been curtailed.

I was waved beyond the immigration line to the Perspex counter. The soldier at passport control offered no smile. He did not welcome me to his country. He did not greet me as a Muslim, even though my last name gave me away as one. In fact, he did not greet me at all. Supercilious, he busied himself reviewing my papers. Following his lead, I didn't engage in small talk either. We made no eye contact. Intuitively I already knew the ways of the Kingdom. With a dismissive wave, he signaled me gone, tossing my passport onto a distant counter. The gold insignia of Her Majesty's Crown lay marooned in an eddy of crumpled-up, handwritten Arabic notes. The sharp taste of nostalgia for my English childhood rose suddenly to my throat. Out of habit, I went to grab my passport anyway. Instead, a hulking figure expertly corralled it, snatching it away from me.

I looked up to see a huge man. He returned my gaze with open distaste. This was Umair, my sponsor. Under his male authority, I could now leave passport control and enter the Kingdom. Umair was my "meet and greet" manifestation of my employer. Intimidated, I felt myself shrink in his male shadow. A bulky, tall Saudi, Umair was dressed in a white thobe[5] punctuated with a recurring filigree of tobacco-stains; a batik of spit. Ancient sandals made almost of camel-hide (they seemed so thick) completed the ensemble, exposing fat, cracked heels. On his head, he wore a red and white checked headdress (the shemagh) that sorely needed

---

[5] A thobe is a loose fitting long sleeved ankle length garment worn by Saudi men. Usually white in color except for brief months in winter when it may be made of darker cloth (brown, black, or navy). Summer heat means the white thobes are usually made of fine cotton. Sleeves can be cuffed or simply loose. The neckline can be collared, in which case it is usually worn buttoned up, or round necked and worn unbuttoned.

pressing. Though dressed in the identical uniform of the Saudi national dress, he wasn't as refined as the Saudi I had been studying on the cover of *Fortune*.

Though meeting me (meeting my passport, more specifically) he failed to greet me. We communicated in sign language, as he spoke no English and my Arabic consisted only of prayers. Stupidly, I still made vain gestures to recover my passport but he retained it tightly in his leonine fist. Irritated, with flabby nicotine-stained fingers, he motioned to me to retrieve my heavy luggage, while he languished, supporting his considerable bulk against a railing. He struggled to coax his fat hand into a seamless pocket, finally retrieving a badly squashed packet of Marlboros. He made no move to help, preferring to watch in unrestrained boredom, scratching his belly from time to time.

The baggage carousel continued to circulate cases which no one rushed to claim. The Malaysian maids remained motionless, leaning against the crawling belt. I lugged my enormous bags off the carousel by myself, surrounded by male onlookers. No man came to my assistance, neither porter nor passenger.

At last, X-raying the bags after baggage claim to ensure I was not bringing anything illegal into the Kingdom, I was allowed to leave the terminal. I sighed with relief. The conspicuous authority in the airport made me uneasy and I felt anxious to get away. I stepped into the November night. A westward desert breeze caressed my face. Without the requisite black abbayah, I was patently out of place. Already I could see Riyadh wore more black than even New York City.

I bundled myself into the hospital van. The windows were blacked out, a cheap film peeled over the panes trapping both air bubbles and me behind a purple haze. Many of the vehicles I would ride in from now on would be themselves a veil, leaving me wondering of the real color of the world outside.

Umair loaded the luggage into the car and started the drive to my new home. The immaculate road leaving the airport stretched for several miles. It was perfectly straight, no need for the mad curves and tight angles of London or New York. Traffic was surprisingly heavy so late in the night. Everyone was driving very fast, as though hurtling to an imminent death. On either side, tumbleweed and desert bushes fell away to interminable sand, an earthbound Sea of Tranquility on a nocturnal moonscape. The only movement, a voiceless ripple of breeze through sand, was soon blurred by our own ridiculous velocity along the roadway.

We entered an arterial highway into the city. Globalization had reached even here. Within minutes, I spied the first signs announcing American pop culture was for sale in Riyadh. Briefly thrilled that my childhood Arabic was good enough to read the signs myself, I started reading the names aloud. Thirty feet in the air, in jarring fluorescence, a sign screamed "Taco Bell" in Arabic. Saudis ate fajitas and tacos! From the van, I could see Saudi families disembarking their sedans and entering the fast food outlets. I was disappointed. This new world seemed depressingly uniform on the surface, so many American flagships of consumption. This Saudiscape revealed an America with Arabic subtitles, where men and women ate burgers and drank Coca-Cola. McDonalds, Pepsi, and finally even KFC followed, underlining the monotony and disconcertingly displaced sense of familiarity. I saw nothing which I could identify as authentically Arabian. The main highway on which we were driving was peppered only with fast food outlets and strips of car dealerships selling GMC Suburbans or Porsches.

Around us, cars raced by, bulging Cadillacs, bellies bursting with Saudi women and their children, at each wheel always a man. I wondered where they were going, so late at night. Every car window in the rear was blacked out with heavy tinted glass or veiled under pleated curtains. These roads teemed with more Cadillacs than Park Avenue. Yet inside the glossy cars, the people were most definitely from here. I allowed myself a first unseen smile.

Regulation black or steel-colored S-series Benzes passed the bumbling Cadillacs, racing one another along the highway. I looked to my left and locked eyes with a long-lashed camel in a battered Suzuki pickup, a jarring reminder that I was no longer in New York. Rubber burns marked the roadway in wide calligraphic Naskh strokes. The new Kingdom of German sedans sliced past the old Kingdom of munching camels, the two worlds dueling alongside each other on this, the Mecca Highway.

I looked at the drivers. Within these obese Cadillac-shaped camels, among the Benz-clad Bedouin, falcon-eyed men lounged at the wheel, each invariably dressed in checkered shemaghs and flowing white thobes. To a man, each carried a cell phone, a near-appendage to his headdress. The men were driving nonchalantly with one hand, reclining. So many commuting caliphs. Of course, there were no women drivers. The absurd, clamorous clash of modern and medieval—Benz and Bedou, Cadillac and camel—was one which would reverberate throughout my stay in the Kingdom. It never became less arresting to behold.

In these first moments, I was already captivated, in more ways than I knew.

Chapter
Three

My New Home,
a Military Compound

We WERE NOW AT THE extreme east of the city. Waiting at traffic lights, the dusty silence was punctuated by rubber burns on slick, vacant roads. Crackling Arabic music carried on currents of exhaust fumes drifted into earshot from a nearby car. I could smell gasoline. We were on a deserted road leading up toward a compound. It was remote; soon there were no lights. In the darkness I could sense the edges of a huge desert.

Sudden floodlights heralded a gate. Barriers blazing, guardhouse gleaming, this was the gate to my new life, my life in Saudi Arabia. I would be working at the King Fahad National Guard Hospital, a hospital for the military protecting the Saudi royal family. I was now an employee of the Saudi Arabian National Guard Health Affairs and so would live on a militarized compound. Quickly, the well-groomed Saudi soldiers, uncovered hair perfectly coiffed and waxed even this late in the night, waved us through the gate without inquiry; I was in a hospital vehicle, with a known escort.

After a few brief turns through the campus-like grounds, we approached one of many buildings. Flat-roofed, cuboid buildings coated in garish terracotta paint extended far and wide. External air conditioning units peppered the surfaces, barnacles on whale hide. No central air, when it would be over 120°F in the summer? I wondered about the furnace of summer ahead, noticing the night air, which tasted of the pervasive dust. I smacked my already chapped lips to get the chalky taste away.

The heaving white minivan, mimicking its driver, ground to a lethargic halt. I looked at a neglected bilingual sign: Building 40. Even in the dark, the building was evidently in poor repair, a stark contrast from the dazzling airport. I entered cautiously, following Umair. I watched with amazement as he expertly gathered the skirt of his thobe. Curiously woman-like, he deftly raised the hem to avoid tripping while he carried my suitcases upstairs. For a time, I digested the strange scene of the heaving bulk of a man who now revealed the distinct gestures of a woman.

We entered an airless apartment, inhaling mouthfuls of dust. A plywood door slammed cheaply behind us. With a clumsy swipe, Umair slapped on the lights. I could smell hot dust burning on bare light bulbs. The apartment had been unoccupied for a while. More animated than at any time yet, Umair now reveled in the role of rotund realtor. Eagerly he showed me the appliances, opening all the drawers and showing me the cutlery for ten. He explained how to switch on the satellite television, smiling as he surfed channels which were broadcasting from a West now as remote to me here as Jupiter. He peered at me closely, reviewing my reaction. Somewhere in between passport control and the apartment it had become appropriate to look at me. Finally, he directed me to a welcome food pack. He left, his heaving footsteps retreating as he clumped down the concrete stairwell, doubtless while clutching the dangerous hems of his thobe. Stupidly, but suddenly, I missed him.

Hours later, I awoke, heavy-headed, disoriented. Slowly my thoughts came into focus. My sandpapered throat was rasping. The bed was facing the wrong direction. As I regained full consciousness, shaking off the heavy vestiges of sleep, I remembered: my entire life was now facing in this new, wrong, Eastern direction. I drew back the heavy black-out curtain, blinking in the stinging winter sunlight. Molten light poured in through windows as I opened them, chasing away every drop of darkness. Above, an interminably blanched sky would soon make me yearn for long-forgotten, gray clouds of England. The view from my apartment revealed that Saudi Arabia seemed now a poor country, despite the swashbuckling Mercedes of my arrival. I would learn that Saudi Arabia was many things to many people: to the rich, a land of boundless wealth; to the poor, a prison of abject poverty; to the expatriate worker, a land of contrasts and inconsistencies, an ever moving labyrinth of contradiction, not wholly one nor wholly the other. I readied myself for my first day in the Kingdom.

Dressing, I noticed a number of typed notes throughout the apartment; detailed instructions from the chairman of the department. Away from Riyadh at the time of my arrival into the Kingdom, he had left helpful details. I read with interest, hungry for information.

I unfolded a map, studying the glossy colors like a child. I felt displaced. According to my best estimations, I was perched on a precipice of encroaching desert. I looked out of the window. Certainly my eyes confirmed this was so. Returning to the map, I noticed the utter lack of detail. Riyadh didn't look very big or very labyrinthine according to this map, the way a city of 4.2 million[6] surely should be. I wondered about my new bearings.

"Think of yourself as in someone's private garden, Qanta. You are a guest in a private retreat, unlike anywhere else you may have lived. I like to call it The Magic Kingdom," I remembered the chairman saying. I wondered what he could mean.

Nearby, I noticed a handbook on Islamic etiquette that he had also left for me. I glanced at it. Cartoonish diagrams peppered short couplets of text, curiously like a child's book. I flicked through the pages, disinterested. These simple diagrams hoped to communicate the most complex cultural subtleties to non-Muslims? Suddenly, I wondered whether the chairman understood he had hired a Muslim woman. Pictures of veiled women and thobed men discussed codes of behavior with which I then believed myself to be familiar: a man greeting a man (with handshakes); a man greeting a woman (without handshakes and never without the presence of her male family member); permitted and forbidden items of consumption (alcohol, porcine flesh, illicit drugs); nature and timing of prayer (five times a day during which shops would always shut). After skimming through this "child's stuff" (stuff of my childhood at least), I discarded it. While I had briefly considered culture shock on arrival to the Kingdom as a possibility in past weeks, I had quickly dismissed it as silly, assuming my Muslim womanhood would give me an immediate and very natural carte blanche of insight and acceptance in Saudi Arabia.

---

[6] Riyadh's population is 4.26 million as of February 2005 and has grown by 4.2% in the eight years prior. Of the total, 34% (1.46 million) are expatriate workers, the remainder Saudi nationals (2.46 million). While the population continues to grow, the rate of population growth has diminished as internal domestic migration to Riyadh has decreased in recent years. http://www.saudiembassy.net/2005News/News/NewsDetail.asp?cIndex=5111.

I wasn't remotely worried about customs and culture here. As a Muslim, I considered myself a member of this club. My trite self-assurance began to ring hollow. Echoes of doubt were already magnifying in my new reality. What I didn't know, as I carelessly tossed the wooden books aside, were the legislated ways of orthodox Islam. Knowing the basic tenets of Islam would not get me very far. I would only make my painful discoveries with time as I bloodied myself colliding in one culture clash after another. I was to need an altogether different guide book for this "Kingdom of Strangers."

I returned to the notes. I was to call Maurag, my secretary, at once, one of them instructed. I dialed the number, speaking into a receiver that smelled of dust. She would be right over to take me to lunch so we could make plans for my essential first purchase in Saudi Arabia: tonight we were going shopping for an abbayah.

Chapter four

ABBAYAH SHOPPING

I HAD NEVER HEARD THE WORD *abbayah* before planning to move to the Kingdom. As Maurag explained, I realized this was the same as a burqa, the outdoor covering that I had first seen women wearing during my childhood vacations in Pakistan. My young mother would wear an ivory burqa when she was shopping in Karachi. I thought she looked like a bride on those special outings. In England she switched this for the peculiarly British ensemble of raincoat and headscarf which still covered her with Islamic propriety.

Though I had spent all my life as a Muslim, my wardrobe lacked any burqa, or chadhur, or in fact any kind of veil. My family, my parents in particular, had never required me to dress anything other than modestly. I was firmly settled in standard Western clothing of trouser suits or modest skirts. My hair was only covered when I prayed. My family allowed me and every other woman in our family to make the critical choice of veiling for themselves. I would quickly find Riyadh to be much less tolerant and much more demanding than my family.

The burqa or abbayah (as it is called in Saudi Arabia) is a thin, flowing robe that covers the entire length of the body, from head to foot. It is fastened at the neck and mid-chest, overlapping extensively to leave no clothing visible underneath. The abbayah has an accompanying and often matching scarf, also called a hijab, to cover the hair and head, leaving the face exposed. Some women additionally wear a cloth covering the face to varying degrees, called a niqab, veiling the face from the bridge of the nose downward.

In Saudi Arabia, women veil themselves in progressive, man-made demarcations of orthodoxy, each vying in severity with the next. Some expose eyebrows which are groomed, others brandish ungroomed eyebrows as a medal of orthodoxy in the eschewal of artificial reshaping, while continuing to veil the remainder of the forehead and the face below the bridge of the nose. Those with exposed eyebrows could reveal their expressions of surprise, dismay, or, rarely, a hastily suppressed joy. Others choose never to reveal even the allure of an arched brow. Instead they wrap the black cloth lower, brushing the center of upper eyelids barely revealing the margins of unmascaraed eyelashes.

Even more canonical were the extreme Wahabi[1] women whose veiling was unlike anything I had ever seen, even during childhood journeys to Afghanistan, Iran, or northern Pakistan.[2] Years later, when I saw blue-meshed bundles murdered at anonymous gunpoint in a forgotten Afghan hellhole, I recognized every Wahabi woman in Riyadh.

In Saudi Arabia, these women follow the most extreme veiling, which engulfs the entire woman. The whole head, every feature, eyes and ears included, is covered in an opaque shroud of black. Even the crocheted face mesh of the Taliban is forbidden. Hands are gloved in thick black cotton, as are toes. Not an inch of skin is visible, every atom of womanhood extinguished by polyester blackness. Many of these überorthodox women continue to wear full veiling indoors, even in the company of women, at every occasion, births, marriages, and deaths, taking a proud stance of zealotry over other women who are less observant.[3] The women are faceless, voiceless fragments of a lurid Wahabi imagination. They are easily forgotten.

This veiling was anathema to me. Even with a deep understanding of Islam, I could not imagine mummification is what an enlightened, merciful God would ever have wished for half of all His creation. These shrouded, gagged silences rise into a shrieking register of muted laments for stillborn freedoms. Such enforced incarceration of womanhood is a form of female infanticide. Throughout the Kingdom, short, tiny prepubertal girls could be seen tripping over their abbayahs, well before Islam asks for female modesty to be protected. While these veils conceal women, at the same time they expose the rampant, male oppression which is their jailor. Polyester imprisonment *by compulsion* is ungodly and (like the fiber) distinctly man-made.

Regardless of whether the face is covered or not, in Saudi Arabia, no woman can go anywhere in public without wearing an abbayah that covers at least the body and her head of hair. In Riyadh, these abbayahs are almost always black, year-round, irrespective of the intensely hot climate. Mine would be no exception.

These were the rules of Sharia law. The Kingdom is the only Arab state that claims Islamic law (known as Sharia) as its sole foundation for legal code. Inexplicably, the Kingdom's clerics compel non-Muslim women to veil also, a rule which is not to be found codified in the Quran. To the enforcers, this was a minor detail easily abrogated. In the eyes of the clergy, there could be no choice for a woman, in veiling or in any other matter; covering the hair and wearing the abbayah was legislated by their version of Sharia law, irrespective of any personal beliefs including fundamental professions of revealed faiths.

Sharia law is expressed in Saudi Arabia as decreed by Wahabi clerical lawmakers, followers of the most extreme brand of Islam. Wahabiism is the movement founded by Mohammed bin Abdul Wahab (died 1792), a monstrous and very modern phenomenon that distorts much Islamic teaching through his myopic, blinkered interpretations of a magnificent religion. In its place, he spawned a rigid movement that dismantled centuries of careful pluralistic Islamic discourse and learned interpretations, denouncing such scholarship as "innovative" and corrupting of Divine instruction.

Over time, the Wahabi stance toward innovation (which is often expressed as a hysterical counter to perceived "infection" with Western ideologies and appetites) has evolved into a number of laws designed to subjugate and oppress women. Citing Sharia, the clerics ban women from driving cars, forbid women from buying music, prevent women from booking hotel rooms in their own names, and attempted (but failed) to dissuade female passengers from wearing seat belts in front seats of cars for fear of defining a woman's veiled cleavage. Earlier, Wahabis had worked hard to prevent the telephone from being introduced in the Kingdom, fearing it would be used as a satanic instrument encouraging male-female interactions and succeeded for a time to keep out television (a heinous portal of evil un-Islamic influence), satellite television (multinational invasion of satanic forces), and even the Internet (unassailable external evil available on dial-up, and even worse, now broadband). New dilemmas plaguing the clerics include illicit Bluetooth interfaces between the sexes, cameras on handheld phones, and text messaging.

Modern Wahabi forces in the Kingdom are very alive today, where interpretation other than that deemed appropriate by Wahabi rigidity is *haram*, or absolute heresy. The clergy has effectively extinguished public diversity and distorted Islamic jurist thought into a harsh, mandated apartheid: men from women; Saudis from non-Saudis; Muslims from non-Muslims; Wahabis from non-Wahabis.

As I spent time in the Kingdom, I was to see just how far removed the state-enforced theocracy was from the truth which is Islam and also how conflicted the Saudis around me, both men and women, had themselves become. Their state no longer represented their personal beliefs. They were just as much victims of oppression as any visitor to their country. Perhaps even the same could be said for some members of the monarchy who bravely fostered the beginnings of progressive reform in this difficult climate.

Thus, even though Islam clearly mandates no compulsion in faith, because of Wahabi Sharia law, it was here I would experience enforced veiling. My oppression had begun. It began with my consent to work in a police state, followed by Umair's authority on my passport, then my subjugation within the robes of the abbayah and my bewildering introduction to legislated male supremacy. Finally I found my own spineless capitulation when all my defiance exhausted me and I too cowered, muted under the perpetual specter of ruling Wahabiism.

For now, I merely wondered how much the abbayah would cost, regarding it no more of a hindrance than I did my doctor's white coat for my work. Maurag promised to lend me an old abbayah of hers to wear so I could safely (as she put it delicately, when we both knew she meant "legally") move outside the compound and enter the mall where we would make the purchase. After the Isha prayer, when shops would reopen after their mandatory closure for evening worship, we would be going abbayah shopping.

Chapter
Five

INVISIBLE AND SAFE

WE TRAVELED IN A TAXI to the center of the city. Along the way, Maurag taught me never to hail a cab curbside but instead to rely on the hospital's own car service. In Riyadh, there was still no enforced registration of licensed taxis. A lone Western woman could be vulnerable alone in a taxi, and how could one tell a genuine taxi from a predator? My dark Asian skin was an added conundrum. Veiled, I could pass as Saudi, and a lone Saudi woman in a taxi was almost in a worse predicament than a non-Saudi. A Saudi woman with no honor or protection, just where could she be going shamelessly unchaperoned? That would be the received message. She would be inviting danger.

The driving in Riyadh was deadly. Turbocharged testosterone without creative or sexual outlet translated into deadly acceleration. The road was supposedly a six-lane highway into the city, but additional lanes appeared at will.

Someone passed us on the hard shoulder traveling at least one hundred miles per hour. I feverishly followed the speedometer in which our un-seat-belted driver displayed no interest. We ourselves were already seventy-five miles per hour in an old South African rust bucket. I began to feel angry with the driver. I stupidly clutched onto the flimsy scarf over my hair. "Shweh," (Slow) was falling on deaf ears. I felt feeble and increasingly powerless.

At last we reached a mall. From outside it was an elegant glass and marble structure, shining with chrome staircases. It was modern and familiar in its Western design. The al-Akariyah shopping center was inviting, ablaze with neon and fluorescence. Inside, Saudi men and women rustled purposefully, focused on Thursday night shopping. The paucity of color was striking; aside from the black abbayahs and white thobes, no other color was apparent. Stocky figures were cast into sharp relief against the gleaming marble canvas; black, veiled silhouettes enshrouding women trailed behind the white-clad, plump men who had married or fathered or been delivered of them. I was entranced.

Little children were shorter versions of their parents, small girls no more than six in abbreviated shrouds, their abbayah hems getting stuck in their brightly colored, open-toed jelly sandals. Their clumsy tumbles reminded me that a childhood was encased within these opaque sarcophagi. Little boys, scuffed and stained, tumbled along in short white robes hurrying to keep up with Dad, always ahead of their sisters, already exerting an infantile male supremacy.

I noticed mainly families with many children, three or four at least to every mother-shaped veil. Saudi children ran amok, far ahead of the parents. Waddling women hurried hopelessly to keep up, clumsy platform shoes and billowing abbayahs impeding their progress. Under askew hems, I could see Riyadh was the home of the rubberized platform sneaker. I watched the clumpy shoes carry ballooning sailboats of veiled women back and forth over the marble causeway. The Dior handbags and Fendi footwear I had seen Saudi women in London wearing were nowhere to be seen. Things were much more kitsch at home.

At the perimeter of the mall, Saudi bachelors condensed in groups at mall entrances, barred from entering during family time when only married couples and women could shop. Security guards dotted the mall in clusters, accompanied by policemen. The officers were dressed in militarized uniforms and red berets, a brief relief of color in the bloodless scene.

Women without families, like us, patrolled in clutches of twos or threes. Many women were Western. It seemed al-Akariyah was a favorite mall for the expat worker. Caucasian faces stared out of the black regulation abbayahs, chatting with one another easily, blue eyes peering out of the Wahabi garb, faces often smiling, strangely relaxed. Here and there a wisp of blonde inveigled its way out of veiled blackness. Sometimes, a Swedish accent punctuated the air, ridiculously displaced.

There were other women out this evening too. Young Saudi millenials patrolled the mall, their pallid anemia partly visible behind hijabs. Some talked incessantly on cell phones, eagerly surveying goods. Wealthier teens wore slim-line microphones under tightly bound layers of veils, microphones nestling provocatively in front of the invisible fullness of lips concealed within. Everywhere I looked, headpieces peeped out from behind headscarves, so many Muslim Madonnas, engaged in secretive, coquettish flirtations, perhaps with their Bluetooth boyfriends.

I watched them closely. The girls often giggled but always quietly, no raucous, jaw-splitting guffaws. These girls were uncomfortable even containing such covert gaiety, ever-vigilant of an impending capture. They were very controlled, with years of training, always hiding their stolen snatches of happiness. Clearly these women were unmarried. There were no entourages of children, no awkward newlywed husbands, no pregnant bellies suggested by the folds of their abbayahs. These were the swinging single Saudi women, the hip elite of Riyadh. I wondered if they were having some kind of fun.

We cut through a food court. I watched people eagerly lunging forward to place their orders for kebabs, ice cream, and juices. Children clamoring, jostling against adults, the unruly wait dissolved into small puddles of confusion. There was no distinct line; it was every man for himself, literally. Nearby, anxious, powerless women waited patiently for their food, eternally dependent. I failed to find any mixed groups. The segregation was pervasive: Saudi from non-Saudi, Muslim from non-Muslim, men from women, married from unmarried. Saudi Arabia was about separation even for the Saudis.

We scurried toward shops in the back of the mall. Here were lines of stores, each a purveyor of polyester incarceration. I looked through shop windows. They displayed seemingly identical black cloaks. I followed Maurag into one store. Entering, we ducked under a low beam. The floor was saturated with blood-colored kilims, rich in their authenticity, yet soiled by the puddled umbras of garish strip lights. The smell alone suffocated me in the heavy, hot lighting and stifling atmosphere of warm wool and dusty abbayahs. Around us, attendants looked on intently.

Every assistant was a male Saudi. The men were dotted around edges of the kilims, like so many sentries. At the time women were forbidden from assisting in shops in the Kingdom and even now can only serve in gender segregated malls which have developed in recent years. Strangely, therefore, only men could sell abbayahs. Their accumulating colognes reached a critical mass of sickly sweetness. They were all in their early twenties, dressed in white thobes and mascara-like beards, the careful grooming marks of their significant vanity.

Abbayah shopping was like renting a graduation gown, deadly dull. Racks and racks of black cloaks and matching scarves, hanging from their perches, stretched in every direction. Perhaps label shopping would help. I started looking at price tags and was surprised to see some were SR 1800 (in excess of $500). Many were decorated with fine needle work, sequins, mirrors, or even Swarovski crystal, priced far beyond my reach.

In that store, Maurag the Australian showed me more about Muslim covering than any woman in my family had ever done, idly mentioning rumors of blue abbayahs being worn publicly in more liberal Jeddah; unthinkable here in Riyadh. I couldn't believe women there were still excited at the prospect of reform in the shape of relaxation of legislated color. Years later, self-expression in Riyadh has evolved to an abbayah trimmed in Burberry plaid or, for the more daring, embroidered animals, flowers, celebrities, or even slogans stitched into the sleeves or the backs of the abbayah. I was left to choose one of my own.

Perfunctorily, I picked one. I tried it on inside a curtained alcove. The abbayah had three tassels on the front and at the corner of each sleeve. It was one of the cheapest there. I watched as the lifeless abbayah took on life. Mine.

The ugly neckline was boat shaped and secured with cheap studs. An internal tie at waist level made of limpid cord held the abbayah together. A plain black scarf of slippery polyester completed my new about-town ensemble. I should have done a "sound-check" before buying it; that stereophonic rustling would drive me nearly mad later on.

As I fastened the abbayah in front of a mirror inside the makeshift dressing room, I watched my eradication. Soon I was completely submerged in black. No trace of my figure remained. My androgyny was complete.

I looked at my face in the mirror, my dark eyes assessing my new public persona, my thick hair squashed completely out of sight. What a small head, I thought to myself, surprised at my resilient vanity. My head seemed out of proportion, not a good mast for a veil. I looked more closely. The veil was a strangely inviting prison. I could be Saudi, I thought naïvely. In this I was one of the crowd, I thought, suddenly excited. I would move within this society unremarked upon. Who knew what I would see or learn with my unseen eyes.

I paid SR 270 ($70) for my abbayah, hurling the garish notes at the attendant. I wanted to wear the abbayah out of the store. The attendant boxed Maurag's old abbayah (that I had now discarded in place of my new one), handling it as carefully as if it were a Balenciaga gown. It seemed stupid to take such care over the black rag. He handed the box to Maurag, who appeared completely unmoved at my transformation; she had seen such metamorphoses already. Ignoring her lack of enthusiasm, I stepped out of the store, eager to try my new armor.

Immediately, I felt safer. This veil would deflect intrusive male gazes. I was shielded, impregnable, and most importantly of all, completely concealed. The abbayah was easy to move in, not at all binding or restrictive of my movements. The abbayah I had chosen was very light weight (in anticipation of the superheated summer to come) and I moved ahead rapidly, unencumbered at my normal Western pace. I was enthralled at my total obliteration.

My social suicide had begun. In some ways, my womanhood couldn't wait for this strange rebirth through my own obliteration, one which would enable me to live and work within this Kingdom. Inside the abbayah, I felt oddly free.

I was discovering what many Saudi women already know: that the only way to enter the public space and participate in public life in the Kingdom was behind the shield of an abbayah. In some respects the abbayah was a powerful tool of women's liberation from the clerical male misogyny. I would be reminded of the abbayah as a banner for feminism time and again as I encountered extraordinary Saudi women who would work alongside me.

Yet there would be plenty of times when I would abhor the compulsion of this incarceration. Only later would the magnitude of my silent contract, the chains of my unseen pact with the world of Wahabiism, begin to dawn on me. Though itself literally weightless, for me and many other women, Western and Saudi alike, my abbayah was to become one of the heaviest burdens I would bear in Saudi Arabia. Only the mantle of my womanhood would weigh more.

As we left the shop, Maurag brazenly allowed her headscarf to slip. She seemed entirely unconcerned. A few steps behind her, I could see the x-rated scene she was creating. Her ripe red hair, lush with pregnancy, was on open display. In the rigidity of the veiled Kingdom, the exposure was nothing short of pornographic.

Though we were in an uncrowded corner of the mall, I felt increasingly uncomfortable. An echo chamber of anxiety screeched inside the amplifier of my polyester veil, cocooning me from the surroundings. I nursed my worries. Maurag was my only guide back to the compound. If anything happened to her, what would happen to me? I was astonishingly powerless.

And then, I saw him. My worst fears became manifest. A Muttawa (a member of the religious police)[7] had been soaking up the illicit scene and now closed in for the kill. He must have approached before I could ever see him coming, even though we were in this desolate part of the mall.

Every Mutawaeen cultivated a religious straggly beard of variable length. This man was no different. His was a religious, untrimmed beard, I learned, which was not cut unless the man could grasp a fistful of hair. The Muttawa wore the same white thobe as the average Saudi man but at a markedly shortened

---

[7] In general, the term Muttawa is used for holy men, community sources of religious scholarship or teachers of religion. However, the Saudis themselves often use the term Muttawa when they are referring to the religious police.

hemline, revealing invariably hairy, unmuscled shins. Over this ensemble he wore a dark brown overcoat called a bisht, made of translucent muslin and trimmed in fine gold embroidery. The delicacy of the material contrasted sharply with his offensive bulk. It was strangely discomfiting. The gold thread was especially disturbing, far too regal for a supposedly ascetic holy man, and so closely reminiscent of the Royal habit, the hallmark of Saudi monarchs, (who also wore bishts) almost as though they were cut of the same cloth.

At the summit of his narrow-browed head, the Muttawa wore a white head covering, draping to his thickened waist. The cloth balanced symmetrically, without any visible traction, minus the traditional black rim of the Saudi male headdress. It came forward over his face, covering part of the brow into a short visor of officialdom. From inside, his vantage was therefore blinkered, his peripheral vision limited by the headdress, a fitting metaphor for his narrow horizons of inflexible philosophies.

In one hand the Muttawa carried a cane, to wield his corpulence along the causeway as he heaved along the tightrope of extremism. His was a path of very narrow and circumscribed dimensions. In his right hand he carried a wooden rosary. It seemed to be a stress reliever, spinning around faster and faster as he became increasingly irritated with Maurag's violation. Overbearing and dangerously arrogant, he began to speak.

"Cover your hair!" he told Maurag firmly. He sounded menacing.

Quickly, worried women around us scurried by, disappearing from view, fearful of being swept up in the fray. How I wished to join them. I watched the scene slightly apart from Maurag, some feet to her right. The Muttawa was accompanied by an emaciated policeman. The officer seemed bored, flitting restlessly behind the obese icon of intolerance he accompanied. Maurag's jaw was set. She was going to retaliate.

"I will not cover my hair! My husband does not require it! He allows me to be unveiled! I will not!" she answered angrily. The opening of her abbayah fell loose and her pregnant belly protruded with indignant authority. Even though Maurag was so angry, she still cited the authority of a man to the Muttawa, rather than exert her own.

"You must cover it!" demanded the Muttawa. "Cover your hair, now!" he repeated, while gabbling an Arabic aside to the bored policeman. Was this perhaps the sum total of his English vocabulary? I began to wonder. The policeman remained mute.

This was the first Muttawa I had seen. Invariably male, I would quickly become accustomed to the patrolling menaces of State-appointed religious police. I was simultaneously repelled and fascinated. And like something horrible, I wanted to take a good, long, forbidden look. The Muttawa was tall and, because of his bulk and his intrinsic power, he certainly looked intimidating. But most puzzling of all, Maurag seemed not the least perturbed and even seemed to pull a face with a sly roll of her defiant eyes. I was surprised by her foolish courage and rightly worried. I couldn't believe Maurag had made us such a spectacle, and on my very first public experience in Saudi Arabia. I was expecting her to be more considerate. Here I was, taking fearful baby steps in my brand new abbayah, only moments out of the store and she was already defying the Muttawa. Instead of being angry with the Muttawa, I was surprised to find I was angry with Maurag.

Grumpily, Maurag pulled her ragged scarf over some of her red hair. She was fuming. The Muttawa began to withdraw, back to the shadows from where he must have been lurking. A sigh of relief fluttered through my veil which I had been clutching up to my face during the scene.

At least the Muttawa had gone. Fearful but relieved, I secured my scarf. No matter how ugly it surely looked, this way it stayed put, firmly tied under my chin with a double knot, a bandage for a head wound. We hailed a taxi to leave.

In one short foray into the world outside my compound, I learned I had made my home in the epicenter of a wasp's nest of intolerance: in Riyadh, home of the Wahabi clergy. The Najd, the central region of Saudi Arabia of which Riyadh was the capital, was the geographic center and the seat of clerical power. In Riyadh the Wahabi schools maintained an uncomfortable status quo with the plebes (of which I was now one) and our rulers, the Saudi Monarchy. This triangular tension of proletariat, princes, and fire-breathing papacy kept the Kingdom grinding onward. During my years in Riyadh, I would remain imprisoned in polyester, avoiding confrontation my primary modus operandi. Fortunately for me, social suicide or not, this was ultimately something to which I could never become accustomed.

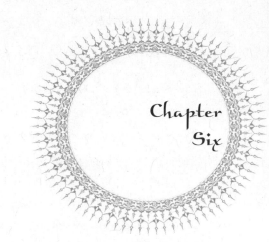

SAUDI WOMEN WHO
DANCE ALONE

A s my curiosity about the Kingdom grew, I began to look outward. Initially my solitary existence was punctuated only by patients and colleagues. I lacked friends and already wanted an exit from the intense isolation. As I walked toward the ICU late one afternoon, I passed the open doors of the hospital library, noticing studious veiled or shemagh covered heads bowed deep in study or peering at computer screens. I was tempted to enter but was already running late. Just as I was about to turn away, I looked up and recognized Zubaidah, the ICU nutritionist, leaving the library and approaching, apparently to talk to me.

She was dressed in a knee-length white coat, fully buttoned up to the throat, and a carefully placed scarf in (what else) regulation black. Underneath the coat, I noticed petrol-gray folds of a chiffon skirt grazing down to her impossibly white feet, carefully dressed in open-toe mules glinting with quiet sophistication. Her toes, I noticed, were unpolished, as was her outstretched hand meeting me in a handshake. Her sleeve lifted a fraction and I saw the unmistakable glint of a dial of Swiss diamonds on her wrist. A single, costly, jeweled band on the ring finger of her right hand indicated Zubaidah was, like me, single.

"Salaam alaikum, Dr. Ahmed," Zubaidah said as she smiled, "How do you enjoy Riyadh?" Her soft voice lilted, suspended in a mid-Continental fusion of Jordanian and French-Swiss accents, somehow endearing her imperfect English grammar. She actually looked interested in my response, revealing an even, pearly smile of patience as she waited for my response. I searched for a diplomatic answer. How could I tell this lovely woman that so far her country had been less than appetizing? How did she "enjoy Riyadh?" I wondered sardonically. I opted not to answer at all.

"Zubaidah, please call me Qanta. I have been meaning to invite you to coffee for some weeks now. It would be lovely to chat if you have time. Let me give you my number." I began to scribble my impossibly long phone number, which all residents of the hospital compound shared, followed by the extension to my landline. Zubaidah shared hers, immediately revealing her home to be off-campus, and a mobile number in addition, a very rare commodity in the late nineties. Zubaidah was privileged.

Even in that first brief meeting, which lasted just minutes, I couldn't fail to notice Zubaidah's elegance despite the mandatory veiling, perhaps even magnified because of the veiling. Properly wrapped around her hair, the hijab still exposed her extraordinary face. Her flawless skin was a creamy alabaster, unlined and of indeterminate age. A light radiated from her face, which the drab blackness of a headscarf couldn't extinguish. She greeted me with genuine enthusiasm expressed in the open and friendly arches of fine, honey-colored brows surmounting gray-brown eyes. Zubaidah was incredibly beautiful. As I studied her gaze, I found it was possible that she was just as curious about me as I was toward her.

I had been wanting to speak to this Saudi woman for some weeks, but so far our conversations had been limited to calculations of caloric intake for our patients. In the ICU she was the model of Saudi professionalism, veiling not only her *body*, but, as becomes a true Muslim, *her entire demeanor* in the mixed gender environment of the ICU. I had noticed that she never made direct eye contact with any of my male colleagues, that she always waited to be invited to render her professional opinion, and that she was overall subdued and reticent in public. I had mistaken her retiring qualities for shyness. Now I found her mutual curiosity surprising. I wondered what else I would learn about her.

So began my first friendship with a Saudi woman, one which led to many others. Zubaidah would open the doors into the Kingdom for me. She would show me the lives of others inside this bell jar.

Some weeks after our first meeting, Zubaidah mentioned she was having a party to usher in Ramadan, on the eve of the holiest month of the Muslim year, and she invited me to attend. I had heard that Ramadan was a time when the religious police were especially dedicated to enforcing the difficult Islamic rituals of day long fasting. I was dreading the beginning of the month. And now when even Zubaidah explained Riyadh during Ramadan would be difficult, I was alarmed further. It seemed my expatriate friends, veterans of Kingdom living, were accurate in warning me about the holy month in the Kingdom. Before the austere days of fasting and supplication would begin, Zubaidah was hosting a party as final festivities. The party would be given at Zubaidah's home and would be my first visit there. Delighted and flattered, I accepted immediately.

On the day of the festivities, I worried about my party outfit. What could I wear that would be suitable? I wanted my first foray into the real Saudi Arabia to be a success, and most importantly, not the last. I rushed home to take stock of my limited wardrobe.

In the dull hours of the late afternoon, I surveyed the closet. My livelier and more daring outfits were stowed away in New York, awaiting my resumption of "Life in the West." Here, in Riyadh, I had brought with me what I believed to be an appropriately conservative wardrobe: wide-legged trousers of every dark color, endless long-sleeved white turtlenecks, long-sleeved shirts, a couple of long, ankle-skimming skirts, and knee-high boots; in sum, one's basic, capsule Wahabi wardrobe. After debating the very minimal choice I did have, I pulled on a pair of beige slacks and a white turtleneck. I dressed the dull outfit up with a shiny belt, some jewelry, and a lively ruby lipstick. This would be fine, I thought; no one would be offended by bare skin or short hemlines. And, after all, it was cool in December, and with the party starting at nine, there would be a chilly desert breeze on the way home.

I cloaked my ensemble with the mask of my abbayah, drowning all my meager efforts at appearing stylish. Firmly tying my headscarf on, I was ready for my first evening out. As I looked at my departing face in the hallway mirror, the only familiar emblem of my dressed-up self was my lipstick, in traffic-light red. Everything else about me was already changed beyond recognition in just these few weeks. I stepped outside my building and waited in the forsaken silence, my cheek caressed by the evening wind. In the glare of headlights a taxi pulled up, with two fellow party goers beckoning me in. This was my ride.

I jumped in, careful that my abbayah and scarf didn't entrap me in the car door and turned to greet my fellow passengers. These women were also compound-dwellers who worked with Zubaidah in the nutrition section, both of them dieticians. One was a pretty, blond Irish girl, the other a tall, imposing redhead, Christine, a Canadian. Christine had been in the Kingdom for some time and knew Zubaidah well. We chatted along the way, talking of home (which was always elsewhere, no matter how long anyone had lived in the Kingdom). We shared our common stories of adjusting to life in the Kingdom. I mentioned to Christine how much I missed my duck-down duvet which I had left in New York. I was astounded and delighted when the ladies told me I could pick up a new one at Ikea! In Riyadh? There was a market for Scandinavian furniture here? Somehow, I couldn't imagine a Saudi assembling flat-pack furniture.

As we drove on, I discovered Christine had been in the Canadian army and had been a UN peacekeeper patrolling the Golan Heights before she was a nutritionist here. The diversity of backgrounds amongst the expats was only beginning to come into focus. Everyone was more than they appeared, often having lived in several other countries, and often having more than one profession.

The driver headed away from the compound in a westerly direction, along the Khuraij Road, as he always did. Our compound was at the eastern-most tip of habitable land before the desert engulfed everything in earnest. Tonight we were headed into town and soon joined the fast-gathering traffic jams. Zubaidah's home was in a discreet corner of the residential and commercial neighborhood of Olleyah. Her home was on a road just off Siteen Street, a chic shopping address frequented by locals. She lived in the heart of Riyadh.

Tonight, the night before Ramadan, was everyone's last reprieve in this city of four million. An ambient urgency of compressed pleasures suffused the air. City dwellers were intent to revel, albeit in private, before the gravity of the month-long fasting set in. For many, there was cause to celebrate the arrival of the most holy month of the Islamic year, a joyous and rewarding time for observant Muslims. Repressed excitement mingled with anxious anticipation, forming a critical mass of novel energy in the usually torpid, humorless Riyadh. The air was charged.

As we coursed along the Khuraij Road, a six-lane highway, to the left and right of us cars raced at a perilous speed, leaving us trailing behind as we journeyed at sixty-five miles per hour in the middle, the supposedly slower, so-called "expat" lane. I fastened my seat belt in the rear seat and focused on buildings rather than cars, anything to distract me from the wildness of the traffic that barely grazed past us at deadly speed.

I strained to see everything through the cheap adhesive tint of the taxi windows. We passed the gleaming Lucent building, empty of employees, then Zahid Tractors with rows of shiny, flat-nosed, sunflower-yellow tractors. On our right, we zipped past the Astra compound, also belonging to the National Guard, where our Saudi counterparts lived, separate, divorced from us, the expat population. On the opposite side of the road, car dealerships stretched out, Toyota, Cadillac, Porsche, cars and trucks gleaming in the evening light, each waiting for an eager, first, *male* owner.

Within fifteen minutes we were well into the city. Brightly lit public areas opened out into shopping centers and market places which tonight were spilling over with Saudis carrying armfuls of shopping in overstuffed plastic baskets and boxes. Neon illuminated the night sky from fast food outlets. Aimless urban planning, dominated by arterial, never-ending roads in turn flanked by commercial businesses, was reminiscent of a generic America. Entire developments were perhaps only a block deep, making for a curiously pockmarked landscape; highly developed commercial buildings and vacant lots side by side, the lots nothing more than mounds of partially dug-up, barren land, a galling reminder of what must have been here only a few years before. No grass, no public gardens, no shade of trees could be seen along the entire route. Riyadh was built of concrete, plate glass, and sand secured with a tarry mortar of oil and cheap foreign labor. Entirely man-made, the only animation in Riyadh was the flutter of litter swirling in the wake of the fearsome traffic.

Overhead, even though it was three hours past dusk, it still wasn't dark. The petrol-blue night sky, its vastness accentuated by squat buildings, was darkest sapphire, never black, backlit by strong moonlight and prevailing light pollution. Devoid of clouds, there was nothing to absorb the moonlight. A filigree silhouette of a mosque made entirely of mesh gently impressed its form against the soft pile of the velvet night. What lacked in the department of parks and services was made up for in houses of worship. Almost every other building, if it wasn't selling goods, was selling God.

Myriad round domes and skeletal minarets catapulted me to my new reality—unmistakably Arabia. No amount of fast food pylons or American cars could distract or dilute. As I admired the mosques extending seemingly in every direction, I was surprised to feel an unexpected yearning for lost churches in New York I had left behind. I missed the neighborhood church around the corner from my first apartment. I missed the damp, inviting silence of St. Patrick's, a relief from the Midtown madding. I smiled, recalling my favorite hymn, "I Vow to Thee My Country," from my distant childhood at a Church of England school. It would never ring out across these plains. Silently I checked. I could still recite the Lord's Prayer, even after all these years. My experience of Islam had been built on a bedrock of books from diverse faiths, foremost among them Christianity. My Islam was not birthed in a monolithic vacuum like this one. Here in Riyadh there was one flavor for all, and only one. Everything else was expelled. Even Islam here was officially of one brand only. I gazed at the multitude of mosques, at once striking and singularly ominous.

The cab slowed and took a right turn off Siteen Street. As we trundled along the side road, we approached a mosque spilling worshipers left and right. Isha (evening prayer) had just ended. A fluorescent umbra cast by the harsh lighting of the minaret bathed the streetscape in lurid green. Short, thobed figures scattered to either side of vehicles, each one a boy playing in the street. One figure, kicking a dusty soccer ball, drew a swarm of boys following him intensely, tackling with dusty, slippered feet. We turned left across from another mosque and stopped. This was Zubaidah's house.

As we clambered out of the car, straightening our abbayahs, I looked around. There was no sidewalk. Underfoot, a thick layer of dust covered the once-black tarmac. Small oil puddles punctuated dirt. Again there was not a single planted tree in sight. The neighborhood looked in poor repair, not particularly affluent. Approaching the gate, however, I saw cars parked by the house, a Jaguar, two Benzes, a few other German automobiles. This was a moneyed neighborhood after all, and those boys with dusty, worn sandals didn't live in these houses; that much was clear.

Christine rang the dusty bell in its fractured casing. An intricate steel gate towered above our veiled heads, the twisting white metal work supported by sky-blue metal plates. It wailed open. The house was surrounded completely by a barricade of high walls, over twenty feet high.

I crossed the threshold, entering the lives of others. Either side, neatly tended lawns were encircled by terracotta planters spilling cheerful scarlet geraniums. From the inside, these same walls which had looked so ominous from the outside now looked strangely protective. I was glad to be behind them, ensconced in privacy and at once immediately relaxed. At the top of a small flight of steps was a terrace, onto which opened white-framed double French windows. No matter how often I visited Zubaidah's home, I never got used to the French window entrance, as if I was entering secretly from a rear entrance.

A Filipina maid opened the door, wordlessly ushering us inward. As I was taking in the Daum figurines and the oversized Lalique coffee table amid a Liberace-esque interior, Zubaidah rushed up to greet us, a riot of color against her white marble home. She looked so different, she moved differently; even her voice was less modulated. Her hair I could now see was a flaxen golden brown, playfully turned upward in deliciously sassy, soft waves. I looked at her as if seeing her for the first time. I couldn't take my eyes from her and in that moment I understood the power of veiling. A woman is transformed by hair. I was agog, and, soon after, embarrassed that I was looking at Zubaidah rather in the way a man might have done. For full moments, I was transfixed by the sight of her exposed hair and her buoyant beauty.

The forbidden becomes much more enticing than what is always revealed. I was astonished at the effect her unveiled appearance had on me. Momentarily, I was jealous at how she caged her beauty, sharing it only with the few, the chosen. Briefly, I wished I had treated my looks with such gravity, with such careful measure, instead of giving myself away, daily, wastefully, indiscriminately. Adjusting to the distraction of her entire appearance and her total beauty, I saw she was smiling her warm and infectious pearly smile, greeting us each in turn, gray-brown eyes sparkling with animation, rapidly speaking in refined English laced with a cultivated Lausanne-Amman hybrid accent, markers of a lifetime of summers spent in her family's Jordanian and French-Swiss homes.

She greeted each of us with brief but sincere hugs, and we responded in perfumed flurries of salaams and good evenings. Unanimously we admired her stylish, heavily embroidered burgundy caftan. Zubaidah had opted to wear the traditional dress preferred by so many Palestinian exiles in Riyadh. I was learning. Zubaidah was born and raised in Riyadh and was a Saudi national, but her father had left Palestine in 1948. She was a Saudi Palestinian.

Quickly disengaging ourselves of our abbayahs, we handed them to the silent maid, and followed Zubaidah into her sumptuous home. She led us down the white marble stairs, and into a refinished basement, a suburban American aspiration once again, except it was finished in marble, with Persian fine rugs and several areas of seating. There wasn't a man to be seen. Instead the room was filled with amazing-looking women. My dull outfit was becoming, like me, more hideous by the minute. Zubaidah was the centerpiece of the room, animated, a little flushed and vibrant. She moved effortlessly, engaging in conversation in several languages all the while skillfully switching music and introducing her guests. Seated around the perimeter of the room, other women coolly appraised us, the newly arrived guests. We were the only Westerners there. I was the only non-Caucasian Western Muslim, a strange fruit indeed. I invited extra scrutiny.

I settled myself into a deep, navy blue sofa, which, by dint of generous upholstery, defied any possibility of sitting up straight. I felt increasingly inelegant, my ignominy around these sophisticated Saudi creatures mounting ever further.

Across from me, a Saudi woman, in her early thirties, sat alone on an armless dining chair, dressed in a tight fitting gray wool dress with a short, fringed skirt exposing a single, chiseled knee peeping beyond the hemline. She smoked Marlboros skyward, her glossy head lazily abutting the wall, a picture of nonchalance. Smooth, waxed legs wore tall, black, high-heeled suede boots. Her shapely legs were idly crossed, swinging in synch to each drag of the cigarette. Slowly, she fixed on me with a steady, unblinking gaze and surmised my clumsy ensemble. As she exhaled languidly, I noticed her cigarette was perched on immaculately manicured, slender fingers. In fact every Saudi woman there was also smoking cigarettes, except for Zubaidah. I looked at the chic woman once more. So this was what women in Saudi Arabia wear: exactly what they wear in Manhattan, even down to their nail polish!

I thought of the hundreds of abbayahs that had scurried by me, perhaps many concealing chic and trendy outfits, free of my critical eye, or indeed anyone else's.

"I love your dress!" I told her, "and the boots are fabulous! Where do you shop?" I asked her in genuine admiration.

"From my own boutique in Oleyya," she replied, coolly, blowing a smoke ring. After a moment, she went on, "This is all from my store. You should visit. Perhaps you will find something you prefer," she replied, only a glint of excitement in her eye giving away her pride. Her accent was harsher than Zubaidah's and the color of her skin darker, closer to my own, though her English was measured and excellent. This was Hudah, born and bred in Riyadh, of an undiluted Saudi family, a family that allowed their daughter to be a business owner! In Riyadh! Immediately, I wondered if she was married but instinctively knew she was unwed. She seemed too independent. I was pleased to recognize some of myself within this woman.

In the Kingdom, women had been asserting their economic independence for some time. I was stunned to discover a number of other women at the party were also business owners, of clothing boutiques, hair salons, or even, like my friend Zubaidah, owners of chic stores purveying hard-to-find European wares like hand-turned glassware or rare porcelain. It is estimated that forty percent of private wealth in Saudi Arabia is held by Saudi women, and even though women are not permitted to hold a business directly, many do so through the front of a male representative, often a family member. More than fifteen thousand firms are owned and operated in this manner, and their women owners are allowed to be elected to business guilds and chambers of commerce in Riyadh, Jeddah, and Dharan.[4]

Elsewhere, a young, sylph-like girl clattered into a small room in the corner of the basement, carrying a series of rather ugly vases. I could see no flowers. Not everything was quite ready for this party, after all. I followed the activity and offered help. With expert, feline dexterity, the young Saudi woman, Sara, quickly assembled the series of thick glass cylinders onto a round base. From one cylinder (the top most) emerged a thick flexible hose of purple silk. At the end of the hose was a wooden carved pipe wrapped with red cloth, ending in a brass mouthpiece. The "vase" being cleaned was not a vase at all. I was increasingly alarmed. Drugs! The Ganja! In Saudi Arabia! Don't they know about the death penalty? Do they really think they are safe in their homes, here in this police state? Hysterically, I began to feel unsafe, even here, in the security of a private home.

Sara carried on, oblivious to my rising anxiety. She pulled out a small packet of dusty gray bricks, each smaller than a deck of cards, unwrapped the colorful paper enclosing them, and placed them carefully on a steel tray to one side. She piled them up loosely like a short, fat tower. Then she lugged the vessel of vases, which was by now almost as tall as she was, into the deep sink, filling the base of the cylinder with tap water. Finally, I could see, she was assembling a giant kettle; it was a "hubbly-bubbly," a hookah. Tonight women would smoke!

I looked at Sara more closely. No more than twenty-six, weighing less than one hundred pounds, her darker complexion was nearer mine in color, not as fair as Zubaidah. She was well made up; her well-dressed darker skin concealed scars from recent teenage acne, carefully covered in camouflage makeup. Sara's features were more Indian than Arab, and there was a coldness in her vivacity. She knew the power of her beauty already at a young age. Her widely arched eyebrows and wide-set, dark eyes imparted a feline appearance, compounded by her elegant, efficient movements. She too was wearing a stylish ensemble, a short skirt ending above the knee accompanied by a slim-fitting sleeveless sweater. Clicking heels added to her momentum. The body-hugging clothing revealed a lean, enviably streamlined figure.

Sara, like all the other women aside from Zubaidah, was dressed in entirely Western clothing. She would have looked right at home

in New York City. What then was the Saudi national dress for
women? These women didn't look anything like my patient Mrs.
al-Otaibi or her relatives. In fact I noticed from my observations
so far, though Saudi men were umbilically rooted in the Medieval
magnificence of robes, immutable across centuries, the modern
Saudi woman was much more Neiman Marcus than Najd.

As I watched her critically, Sara scurried amid peels of laughter
and placed the hubbly-bubbly down on the floor by the spineless
sofa. Clearly she was expert at doing this. The steel tray of char-
coal bricks was now at the apex of the glass tower and, with matches,
a flame was lit beneath. Soon water bubbled and bricks glowed,
perfuming the air with roses. Women puffed on the hubbly-bubbly,
offering each other the same mouthpiece, each carefully wiping it
before passing it on. As I sat, flanked by the Irish nurse and the
Canadian peacekeeper, the hubbly-bubbly was offered to me. I was
surprised to find myself taking the long, purple, silk-covered hose
between my fingers. Even if I was a lung specialist, finding no
excuse to refuse and not wanting to offend my hosts, I inhaled
deeply. Someone snatched a photo documenting my efforts. It was
surprisingly pleasurable, leaving a brief race of nicotine pounding
in my chest and a soft aftertaste of rosehip. So I had engaged in
smoking—a *macrue* activity (undesirable, but not forbidden) in
Islam. These women were not at all rigid, in the way I expected.
Already they had me pushing my boundaries.

I passed the pipe on to the next guest, satisfied that I was partic-
ipating in the joviality rather than just spectating from the sidelines.
I settled back to enjoy the scene, as they laughed, smoked, giggled,
and generally had fun. Soon the conversation lapsed into Arabic,
but our hostess never forgot to see that we were included in conversations in English whenever possible. All women there spoke perfect
English, and many spoke excellent French too. Finally, hours after
I had lost my appetite, around eleven p.m., food was served,

elegantly displayed in silver trays and porcelain platters. Zubaidah had personally prepared much of the menu: hummus, tabouleh, kibbe, rice, motabbal, kebabs, babaghanoush, yogurt sauces; a dazzling array. The food was predominantly Lebanese, Mediterranean, and Jordanian.

As we started eating, Zubaidah's mother descended the stairs. She floated into view without intruding yet somehow immediately causing a stir. She was an elegant woman, wearing her hair short in a stylish, well-cut bob dyed a tasteful auburn. Smoking a ciga-rette, leaning one hand languidly on her hip, she greeted her guests with soft, liquid salaams. She had presence and superb dress sense. Tonight she was swathed in a chic outfit of neutral wools and silks, draping her tall figure in softly pleated slacks, a silk blouse, and a warm shawl casually thrown together with effortless precision. The generational contrast was intriguing. I wondered why Zubaidah had chosen a traditional Palestinian costume when her mother was much more MaxMara.

Zubaidah's mother spoke French with more ease than English, though she fluidly swirled between both. Eager to welcome me, she seemed to know about me already; being the first female physician in the ICU had apparently been some news. Immediately she enquired of my parents and then asked how I could leave them so far away. I was beginning to get used to my parental lineage as an opening gambit in any conversation in Riyadh. People wanted to know where I was from, but more importantly, to whom I belonged. Without family, I was an unmoored puzzle. Quickly however, and unbidden, she told me her memories of Riyadh before the Mutawaeen had become so powerful.

"Riyadh wasn't always so difficult, Qanta," she began in a cultured, tobacco-bruised voice. "When I was newly married in the '50s, we never covered! No abbayahs, no scarves. I could go out alone without my husband." She released a poignant gravelly laugh.

"Khallas, those days are over now," she went on, sounding defeated. "The Mutawaeen spoil everything. These days it's really bad, Qanta, really bad." She studied me for the full effect. "We hate them!" She looked suddenly defiant. "I still hate them. I am never used to veiling. My mother also never veiled. We are not from this orthodox Islam. We are not Wahabis!"

I was astonished to learn there had been a time before the menace of Mutawaeen and the mandate of monolithic religion.

"It started in 1979," she explained. "In the Islamic calendar this was 1399, so at the beginning of a new century, the radicals believed this was to be the century of Islam. At the same time, you remember, Khomeini was taking control of Iran. The revolution was in full swing." She stopped to expectorate a fruity, bronchitic cough.

Inhaling a drag on her French cigarettes to calm her spastic cough, she began a detailed explanation beginning with the assassination of King Faisal in 1975.[5] Shortly after that, in Medina, a new plot was suspected against the royal family, directly threatening the monarchy. The danger appeared to be coming from among the community of Wahabi clergy. They were looking for the right Muttawa leadership figure who could spearhead their cause. Zubaidah's mother snorted in distaste at various intervals in the story. I was surprised; Zubaidah's mother had a deep loyalty for royalty.

She continued explaining, mentioning Juhaiman bin Mohammed al-Otaibi, who had served in the Saudi Arabian National Guard for around 18 years. Together with the rector of the University of Medina (a man called Ibn Baz) they formed a group called the Ikhwan (which means spiritual brothers) but it was nothing to do with the original Ikhwan who were involved in the formation of the Kingdom earlier in Saudi Arabia's history. I was listening rapt, only now realizing that several other women had gathered to listen to Zubaidah's mother recount the recent history which had become modern folklore. She had more to tell.

Al-Otaibi was a radical critic of the royal family.[6] He believed Wahabi doctrines could somehow become a political program that would avoid creating either a republic or a monarchy. Instead he wanted the rigid, archaic teachings to form a philosophical basis on which to run the Kingdom. Soon he declared himself "Mahdi," an emissary of the Prophet from the end of time, and on the threshold of a new century he began calling for the downfall of the monarchy. That November more than one thousand Ikhwan had mixed with Iranian pilgrims who were celebrating the revolution's success at eliminating the Shah from power during their Hajj. They were able to give special prayers of thanks during Hajj. The day before Hajj was complete, on the morning of November 20, 1979, the Ikhwan (who were heavily armed) swarmed through the al-Haram mosque around the Ka'aba. Many of them were from within the National Guard itself, friends and allies of al-Otaibi. Zubaidah's mother stopped, interrupted by cries of "Astagfarullah" (God forgive me) that echoed through the cluster of women around us. She went on:

"Can you believe these men occupied the holiest place in Islam and with weapons? Russian weapons! They held a siege there for nearly two weeks. It was a terrible time. Many died, hundreds of soldiers, pilgrims, and clerics and even more, more than five hundred were injured."

I began to understand that at that time both the monarchy and the clergy were vulnerable. Both needed the other to survive, so the crisis actually strengthened their parasitic relationship. The monarchy needed the clerics to control the population, authorizing some very oppressive laws. Another woman chipped in:

"So here we are in Riyadh today, controlled with abbayahs, and bans on driving and not being allowed to travel without our men. We lost our freedoms while the monarchy and the Mutawaeen got to keep their power."

Zubaidah's mother nodded to the other guest. After a deep sigh, she threw back her stylish head and blew a smoke ring, self-medicating her frustration with tobacco. Tapping the glowing embers aside into a Baccarat ashtray, she went on.

"And meanwhile the royal family feels safer, but not until they also made a special unit in the National Guard for special operations. You know they rewarded the army which protects them, kind of protection money. Somehow this arrangement works, for the Mutawaeen and the monarchy. Only the people are fed up!" Smiling, she began to rise to mingle with other guests.

"This is a depressing topic, not good for a party, but at least you know. After 1979, they decided women have to wear abbayahs always because they allowed the Mutawaeen more freedom to impose their ways, and Sharia law was everything. Luckily a lot of us still remember Riyadh before the Mutawaeen were so powerful. I used to be free in Riyadh, walking around like this," and she ruffled her hair with her elegant hands. "Can you believe, Qanta, I used to walk alone in Riyadh, no man, no maid, just relaxed like in Paris? Now that is all over, just like that. Makes Riyadh very hard to live in, huh, Qanta? That's why we spend time in Amman and Lausanne every year. We can stay in Riyadh only three months at a time." She looked at me for agreement.

"Are you ready for Ramadan, Qanta? It will be difficult here. You will have to get used to it. Next year will be better, Inshallah." She stopped as abruptly as her grammar, rearranging her tense face into a relaxed, chic smile. I couldn't imagine being here more than one year. I couldn't see beyond the next thirty days.

Looking at my grave expression, Zubaidah piped up, "I veil because I choose it!" Defiant, her gray-green eyes gleamed. "My parents never required but I always wanted. It is what Allah wants for me. I am not yet strong enough for full niqab, for full veiling, but I do what I can. It makes me happy, Qanta. I don't hate the veiling. Not like my mother!" She exchanged a goading chuckle with her resigned mother. Her mother looked at Zubaidah in dismay, rolling her eyes in contempt.

As I looked at Zubaidah's shining eyes, which glowed with idealism and spiritual enlightenment, I believed her. There was no doubt that Zubaidah's enthusiasm for veiling was genuine, her passion for her beliefs not fanatical but quietly steely, and I wondered if the glow she had about her, which her mother, in her bitterness and resignation so lacked, was more spiritual, more God-given than simply the elixir of youth.

I was puzzled as to how such radically different views could emerge from the same family and societal environment, and I wondered how much of her enthusiasm was founded on unques-tioning submission to the prevailing norm, following the peers of the day, rather than an active, living choice. After all, unlike her elegantly bitter mother, Zubaidah had never known life before the Muttawa, so in reality how could any of this be a choice, when the head scarf was mandated by law?

As I cast my eye around the marble room, the amount of hair on display struck me. In a short time, what would have never caught my eye previously was now arresting. Outside, bare heads were a rarity in Riyadh, when all men wore headdresses and all the women were veiled, even the patients. Here, amidst all these exposed manes, I could see I was the only woman with undyed black hair; everyone else was an aspiring redhead or a blonde-in-evolution. Kingdom-wide, female hair was colored along a continuum between the two. Next to these women I was plain, ungilded, colorless.

Hair had never been a particular concern of mine except that it be quick and easy to manage and above all, in place when I woke up in the dead of night to answer to my patients. Here, where hair was veiled, concealed for most of the time, enormous energy and money went into making it attractive. For whom was all this effort?

For the women themselves, I suspected. After all, how many men in a woman's family could care either way? And if no unrelated men were to see one's hair, how gratifying could it be to repeatedly beautify one's own lonely reflection? On a practical note, where did they get their hair done, I wondered. I was acutely aware I would have to find a replacement for Gerard, who had tended my hair for years. For sure, there would never be anyone as skilled here, but didn't these women all look great without access to Fekkai, Licari, Zouary, or Désange?

As I pondered these observations, an uproarious whoop let loose. I turned to witness a tall and extraordinarily beautiful woman entering the room. Simultaneously stately and mischievous, she caught my eye at once. I signaled her to sit near me. This was Ghadah, another dietician colleague of Zubaidah's. Ghadah had deep, shining, brown saucers for eyes, surmounted by long, pharonic eyebrows and flawless, creamy skin. The expressive, extraordinary eyes dominated her face. She bubbled over with joy. Impala-like, Ghadah was spectacularly beautiful. Hers was the index against which all the women present here measured their beauty in meager, modest comparison. White gold jewelry adorned her throat, wrists, slender fingers, and ears, reflecting against her luminous porcelain complexion, glinting with her every animation. A wedding band studded with diamonds graced her left hand, accompanied by the de rigueur Geneva timepiece. A deep, guttural laugh interspersed her speech, infecting everyone around her. She laughed full-throttle with her head tossed back, mouth wide open revealing imperfect and uneven teeth, an irregularity which seemed only to enhance the authenticity of her incredible looks.

She was dressed in easy, wide-legged slacks and a billowing Etro shirt. Casually she flung a substantial Dior bag into a deep recess in the sofa and rearranged herself. Rangy and lean, she crossed her legs and stretched out her arm on the back of the sofa. Ghadah exuded confidence and unabashed sex appeal. Chanel footwear completed her relaxed elegance. Her silky black hair was shot through with subtle ruby highlights framing her translucent skin with a pink glow, blushing like the inside of a smooth, polished shell.

Ghadah, it emerged, was my immediate neighbor, living in a row of villas opposite my apartment. She too had just relocated to Riyadh after years in Toronto, where she had accompanied her husband during his years of training to become a cardiothoracic surgeon. Haydar, her husband, was a talented surgeon, and I had already met him at work where we shared patients post-operatively. Ghadah already was a mother of two and, while raising her children, had pursued her own deepening interest in work outside the home, ultimately training in nutrition and also qualifying in Canada. Ghadah seemingly had it all: marriage, children, and a career. Riyadh was her home; she was a Saudi daughter of a Saudi father. They represented the crest of modern avant-garde professionals returning to Riyadh in the late nineties; the New Saudis. Haydar and Ghadah were committed to bettering their nation.

She invited me to her home for a longer talk and we quickly exchanged numbers. I was delighted at my good fortune: I would befriend this gazelle. Maybe some of her grace would fall like diamond dust on me too. Already, part of me wanted to be more like these glittering, extraordinary women.

After dinner the music began to rock, reverberating with unpent energy in the marble basement. The soundtracks were a mix of cutting-edge Beirut house and traditional Arabic melodies. I wondered where Zubaidah's father could be hiding in this noisy, tumultuous house. Clearing a space in the middle of the room, the women began to dance. They tied their scarves low around their hip bones, accentuating their movements, the hip-scarves forming a visible line of gyrating iliac crests that moved to a beat. The wider the hips appeared the better, it seemed. Unlike the fashion world of the West, where androgyny was king, here womanly, voluptuous figures were admired. The lights remained bright, not turned down. And one by one, each woman took the lead, dancing wildly and without inhibition, so self-confident even bright lights were no deterrent.

No one was intoxicated either, because alcohol was never served in Zubaidah's house, in keeping with the strong Islamic faith she shared with her family. Though illegal and punishable, black market alcohol was readily available in the Kingdom, but these ladies needed no alcohol to have a riotous time.

Among the sober Saudis, no one danced *with* one another; rather they danced *for* one another, the dancing woman surrounded by an enclave of clapping, laughing, shrieking joviality. The dancer was a performer for all to enjoy. I clapped to the music and collected my disordered thoughts.

In a few short hours, Saudi Arabia and its women were slowly demystified. These women were becoming three-dimensional, less like hooded holograms as I learned more about them. They were real women, coming into sharp focus through my very privileged lens of fellow womanhood. Underneath the swathes of veils and abbayahs, dancing feet and gyrating, curvaceous hips were scurrying by all over Riyadh. The daylong sedated, veiled torpor, the mask of Puritanism was just that: a bland façade to the uninitiated, lifting privately to unveil carefully guarded energy, made all the more delicious and potent in its illicitness. These were buoyant, spirited women, made stronger by the layers of oppression in the public world. These were women of appetites, complexity, and deep convictions. Through Zubaidah I was inducted into a multilayered, complex, cloistered world. Under an impassive, forbidding surface, Saudi Arabia was very far from monolithic.

As Christine and I tapped our feet to this scene, unable to join in the day-lit disco of dervishes, trapped in very Western inhibitions, I asked her about her relationships with her fellow Saudi nutritionists. She had worked with them for some years. I wondered how she felt toward them.

"How do you get along with these Saudi women?" I asked, mentioning that I hadn't any female colleagues in my section.

"Saudi women are incredibly manipulative," she answered flatly, in a low determined voice. She watched the scene with an unflinching, aqua-colored eye. I looked at her, stunned at her criticism, especially as she partook of their hospitality. What did she know of these women? What had she learned in her years here?

"They have to be manipulative," she went on. "Their goals and dreams and their places in the workplace are achieved only through the manipulation and influence of husbands or fathers or brothers or sons. Without their influence, they can never express themselves." She sounded bored. Evidently she had theorized on this before.

I listened, taken aback by the venom in her conviction. Christine explained how she believed Saudi women cannot realize their needs by assertion, in the way women in the West traditionally do. The ambitious Saudi woman, therefore, becomes skillful in influencing men within the family, a subversive manipulation, calculating, persuasive, and highly intelligent. I knew already that the women at this party, the Saudi women who worked at my hospital, were unique and rare within the Kingdom. These were some of the first women in the workplace in Saudi Arabia. My hospital was exceptional in encouraging Saudi women to work, with the support of the liberal and woman-promoting CEO, Dr. Fahad Abdul Jabbar. I had not yet met him, but among the Saudi women at the National Guard Hospital, he was revered.

These women must have overcome tremendous traditions that would normally encourage them to remain at their father's home until it was time to relocate to a husband's home. In this stratum of Saudi society, the families were wealthy and the women would have no material need, no economic compulsion to earn. The goal to live in one's own apartment was one which I never encountered amongst these women. Though they longed for the freedoms I had enjoyed—driving cars; wandering the world with short hair and no scarf; traveling alone; pursuing a career as avidly as a man; simply being free—there was no driving force urging them on to leave their families and be independent in any real sense. The hunger these women did have was for education and autonomy in the workplace; a need for purpose, one greater than that of their mothers.

Whatever their methods, of argument or debate or attrition only in the way a beloved daughter can exact upon any indulgent father, these women were indeed very strong. I was not sure that "manipulative" was the most encompassing description for such determined women, and I wondered how much of that observation was a reflection of Christine's frustrations. I could see that matters I had taken for granted—education, freedom, travel, independence—were hard-won prizes, even for these privileged, wealthy creatures. And yet, when allowed in the workplace, they had to be tough, just like I did, competing not only against men, but against legislated male supremacy—men who believed women belonged in the home and at the hearth, not in the hospital or headquarters, not in offices or operating rooms. Facing that everyday was a feat. As I spent more time in Saudi Arabia, I would see how much strength would be asked of a woman at work. I would learn from them and observe them in action. Saudi women indeed were a force to be reckoned with.

It was after one a.m. I had work in the morning, and we faced a long drive back to the compound, far from the pulse of downtown Olleyah. Christine signaled that it was time to take our leave, and we began our thanks and farewells. Already a good neighbor to me, Ghadah volunteered to run us back home. As the steely gates closed on an exceptional evening, we clambered into Ghadah's green minivan, which was waiting for us, engine running, outside the house.

A sinewy Bengali sat hunched over the wheel. The streetscape shimmered by in the velvet night. The city was still busy even though it was late. Traffic packed the highway and the side streets were congested. Everyone had been out tonight, on the eve of Ramadan. We all wore our veils properly, covering our hair, even though the windows were heavily tinted. Ghadah's veil was the most beautiful, with deep borders of purple and silver embroidered flowers; she drew the veil into a perfect frame around her face, showing off her chiseled jaw. There could be no hiding this kind of beauty. Ghadah's beauty was radiant, unquashable. No abbayah could vanquish this resilient, gleaming woman.

As I sat enfolded in my own clumsy veil, I smiled: I really had enjoyed myself. It was extraordinary to gain entry to the matrix that is Saudi. Without the abbayah, in the privacy of a home, these women laughed and danced and joked and smoked like anywhere else. In unveiling ourselves, we had revealed our womanhood in common. Saudi women were no longer alien. During the day, or in public, these women not only veiled their beauty and their clothes in those black abbayahs, they veiled their spirits, their souls, their joie de vivre.

With a jolt, I noticed this was the first time I had heard out-loud laughter in the Kingdom. Within weeks of my arrival, the public Saudi Arabia had already become pervasively oppressive; like a vapor, nothing escaped its suffocating touch. Invisible tentacles of control had smothered me into submission. But underneath this miasma-mask, in the far marble pavilions of Saudi homes, in the recesses of the private Saudi, it was already alluring, intoxicating, and profoundly conflicted. I wanted to know more.

My joyful reverie was aborted minutes later. Caught in a snag of unruly traffic, we came to a juddering halt on the highway. An impasse of SUVs ("James's") and loitering Land Cruisers barred our way. Music blaring, pulsating windows reverberating to the subwoofer bass beats within them, surrounded the diminutive minivan. Our entrapment was sudden. The bass beats were more Cross-Bronx Parkway than Khuraij Road; once more a crass cultural shard of America in the heart of Arabia.

As I looked out of the tinted window, I locked eyes with a Saudi man staring straight back, window rolled down, his shemagh flowing in the night wind, billowing in the breeze. From the front window I could see their driver, arm hanging out, gangsta-style. He slouched in the unspoken language of the ghetto, slumped at the wheel, barely sitting upright. These men were reclining at the wheel less like caliphs and a lot more like boys from the 'hood. This cruiser was prowling for "chicks," and we, it appeared, were the chicks in question. Ghadah was already screaming instructions to the dull driver to move the car, except he couldn't; the cars were packed ahead. In the impromptu jam, the guys were taking time out to pick up women.

On the left-hand side of our car, another vehicle heaving with young men prowled menacingly. They had caught on that we were six women in one car, the odds were good. Ghadah became more alarmed.

"Ladies! Please! Cover yourselves! Please cover your faces." Immediately she tossed the end of her scarf over her face. She continued to bark orders to the driver through a mass of chiffon, like a crazed but very commanding Muppet.

I felt ridiculous. I tried harder to see through the opacity of polyester and tinted glass. She was overreacting, but her fear was real. I couldn't tell her to calm down. Surely, they couldn't see us through the smoked windows, except maybe our silhouettes. We were now transformed to six shrouds. With my eyes firmly covered I found I could stare about with much more abandon. Donning my mask was perversely liberating.

Then the missiles began. Through the driver's window, which in his torpor he still hadn't closed, a piece of crumpled paper came up, thrown in from the black Land Cruiser. Unraveled, it was a cell number. The shrouds collectively laughed, partly inhaling our scarves. The other ladies were only half-amused. It was impossible to know which of the men had sent it and to which lady it was intended. Ghadah's anger was now ablaze.

"This is what they do, Qanta," she said, exasperated, Impala eyes flashing with anger. "They are trying to pick us up!"

It seems this was how Saudi men met girls or at least tried to meet them. Sometimes they threw in crumpled paper. Other times the paper was wrapped around empty cassettes for a more aerodynamic missile-missive. As I looked at the leering faces, there was no mistaking that hungry, prowling look of cowardly men who hunt in packs. I wished the glass had been darker. I wished I was more concealed. I wished we were home.

It made perfect sense, once I considered it. Without a religious policeman installed in every vehicle, men simply could not be prevented from doing this; the law could not be enforced here. And, with so many men and women in a small place together, stuck in a jam, it was only natural that the walls of segregation would strain under the proximity. Necessity was indeed the mother of invention, it seemed. I recalled a recent trip to Miami. This was after all just a slight distortion from cruising South Beach on a Saturday night.

I found the exaggerated panic of Ghadah even more startling. She was planning to drop off her sister who was also in the car with us at her married home before reaching our compound, but, given the SUVs pursuing us, immediately cancelled that plan. Ghadah called her father on the cell phone for advice. After a tense discussion in staccato Arabic, Ghadah's sister was to come to her father's house instantly. She was not safe in her home while her husband was away on business, and the Land Cruiser seemed intent on following us. Ghadah decided to drive everyone, all of us, to her father's home first, before taking us back to the compound.

No matter how much her sister protested, first to Ghadah, then to her father, there could be no discussion. She would not be allowed to travel to her own house. She was quite powerless in the face of her father's decree. She would manage without her bed that night; they had everything she needed to stay over. The illusion of our power had evaporated.

As we continued on and the road ahead opened up, the Land Cruiser kept up constant pursuit. Driving in parallel, windows open, men leering, hanging out of the windows, and calling out in Arabic, we were prey. Music blasted louder still. Effectively only a malnourished and silent Bengali was our protection. Where were the Muttawa now, when they could have done some good after all, protecting us?

We traveled deeper into the city, away from our compound. At last we arrived at Ghadah's father's house, and the Cruiser entered the mouth of the street. Instinctively it hung back, exhausts growling as the engine idled. The Cruiser blocked off the only exit to the small lane leading to the house. Again, Ghadah called her father. It was now two a.m. She refused to unlock the car doors until her aging, silver-haired father came into the street to receive his daughter. Immediately on the appearance of the septuagenarian, an arc of blazing headlights swept by, illuminating the scene, recognizing his male authority. The Land Cruiser retreated, double-lumened exhausts growling a low roar. Soon, it was merely a drop of brake lights joining the red stream of traffic in the distance. We were safe.

After seeing Ghadah's sister into the house, we headed back home in silence. The mood was one of subdued relief. I recalled my question at orientation, "What should we do when we are followed?" and the disdain with which it had been received, remembering the irritated dismissal of my alarmism. I felt indignant and newly vulnerable. The repressed, inhibited men sought conquests, just like men in other countries, but the strain of their leashes wore thin. What was unfathomable to me was how they could be attracted to follow us to such lengths. After all, there were so many other vehicles carrying bundles of women.

But which women would respond to such overtures? In the late nineties these missile missives were common, but in a few years, these comically desperate attempts of the segregated lone male would be replaced by a wireless Bluetooth assault of tracking devices looking to make an electronic connection with bored, lonely women longing for Bluetooth boyfriends.[7] Now women in Riyadh and Jeddah can flick on their cell phones and BlackBerrys, activate the Bluetooth icon, and simply wait for messages to appear. Very quickly they do indeed pop up on screen, by the dozens and often with very flirtatious screen names looking for cyberdates. These not-so-shy cybersuitors, themselves veiled by virtuality, are within a radius of only a few meters, flirting from within the wireless confines of the Bluetooth signal.

I looked over to Ghadah, her face uncovered and veiled as she was normally, silently staring into the road ahead. Her gaze was steely. She seemed furious. Her angular jaw, her liquid eyes, and those endless brows were indeed alluring. In the moonlight, her pale skin gleamed. Now I could see the enormous price she paid for her beauty; it was a weight, a burden, a tiresome responsibility. It was probably her profile that had fueled the chase. When I pressed her, she admitted this happened to her often. Her screaming instruction had been less anxiety and panic and more anger. Ghadah was constantly a victim of her beauty. While perhaps it sounded exotic to be chased in pursuit, even when recounting the tale now, it left all of us feeling exposed, powerless, and above all, defenseless.

The gatehouse loomed up out of the darkness and the military guard waved at us in recognition. The gates closed behind us. For the first time I was pleased to see the walled compound. I was relieved to be secure under military patrol. It was then that I drew the parallel that stayed with me throughout my Saudi years; the safety in my home in Riyadh was based on armed security. I could relax only in private, high-walled homes. For me, Saudi Arabia was becoming clear: while now my home, it was also my prison.

Chapter
Seven

VEILED DOCTORS

EVEN THOUGH POST GRADUATE MEDICINE in the Kingdom was legally a desegregated environment, where men and women were employed and could interact as work dictated, the voluntary gender segregation remained extreme. Rounds were a male-dominated event. More often than not, I found myself the lone female in the team. If any other women were present, they had only silent walk-on parts, mute props watching from the sidelines. I was slowly becoming aware that chauvinism and sexism was just as marked among many of the Western attendings as it was amongst many of the Saudi and other Arab physicians, as though the climate of the workplace promoted an infectious transmission of male supremacy.

With time I began to understand how this could have developed. State-legislated Wahabiism endorsed male supremacy, which was pervasive throughout the Kingdom and in all aspects of life; a rather heady mixture for weaker men from all parts of the world. Porous to the noxious waters they found themselves steeped in, they sucked in male supremacy with surprisingly little aversion. Quickly they themselves became vectors of oppression. It took an extraordinarily strong, sound-minded, and secure man to protest to the benefits and intoxicating ascendancy being a man in the Kingdom entailed.

Male physicians consulting on my patients would arrive at the bedside where I would be attending the patient. Frequently, they would breeze past me. I was invisible to them. In medicine, it is usual to offer an opinion about a patient's illness that could sometimes be quite different than one's colleagues. This medical exchange is vital for the best diagnosis and management of disease. In Saudi Arabia, if I failed to support the tentative diagnosis or, worse, tendered an alternative, male Saudi attendings would sometimes show deep personal affront. Missing the subtle indicators of displeasure in a silent, curled male lip, I was, for a time, puzzled at the unspoken injury it seemed I often caused. Eventually I realized a difference of opinion was sometimes received no differently than a personal insult. No amount of Harvard or Cleveland Clinic could ever quell the tribal pride of the wounded Saudi male. My stubborn clinical disputes were deeply upsetting and anathema to them. I was told quite bluntly that while my clinical acumen was valuable, personally I was considered "intolerable." I was surprised how wounded I felt to hear this. It would be a long time before I would be inclined to be more diplomatic. In my beginnings in this world, I was just too angry.

An insidiously advancing invisible status engulfed me. As a woman clinician, even unveiled at work, but always covered in my white coat and trousers, I was at best an obstacle that was to be circumnavigated, quite literally like an awkward piece of furniture indecent enough to lack wheels. In typically female fashion, I began to search for my mistakes. Perhaps this lack of recognition was rooted somehow in my own fault? After all, I was a guest in this Kingdom. Why couldn't I communicate more diplomatically, like my other (male) peers, the quiet Poles who always smiled and were able to be incredibly pleasant to the most arrogant of Saudis. Later I would discover them privately, defusing their stress in a flurry of muttered Polish expletives and intense chain smoking, as they only half-jested at comparisons of Kingdom life to Communist rule.

I turned to my Saudi female colleagues. I knew they were a rarity in this society and must have overcome many obstacles to be able to practice medicine in this world. The statistics were astonishing and these women were valuable for both their experiences and their expertise. Very few Saudi women could do what they could.

At the time, the Kingdom was not self-sufficient in terms of the number of Saudi doctors its population needed. Only twenty percent of all doctors in the Kingdom were Saudi, with eighty percent being expatriates. This is an exact reversal of the United States, where between twenty and twenty-five percent of all doctors are migrants and the remainder citizens. Of the twenty percent in the Kingdom who were Saudi clinicians, only a tiny minority were women. This I could see reflected around me. I had almost no female peers.

The prospect of women in the workplace was not necessarily an accepted reality. The women who worked with me were a reflection of the extremely progressive views of our feminist Saudi CEO, Dr. Fahad Abdul Jabbar. In fact, some muftis (senior clerical scholars) had even chimed in with the prospect of women-only hospitals as a solution to what they considered the avoidable evil of bringing women into the public workforce. Sheikh Abdul Aziz al-Asheikh, the Grand Mufti of Saudi Arabia, recently proposed the same during a symposium in Riyadh on applying religion in medical issues. He described the intermingling of sexes at hospitals as a "disaster" that challenged the intrinsic modesty of Islamic societies. The Grand Mufti even went on to suggest medical professionals should only treat patients of the opposite gender under clinical extremis.

Saudi women are reported to have had a mixed reaction to this. Some orthodox women from very conservative families now newly considered medicine (regarded even by the most vehement mufti as a humane profession) as a possible career choice if she could be guaranteed practicing in an all-female environment; for instance, in a hospital devoted to obstetrics and gynecology. To many women in the Kingdom, however, this was simply another way of their marginalization, this time through limiting work options for professional women. The *Arab News* reported[8] these objections to single-gender hospitals in the words of one woman in particular:

"I don't think this is a good idea. We all live on one planet so we cannot segregate the genders. If the Holy Mosque in Makkah, which is the holiest place on earth, does not segregate women, then why would the Ministry of Health want to segregate them?" said Maha al-Nuwaisser, 26.

She also went on to object to the selection of a physician based only on gender and not competence, expressing her disdain as follows: "I prefer doctors who are professional in studying my situation and solving my problem, regardless of whether they are male or female. I cannot imagine a men's hospital without female nurses and doctors, and I also cannot imagine women's hospitals without men playing a role in them," she added.

Even though I and the women around me agreed, we knew anything was possible here and were unsurprised when we read the expected response of the Ministry of Health to the Grand Mufti's declaration. Dr. Khaled Mirghalani, official spokesman for the Ministry of Health, did admit the Ministry was considering the formation of such single-gender hospitals, but rapidly added that this had nothing to do with the mufti's recommendation. For now, I found myself in a mixed environment where, whether expatriate women or Saudi citizens, female physicians were a rarity. I looked to my few female colleagues for support and guidance. Perhaps I could learn how to cope in my new environment by studying these women.

All Saudi female residents were entirely veiled. They would join the rounds covered from head to foot in black abbayahs, over which they would wear cartoonishly long white coats, tailor-made, which were always fully buttoned up to the throat and often closed with round mandarin collars rather than the standard neckline of a jacket. On their heads, black nylon hijabs would brush down to their mid-backs over the stuffy white coats. All features and any suggestion of shape or even weight were obliterated. It was impossible to distinguish one woman from another. Often in corridors, I would be greeted by a woman whom I had taught in the ICU and could not recognize her because of the uniform guise of anonymity required of women in Riyadh.

On rounds, invariably the women would be glued to the back of the group, standing always to one side, a single invisible organism. Frequently I would try to move each female resident with a gentle but firm guiding hand to their draped elbow or shoulder, encouraging them to move to the fore of the group. Like a phalanx, they moved only in a cohort, afraid to stand alone, sheltering each other in a cumulative shadow of their opacity. They remained silent and respectful during acrimonious exchanges, inscrutable behind their hijabs, rarely tendering any opinion, and certainly never questioning anything that was said. I watched them at this strange nexus of Wahabiism, womanhood, and Western medicine. They shuffled heavily on rubber-soled shoes in their airless mantles of the modified white coats and helmet-hijabs. How hot they must be, even in the air conditioning of the unit.

From time to time, I would direct them to listen to the patient or examine for a particular sign. I watched as they stuck the rubber ear pieces of their stethoscopes into veiled ears, pushing the ear buds over their fabric masks of blackness which extended, here, even deep into the recesses of the female ear canal. I knew it would be impossible for them to hear a soft diastolic murmur against the deafening (and now acoustically magnified) crunch of itchy polyester.

When we made rounds visiting our burn patients who were nursed in strict isolation, I knew these stoic women were even more uncomfortable, dressed in the sterile, bright yellow protective garb over shrouds and coats. Isolation masks or orange duckbilled TB masks snapped on over full-face hijabs. Sometimes metal-rimmed eyeglasses perched bizarrely over entirely veiled heads, like so many bespecled puppets. The intensity of veiling even engaged in procedures within the privacy of isolation rooms was astonishing. These women had to be very dedicated and able to withstand uncomfortable conditions, sometimes for hours. They were tough and capable of seemingly enormous tolerance for the intolerable.

Over time I found myself full of fascination and admiration, while somehow also brimming with enormous pity for these mysterious women. Judging by the miserable rounds we were making, their approach to medicine mimicked what I guessed must be their approach to Islam, mute and unquestioning obedience, always prescribed by a man. As the women rarely spoke to me on rounds, I wouldn't be corrected in my simplistic views until much later, when I befriended more Saudi women. For now, I made my own wretched conclusions and began to wonder how long I really could last in the low-grade hostility I felt at work.

The rounds at least allowed me an opportunity to observe the Saudis in their workplace. Occasionally, other specialists would visit our patients while we were at the bedside. While presenting a patient for the benefit of Waleed, a young Saudi resident, and his fellow surgeons, I pointed out an important physical sign. I spent a significant amount of time explaining the patient history and nudging him toward the expected findings. Waleed's long moustache drooped into an expression at the intersection of abject boredom, indulgent tedium, and ignorance. I tried harder to animate him. As I focused on striving to unlock his medical imagination, at the periphery of my vision, I slowly became aware of the rustling of crumpled cotton. Mid-auscultation, around me I began to hear greetings in Arabic, followed by the preeminently disturbing and unmistakable sound of kissing! Filled with disquiet, I looked up. The stethoscope slipped from my hand clattering noisily against the bedrail.

Coteries of male surgeons from the vascular service were greeting Waleed and the other male residents. They had just stepped out of the operating room. Some still had their surgical masks dangling rakishly around stubbled necks. Green clumps of Saudi men dressed in surgical scrubs intermittently disentangled into single green entities. Slowly, methodically, the men were kissing one another on each side of the face: each cheek, twice, thrice, four times, even more, as I lost count. At the same time, they shook hands and embraced in endless combinations of two—a strange, synchronized kissing geometry.

Nothing could proceed until every Saudi scrub suit had greeted every other Saudi scrub suit. Of course, all women were excluded. The veiled phalanx stood wordlessly, as usual, to one side. For once I joined them in my own silence. I was annoyed at the interruption, but even more flummoxed at the overt lack of concern for my time and the uncovered patient who lay half-examined. Beeping monitors and alarming machines faded into the background. I lost my train of thought in its entirety as I stared at the scene.

Their greetings were slow, languid, and relaxed, as if we had all the time in the world. Did they know we had critically ill patients to attend? What a contrast from New York City, I thought, imagining all the red-blooded, monogram-cuff-wearing men who had worked with me there; a quick back slap to a male colleague followed by a rapid hand scrub with sanitizers and it was back to work immediately. Nothing could be more alien to this display. "There will be no kissing on my round!" I wanted to scream, but of course, as usual, I bit my tongue and waited for every man to greet each of his compatriots.

Truthfully, if I looked inside myself, it was disconcerting to see so many men kissing one another. This was the first display of public affection I had ever seen in the Kingdom. Subconsciously perhaps, I had assumed Saudis didn't kiss. Who knew Saudi mouths could make such sounds of tenderness and grace? After all, for months now, I had never seen anyone kiss or hold hands or embrace one another here. Physical contact seemed unthinkable in the Wahabi state.

Observing the kissing surgeons, I couldn't help thinking I had wandered into a Halloween party in the West Village by mistake where gay New Yorkers masqueraded as sheikhs, greeting each other girlishly, almost camp displays of affection. The themes of homosexuality seemed strangely near. Nevertheless, I could tell there was a sense of real connection here. The familiarity and physical intimacy with which these men greeted one another was astonishing. Not only did they shake hands, but men continued holding each others' hands in greeting quite some time after the initial pleasantries and salutations, intertwining long slender fingers almost wistfully.

The actual kiss was in fact a gesture, the pink, full lips rarely contacting skin, but making a quiet sound of lips touching softly. The kiss of a Saudi man was a caress, warmer than a plastic Park Avenue pout, more sophisticated than a clumsy kiss planted on a cheek. This seemingly intimate act was an effeminate and highly choreographed, practiced maneuver: the man closing his eyes as he caressed the air around the recipient's cheek or shoulder, a small quiet gesture of closeness and undeniable elegance, carried over across the ages; an elegance not of my world, not of the West, nor of this time. It made for an arresting dichotomy: the harshness of male supremacy and sometimes visceral misogyny juxtaposed with the intensely tender relations between the men themselves, as if the only sensitivities that could be safely displayed were deeply gender segregated.

It would take time for me to be accustomed not only to this public courtliness among Saudi men but the far more unsettling sensation which often accompanied it. The fact that perhaps among these men a homosexual was compelled to hide, at risk of the penalty of decapitation, filled me with unease. Did a gay man move comfortably among these men, or was he full of fear? Could men even acknowledge these possibilities among themselves?

My unease was not homophobic, but at how difficult it was to make sense of anything that I witnessed here. The opacity was overwhelming and blinding; I could see, yet I couldn't. Sometimes I could feel myself literally widening my stare, as if to catch more light to decipher the unintelligible images. How well invisible gay men could blend in, how well-concealed, how protected and ensconced in this male-dominated, severely segregated society. I couldn't distinguish men in any way, the homogeneity was extraordinarily powerful. The feeling of not knowing quite what I was privy to at the moment I was privy to it, and that things were (as usual) not what they appeared to be, never left me in the Kingdom.

Once again, even the familiar salaams which these men were exchanging, almost the first Arabic words I had learned as a child, were rendered unfamiliar because of the social dance in which they were contained. At the end of this dance, Waleed and his fellow residents reluctantly returned to the round, grudgingly restoring their attention to me. They failed to notice my stony silence as I had waited for them. Mercurially, their moist smiles changed to impassive masks of severity and boredom. The warmth and politesse drained quite suddenly away. We returned to the patient. Mentioning nothing of the intrusion on my round, I continued seamlessly from where I had been interrupted. Invisible or not, I had a job to do.

Chapter
Eight

THE LOST BOYS OF THE KINGDOM

I RACED TO THE EMERGENCY ROOM. Arriving, I was immediately sucked into the gravity of crisis. Three bodies were laid on steel trolleys, dead on arrival. An orderly draped them with sheets. A fourth stretcher bore a shorter bundle already shrouded; one of the dead had been a two-year-old, sheets around him purpled with cold blood. In the far corner, a bleeding body lay limp on the final stretcher where a cluster of doctors worked. It was this man whom I had been called to attend.

I pushed through the anxious mass surrounding the bed. The man's head was split open, the scalp a bisected, bloody coconut. An intense smell of alcohol exuded from clammy skin. He had been drinking, probably Jack Daniels, likely chased down by whole bottles of Finnish vodka, I guessed, by now experienced in the poisons of choice in the Kingdom. Eyes swollen shut, now purple figs, and a trickle of thick blood from the left ear confirmed my suspicion: a basal skull fracture.

Lush, long lashes revealed the prime of youth. A single mole on his right cheek conferred aristocracy to the young face. A finely manicured beard betrayed a man of vanities and panache.

His once-aquiline nose was ignominiously collapsed into itself, a "dishpan" fracture indicating enormous impact to his face. Around it, his dreadlocked mane was startlingly lush. His elaborate hair was his private rebellion. The airway had already been protected with a breathing tube, rasping with bloody secretions at each mechanical shudder. His chest was severely bruised. I could feel the sickening give of fractured ribs crumpling like wishbones in roast chicken. A collar bone was wildly displaced. Scanning for the telltale marks, I realized he had been unrestrained. His belly was disturbingly swollen and bruises were beginning to form on his cool flanks. A leg was rotated outwardly at a queasy angle, the swollen thigh pooling with liters of blood. He had fractured at least one hip, perhaps also the pelvis.

I checked his pulse. His digits were icy. An unpleasant mottling was beginning to show on the palms of his hands. He had already lost liters of blood. As quickly as I could, I placed a line to deliver massive amounts of intravenous fluid. I managed to insert it in his hollow, left groin. Even his femoral artery, normally a booming pulse, was deflated, fluttering like a frightened, dying sparrow.

Stitching, I noticed the glittering wristwatch on his left hand. The diamond surround of the sapphire dial was flecked with his own blood, the P of Piaget obscured under a mossy clot. I unbuckled the thick crocodile wristband, handing the precious timepiece to the nurse for safekeeping. Studded Vuitton wrist cuffs dressed a broken spirit of stylized angst. Above, where his Gucci flying jacket had been sheared open, his inner arm was a crisscross of fresh track marks, revealing a heavy drug habit. My patient was a privileged man with addictions to alcohol, heroin, and, I suspected, several other substances.

After intense teamwork, we rescued the falling blood pressure and could safely move him to the CT scanner. I accompanied him to the scanning table, blood transfusions running. Satisfied he was secure, I returned to the ER to finish up.

A Filipino janitor cleaned the bloody floor where we had been working, smearing the viscid mess across white linoleum. The adult bodies were wheeled away, awaiting identification in the hospital morgue. Parents numbed in their grief prayed over the smallest, still body. The brutal fluorescent lighting stole any semblance of privacy. A nurse whispered the details of the dead child to me as I wrote at the station.

The child had been their eighth, a youngest son. He had been killed by the Mercedes which had carried the four men returning from a weekend of high jinx in Bahrain. These parents had lost another child in a motor vehicle accident only a year earlier. I listened, unflinching. Months of working in the traumatic environment of critical care in Riyadh had already numbed me. Children were killed every day. I watched the parents weeping and allowed myself to feel nothing. The cruel, tasteless expatriate joke was based on a hideous reality.

"What do you call a Saudi airbag?"

"A five-year-old."

Follow with black laughter.

It was common practice for fathers to drive with their sons at the wheel. Often the child, flying unrestrained headlong through windshields, died in the collision while the father lived. A massive effort was underway to teach parents about car seats and seat belts, spearheaded by the National Guard Hospital, yet safety of children in Riyadh was not the neurotic obsession we were familiar with in the West. Often one could see actual children driving, their button noses barely peeking over the steering wheels of American SUVs. Motorists as young as twelve were an unremarkable sight in Riyadh.

As I finished writing, I looked at a young Saudi man pacing in the area, unable to settle in a chair which had been provided. His thobe was scattered with the blood of others. He must have tried to stem the bleeding of his fellow passengers before help had arrived. In his left hand, he clutched remote entry keys to the now-mangled monster Benz. I realized he was the sole passenger unscathed by the apocalyptical joy ride. He must know what had happened.

Before I could approach him, he rushed up to me. He had been watching me treat his brother.

"Doctora, Doctora, is Tahir going to live? Please, I have to know. God, I can't believe this is happening." He rushed up to me, then dissolving into sobs, frantic. In his distress, he reached out to grasp my forearm but at the last minute, inhibited by tradition, snatched his hand away. Traces of $185 Creed wafted from his Dunhill thobe, despite the carnage wrought on his clothing. I waited for him to become calm. He wiped away tears of pain with soft, manicured hands. The sharp scent of absinthe on his breath startled me. He had also been drinking it seemed. When he finally spoke, it was slowly and in a British voice, smoke-laced and Eaton-educated. He sounded exactly like Jeremy Irons.

Yaseer, the brother of the wounded man, described the night I had predicted. They had been returning from a weekend of drinking, coke, and heroin. Tahir had just taken delivery of the monster Mercedes McLaren. They had opened the 5.4L engine full-throttle to see what it could do. They clocked speeds of almost one hundred twenty miles per hour. Tahir had been drinking for hours, trying to "sober up" with lines of cocaine. His brother couldn't persuade him to relinquish the keys, and so the death ride began.

At the end of an especially straight stretch of the Damman Highway, Tahir saw the Suzuki pickup—in the back, a dozen long-eared goats. It was stalled halfway into the road. There was no time to prepare. Yet he swerved, even at these speeds. A sound of screeching goats, roaring rubber, buckling steel, and it was all over.

When the noise stopped, Tahir was crushed between the steering wheel and dashboard, his head through the windshield. Powder from the airbags mixed with goat fur and blood. From the Suzuki, a Bedouin mother cried for her child. Yaseer stopped talking, spiraling deep into the memory. Pulling out a cigarette, he wiped away new tears for long moments. Finally he crumpled the filter between his orthodontically perfected clench.

"How long had Tahir been doing drugs? And how did he become an alcoholic?" I began. The brother was surprised I had exposed my patient's addictions, but after a long sigh, he began to tell me the sad elegy of his brother, an anthem to so many other privileged men in the Saudi Kingdom.

The brothers were the youngest sons of a wealthy Saudi merchant, born to his fourth wife. The father was already seventy-two when Tahir was born. He was also a severe alcoholic, disappearing for weeks at a time to seek shelter with his other wives, away from the needs of his youngest children.

Despite, or perhaps because of, his alcoholism, the father wanted Tahir to have the best education possible. At eleven, he was sent to boarding school, first in Switzerland and later, after expulsion for delinquency, to an English boarding school in Norfolk. Away from his mother, he became even lonelier.

Before long he was playing truant. By thirteen he had started drinking. By fourteen he had been to the ER for intoxication. At sixteen he was expelled again, returning to the Kingdom. His family noticed a change. He was withdrawn, sleeping for long hours in the day.

It was at this point that Tahir started using coke seriously. With his family money and connections, drugs and alcohol were easily accessible. Yaseer explained how Tahir started out doing lines of coke in private homes and some of the better hotels. Soon, he was hanging with a fast set from Bahrain and later an elite jet set from Dubai. His life for the last three years had been a series of drug and alcohol benders. Amman one weekend, Milan the next, returning to Dubai, then Paris for Fashion Week. And so he moved, constantly, partying everywhere, until he was trashed. He never felt at home anywhere, preferring instead to live in suites at the Lanesborough in London or the Hotel de Crillon in Paris.

Tahir, a product of a broken polygamous family wracked by alcoholism and jealousies, couldn't sink any roots. He had even tried the conventional Saudi life expected of him, marrying endogamously several years earlier. But like so many privileged, sheltered Saudi women, his wife had been groomed only to be a bride, not to become a wife.

Newly married, Tahir would return from a day at his father's office to find an empty married home, his wife bored, stationed instead at her parents' house. He discovered he had married a child still umbilically connected to her mother. The drinking soon returned. His brother looked on, powerless, and so ended the story in the carnage of tonight.

I returned to the ICU waiting for the scanning to finish. Yaseer's tale of his tragic brother had filled me with sadness, yet it was already an all-too-familiar story.

I called them the Lost Boys of Riyadh. They shambled around town in anti-establishment T-shirts, sporting low-slung, studded belts and black jeans, so many Riyadh Rappers. Now and again, an irreverent witticism on a T-shirt would catch my eye, sometimes reading "Made in England" on the back, causing me to smile. The slump in their shoulders, their heads bowed under the perpetual weight of shame and loss, pulled at something inside me. I felt sad. These men were broken.

Often, I saw cohorts of them milling in the ER after a night of high carousing. Other times, like the prowling Testarossa coxswains issuing cat calls in Olleya, I watched them, intrigued by their behavior, at once threatening and cowardly. Always, a defiant jaw line belied bravado rather than courage. Manicured beards revealed a peacock's vanity, reddened, always runny nostrils, gave away a voracious appetite for blow.

The glossy accessories and costly playgrounds only defined the void these men carried within them. They felt abandoned, lost, and unvalued. These were men raised without fathers, sired by those old enough to be grandfathers. They were sons spawned of men who had lost interest in children, even a male. The Lost Boys grew into men without direction or future. For all their privilege, which torpedoed them into the echelons of Western societies and appetites, they lacked the substantial anchors of a place and an identity in their own families, culture, and religion. Outcasts in their own families, unable to bridge the generation abyss between aging polygamist fathers and modern bachelorhood, they failed to find belonging anywhere else. These were the New Nomads. Unlike their forebears, however, there was no purpose to their painful and very isolating wanderings. They roamed in search of an escape from self, often finding it in drug-induced oblivion. The Kingdom was losing whole generations of Lost Boys in this way. They became strangers in the very Kingdom that had birthed them.

Chapter Nine

A Father's Grieving

SEVERAL DAYS OF PROPER SLEEP had invigorated me. I was ready
for anything on duty. As I sipped the first of many coffees, I
spoke to the charge nurse running the ICU.

"Don't tell me, Floriana, bed 16 still hasn't gone to surgery?"
Floriana nodded in placid agreement.

A pleasant enough Saudi, Hesham was a rather timid surgeon.
I suspected he recognized the fear of operating within himself.
Floriana and I took a long look at the patient.

"His spleen has been oozing for a while now, Floriana.
Hopefully that sack of boggy clot will hold. This spleen could
rupture at any time." We exchanged a pained look.

"Maybe I should call him to take a second look? What do you
think Floriana?"

"Oh Doctora, you didn't hear the news?" Floriana looked at

me, puzzled. "The news about Hesham's son?" I looked at her blankly, absorbing her concerned tone.

"Hesham's son was killed on Thursday. He was only six. We don't know the details, but there was an announcement in the staff meeting. An accident. He died shortly after arriving at the hospital."

Floriana fell into a silence, thinking about her own children who were living thousands of miles away in Manila. As the only bread-winner in her family, she sent them money every month. As a mother she was wounded by the death of another's child. Years later we would all be broken when Floriana herself was killed in a motor accident weeks before repatriating to Manila for good. Riyadh was notorious for motor vehicle accidents.

Instantly I regretted my contempt for poor Hesham. I separated from Floriana and went for a walk outside on the ICU lawn. It was past dusk. The sparrows were twittering their final birdsong before moonrise. I felt acutely sad for the bumbling surgeon, remem-bering how eager he had seemed to be friendly to me.

"And if you need anything at all, Doctora Qanta, anything in Riyadh, please let me know," Hesham had urged, leaning his tubby shoulders against the steel doors of the ICU late one night after I revived one of his patients. I remember looking up at the overweight Saudi who was beaming a surprisingly friendly smile. I wondered exactly what he could mean, "should I need anything." I was so unaccustomed to casual friendliness with Saudi colleagues that now I regarded good will, especially from Saudi men, with intense suspicion. That night, I had dismissed him with the briefest of nods, my disdain for him secured behind my surgical mask.

Recalling his friendliness now cut me to the quick. Though I knew him only from caring for our shared trauma patients, I knew him to be well-meaning. He was a man who did his best in spite of the fact he wasn't particularly able. That was a bravery and persist-ence in and of itself.

In a moment of clarity, I knew at once I wanted to visit Hesham's home and express my condolences. It was the only way I could express penance for my disgraceful condescension in past months. Perhaps, now that I could see my own arrogance, I would finally learn some much-needed humility. Riyadh was making me very hard. There was a sharp edge to me which wounded everyone around me. I didn't like the angry, aggressive woman I was becoming. I wanted to change. I would start by doing the right thing for Hesham.

The next morning after signing out my caseload, I spoke to Faris (the ICU chairman) about Hesham. A Saudi Hijazi and a trained scholar in Islam before he ever practiced medicine (actually himself a Muttawa), Faris was well versed in the traditions both of Islam and the Saudi Kingdom. He would know how I could arrange a visit for such a delicate matter as the death of a child.

"Dr. Faris, I know it is unconventional, but I wish to visit Hesham himself. This is just terrible news. I cannot believe this has happened. When is the funeral? I want to see him, give my condolences."

"Yesterday. And, Qanta, in our tradition only men can attend funerals. So you wouldn't have been able to go anyway. I was there with many of our other colleagues. It was terribly sad. After the funeral, Allah recommends three days of visiting for people to pay respects to the bereaved, but after then we really shouldn't intrude on them. The family is given forty days to grieve in privacy. Allah wants them to try and recover from this terrible loss. We should not make it more difficult for them by visiting outside this period."

"What about tomorrow, Dr. Faris? Could we please visit Hesham, perhaps as a group of colleagues from the ICU? You know I cannot visit alone. I have never met his wife. Maybe if several of us went as his ICU colleagues it could be possible for me to go there this way?"

Faris burst into a wide smile. He was renowned for his appetite for community service whether visiting the sick, the bereaved, or others in need. He was a very social Hijazi. Recently divorced, I wondered perhaps if he was also lonely. An outing even of this nature was one he would certainly enjoy arranging, if nothing else other than to pass a solitary afternoon.

"Qanta, that is an excellent idea. I think in the company of your colleagues there would be no impropriety." I was taken back by his genuine praise. "Let me talk with Hesham and see what I can arrange. Perhaps we will ask Imran and Imtiaz to join us? I know they are friends."

"I will tell the others," I agreed and rushed home to start making the calls. Faris retrieved his cell phone from a deep pocket in his thobe and was already dialing numbers before I had left the room.

Imran and Mobeen (my fellow New York City-trained colleagues in the ICU) were at once supportive when I told them the plan. They agreed to come. They promised to invite Imtiaz too, our other Pakistani colleague who, like us, had trained in New York.

The next afternoon we were to gather outside the ornate hospital VIP entrance. At the appointed time, I scurried through the brown-and-gold marble atrium which ushered influential and sometimes royal Saudis who came to be treated at our hospital. The mid-afternoon light was blinding, and my eyes smarted even from behind shades. On the portico, pacing up and down with a cell phone, Faris, our escort, awaited us. In his white thobe standing next to his white Cadillac, Faris cut a fine figure. Admiring his surprising elegance, I spied on him unseen for some time before stepping over toward him.

Faris was probably six foot two in height. In recent years he had gained weight, conferring a prosperous yet warm countenance to the man. His face was almost round, lined with an unobtrusive but maintained beard. His eyes were always on the verge of sharing a joke and in fact he was renowned for his excellent sense of humor. Faris was a comedian and the antithesis of the forbidding stereotypes that powerful men in the Kingdom somehow bore.

Today, in place of his clumsy white coat and ill-fitting scrubs, he had chosen to dress in traditional attire. His white headdress fluttered in the blustery afternoon breeze. As he took a phone call, pressing the black cell phone to an unveiled ear, the aerial slid upwards, cutting a startling contrast against his ancient headdress. His shaded eyes looked out pensively into the distance. From time to time the wind tugged at his white shemagh, pulling it away from him, revealing a shaven, scented neck and plump sides of a smooth, unlined face. His skin color was deep brown, almost Indian in coloration, adding contrast to the striking cream ensemble of his dress. I was struck by his panache and glamour, made even more beguiling because he was so obviously unaware of his own allure.

He moved toward his white Cadillac, as immaculately spotless as its owner. Spying me, he signaled me to hurry. Imran and Imtiaz were already in the car, expecting me to take the front passenger seat as a means of providing me, the lone female, with personal space. Faris got into the car carefully so as not to disturb his headdress. Once settled in the driving seat, he glanced in the rearview mirror and adjusted the peak on his hat, exactly like a cattle rancher fixing his Stetson. He signaled to me to sit beside him. In response I froze, remaining outside the car.

In my observation inside the Kingdom, the front seat was reserved only for wives. In the glare of the wide expanse of windshield, the Mutawaeen might easily spy me if I sat there and ask to see my papers. As an unmarried woman I wasn't sure that even Faris, the head of the National Guard Hospital's prestigious ICU, could protect me. Worse, I feared fueling the fantasy that I might take the place of Faris's partner. His recent divorce was common knowledge, one that was widely discussed in the hospital. I didn't want to encourage even a remote chance of inviting his attentions. My paranoia was paralyzing and completely disproportionate. What would never give me pause in the West somehow had monumental connotations in Riyadh.

Despite protestations, one of the men finally moved from the back to sit next to Faris and I sat instead in the rear seat. The windows at the back were deeply tinted, a practice widely adopted in the Kingdom at the time to protect the female cargo from intrusive stares. These cultural shades on all motor vehicles have since been discontinued to make it easier to search for potential terrorists in the Kingdom. We were still pre-9/11 at that time. But today I was glad of the concealment. After months of living in the Kingdom, I couldn't tolerate the vulnerability, both physical and social, of sitting in the front seat.

At last, Faris put the car in gear and began our journey to Hesham's house. As he pulled on the gear stick which, pathognomonic of truly American cars, was attached to the steering column, I couldn't help laughing at the thought of Seinfeld's dad. Faris was a Saudi version of the same. His car was pure Boca. I sank into the deep leathery seats. Semi-recumbent, we floated through the afternoon. Soon, thinking of the sad visit ahead, we fell into a silence. Riyadh was rather empty. It was a quiet Tuesday. Most were either at their workplaces or taking a customary afternoon nap, and pedestrians were almost never seen in the Kingdom. Most streets were devoid of sidewalks. In Riyadh, a city which had been constructed at warp speed, roads had been built without sidewalks for a population which had made the transition from camel to pickup, SUV, or sports car in one fell swoop. Here everyone traveled by car, Saudis and expats alike. Even the poorest of the poor, the foreign laborers, relied on rickety cycles, but few were in sight at that time of day. I watched the scenes as they fled past the window, lifeless and unpeopled.

Just as we passed a shopping center I recognized, we turned off the main road and began weaving through a maze of half-finished streets. A couple of boys lurked around a corner shop, watching traffic and kicking a dusty ball. We turned off a busy two-lane road lined by small shops on either side.

Faris squeezed the fat Cadillac along the narrow road, creeping ahead to find the house. No properties were numbered, but he had been to the house before. He finally identified Hesham's home by a palm tree that hung into the street from the front yard. Making an impossible turn, he pulled into the narrow driveway. The steel gates had been drawn back. We were expected.

The silence after the engine stopped engulfed us. Only the ticking of the slowly contracting metal under the hood punctuated the vapors of grief emanating from the house. We were parked on a small drive, large enough for one car, covered in crazy paving. This was a lower-middle-class home. Like many Saudi employees at the hospital, Hesham chose to live in a private dwelling in the city rather than in the generic Medical City accommodations where, segregated onto different compounds, many Saudi and non-Saudi employees lived, free of charge.

Neatly weeded flower borders gave Hesham away as house-proud, though I imagined a poor Bengali gardener probably toiled over these beds for him. The breeze fluttered through a rose hedge. Distant sounds of boys playing tag magnified the sound of the loss at this house. Faris dropped his voice into a whisper and lead us towards the house. Before we could ascend the terrazzo steps, Hesham opened the door. He greeted us with a weak but genuine smile and with a heart-rending humility welcomed us into his home.

"Innalillah e wa inna ilayhe rajioon," (Surely we are from God and to Him we are all to return) echoed among us as we greeted him with salaams. We tried to soothe him with the mantra of the prayer for the deceased. Hesham responded with the same prayer. I could tell he was trying hard to believe his son had indeed returned to his Maker.

Hesham was dressed like a man about house. His head was uncovered without the formal headdress that Faris wore, yet he wore a similar white thobe. The throat was undone, unlike the peaked collars of Faris's formal thobe, which were closely buttoned. Hesham's bald pate gleamed, a bluish bruise in the center of his fore-head, a mark of his devotion to regular prayer. His moustache was tidy, the rest of his face clean shaven and freshly cologned. In the few days since I had last seen him, his customary cherubic glow had faded and his round, Reubenesque face had thinned under the burden of recent grief. He leaned against the doorway of his home, shoulders forever broken by sadness.

"Salaam alaikum, Salaam alaikum!" (Peace be upon you! Peace be upon you!) He greeted each of us warmly. Each man took his hand and kissed the side of his face several times in the usual Saudi custom. Faris stopped longer, consoling him in Arabic, his hand pressed on top of Hesham's. With a quick swipe of his hand, Faris brushed his ready tears, which had already wet his face in empathic sorrow.

"Salaam alaikum, Doctora Qanta," Hesham addressed me. "Welcome to my home. I am so happy to receive you." Even in grief he was gallant. "I have to apologize, my wife is still not returned. Since we lost Raeef we have been staying with her parents in Riyadh. I apologize there are no ladies in the house to greet you." Hesham trailed into a silence and then, after seeing we were all properly seated in his living room, he vanished, assuring us of a rapid return.

We looked around at each other, awkward in this newfound inti-macy linked by a crushing bereavement. We sat on one of three sofas. I perched on a distant end so no man could feel squashed by proximity to a woman. The room was still. The carpets seemed to have been freshly vacuumed. The faint aroma of heated dust filled the air. A low coffee table was laid out with Arabic coffee sets, plates of dates. Fruit had been freshly sliced. Plates, cutlery, and napkins were laid neatly in our anticipation. Some incense burned on a credenza near by. The home was prettily decorated. Decorative brass plates lined the walls. A sole house plant was the only sign of life, motionless in a terracotta pot. The shades on high windows were lowered. The sunlight struck blindly against the sealed shades, bathing us in a muted white light. No one said anything.

Hesham returned, bustling in with a heavy tray of coffee. The heady aroma of cardamom filled the room. Once ready, he poured it into a shiny steel Alfi thermos, a chic German variety which was very popular in the Kingdom at the time. As he busied himself unloading the tray and distributing first the tiny egg-cup-like coffee cups to each of us, I realized he had prepared all the food himself. There was no assistant, no cook, no maid (all very common in a Saudi physician's household) at the house. All the staff had been given time to grieve while the family had repaired to the grandparents' villa. The servants had been very attached to his youngest child.

"Today is my first day at home since the funeral," Hesham began, straining to be cheerful. Our silence was becoming painful. I had to break it.

"Thank you for receiving us, Hesham. Your house is very beautiful. Please, you should not be serving us like this. May I assist?" It seemed incomprehensible that the grieving father should serve us in this manner.

"Absolutely not. You are my guest. Please remain seated." With these words he stopped me mid-ascension from the sofa. I was relieved. I was still wearing my abbayah and with the hot coffee and high heels I was likely to fall had I actually had to serve the men myself.

"Hesham, we came here today because we feel so unspeakably sad about the death of your son. We wanted to see you to tell you this, to express our sympathies. What can we do for you?"

I spoke for the whole room. The men shifted uncomfortably in their seats. There was a loud and awkward creaking of leather. Pouring the last cup of coffee, Hesham at last took a seat on a sofa to my right. Faris sat opposite me in an armchair, his eyes downcast. Imran and Imtiaz were to my left, just out of my peripheral vision. I could feel their relief as I spoke our feelings.

"Thank you, Qanta. You are all very kind for visiting me. It helps a lot to see friends—"

Faris interrupted him. "This was Qanta's idea. We are so happy she thought of this opportunity." And just as abruptly he fell back into a strangled silence.

"Tell me, Hesham," I asked, "can you speak about what happened?" Hesham turned towards me, wrapping a fat ankle behind his bulging calf. His thobe rose over the stretch of his belly revealing the hems of his sirwal, the trousers which Saudi men wore underneath their thobe. He looked directly at me, stretching one bulky arm across the back of the sofa. He began to tell us of the death of his child. I had a feeling the story had already been often told. He spoke in a resigned, small voice.

"I was beginning my vacation last Thursday. I had been stuck closing an abdomen on my last case. My cell phone was ringing constantly. Finally the OR nurse answered it. It was my wife saying that I should leave the hospital immediately, our son had been hurt. I dropped my instruments at once and the resident took over. I think Dr. al-Naimi continued, though I don't know. The OR nurses took care of everything. I ran to my car and raced to the house. I didn't know where my wife or son were. I was driving down the main street, the one just here before you turn into our lane, when my wife reached me by phone again.

"'We are at the Security Forces Hospital. Hesham,' she said, 'our baby was hit by a car!' And she was hysterical. I couldn't understand the rest." Around the room several of the men were already weeping. Every man who had accompanied me here was a father to at least one son. In fact Faris had a son who was exactly the same age as the slain Raeef.

Hesham continued, "I drove there like a maniac, running red lights. I don't know how I reached there in such confusion. I drove up to the main entrance and left the engine running with the keys inside. I ran like a madman to the ER. I remembered it from when I had to come in and assisted with cases here. It was already over, Qanta. When I entered the room, he had just died."

Hesham stopped, sobbing for a long time. I listened, unable to bridge the gulf of grief and gender between us. I wished I could touch his shoulder in sympathy but I was immobilized by the rules of Saudi culture. No one moved in the room. Faris expressed our sadness as he uttered several verses of the Quran aloud in a soft, soulful voice filling the terrible space.

After a time, Hesham continued, "My small son, my little boy, was lying there on the steel stretcher. The ER attending was there. He was crying himself. Raeef had horrible head injuries. I actually saw some brain tissue there on the stretcher. I think his neck was broken too. My wife had fallen to the floor. Her abbayah was covered in Raeef's blood. She had reached him before me. The doctor finally told me Raeef had arrived in cardiac arrest, but the team could not revive him. My poor wife had waited alone outside for thirty minutes. I can't believe it… I can't believe it."

There was nothing we could say to assuage his pain. He slumped again into a heap of grief. The white sleeves of his thobe were now damp with his tears. He ran his hands back and forth over his pate, tearing at the few strands of hair that remained.

"How did the accident happen?" I prodded gently. "Are you able to tell us?"

He looked up, wiping his nose with the back of his hand. I passed him some Kleenex. With red-rimmed eyes, he smiled at me with gratitude. Somehow it was helping him to retell the ghastly story. In a loud gulp, I swallowed some coffee. My throat was contracting under the terrible grief so concentrated within the small room. Immediately the others followed suit. There was a clinking of coffee cups on glass tabletops. Someone chewed a cardamom seed. We waited.

After taking a deep breath, Hesham began to speak again,

"Raeef was a very special child, Qanta. He was very good. He was very obedient. He was a follower. He never once angered me. We worried about him because he was so trusting, a small friendly angel. He was so different from the other children.

"I had always told the children to play inside the yard, not outside. You have seen the traffic out there. And our street is so narrow that the boys cannot play there because of the passing traffic and the heavy parking. So they always want to go out toward the shops where they like to play in the parking lots.

"I know our yard is small, but there is a small lawn where they could play, and when I go to work the drive is empty and they are allowed to play football behind the closed gates. Without the car there is enough space. It is not much. I am not a rich man. But Alhumdullilah (by the Grace of God) we have enough. Everyday for years I am telling them to play inside, not on the street. And the children always listened. My children listen always to me. I never have to raise my voice. Their mother is the disciplinarian."

With a sidelong glance to the other men in the room he allowed himself a watery chuckle. The room eased under the mounting strain just a fraction. Recognizing the universality of marriage, a quiet ripple of smiles flickered through the room of men, vanishing almost immediately.

"Raeef was excited that day. He knew I was to be on vacation for two weeks. We were planning a trip to the sea in Bahrain, a special treat for my family." He trailed off looking wildly around the room, in utter disbelief at his new reality. "On the day of the accident he was playing with Wissam and Mourad, his two cousins. He loved them. He wanted to be like them. You know, they were older. They could climb trees. They could play football. Raeef just adored them. He couldn't wait to grow up.

"My wife was in the home supervising dinner. Tutu, our Malaysian maid, was finding some difficulty in preparing the omali (my favorite dessert) which my wife always likes to make for me on the first day of my vacation. So, my wife," he stuttered under fresh waves of grief, "… Raeef's mother…she was therefore in the back of the house and didn't realize that the yard had become quiet. When she called for Raeef to wash his hands and bring the others in for a snack, she realized no one was in the yard and the gates were opened. She went into the street and couldn't see them. She followed the road, remembering there were shops which sold some candy and Pepsi nearby. She also remembered the boys had wanted a new football because the one they were playing with had somehow lost the air pressure. She noticed it, deflated, in the corner of the garden. It was then she realized they had gone to buy a new ball with their pocket money.

"Now she started running and right away she saw Mourad and Wissam across the road, entering the shop. They seemed to be laughing. But Raeef, who was not able to keep up, had been running behind them. Suddenly my wife saw him in the road, actually in between the lanes. His cousins told him to stay back, that they would be returning in a minute, and Raeef looked confused. He recognized his mother and just at that time Hayyat, my wife, saw a black GMC Suburban racing toward our son. I think, we think, Raeef saw it and got so scared he couldn't move. The truck was so big the driver didn't see the child until he was almost on top of him. Raeef was hit by the fender and went up over the windscreen. It was horrible. The driver immediately stopped the car and was so distraught, but he was a good man. He called to my wife and put them both in the car and drove them to the security forces. When I arrived there, his Suburban was standing at the ER entrance, covered in my son's blood. I didn't realize until later... well... you know the rest."

Hesham was inconsolable for a long time. Even under his tremendous grief, however, his weeping was soft and controlled. He was trapped in a monumental silence of shuddering sobs.

At last, in a voice swollen with emotion, Faris spoke, "How is Raeef's mother?"

"Faris," Hesham responded, "she is terrible. She has eaten nothing since Thursday. She cannot stop crying. It is so distressing. She is a very strong woman but I seem to have lost her in this tragedy. I pray Allah sends us relief. This is a very difficult pain for parents."

Suddenly Hesham turned to me. "You know, Qanta, we have to be very patient. Everything we have is because of Allah's bounty, His Grace. We have nothing without His Benevolence. He is All Powerful, and we must remember whatever He gives to us, He can also take away at any time. Everything comes from Him and everything returns to Him. As parents we have to be prepared to return our children if He asks for them. I tell my wife, Raeef was so dear to Allah, he wanted him back very soon."

Hesham stopped to pause for breath. Stirring finally out of his empathic sadness, Faris finally rose to the occasion and began sharing some of his monumental scholarship of Islam. He often surprised us with his vignettes of Islamic philosophy in between making rounds in the ICU.

Addressing me, he began to explain, "Hesham and Hayyat are being tested in the most difficult manner. If I can explain something to you? The death of a child is a special trial for parents. There are three fundamental beliefs in Islam about the death of a child which

Allah teaches us to make the parents' suffering a little easier." He glanced quickly at Hesham who nodded, encouraging him to continue. We listened, rapt while he explained the bereavement reaction to the death of children from an Islamic point of view. As Faris explained, speaking slowly and carefully, sometimes pausing to recollect a precise detail, Hesham periodically sighed and filled with tears. At one point he felt compelled to interject, "Did you know it is said a mother who has lost one child is being pulled to heaven by one hand by her deceased child? And that a mother who has lost two children is admitted to heaven by her children each of whom leads her through the gates by one hand? Raeef is pulling his mother through to heaven even now. I try to tell her that, to make her feel better."

"Hesham is describing intercession." Faris continued, "Allah wants us to learn patience. The death of a child is perhaps the most difficult test to develop this, Qanta. Patience is a tremendous virtue in Islam because Allah wants us to cope with difficulties and trials always with acceptance."

Faris went on to explain how the Prophet Muhammad (PBUH) himself emphasized that the person who praises God both in good times and bad is the true believer and most worthy of God's Grace. He continued, "Raeef's death is terribly painful for his parents but they have been given a special opportunity to grow closer to Allah."

As I listened I was reminded of the amazing tolerance of the patients I had attended in this country. The principles Faris was describing were probably why my patients, no matter how ill, were surrounded, by and large, by nonjudgmental, accepting relatives who seemed equally pleased and comfortable with my efforts no matter what the outcome of their family member. Relatives of patients in Saudi Arabia were surprisingly devoid of the recriminations despite the severity of disease, the unexpectedly precipitous deaths, or the difficult course their family members often faced in critical illness.

I used to explain this away by the absence of litigiousness in the Kingdom where medical malpractice suits do not exist, but now from Faris's careful explanations I understood that this belief that one must be patient in the face of terrible ordeals and terrible tribulations was evidently dearly held among all Saudis in the Kingdom.

Faris continued, "A child who has passed from this life, at the Will of God, is allowed to plead on behalf of his parents. God's heart is soft to these young, innocent souls. Always tell a suffering parent this, because it will soothe their grief. Allah allows the deceased child to speak to Him on his parents' behalf. Raeef will intercede, meaning, plead to Allah for His mercy when He must make judgment on his parents in the afterlife, asking Allah to excuse their mistakes. Normally only special souls can appeal to Allah at the time of judgment, asking Allah to be merciful in his judgment, for instance like the Prophet Muhammad (peace be upon him) or holy saints may speak on behalf of the soul. But the soul of a child can speak for his parents too."

Faris felt compelled to add more, "The Prophet Muhammad (peace be upon him) taught that a child who dies, whether a boy or a girl, will always appeal on their parents' behalf. Not only for the mother," and he looked significantly at Hesham, "but also on behalf of the father. Allah will look very compassionately on these parents who will suffer lifelong for their precious loss and of course, the child is always admitted to heaven in the afterlife, to Jannat." Faris used the Arabic word for special emphasis. "Because children are pure, without sin, and die in a state of innocence, like Raeef. And what is most important of all is to remember it is said the child will not bear to be separated from his parents in heaven and so when Allah is calling him to Jannat, he will refuse to enter the gates of heaven without his beloved mother and father's admission. In this way he takes each parent by the hand and leads them towards Allah in Heaven. And God takes pity on them."[9]

"How beautiful," I couldn't help saying. Hesham nodded.

"Raeef is taking us by the hand. I know he is," Hesham murmured. "Maybe we will stand before Allah in judgment and maybe Raeef will plead our sins to be forgiven. And you know, Qanta, God may take with one hand but he gives with another. Inshallah he has given us much, and he will give to us again."

I looked at him puzzled, wondering if he was considering replacing Raeef with a new baby. I didn't dare ask such a sensitive question. The grieving father was too raw. Identifying my confusion, Faris again helped me understand and explained how another belief about the death of a child is substitution, though as humans we cannot begin to comprehend His wisdom. Some parents think that one child has been taken so that they might receive another who is even more pious. Or it could be Allah wished the child a sinless, innocent death in order for him to appeal for his imperfect parents on the Day of Judgment.

Hesham was calm now, approaching tranquility. "You know, Qanta," Hesham began, "my wife always thought Raeef was special. Mashallah, also I think he was. Sometimes it worried my wife, because he was so adoring of Allah. His request every night at bedtime was, 'Mummy, please read me the Quran.' And even when my wife tried to read him a storybook or children's story he was not satisfied. She was worried by his piety. He seemed to have a maturity way beyond his six short years. He liked best the stories about the Prophet and he liked very much to picture Allah. None of our other children were like this. He was very pure, Qanta. That is why we really believed he was angelic. I think that is why he had to return so soon.

"You must know, Qanta, that the Prophet Muhammad (peace be upon him) was himself an orphan. You remember he lost his parents and his beloved uncle and grandfather at a very early stage in life. His parents died when he was a young child. His life was marked by loss, Qanta. As a father, he went on to lose every single son and numerous daughters. We always tell one story to teach Muslims about grief following the death of a child. It is the story of when he was burying his son, Ibrahim, who had died in infancy. Do you know this example?"

I quickly admitted my ignorance. Quietly Imran switched on a lamp. Imtiaz poured some more coffee. A stray cat called for its mate in the alley outside. Looking through the shades I could tell it was finally growing dark. We listened in silence. Faris's explanations of Islamic teachings were very compelling. We were ensconced in this unfolding beauty of Islam.

Faris began to recount the story about the Prophet Muhammad (PBUH) when he buried his own son. "It is recorded that when the Prophet Muhammad's son died, he held him one last time, pressing the body against his chest. Witnesses saw the Prophet's face became wet with tears as he said to the small body, 'Oh my son, I didn't own you. You belonged to God and now you are returning to Him... If there had not been the true and certain promise of Allah that we too shall come after you, I would have wept more and become more grieved at the separation from you.'"

Hesham began to cry softly again as he imagined the parallel grief of the Prophet. Faris sniffed a little, stemming back his own tears. He continued, "After the corpse of the child was washed at the Prophet's instruction (which in Islam must be done by a same-sex member of the family) they approached the place of burial." Hesham seemed lost in his own memories of his son's burial only two days earlier. "The gathered men—and in fact women as well, women in the Prophet's family were there too—saw the Prophet crying and they too were grief-stricken. Yet even in this state of distress, still the Prophet showed us the correct example and chastised the noisy mourners gently saying..." (again Faris lapsed into classical Quranic Arabic, translating quickly for me) "'Shed tears from your eyes and grieve in your heart but don't wail and moan!'"

Faris was finally silent. All that could be heard was the occasional sniff and the silent weeping of the grieving father. By now my own eyes were wet. I rummaged in my bag for tissues, pulling out a residue of crumpled Kleenex.

"We should not be ashamed of tears," Faris suddenly announced in a louder, more impassioned voice, making no effort to hide his own tears which streamed into his beard. "The Prophet always said crying indicates a subtle and spiritually refined heart. Crying is a mercy from God that He gives only to whomever he pleases. He shows mercy only to those people who are merciful to others. It is a sign of tenderness that pleases Allah greatly."

In these quiet, extraordinary moments of inclusion into the grief of a Saudi father, I was learning what I needed most, humility. Around me, these Saudi men, one, a new divorcé, and the other, a bereaved young father, were clumsily but gently showing me the way to be a better Muslim, perhaps even a better woman.

Hesham offered me more coffee. I nearly crumbled at his simple kindness, accepting some quickly to hide my quivering chin. The Azaan rang out, indicating time for Isha.

"We have stayed too long, Hesham," Faris stood, suddenly, at once filling the room with his height and a recovered bonhomie. The men began their courtly procedures of farewell salaams. I flouted convention and shook Hesham's hand. He received it warmly.

"Please give my regards to your wife," I volunteered.

"Yes, yes I will," he responded, almost excited. "Hayyat knows you are visiting. She was very pleased, Doctora Qanta. You will have to meet her when she returns home. When she is stronger."

"Inshallah," I responded. "I will be glad to."

We left him standing at the doorway, a forlorn figure forever framed by his loss. The solitude around him was overwhelming. Faris started the car, pausing momentarily before lurching the

Cadillac into gear and rolling out of the driveway. I could tell he was reluctant to leave Hesham, but we all knew none of us could shelter Hesham from his loss. We knew there was no escape for Hesham from his grief, no peace or tranquility, either with the company of others or without.

The cocooning silence of the Cadillac muted us once more, each lost in private thoughts. The white road marks disappeared under the heavy American tires that carried us over anonymous roadways, the same roadways which were carrying me on so many strange journeys in this Kingdom of Loss, and the same roadways which had cut little Raeef's journey of lightness so unbearably short.

Chapter
Ten

AN INVITATION TO GOD

INSIDE THE KINGDOM, HAJJ SEASON was upon us. Something approaching national fervor was beginning to take hold, quickly erasing the somber weeks of Ramadan, which had just elapsed. Each year, Hajj draws millions of Muslims from around the world who descend upon Mecca into an unparalleled pandemonium of worship. In Riyadh, several hundred miles northeast of Mecca, I could already feel the reverberations of Hajj. I wondered if I would glimpse some inkling of this extraordinary mass migration washing over the Kingdom.

Early one morning, I entered the doctors' office in the ICU and walked into a discussion on scheduling. I looked on with disinterest as colleagues negotiated leave for Hajj holiday. Most had already booked trips with Hajj agencies for their families and would be making Hajj themselves. Within me, the slow stirrings of a new curiosity tugged into life. Before I could investigate my thoughts any further, an emergency halted the meeting.

* * *

Forty-five minutes later, Imtiaz and I looked at each other with the intense release physicians know to follow extreme pressure. We had just pulled Halima (at sixteen, our youngest patient in the ICU) back from the brink of death. Thankfully she would get to live another day. We joined Mobeen, the other physician on duty, and together headed toward the South Indian's stall to buy ourselves tea. As I was leaving the ICU, pulling me to one side, Mobeen stopped me just inside the steel doors.

"Qanta, I must talk to you about Hajj." His urgency stopped me in my tracks. We had hardly had any conversations outside of patient care. I leaned against a cool wall. Beads of perspiration slowly evaporated from between my shoulder blades. An air conditioning vent whirred directly overhead, dissipating the last remnants of my adrenalin. Intent, I listened, still keen from recent crisis.

"Qanta, you must go to Hajj. You must." Taken aback, I listened. I hadn't been thinking of going to Hajj at all.

Mobeen's soft voice was unexpectedly impassioned. The room contracted to a single, shared moment. Conspiratorial, he urged on:

"It is every Muslim's right. It is your right, Qanta. No one can stop you from going because of the schedule. This could be your only year in the Kingdom. Who knows when you will get a chance to attend Hajj again, Qanta? You must take this chance. You are a Muslim and this is an Islamic Kingdom. It will be impossible for anyone to deny your request to attend."

Triumphant that he had made his point clear, he left, looking suitably pleased. He had made an indelible impression. I was slightly shaken. In a bland instant, amid the humdrum of critical care, I had stumbled upon my *niyyat* (intent). I had clasped the fleeting Muslim within me and started a journey which would carry to the innermost sanctum of Islam.

Mecca is the place on earth where a Muslim can meet his Maker in this lifetime. Until now, the force field of my Maker had escaped me, but since I had moved to the Kingdom, I was beginning to feel His rumbling magnetism. Now, with my own Hajj days away, I realized I had never been so badly planned nor so spontaneous. I was a mixture of elation and fear as I began to find the edges of my ignorance.

I hurried to arrange leave and find a means of getting to Hajj. Mobeen had read the situation precisely. When I told him, my chairman was surprised but coolly complied with my ill-timed request. He couldn't deny a Muslim the opportunity to visit Mecca. The ICU would have to manage without me. I needed to find a carrier who would take me to Hajj, a Hajj agent. I soon realized that most had made arrangements months earlier. Helpful colleagues advised me to speak to the hospital's travel office. As soon as I could, I went to the hospital's Hajj office and booked a last minute package.

Later that afternoon, I made more tea. Switching on the computer, I surfed the Internet for information on how to do Hajj. On the verge of the most fundamental pillar of being a Muslim, I found myself an imposter. I didn't even have a copy of the Quran here in the Kingdom, let alone a book about how to do Hajj.

At last, I found a diagram explaining the stages of the journey. Designed for children, it was one of the few explanations I could find in English. I gathered up the pages as they unfurled from the printer. Fat arrows depicted steps that would soon be mine. I read hungrily.

In the beginning, I would express an intention to make Hajj. I would assume the required purified state, the ihram, through ablutions and prayer, before departing for the airport. As I traveled, I would acknowledge the Holy Sites of Medina and Mecca when I flew over them. (The pilot would notify us of precise moments to do so.) On arriving in Mecca, I would make my first Tawaf, circumambulating counterclockwise seven times around the Ka'aba, before embarking on Hajj proper. There was so much to remember, I found myself filling with a rising panic.

Returning to the map, I read more. After that first night completing the first Tawaf, I would depart the next day to a place called Mina where, for three days, I would spend the time in a reverie of supplication, along with several million others. From there I would go to the plain of Arafat. I would stand on the ground where Abraham had stood before God and prayed all night long. This was the most important part of Hajj: "Arafat is Hajj," was repeated everywhere on any explanations I read. This was the essence of Hajj.

After a day at Arafat, in the late evening, I would spend the night outdoors on a plain called Muzdullifah. Finally, I would return to a place near Mina, called Jamaraat, where I would throw seven stones at three pillars which symbolize Iblis, the Devil, showing him appropriate scorn. This would mark the end of my Hajj, and I would cut a small lock of hair and discard it; a symbol of my purification. If God accepted my Hajj, I would be reborn, without sin.

If my Hajj was complete, I must sacrifice a sheep to distribute to the poor. How would I do this? Things seemed complicated enough without sheep shopping to boot! Only then, after finishing all these steps could I celebrate Eid, the end of Hajj. With a frantic rushing back and forth in memory of Hagar's search for water in the desert (a ritual called the Sai'ee), I would make a final Tawaf, at the end of which, with a final backward glance at the Ka'aba, I would pray that God allow me to return once more in my life to the Ka'aba, and leave the city limits immediately. I would thus become a Hajja (the official title of a Muslim woman who has completed Hajj).

As I looked at the crude diagram, it seemed straightforward enough and, thankfully, at eight days, apparently quite short. I kept the map in my bag and transposed some of the rituals into my diary. My Hajj was beginning to materialize from a mirage. I went to the phone. I wanted to call my Saudi friends and tell them I would go to Hajj. Maybe they would know what I should wear and exactly what else I needed. They would fill in the details.

"I will just get her, ma'am," said Tutu, the Malaysian maid who answered the phone in Zubaidah's house. I heard Zubaidah's couture heels echoing across the cool marble floors of her villa. Barely allowing her time to greet me, I gabbled my news into the receiver.

"Mashallah, this is wonderful, Qanta, really wonderful." Her deep, cultured voice was infused with joy. I could tell her pearly smile was slowly curving into a wide bow.

"I am so excited for you, Qanta! How did this happen so suddenly? Tell me everything!" exclaimed Zubaidah. I explained it all. As I told her the madcap events of prior days, I was taken aback by her exuberance. She was clearly thrilled at my decision.

"Well, Qanta, this is something incredible. I haven't performed Hajj myself. I don't think it is the time, I don't believe I am ready for the responsibilities that follow. I am too weak. I wish I was stronger, like you. Maybe Inshallah if I am ever married, I will go, Inshallah, Inshallah." I wondered if she was as wistful as her voice sounded, trailing off into silence. Before I could ask, Zubaidah quickly returned to her genuine glee for me.

"Wa Allah, Qanta, let me tell you something, something very exciting; one can only go to Mecca when invited by Allah." I listened, rapt, pressing the receiver even more tightly to my ear.

"Clearly, Qanta, your invitation has come. Allah Himself has invited you to Mecca. You have been invited to meet God! There can be no other explanation for why this happened so suddenly.

Only He knows when the time is right for you. My invitation has not arrived yet but yours is here now!"

I called my astounded parents in England. My mother sounded remote, bemused, but I could sense my father's thrill. I emailed friends, family, colleagues, mentors. I wanted them to know! I made a list of friends to remember in Mecca. On a piece of paper I assembled a list of those I loved. I wrote the names of my beloved, recording them carefully in pairs: husbands and wives; parents and children; families, friends, and relatives. I wanted to forget no one in my prayers.

The next morning at work was a busy one. I chatted easily with Nadir, the surgeon who was my assigned resident for the month. Nadir was a Hijazi Saudi, an officer in the National Guard and a recently divorced father of a small daughter. I watched Nadir as he placed final stitches in the patient we were working on. "Nadir, I didn't tell you, I am going to Hajj on Saturday!"

A wide smile splayed Nadir's beard, carefully maintained at a straggly religious length. "Mashallah Doctora! That is great news!" I was surprised by his genuine joy. He hardly knew me, yet he seemed so pleased. Saudis could be so spontaneous and warm, but I never knew quite when to expect this.

"I am worried about Hajj, Nadir. How will I know what to do? It all seems so complicated, and I am going alone, with no one to ask."

He threw back his head and laughed out loud, a rather shocking sight in Riyadh where I had already seen that public displays of joy were rare and looked upon oddly. Nadir stopped laughing, discarded his surgeon's hat, and smoothed his glossy black hair. I was glad of the glass isolation doors. While we could be seen in the patient's room, at least the laughter would be muted behind soundproof panes. Saudi relatives of other patients were already glancing toward us askance, wondering about this fraternization between a Saudi man and a Western woman.

"Please don't worry, Doctora," Nadir said. "Nearly everyone who attends Hajj is going there for the first time. No pilgrim ever knows what to do. Everyone takes small books with them, books of prayers and instructions." His face lit up. "I will bring them for you!" Pleased with his plan, Nadir turned on his Birkenstocks and left, squeaking quickly along the hallway.

Sure enough, a day later, he arrived with three books in both English and Arabic. He assured me they would explain everything. I was taken aback by his generosity. He must have run out to the market after work and bought them at once, especially for me. They were obviously new, with the price tags from the Jarir bookshop still in place.

I couldn't have received better counsel and would think of Nadir's simple, kind advice many times during my Hajj when I did indeed ask others for help or directions or simply studied their actions in order to emulate them. This Kingdom of Strangers just seemed to become more unintelligible with time. A Saudi Hijazi surgeon, a military officer in the Saudi Arabian National Guard, and an orthodox Wahabi couldn't do enough to help me on my Hajj!

I called Zubaidah for more counsel. Zubaidah was sipping her customary mint tea on the veranda as she took my call.

"Zubaidah, what shall I wear to Hajj?"

"Qanta, just your usual clothing is fine, always with your abbayah on top when you are in public," she advised. "Wa Allah Qanta, you know, Jeddah is on the Red Sea and Mecca is forty minutes away. It is extremely humid, really, Qanta, even in March; unbearable. But please, it is very important, Qanta," she continued, "be sure to cover all your hair inside your veil; not a wisp of hair must show. That is critical, a must!

"It's OK, Qanta, please don't worry. I will help you get the right kind of scarf for Hajj, one that doesn't slip. How is after Isha prayer for you?"

At the designated time, Zubaidah's burgundy Mercedes sedan pulled up to my building to drive me to her house. Raheem (her Pakistani driver) and I chatted in Urdu during the journey back to her villa. As we pulled up, Zubaidah swept out of the steel gates, impossibly elegant in an evening abbayah sparkling with subtle mirror work. She was a vision.

A cloud of Chanel enfolded me in Zubaidah's mystery as she settled in the car. She shielded her sparkling gray eyes with Gucci visors, even though it was well after dusk. She wound up her phone call to her sister in Amman and leaned over to give me the customary two-cheek-seven-kiss greeting, all the while her cell phone jewelry jangling, her Swiss watch sparkling in the dark. I was dazzled by her femininity. I made a mental note to learn such mystery from her. Briskly (but never rudely) she instructed Raheem in Arabic in which he was also fluent. We chatted along the way.

"Qanta, really! I am so excited about your Hajj! Mashallah Mashallah Mashallah!" she cried, the moon light dancing off delightful dimples set deep into her porcelain skin framed to perfection by a gossamer chiffon veil. Zubaidah became more beautiful each time I beheld her.

Raheem dropped us at the ladies entrance to the al-Sahara shopping center. Quickly, Zubaidah and I chose a veil of thin silk georgette. Then she led me to a small store that sold hair accessories. I paid for the purchases, adding steel hair slides to our booty. We scuttled back to the rumbling Benz.

"But Zubaidah, what is the purpose of covering our hair as women? Why do you think it's so important in Islam?" I was dissatisfied.

"Why do you think, Qanta? What are your thoughts?" she challenged me, softly.

"Zubaidah, all I know is that this is what I was told when growing up. Always, 'a Muslim daughter must not do this,' 'a Muslim daughter must not do that.'"

"Well, Qanta, the hair is the crown of a woman's beauty. You recognize the difference well. Without our hair displayed, we all look plain. That is because we preserve our beauty only for those entitled to look at it. It is not for everyone to see, only for our families and husbands. At Hajj this is most important. You guard your beauty to maintain your respect. And you must not be in any way provocative to any of the men struggling in their pilgrimage. That would be wrong and additionally difficult for them.

"Now at Hajj, if you find yourself surrounded in a crowd of men and you feel uncomfortable, you may use the end of your scarf and veil your face. But otherwise covering your face inside the Holy Mosque during Hajj is forbidden, even for women who normally cover their faces in Riyadh or wherever else they may live. Do it only if you feel exposed or afraid or uncomfortable, otherwise this arrangement with the hair pins and scarf will be fine." She glanced over at my knotted brows, sensing my concern. "Don't worry, Qanta, I assure you, your niyyat is pure."

Back in my apartment, Zubaidah scrutinized the back of my head intensely as I fixed my hair in front of the mirror. We put the silk veil over an ugly scaffolding of hairpins and headbands. Zubaidah tucked the material tightly around my face with an expert dexterity borne of decades of veiling. A couple of rotations of her slim, braceleted wrists and my hair was hidden.

I glanced at my new reflection.

Gazing back was a pilgrim.

* * *

It was now Friday morning, the day before Hajj. The week had flown by in a blur. Yet even at the ninth hour, still no sign either of my plane tickets or of details of the group to whom I had been assigned. I called the Hajj office impatiently.

"I am waiting for the man to bring the tickets, Doctora." A woman responded, "He promised me that they would be here today." Her voice trailed off under a burden of anxiety. She mustered some empty assurances.

"I can't make any calls now because the agents are closed for Zuhr prayer. I will try after four when they reopen." She hung up.

I was incredulous. I was due to fly at 9:30 the next morning! How maddening that everything was always closed for prayer, especially at a time like this! Dejected, I replaced the receiver and asked myself of my real intent. Perhaps I only wanted to go on Hajj to feel included. Maybe my niyyat was impure, or worse, maybe the invitation hadn't ever come. It seemed time for my humiliation. I cowered into the long shadows of my shame, knowing I ill-deserved to go to Hajj, aware of how much I had neglected Islam in my life.

Early the next morning, the day of my now-fictional departure, Leila, the woman from the travel center, rang and informed me the agent would be hand-delivering my plane ticket at 8:30 a.m. I was to be at her office to receive the ticket and be driven on to King Khalid Airport for my flight to Jeddah, departing at 9:30 a.m. She told me to hurry. Incredulous that there still seemed hope at this, the eleventh hour, I began making my ablutions to enter the state of Ihram. My Hajj had most certainly begun.

A furry kiss goodbye to Souhaa, my flummoxed cat, and I was on my way. I stepped out into harsh morning light, slipping on sunglasses as I scurried down cement stairs and rushed towards a compound center.

The compound was deserted. Everyone was already away for the Hajj holiday. An eerie silence magnified my staccato steps ringing echoes across the precinct. It was almost time to leave for the airport. I was beginning to grow nervous, when the sound of tires on gravel punctuated the silence. A cloud of dust delivered a perspiring man. Rushing forward, he thrust two slivers of paper toward me. I had my ticket to God!

Folding them into my needy fist, he urged me into the waiting car. Inside, another single woman, an African American nurse from Newark, would also be traveling with me. Her name was Qudsia. The driver raced to get us to the King Khalid International on time.

Soon, we entered the airport grounds. For once I was thankful for the crazy, fast driving in Riyadh as our small car hurtled into the chaos. The terminal was submerged in a biblical scene; no movie set could have been more authentic. Millions were locked in the same force field. We were being magnetically drawn to Mecca. I could feel the gravitational pull of God.

The terminal was besieged by pilgrims who were unloading luggage, carrying children, wheeling the disabled, counting money, prostrate in prayer, swirling rosaries; all the while announcing aloud their intentions to make Hajj in the special prayers of the pilgrim. These Labbaik prayers, distinctive to Hajj, echoed in unison, a single powerful voice of the giant pilgrim vortex. I was reminded of my favorite childhood movie, *Close Encounters*. The unity of voices felt almost supernatural. Even Spielberg couldn't imagine this scene.

Throwing money at the driver who would accept none, seeing his duty to help two unescorted pilgrims by transporting us for free, we spilled into the oceanic current of believers. We met with a sea of whiteness, all male pilgrims draped in the Hajj clothing of white unseamed cloth. Many women too had adopted the ubiquitous white veils preferred by pilgrimaging Muslims. In the melee, we merged instantly and our voices joined the low-grade hum of a colossal swarm. I looked around from within the pandemonium. Pilgrims were carrying giant baskets and enormous bags (some large enough to hold a man). Everyone was carrying some form of bedding.

After a rapid check in, it was time to start believing Hajj was really going to happen. Stunned as my pilgrimage began to materialize into reality, I headed to the plane.

Inhaling the familiar smell of octane and hot asphalt with which all journeys begin, I mounted the staircase. The warm whispering Shamaal wind of Riyadh billowed around me, urging me on, my sole murmuring witness. With a final backward glance at Riyadh, I boarded the plane that would take me to the Ka'aba, the House of God. I wondered what I would learn of the millions of Muslims who would soon engulf me, and even more so, of the Muslim within me.

My transformation had begun.

Chapter
Eleven

THE EPICENTER OF ISLAM

THE SHORT FLIGHT PASSED QUICKLY. The seat belt sign came on and the 350 pilgrims prepared for landing. Internally, I braced. In a few minutes, I would be delivered into a Niagara of humanity. A squeak of rubber on burning hot runway and we landed in Jeddah. Minutes later the door of the plane opened, admitting a torrent of noise. Sounds of a million men swarmed into the cabin.

Hajj was here.

We disembarked the plane in a tumbling mass, slamming into a sweltering wall of moist heat. The humidity from the Red Sea was staggering. Like a live beast, it traveled insidiously under my abbayah, entering at the wrists, snaking over my body, leaving a sticky trail of perspiration in its wake. I peered for Qudsia. Spying her a few steps behind me, I went to join her, and abreast we walked from the runway into the terminal ahead.

Pilgrims from our plane disappeared into dank darkness, scurrying to baggage claim. We hurried to follow, soon noticing all signs were in Arabic which neither of us could understand. We would have to rely on our fellow passengers to take us to the right carousel. Overhead, announcements in guttural and precise Saudi Arabic peppered a hubbub of whirring air conditioners and asynchronous praying.

The male pilgrims were surprisingly adept at handling their robes and carrying luggage, all the while moving at a rapid pace. They were possessed with an urgency which I now noticed I lacked. I felt more fearful of being lost than concerned about rushing toward Mecca. These men were anxious with an urgent joy to meet their Maker. Even clumsy Hajj garments seemed not the least encumbrance. I continued my customary staccato forward rushing and periodic arrests backward, tripping on the rear hemline of my abbayah, and made considerably slower progress, but already I was glad of my low-heeled moccasins. I would be doing a lot of walking and already, even mid-morning, the tarmac was heating underfoot.

Inside, the terminal at the King Abdul Aziz airport was surprisingly small given the fifty thousand pilgrims who had been arriving here daily throughout the weeks leading up to Hajj. Many of these pilgrims were likely to be from Southeast Asia—450 flights arrive each day from Indonesia and from Pakistan another 376.[10] But today I was arriving with the final influx of domestic pilgrims, traveling from within the Kingdom.

A year before my arrival in the Kingdom, the Saudi authorities had placed a quota on domestic residents, to ease pressure on Hajj. Now Saudi citizens were required to apply to local pilgrimage boards to seek a permit for Hajj, granted only to those who had not performed Hajj within at least a five-year period. This prevented Saudi residents from arriving annually for Hajj, magnifying the congestion. Though controversial at the time, these sensible restrictions had been effective and reduced domestic pilgrims from fifty percent of all pilgrims to under thirty percent and, because of the specific restriction to those who had been on Hajj within a five-year window, most of the thirty percent now traveling to Hajj from within the Kingdom were non-Saudi expatriates.[11]

Amazingly, our bags were waiting neatly alongside the moving belt, already loaded with luggage from a subsequent flight. I turned, glancing backward. Behind, I could see more pilgrim passengers disembarking just as we had done moments before. In the window of white light at the end of the terminal, I counted scores of Saudi planes lined up, waiting to deplane. This was an operation of extraordinary magnitude and remarkable efficiency. Wheeling my suitcase behind me, I stepped outside.

We were deafened by the growl of a thousand diesel engines. As far as the eye could see giant buses lined the airport. They stretched in lines across the horizon and towards the vanishing point. Dragging our suitcases awkwardly behind us, Qudsia and I struggled to find our ride. We began walking through the diesel forest, spluttering, eyes stinging from gritty exhaust fumes, heavy and hot in the humid heat. Nose to bumper, the trucks barely allowed passage between them.

After about thirty minutes of searching, we spied a sign which looked like our group. We rushed to join the passengers embarking on this bus. They formed a neat line. A bald pilgrim with a thick beard reaching mid-chest checked passengers off on a clipboard. This was the pilgrim tour Imam. He would lead our Hajj, take us to the correct places at the correct times, and pray at the head of our group so that we all could follow.

"Salaam alaikum," I offered, my Urdu-influenced Arabic stretching out the words.

"Wa alaikum Salaam!" barked the tour leader, responding in chiseled Najdi Arabic. He glanced toward us, never making eye contact, and we showed him our leaflet confirming our place in his bus. Tossing his white sheet over his left shoulder with what can only be described as panache, he began scribbling on the clipboard. In short moments he had cross-referenced us on the clipboard and, miraculously, he waived us into the bus. We had found our place in this chaos.

As we entered, climbing the tall steps inside, I could see no other women, even though I had asked to be sent to Hajj with a group for single women. Most of the bus was filled with men. As I moved to the back, my eye fell on the final windows in the bus, covered in orange pleated curtains. So this was where the female pilgrims in the group must be. I climbed the steep steel steps, my first steps to Hajj.

Settling into an empty seat, I pulled the orange curtain slightly to one side and peered into the daylight. We were surrounded by rows and rows of buses and motor coaches and pilgrims rushing to join them. A family tried to stay together in strange human-chain formation, linked by hands gripping stretches of thin rope. Some women carried babies, some children trailed afoot behind their mothers, and others were in wheelchairs, being pushed by younger pilgrims.

While many buses were motor coaches, some were less grand. A clutch of bright yellow buses (exactly like American school buses) carried rows of pilgrims (all male) on the roof. They sat in neat lines, some squatting, some cross legged, all of them bareheaded under the relentless sun. Underneath, inside, heavily veiled women peered out, just like me, from behind the makeshift curtains. Not every pilgrim could afford to be inside an air-conditioned Mercedes Benz like this one, the one that would take me to Hajj.

Minutes turned into hours, and the hours became afternoon. I had brought nothing with me to eat or drink. I was unprepared in every sense for the rigors of Hajj. Everyone on the bus spent the time engaged in repetitive prayer, and for some time the Hajj leader led us in various prayers, which all of us, men and women, started to follow to pass the time. All the while the engine idled in an attempt to power the feeble air conditioning. In the distance, rows of buses peeled away, moving at the slow speed of Hajj. At last, just before two, our bus creaked away from the curb, and we were leaving the terminal. Heaving like a tired old man, the bus lurched forward, stiff with its hours of waiting. We were moving to the first stage of Hajj. Beyond the battalion of buses, Mecca was waiting, and at its center, the Ka'aba.

Next stop, the House of God.

* * *

It would take us the better part of half a day to reach Mecca, normally a forty-minute journey from Jeddah. We creaked forward in suspended animation, the scenery barely changing, the angle of the sun descending imperceptibly, and around us a cacophony of buses, trucks, and vans, an interminable growling, which even thick plate glass could not obliterate. As the day lengthened, the bus grew no cooler even with the air vents fully open. My fellow passengers passed time engaged in prayer, some reading the Qurans they had brought with them, and others following the Hajj Imam in loud prayers. Eventually I could see the mountain ranges circling Mecca; dull brown, baking in the intense heat, remote and impassive to monumental traffic trickling by.

We were approaching a subterranean tunnel, hewn out of a mountain. Instantly, at its threshold, we joined a turbine of noise spinning on the cumulative growl of thousands of engines. Drawing the curtains back, I saw we were now pitched into darkness. Arabic letters on the license plate of the vehicle ahead of us were all we could see. The pallid light of our headlights cast a feeble beam in smog thick enough to bite. Tailgating, we made a giant articulated caterpillar; our bus a tiny segment of the gigantic mechanical centipede oozing its way deeper and deeper into the center of Mecca.

Already I was losing track of time. As I approached my Maker, all dimensions were magnified. His vastness was beginning to over-shadow man-made measures of reality. I was entering a new universe where all human landmarks, whether of time or place, began to fail, pushed away by the spinning vortex of force that lay only a few miles way. We were in the central rip currents surging towards the Ka'aba. I could feel a tide pulling us forward.

Our driver, already fragile from his ordeal, sweated silently at the wheel, all the while the Hajj Imam standing at his side praying for Allah to open a route forward. We entered an eight-lane under-pass and still we ploughed ahead. A couple of male pilgrims hurried to the driver and after several minutes of discussion, the bus stopped in the tunnel, alongside the curb. Parallel to our bus I could see the mouths of four escalators swallowing pilgrims whole and sucking them upward. All escalators were going up, none descending. Further along the tunnel I could make out other escalator entrances, peppered along the roadside, each surrounded by a static knot of white-clad male Hajjis enclosing their female folk. This seemed an impossible place to stop, rather like getting out in the Midtown Tunnel in rush hour. I turned to ask the woman next to me, Randa, for an explanation.

"Oh Qanta, they want to stop here to go immediately to the Ka'aba. They can't wait to go to the hotel first and then come here; they want to go now. Those escalators led directly to the Masjid al-Haram Mosque (the Grand Mosque). The Mosque is directly above. We are passing underneath the House of God!" She stopped, smiling at me. "We are underneath Hajj!"

I watched the men leave our bus and vanish into the maelstrom of worship outside. Soon they were disappeared from view. We continued onward through the traffic toward our hotel for the night. Without sense of time, direction, or perspective, I hadn't realized I was already in the epicenter of Islam; surrounded by it, in fact. I watched the escalators aspirating more and more pilgrims as though an organism with an insatiable appetite; dumbfounded by the volume of humanity which seemingly vanished into an infinite oblivion. Everywhere was in motion, nothing was static.

We were at the vortex-edge.

* * *

A couple of hours later, the bus stopped outside a building in the center of Mecca. We quickly disembarked for refreshments and a brief respite. Men and women entered separate quarters. It was not the "hotel" I had expected. Instead it was clearly a wedding hall, opened up for traveling pilgrims during Hajj season. Along the floor were rolls of bedding and small cylindrical pillows. Quickly, women corralled various areas.

Most of all, I wanted to be in a space alone, already tiring of the crowds so soon into Hajj, but this was not possible. There was no privacy. I arranged my suitcase and leaned against it. Some alpha-female Bedouin pilgrims gathered on the stage, leaning against the lone wedding sofa devoid now of bride or groom. The rest of us congregated on the floor. Randa waved to me to move closer. Food was being served. Hijazi women, their dark skin revealing a Sudanese ancestry, began to move among us, proffering trays of food and cold sodas to drink. I hadn't seen them on our bus, so they must have been from Mecca, assigned to cater and serve the women in our group. A stainless steel tray was pushed toward me by one of the maids. I thanked her in Arabic, "Shukran."

"You are welcome," she responded, beaming with pride at her English. This was Rashida, supervisor of the other maids. She recognized I was not Saudi. Perhaps she had heard Randa and me speaking English earlier. Rashida had sparkling brown eyes made large with joy, and her scarf framed a substantial, defiant double chin. I liked her immediately. Though she was big, she moved quickly and tirelessly, bending down to serve food on the floor where we ate (there was no furniture in the hall) and rising again to serve others. Then she returned with an ice box full of sodas, dragging the entire box alone. I looked at my Coca-Cola. "The Real Thing" had reached even Mecca.

Along with other markers of time I found even appetite was lost. Forcing myself to eat, I took a small portion of rice, unable to face the meat. By the end of Hajj I would lose ten percent of my body weight. Randa had finished eating already. She came to me with an invitation. "Qanta, my husband Sherief and I are going to make our Tawafs at the Ka'aba. Perhaps you would like to accompany us? If we hurry, we can be there to pray Isha."

I leapt to my feet and followed Randa into the evening. We were going to the Ka'aba!

INTO THE LIGHT

RANDA AND SHERIEF HURRIED THROUGH the streets of Mecca, leading me to the Ka'aba. I kept pace immediately behind. We scurried through the loose crowds that were swirling in narrow streets. We strained to see ahead, pitched into deep shadow by outcrops of buildings rising high above our heads. No two buildings were alike, each a higgledy mass of extensions that toppled dangerously close to each other, almost closing out the sky. Some were still partway under construction yet already inhabited—a town planner's nightmare. Everywhere I looked, pilgrims were in progress: robed at the wheel of cars; riding shotgun on motorcycles; perched on cycles; piled high on roof racks. Most, however, were now on foot, having left vehicles far behind them, or perhaps having arrived by sea. I was reminded of the famous verse in the Quran speaking about Hajj:

They will come to thee on foot and (mounted) on every kind of camel,
lean on account of journeys through deep and distant mountain
highways... (Quran 22:27)

Sherief led our trio steadily into the surging eddies of belief.
We hurried. We wanted to reach the Masjid al-Haram by Isha, the
nighttime prayer.

We spilled into a curved plaza, joining a crowd of a hundred
thousand. We had reached the edges of the Masjid al-Haram. Crests
of humanity dissolved into surf, rolling first to the marble forecourt
that surrounded the mosque and then, in the far distance, surging
into it through innumerable gateways like a gaining tide. Dusk was
falling, above the sky was clear, the heat of the day was finally dissipating and a gentle breeze tugged at the edges of my scarf. Randa
and Sherief pressed forward, pulling me out of my stupefaction. As
we crossed a final road cleared of traffic which separated us from
the marble forecourt of the immense oval al-Haram Mosque at the
center of Hajj, the Azan rang out. All motion began to slow. We
had to answer the call of prayer.

At once Randa turned. "Let's pray here," she said and stopped
exactly where we were standing. She stood next to Sherief, shoulder
to shoulder, and I stood next to Randa. We removed our shoes, placing
them in plastic bags we were carrying, and set them between us. I
looked at my feet. We were immediately adjacent to the curb of the
road. We would be praying on tarmac, yet the ground was clean, not
even a single wrapper or piece of litter. We began symbolically patting
the dusty ground around us and went through the motions of our ablutions, using dust in place of water, allowed precisely for the traveling
Muslim who cannot reach water before prayer.

Around us the mass of a hundred thousand had silently arranged
itself identically. Where once a tumultuous crowd had surged, a
peaceful, patient congregation now gathered, perfectly aligned in

every direction. To my right and left, ahead of me, behind me, I found I had become part of a massive circular crowd, every pilgrim abreast of another, the sides of our feet touching, planted a little astride. Like a magic organism forming out of ether, the Hajj crowds had become a parish. After prayer, we would again dissolve into the Hajj ocean, leaving no trace of an assembly.

To the rhythms of familiar prayer, we bowed our heads, kneeled, and finally prostrated in unison. The holy ground radiated warmth, pulsing with absorbed heat. Something lived here. Mid-prostration my veiled head grazed against the inches-high concrete curb. A smell of carbon, petroleum, and heated dust rose into my nostrils, yet I remained unsoiled. Completing both rakats (each rakat consists of two prostrations in Islamic prayer) of the prescribed pilgrims' abbreviated prayer, I expected to leave, but the invisible Muezzin called onward. There seemed to be more prayers due. These were unfamiliar, and the particular choreography not in my repertoire. I constantly muddled the correct order, exposing myself as a novice Muslim. I struggled to copy the veteran worshippers around me. As the prayers ended and the rows began their magic dissolution, I turned to Randa, "What were those final prayers? I did them all wrong."

"That was the funeral prayer, Qanta. Every prayer in Mecca during Hajj ends with the Janaaza prayer for the dead. We have to remember all the pilgrims who have died since the last prayer time. People die here all the time. We have to pray for them. You'll see, the funeral prayers are held at every prayer time while Hajj continues."

This was why they were unrecognizable. I had prayed at only one funeral, at the age of twelve. I had relied on mimicry then, as I did now. Death walked among us and with it followed a sense of both time and scale. Some spiritual lives would end at Hajj while others, like mine, would begin. Many came here at the end of their lives and some would die in the process; not as a result of trauma or disease, but because to die at Hajj was their destiny. Some pilgrims actually hoped for death during Hajj, and the salvation which would follow. Pilgrims know that the Prophet Muhammad (PBUH) had said that should a pilgrim die during Hajj, he would be rewarded like a pilgrim who had successfully completed Hajj, absolved of all sin, tantamount to the day of his birth and spend his afterlife in Heaven until the Day of Judgment. Many pilgrims therefore preserve their Hajj robes to be used again at the end of this life, as a burial shroud, so that when resurrected on the Day of Judgment (when Muslims believe all souls will stand before the Maker) they could appear in the same white ihram clothing again. I realized I was at the nexus of mortality and divinity.

We continued forward directly to the threshold of a marble gate, one of 129 on the circumference of the oval mosque. Now as the crowds condensed around these bottlenecks, I was especially glad not to be on an escalator handling my long, deadly abbayah. One misstep and a fall could result in others stumbling and, quickly, a stampede. Gradually, in the dense mass of people, we edged forward, Randa, Sherief, and I; sometimes in single file, sometimes swinging out into a horizontal formation, molding ourselves according to the forces of the crowds around us. Always we remained connected by handhold.

At the threshold of the gateway, under a towering arch, black-clad Saudi women stood as posted sentries, taming the human tsunami. These were the so-called female Mutawaeen. I had never seen them in Riyadh. Rather than state appointed, they were self-appointed arbiters of orthodoxy. Veiled totally, a short black specter gestured toward me, seeking inspection of my plastic bag. Her gold-rimmed glasses, eyeless, clung onto the side of her veiled head, almost outlining her veiled nose. After waving me on, the anonymous black-gloved hands searched Randa's purse. This force of women searched every bag carried by every woman pilgrim, quietly and quickly returning the items to us. Men were searched by Wahabi clerics, dressed like the Mutawaeen which patrolled Riyadh. Perhaps these women were their wives, I wondered, or maybe their sisters. The sentries, whatever their relationships, searched for weapons or other suspicious items, protecting the House of God and its guests. No one wanted a repeat of 1979. We had entered the Sanctuary.

The Masjid al-Haram (haram literally means "sanctuary") is historically delineated a zone free of bloodshed. No creature can be hunted, no animal kill made, and any violence is forbidden from defiling this holy place and its environs. It was and remains sacrosanct.

Before Islam, the Ka'aba had been a site of worship and focus of pagan rites. Warring Bedouin tribes agreed on a truce to their enmity while performing their religious rites centuries earlier, and peace had been mandated ever since.

In a way, Hajj itself is a sanctuary to all conflicts between Muslims. Hajj is a symbol of how the Islamic ideal of coexistence and tolerance should be practiced in wider society. Islam forbids any destruction of life at Hajj; no animals can be hunted or blood sports practiced in Mecca or any of the surrounding regions, either.

The silent sentries searching us were therefore safeguarding a fundamental aspect of Hajj and a central theme of Mecca. We were truly within a Sanctuary. As I entered the Masjid al-Haram, I was taking the first steps of a ritual which long predated Islam. Countless millions had travelled to Mecca before me.

The Ka'aba in Mecca had been the site of an annual religious gathering for centuries before Islam was revealed to the Prophet. The Ka'aba itself, at the center of the Masjid al-Haram, was originally built by Abraham to blueprints said to have been revealed to him by the Angel Gabriel. But in the centuries since Abraham's initial building and before the Prophet

Muhammad (PBUH), spiritual deviancy had almost extinguished monotheism in the region. Instead a pagan, polytheistic ritual had overtaken these holy sites and severed, (until the coming of Muhammad (PBUH)), the only uniting tie in a deeply fissured and warring region. Nevertheless, this pre-Islamic Hajj provided an opportunity for lucrative trade, while becoming a powerful political actor in its own right. As a result the ancient Hajj became a potent economic force, driving migration and ultimately explaining the racial heterogeneity of today's Hijaz region of the Kingdom (in stark contrast to the monolithic Najd).

The Prophet Muhammad (PBUH) was the modern reformer of Hajj, and his personal efforts dispelled the heinous pre-Islamic associations with idolatry. He restored the Ka'aba as the House of God and cleansed it of statues and symbols of pagan worship, which were sometimes stored even within its hollow core. He returned monotheistic worship to Mecca, making Hajj the pinnacle of Islamic worship, as the Quran specified. Abraham, the founder of monotheistic belief, and his profound love for and unwavering worship of God are symbolic Islamic ideals which were a central part of the Prophet Muhammad's (PBUH) Message from God.

Today this precious and monumental ritual is controlled by the Saudi dynastic monarchy and its Wahabi theocracy, referring to themselves as the self-appointed Custodians of the Two Holy Places. They are enormously powerful in controlling who can make Hajj and how often. They take their duties seriously and discharge their responsibilities with enormous care and attention to detail, spending hundreds of billions of dollars to ensure a safe and healthy Hajj for millions of Muslims each year. Yet it is this supreme, self-appointed authority which the non-Saudi Muslim world particularly begrudges. While I was attending Hajj unimpeded, and completely identical to the Hajj of any male pilgrim there, whether women could do this to the same extent in the future was less clear. Short years later, these same authorities would issue some fearful recommendations exposing just how authoritarian they actually were.

In August 2006, Reuters reported on new limitations Saudi clerics wished to impose on women who were praying at the al-Haram. Interestingly, the al-Haram is one of the few places where male and female worshippers can intermingle. (Normally mosques are segregated with sections for male and female worshippers strictly separated.) The clergy wanted to ban women from the immediate vicinity of the Ka'aba.

Even within the conservative Kingdom, this suggestion by the religious authorities has raised enormous ire, especially among Saudi women activists. Correctly, they accuse the theocracy of misogynistic discrimination. Currently, women are able to pray immediately next to the Ka'aba, in its forecourt, within its shadow, even to touch its perimeter. But the orthodox theocratic forces controlling the all-male Hajj committees overseeing such matters suggest quite openly that women should be barred from this central area of the sanctuary and plan to assign women to a remote area from where they could have a vantage of the Ka'aba but not approach it.

Worse, they suggested this was a considerate move for the protection of women, conveniently disguising their discrimination with a thin veneer of patronizing gallantry. Effectively they hope to remove women from public view in all Holy Sites, just as they were succeeding in doing in public life in the Kingdom. Reuters quoted one committee advisor:

"The area is very small and so crowded. So we decided to get women out of the sahn (Ka'aba area) to a better place where they can see the Ka'aba and have more space," said Osama al-Bar, head of the Institute for Hajj Research. "Some women thought it wasn't good, but from our point of view it will be better for them…. We can sit with them and explain to them what the decision is [about]," he said. "The decision is not final and could be reversed."

I knew I was privileged to be at Hajj at such a young age and as a single unaccompanied woman. I didn't know that one day I might be restricted from approaching the Ka'aba by the invisible and very devious forces always at work in the Kingdom. For now, I was already looking beyond the representative of the Custodians of the Sanctuary, already searching for my Maker. As our personal search was completed by the voiceless shrouds, I began to understand. Arriving in Mecca, at the threshold of the Ka'aba, I was entering a pristine, divine garden where all creation was welcome irrespective of what a male committee of mullahs might think. Here every life was equally valued and had been so for more than a millennium. I was walking in the footsteps of the Prophet Muhammad (PBUH) into the House of God. I was walking into the light.

There could be no turning back.[12]

THE CHILD OF GOD

CROSSING THE THRESHOLD, WE ENTERED the brilliantly illuminated marble mosque and walked onto a glossy causeway.
Lanterns suspended from a ceiling high above our heads (each large
enough to cage a man) spilled their molten light, bathing the sea of
pilgrims in white brilliance. Dazzling rays chased out the encroaching
night, left bereft at the threshold. Wave upon wave of pilgrims carried
us forward like flotsam. Pilgrims moved no more than a quarter-stride
at a time, edging cautiously, as though on the verge of a precipice.
Each footstep of mine dissolved into the collective footfall.

We were on the ground floor of the three-story mosque, able to
hold seven hundred fifty thousand at once. The oval-shaped mosque
was a product of four expansions since the 1950s. The Saudis had
dedicated more than $25 billion just to the renovation and modern-
ization of the Hajj sites.

I gingerly moved forward, carefully judging my steps. The ground was cool and refreshing underfoot, a brilliant feat of underground water engineering. A network of pipes conducted cold water under the marble, vital when Hajj occurred in the hotter seasons and air temperatures here could exceed 129°F.

To the sides of the causeway, carpeted areas were filled with pilgrims in different stages of supplication. Many sat, simply reading the Quran, or stopped to take sips of ice-cool ZamZam[8] water, stored in orange plastic urns stationed all around the mosque. For the first time I noticed my thirst, despite the humid night. They were drinking holy water, the same water that had arrived while Hagar searched desperately in the desert, fearful that her son Ismail might die without it. I remembered the story well:

While she ran frenzied, she left her child on the dusty desert ground. As the crying babe's heel struck the barren earth, ZamZam flowed for the first time, at exactly his footfall. The ZamZam still flows today deep under the ground below the Mosque, and has never run dry in the centuries since. Each Hajj, 141 million liters of ZamZam water are consumed by pilgrims and taken in containers to their friends and families at home.

In Riyadh, a blue-eyed Bedouin father had asked my permission to anoint his 16-year-old son with ZamZam water while the son lay in the ICU dying from terminal lymphoma. I watched as he applied the precious drops with his gnarled fingers, daubing it on like costly French perfume. His arthritic, roughened fingers, wet with ZamZam water, ran over the broken skin, bleeding, blistered, the holy water mixing with blood in wounds that had failed to heal themselves. The boy died hours later, but the family still thanked me, accepting his death as "God's will." ZamZam has

---

[8] Originates from the phrase "Zomë Zomë" meaning "Stop flowing," a command repeated by Hagar in her efforts to contain the spring water when she found it. Saudi Geological Survey ZamZam Research and Studies Center.

healing properties, and the poor father had wanted to try every last hope.

I looked at the lines of orange vessels surrounding the worshipers around me (more than 6,300 peppered the mosque) and at once knew this father must have collected the water here. ZamZam had galvanized his final hopes until lymphoma snuffed that flame too. Even ZamZam cannot change God's will.

At the very perimeter of the causeway, lines of wooden cubby holes no more than two feet high contained the shoes of pilgrims. Muslims remove their shoes to recognize the purity and cleanliness of any place of worship. Most were wrapped in small bags and stashed carefully away in the white wood pigeonholes until the pilgrims returned for the footwear when leaving the mosque. I kept my shoes with me in the small plastic bag, knowing well I would never be able to relocate them in the massive mosque.

As we descended yet another set of steps, the pilgrims ahead of us came to an abrupt standstill. Quickly we halted. I strained to see the cause of the delay ahead. Sounds vanished into silence. Thousands melted from vision. I found myself alone, standing at the gate of God.

I gazed upon the Ka'aba, eyes widening with wonder. The unobstructed view blurred with salty, unexpected tears. I was over-whelmed. A lump constricted my throat, then released, dislodged by a torrent of undammed, silent emotion. Tears were now flowing freely across my face, dampening the shabby veil around it. Unashamed, my feelings were vibrant with a divine energy.

I continued gazing. I was unable to peel my eyes from my Maker. He was here. He was everywhere. He had gathered me. He had forgiven me. My shoulders straightened, relieved of a heavy burden. My head lifted, unbowed without the weight of perpetual shame. My heart ached as it lurched open, stretching, suddenly swollen with relief. Inside me, the force chased away debris accumulated within once narrow, dark corners. I could hide nothing from Him and found myself no longer fearful of discovery. All my follies were exposed to my Maker and yet He loved me still.

In these brief private moments, I placed the burdens of my broken life aside, discharged of shame. I stepped forward lightened, free, absolved. In a cast of millions, in that moment of electric intimacy, my Maker welcomed me. Like the Prophet had said, "If you take one step toward God, He takes ten steps toward you." I could feel Him hurtling toward me, a colossal, joyous Father. I stood before Him, at last, His child.

It was full minutes before I returned to my surroundings, to my senses. Other pilgrims were in a similar state of ecstasy. None was aware of any other pilgrim. I reminded myself of the effect of group dynamics in such a huge crowd but no rationalization could explain what I felt. I stared and stared at the cuboid building, bewildered at the energy emanating from its black-draped walls that beckoned me closer. It radiated light that even its sooty blackness couldn't extinguish. Here, there could be no shadow, only light.

My eyes strained to see something, anything, to explain the phenomenon. The black building reverberated with animal vitality as though a heart pumped within it, or a soul stirred under the black Kiswah. The Ka'aba actually seemed to throb. My eyes were liars. While I could see nothing, I knew what I felt: palpable Divinity, proximal Grace. God was very near.

Before Islam was revealed to the Prophet Muhammad (PBUH), when he was about 35 years of age, the Ka'aba had fallen into terrible disrepair, losing a roof, and the wealthy Quraish tribe set about restoring the former House of God to house their symbols of pagan worship.[13] Their efforts were thwarted by infestation. Symbolically, a snake had come to dwell in the walls of the Ka'aba. Eventually an eagle soaring overhead descended, snatching away at the frightening serpent which had a habit of emerging in the sunlight, scaring away the Quraish who wanted to rebuild the shrine to their idols.[14]

During this time, four of the most powerful tribal leaders of Central Arabia disagreed on who should be allowed to place the revered Black Stone into its proper eastern corner in the Ka'aba after the building's renovation. Each leader believed himself the most worthy of this rare honor. Even though the Prophet was repelled by their pagan beliefs, he still mediated with dignity and kindness as the invited arbiter. Muhammad (PBUH), who by now earned the name "al-Amin" (most trusted), displayed his famed diplomacy, memorialized in a famous parable.

Rather than choose one leader over the others and so engender the perpetual enmity of the remainder, he sought to appease all. He asked each leader to grasp the corner of a four-sided robe or cloak, himself placing the Black Stone upon it. Together the leaders lifted the stone in the makeshift hammock, carrying it to the correct site in the building. The Prophet then lifted it from the cloth, returning it to its resting place, where it remains today. The leaders accepted the solution because of its perfect equality. So the stone has remained at the corner of the Ka'aba. Some choose to believe the Black Stone has been blackened by the absolution of human sin over the centuries.

I looked at the pilgrims kissing the Black Stone. I was disturbed by the paganistic and ritualistic qualities of the scene. But I knew this was an ancient rite utterly distinct from the stone worshipers of centuries earlier.

Muslims are very clear that only God is worthy of worship. The stone is only honored because Muhammad (PBUH) demonstrated his reverence for it by kissing it, but never worshipped it, worshiping only his Maker. The second Calipha of Islam, Umar ibn al-Khattab (580–644), came to kiss the Stone, and made the critical distinction once more.

"No doubt, I know that you are a stone and can neither harm anyone nor benefit anyone. Had I not seen Allah's Messenger kissing you, I would not have kissed you."

Even from this remote distance, hundreds of meters away, I could see pilgrims struggling to touch the Black Stone, emulating this reverence stretching into lost centuries.[9] Some fortunates were close enough to kiss it as they revolved around the Ka'aba in ever-decreasing circles. Seized with fervor, others had stepped partway onto surrounding men in a quest to reach the stone which lay encased in silver housing about five feet from ground level.

So I found, as I would time and again in the days ahead, that in this holiest of Islamic rites, deeply pagan rituals had survived the passage of time, persisting even after the dawn of Islam.

The crowds ahead had eased enough for us to see that the congestion would be too great for us to make circuits on the lower levels. We headed for the immense roof to begin our Tawaf.

We hurried to find the green marble demarcation in the floor which specified the site of the Black Stone far below us, the marker for each one of the seven counterclockwise circuits we would perform. In these circuits, we were following in the footsteps of the Prophet Muhammad (PBUH) who had circumambulated the Ka'aba in the same way.

I looked upward into the night sky. Above us in the heavens, angels were similarly revolving around the Baitul Mamoor, the heavenly home to the Throne of God said to be directly above the

---

[9] Centuries earlier, ancient tribes had guarded the Black Stone, revered as a magical talisman, even as an object of worship. They kept it inside the Ka'aba. This stone is said to have fallen from heaven during the time of Adam and Eve to this site. Non-Islamic scholars suggest it may have been a meteorite, since stone worship was then prevalent in pre-Islamic Arabia. Others believe it was handed to Abraham by the angel Gabriel himself or that Abraham found the stone and recognized its special worth, using it as a key cornerstone in the foundations of the Ka'aba.

Ka'aba. When we identified our starting point, we made the Takbir. Lifting our right hands up to the Ka'aba, facing it with our palms, we hailed God, "Allah hu Akbar! Allah hu Akbar!"

Randa and Sherief led the way at a brisk pace, counting our first Tawaf.

It would be hours before we could finish. My pilgrimage had begun.

THE MILLION-MAN WHEEL

WE MILLED, ALONG WITH A million others, on the first Tawaf, or walk, around the Ka'aba, which would take forty minutes and span three-quarters of a kilometer. My eye was invariably drawn to the black cube at the center of a million supplications. Each pilgrim circulated facing the Ka'aba. Its magnetism was palpable. Here, from the roof, the vantage was God-like. Above the Ka'aba, birds fluttered, also in circular formation, as though on their own Tawaf. My overwhelming relief was replaced now by joy. As I counted my circuits, I found my mouth curving into smiles frequently, inexplicably.

Below, the million-man wheel continued its massive revolutions. Studying the incredible crowds, a memory of Shea Stadium full to the brim returned to me. I recalled a ripple on the floor of the stadium. A hooded figure slowly worked through the masses of fans. A small phalanx moved ahead through the giant seaweed of waving arms, until at last, leaping boxer-like onto the stage, Bono revealed himself. In a moment, I had understood stardom, fifty thousand focused on one. The small figure connected with each fan and that night, in his music, we touched celebrity.

Now looking down onto the five hundred thousand below me and the three hundred thousand around me, I understood Divinity. I watched the endless cycle of pilgrims below and began to understand worship, reminded of the last crowd I had joined. No human could move others to this extent; no force could direct worshipers other than the holy.

We were partway through our third Tawaf when again the Muezzin's soprano voice announced the time for Isha prayers. We would offer them here around the Ka'aba. Again the revolving wheel of worship halted and we formed lines ready for the beginning of prayer. Smoothing our clothes, we stood shoulder to shoulder, ready to pray.

The Azaan was magical. (*Azaan* means "inform" or "announce," and must be called five times each day, at the hours prescribed for compulsory prayer.) The muezzin's crystalline voice called out as though from the sky itself, speakers on the nine minarets which towered over the entire Mosque complex, ricocheting the Azaan throughout Mecca. The tallest minarets, over the giant Fahad gates, propelled the sound beyond the mountain ranges surrounding the city. Throughout Mecca and at Hajj, on hearing the Azaan, every pilgrim stopped their own private prayer, readying himself or herself for prayer in congregation. Somewhere in this mosque the muezzin was standing at a microphone, unseen, and after touching his thumbs to his earlobes with his palms facing forward (a symbolic gesture of cutting himself from worldly distraction) he called to everyone everywhere, literally, to gather, both from the East and the West.

I too lifted my hands to my ears, yet still found it difficult to focus my thoughts on my prayer. Ahead and slightly below, the

Ka'aba tugged me magnetically toward it. It was very difficult to bow my head to my Maker when I constantly wanted to meet His supernatural gaze which sought my eyes wherever I turned. I directed my smiling face downward toward my unvarnished toes. Muslim women at Hajj must be devoid of any adornment including nail polish, perfume, or jewelry, as a sign of purification.

I was surrounded by diversity. Two rows behind, strong American accents gave away Muslims as Southerners. To my right, a gray-eyed man from Kosovo prayed. Ahead, Ghanese men, ebony faces gleaming against their white Hajj robes, responded to the muezzin in their beautiful African-accented Arabic. Everywhere, pug-nosed Malaysian women could be seen, identified by the neat flags sewn onto the back of their headdresses.

On my left was a half-English, half-Egyptian woman, Randa. Nearby, nervous Saudi women were distinguished by their face coverings, which they found so difficult to relinquish especially in dense crowds. I could hear a Pakistani mother soothing a child in Urdu and another pair of pilgrims noisily chatting in uncultivated Punjabi until others nearby shushed them silent.

As I looked up and surveyed the multistranded circle of humanity adorning the Ka'aba, a giant, rich choker of pilgrim pearls, I found myself among them. In this diversity, finally I belonged. Islam was many-faceted and I was simply one. Our diversity had obliterated the Wahabiism of the Najd, save for a few sentries at the periphery or the odd patrolling Muttawa cleric too forbidding for most pilgrims to approach. This was Islam: Hajj! Not the Muttawa with their nightsticks and nihilism. Equality in the eyes of our Maker, whether we be men or women, rich or poor, able-bodied or deformed, black or white, was all that mattered. The frenzied, fascist supremacy of Wahabiism had simply been washed away by a torrent of truth: the multiracial, spiritually hybrid Muslims now flooding Mecca.

As our prayers ended, again after the customary funeral prayer for the dead, we resumed our Tawafs. We could easily keep a brisk pace, as the crowds had begun thinning on the roof-top level, but below the vortex churned on. On the marbled floor, my feet were beginning to ache in new ways, unused to so much walking without shoes, but I was amazed to see the cleanliness. My feet weren't even dusty. With so much humanity here, somehow the mosque remained pristine. Below, I watched a blue ballet of boiler suits hard at work.

Teams of barefooted cleaners, all men from Southeast Asia (most often Bengali), were dressed in royal blue boiler suits, hard at work inside the mosque on every level. In a perfectly synchronized choreography, they cleaned and polished, barely disturbing the perpetually moving pilgrims. My eyes followed the bright blue figures and their complex theatre in the sea of white. Ahead of others, one man threw whole bucketfuls of water countercurrent to the revolving vortex, spilling water onto swathes of white marble flooring. Immediately, a single file, a dozen strong, pushed the water into broad brushstrokes, swiping perpendicular to the wet stream with wide, bristled brushes.

They worked fast and simultaneously. The men were universally thin, many underweight. Running full-tilt towards the streams of water, their brooms gathered speed on the moving aquaplane and their momentum lifted their lithe lean bodies upward, briefly airborne on the broom handles. With trouser legs and sleeves inflated in the night breeze, buoyant, blue-flagged yachts, they sailed forward on their bristled boats. Behind them, a third crew followed, mopping every trace of water dry with wide chamois mops. The joyful dancers moved on, leaving a fragrant wake of warm, dry marble. Without missing a beat, the pilgrim wheel ratcheted forward in the steps of Muhammad (PBUH) and Abraham, most unaware the floor below them was newly cleaned.

The Ka'aba's mystery only grew with time as evening turned to night. The blackness of the Kisweh veil, draping the cube on all sides, seemed almost to billow in the night wind. At the bottom of the Ka'aba, demurely, the Kisweh had been pulled up, like the hems of a dress, gathered to avoid a rising tide of worship swirling below. Though the Ka'aba is forty-nine feet square, its walls seemed to tower over us. Surreal from every angle, seeing it in each new gaze was like seeing it for the first time. I was continually enthralled, yet uncomfortable at the effect the building exerted upon me. As a Muslim I worship only God, not his House, but the building called to me magnetically.

Revolving around the Ka'aba, while intensely pleasurable, was also deeply disturbing. Even without understanding the symbolism of my actions while I performed them, a palpable primordial connection was pulling me inward, deeper into Islam.

The Kisweh drapes veiling the Ka'aba barely stirred, despite the night breeze and the revolving maelstrom around it. I knew the billowing of the cloth, which weighed more than a ton, was likely my imagination. So like everything relating to Hajj, it was a monumental feat of construction.

In the night light the golden Thuluth Arabic calligraphy glittered on the Kisweh, its brilliance enhanced by the velvet blackness of the surrounding silk. I was bewitched by its beauty. With the distortions of Wahabi extremism, beautification of any object was considered an offense, resulting in a Kingdom without ornate decoration, other than repetitive geometry which peppered public walls and even highway underpasses. Anything else was considered futile vanity by Wahabis, but at least the Wahabis had not eroded what seemed the final remaining evidence of Islamic craftsmanship: unparalleled calligraphy. For the first time in the Kingdom, I appreciated beautiful Saudi craftsmanship.

At last, some five hours after we had started, our seventh Tawaf was complete. We terminated with a two-rakat prayer of thanks and made our way back to the wedding hall. Unrolling my bedding to a snoring orchestra of Saudi women, I drifted into a deep sleep. I couldn't wait for tomorrow.

Chapter
Fifteen

COMMITTING HARAM

SOON WE BEGAN PACKING OUR personal items, leaving the bedding behind. Today we would move to Mina, the pilgrims' camp, a station several miles outside of Mecca where we were to spend a day in supplication until we prepared to move onward to the plain of Arafat, the most critical day of Hajj. It was at Arafat that the Prophet Muhammad (PBUH) delivered his final sermon, in the same valley where Abraham too had stood in front of God centuries earlier.

The congregation of pilgrims at Hajj at Arafat represents the gathering of Muslims who listened to his last sermon just months before his death when the final verses of the Quran were revealed during the Prophet's Farewell Pilgrimage. All two and a half million would assemble on this plain, standing from noon until sunset. Many would crowd around the Mount of Mercy, from where the

Prophet actually delivered the sermon. Some would actually climb the Mount of Mercy, believing prayers offered here to be the closest to God. "Arafat is Hajj" was repeated many times, because this, the Day of Standing, was the most important day of Hajj.

Rising with difficulty, I performed a stiff rendition of Fajr (the morning prayer), eternally grateful it was so short. We hurried to prepare for the journey to Mina, where we would stay with millions of others in the Tent City. After hours of traffic jams and mayhem, the bus finally entered the Tent City, a settlement consisting of hundreds of thousands of tents and, for the brief days of Hajj, a population of two and a half million. (A week from now the entire city would be vacant for the rest of the year.) I checked the leaflets and found I would be staying in tent 50007. Printed in Arabic, I memorized the number; this would be my home until the end of Hajj.

Looking at the Tent City through the dirty pane, I could see it would be easy to get lost here. Awkwardly the bus negotiated the narrow tarmacked roads between terraces of tents. Like a searching sea monster, the huge vehicle prowled through acres of fiberglassed canvas. Eventually we found our section.

As I stepped into the large and airy tent, sixty pairs of scanning eyes turned to assess me. None smiled in greeting. I ignored the cool scrutiny, accustomed to it after months of living in the Kingdom where I was always watched both by men and by women. I moved quickly to find a relatively unoccupied place in which to settle. The hours of cramped proximity since Riyadh left me craving space.

I began to disrobe. It was a relief to unwrap myself from the noisy rustling prison of my abbayah. As I released myself from the tangle, the familiar freedom of discarding it still rushed back to me. Wearing it continuously since I had left Riyadh, the longest period of contiguous veiling I had experienced, still was not making the adjustment to veiling any easier. As I shook my head free of the veil, I found I could hear again.

I looked at the women around me in various states of dishabille. Some continued to wear their abbayahs fastened closed and, retaining most of their headdresses in place, they pushed back the facial veiling to the top of their heads, securing it back with a small ribbon under the chin or a deft twist of cloth. While their faces were exposed, their hair remained fully covered, reminding me of Holbein's Elizabethans who dressed in coifs. Literally, these Saudi women covered their hair indoors around women much like the Tudors did in the 1500s. Already the medieval flavor of Wahabi Islam was intensifying. Others had decided to take off their head coverings entirely. Against the far wall of the tent, a row of women sat on the floor leaning against the tent wall, their fleshy backs sagging into the curve of the canvas. Unmanicured fingers combed their long tresses intently, a row of strange mermaids unexpectedly washed ashore.

I was glad to be uncovered, even behind the scenes. I wondered why all the women didn't immediately disrobe their outer garments entirely. Surely, they were just as hot and irritated from the long journey. Yet still they were compelled to maintain a forbidding boundary, even from women, distinguishing themselves as ultra-orthodox. Overhead industrial-size air conditioners suspended from aluminum beams blew gales of icy air. For the first time since landing in Jeddah, it was actually cool. Elsewhere, a row of women were dressed in their daytime clothes, having discarded their external clothing, and sat together, in various states of repose, one massaging her meaty foot, her ankle edema giving away a heart condition. Next to her, a Caucasian woman with short, wavy hair, almost ginger in color, was rubbing the nape of her neck, easing a knot of pain. These women were not orthodox Saudis; if I could guess they seemed Lebanese or Jordanian.

In time, I began to unpack a few essential items. I glanced up, meeting a hard stare. A woman, perhaps forty-five years of age, was watching me intently.

She was already settled in a spot just across from me. Her thin daughter cowered just behind her left shoulder, flinching from attention. The mother assessed my attire, revealed now that the abbayah lay crumpled on the ground. Across my chest, a snug Guess T-shirt gave away its American origins and my Calvin Klein trousers, secured at the waist with a shiny Italian belt, divided my legs, identifying me as an unmistakably Western woman.

She visibly grimaced. Physically, I offended her. I tried to ignore her disapproval, wondering if I had somehow made a faux pas of some kind. As I was reaching for an item deep in the back of my case, stretching my torso and arms bared by short sleeves, I looked up at her and smiled casually, trying to be friendly.

"Hi," I said, rummaging around in the case.

"You say 'Hi' to me? Hi?" she snapped, immediately, as if primed for an angry response. Her English was precisely enunciated. Her face flashed. She was Saudi for sure, probably also Najdi and maybe even from Riyadh but obviously, by her English, she had studied overseas. "As a Muslim at Hajj greeting another Muslim, you say Hi!" she went on, practically spitting with fury.

I looked at her nonplussed. There was such latent energy in her rage.

"You say to me: 'Salaam alaikum,' as a proper Muslim deserves!" she hissed, exhaling in annoyance. By now, I had completely abandoned the search in my bag and was staring at this woman who, while absolutely correct, was surprisingly angry for one performing Hajj herself. I decided to hold my tongue, partly because that was my job as pilgrim, and partly because she was correct. I should have greeted her as a Muslim deserves. I met her flashing eyes with a cool stare and held it, feeling guilty even for this defiance, but she had infuriated me. Her mute teenage daughter remained behind her mother, voiceless, irrelevant.

Again it was time for food. Rashida and her crew of maids arrived, bearing trays of food for the tent. As they shyly offered the rice and lamb, the young ladies barely met my eyes. Some of them watched me askance, giggling with their scarf-endings held up over their mouths, muffling the offending sounds of laughter.

Rashida's bustling bonhomie diffused the tension that had spilled from the angry woman opposite me. Rashida didn't seem offended by my person even now that she could see my Western clothing. I was silently grateful to Rashida for her acceptance. I found myself more confident when she was in the room. I thanked her for the tray of food, "Shukran, Rashida."

"Afwan, Qanta. Maalish." (You're welcome, no problem.) She responded, revealing a perfect set of strong, white teeth framed in her huge booming laugh. Even though she was raised in Mecca, and veiled life-long, never traveled, and married at an early age, her spirit remained indomitable, confident, down-right brassy!

Touching nothing of the main meal, I peeled and ate an orange. My appetite was already waning; by week's end, it would be gone. The late lunch ended in time for Asr (late afternoon) prayer. Women began readying themselves for worship. It was time to make a trek to the bathroom facilities. Before I could step out, I had to put the abbayah back on again. Haneefa and Rashida waited for me patiently, until at last I was ready. I took my toiletries and a small towel with me in a plastic bag. Like a visor, Rashida pulled her veil back down over her face, peeped out of the canvas door, and signaled to us to follow. I stepped into the incredible heat of a Hijazi afternoon.

I began to sweat almost immediately, especially at the surprisingly brisk pace that Rashida was keeping. She moved swiftly, her veil inflating behind her like cape. Haneefa followed behind me, a thin bundle of nerves. We walked between rows and rows of tents, making several turns in sequence. I was utterly disoriented because at every turn the tented tarmac avenues repeated themselves endlessly in a kaleidoscopic confusion of symmetry.

Completing my ablutions quickly, I returned to my veiling. This time we positively rushed back to the tent in time for prayer. Rashida moved like a motorized mannequin. Boy could she move! I stumbled to keep up to the best of my ability and was already dying to get out of the hideous veil.

Flinging back the canvas door, we again entered Tent 50007. Most women were relaxing after prayer, some folding up their prayer mats having just finished. I went to my corner, removing my shoes and hurriedly oriented my prayer mat to Mecca based on the direction of the women praying around me. Disrobing my abbayah but keeping my head covered, I began the short afternoon prayer.

"Allah hu Akbar," I began softly, speaking the words just under my breath. I bowed my head, folding my arms, and tried to block out the surrounding chatter, surprised that the pilgrims were not more respectful to the few of us who were still praying. They were chatting noisily.

I bent forward at the hip, immediately before descending into my first prostration. As I kneeled, the ground was hard and stony underneath the thin durries. It was distinctly uncomfortable. As I sat at the end of the first rakat, I prepared to rise to complete the second. I began to hear some clucking from behind me, the sound of pursed lips snapped in disapproval.

I frowned trying to concentrate, reminding myself that I stood in front of God while in prayer, yet even here in this holy land I was still so distracted. I descended again, flexing first at the hip, then standing, then descending into my second set of prostrations. As I held my forehead flat to the ground, my palms either side to my ears, supporting my weight as I kneeled in front of my Maker, I heard a rising chorus gain momentum.

"Haram! Haram!"

"Wa Allah, Haram! Haram!"

I was increasingly alarmed. In Islam, Haram indicates the most heinous, disallowed substances or behaviors for Muslims: alcohol, swine flesh, sinful actions like murder, blasphemy, or suicide, among many others. What could be going on behind me? It was a monumental effort to stop myself turning to see what was unfolding in the tent. Something atrocious must be happening to trigger such an outcry. I couldn't imagine what it was. I rushed through the rest of my prayers at breakneck speed. Then I remained seated this time gabbling the requisite one hundred chants, a combination of Allah hu Akbar (God is Great), Subhan'allah (all Grace belongs to God), and Alhumdullilah (all thanks be to God). Bowing my head as I marked off my chants with the creases of my fingers, I was breathless but I had to know what was going on. The sounds of "Haram" were coming from somewhere near me in the tent.

At last I finished. Before I could completely straighten myself, a Saudi woman came straight up to me. Her Holbein hat framed her fury. I shrank from her.

"Haram!" she said, touching my exposed ear, which was peeping out of my head scarf.

"Haram!" she repeated defiantly, her chin upturned, scanning the room for any who could have been unsure of my disgraceful ways. I colored with shame, though only the puce tips of my Haram ears could indicate it. I had deliberately pushed the headscarf behind my freshly washed ears immediately after entering the tent. The exposed ears allowed me to listen more clearly and formed a useful anchor for my slippery headscarf, which could stretch tightly behind my ears to keep the whole scarf secure during my various movements in prayer. Because I was surrounded by women, I was sure this was acceptable.

I had no response for her. She spoke no English and I spoke no Arabic but, my pride getting the better of me, I managed some defiance.

"Mafi Haram!" (Not Haram!) I answered her, gathering indignation from the remnants of my shame.

"Mafi Haram?" she mimicked, provocatively. "Mafi Haram?" and she stamped off muttering to herself, as if to say, "We'll see about that." Around me the noisy tent had fallen into an uncomfortable silence. Randa's row of Palestinian and Jordanian moderates didn't enter in the fray. No one wanted to anger another pilgrim, even if she was unjust in her comments or behavior. No one wanted their own or anyone else's Hajj defiled, but already I had offended two of these women deeply, women who seemed to have no regard or fear of defiling my Hajj.

In the rising heat of my deepening chagrin I returned to my isolation. All I had to rely on was the knowledge of Islam my parents had passed on to me. I was not formally educated in an Islamic school. Instead, my family had always instructed their children in the home. These women were correcting me in ways I had never experienced before—severe, categorical, critical. There was no softness in their guidance. I was disappointed for myself and yet also for them. The spirit of unity among pilgrims seemed to have been left behind in Mecca.

After an hour or so another Saudi woman approached me, waving an olive branch. She smiled at me. "Salaam alaikum," she offered. She sounded friendly.

"Wa alaikum Salaam," I responded, afraid to be hopeful.

She paused beaming at me, as though choosing her words. In carefully constructed English, she ventured a question. "When you converted to Islam, Mashallah?" she smiled, thrilled at the courage of her curiosity. I was dumbfounded.

"I have always been Muslim," I began, not sure if she knew what I meant exactly. She continued to smile, revealing uneven, stained teeth.

"And your parents," she asked, "also they converts?" I laughed, startling her. If only my parents could have heard this!

"No, Alhumdullilah, we are all Muslim." I smiled at her confusion. Her question answered, she retreated back to a clutch of Saudi women and translated for them in Arabic. It seemed she was their spokesperson. They digested the new information and appeared to discuss me at length, finally sinking into a silence. Dissatisfied with my answer, they followed my every move with their cumulative gaze.

I hadn't convinced them. They genuinely believed I was a newcomer to Islam, so alien was I in appearance, dress, and yes, so obvious my mistakes. I was just as enigmatic to them as they were to me. Like wary predators in a forest, we were circling one another, each creature assessing the other in the undergrowth of the huge jungle of Islam we had found ourselves in. Within myself I admitted their observation of my naïveté in performing my prayers was a sign of my poor practice and observation. Though born a Muslim, the fountainhead of my faith had just begun to flow. Inside I knew, these strangers were right: my conversion had actually begun.

The day passed punctuated by regular prayers, food, and private supplication. I spent time burying myself in guidebooks which Nadir had given me. I was constantly grateful to him for helping me. I wanted to know more about the women in my group, but my stumbling follies had subdued my curiosity.

Night fell, sleep overwhelmed me, and as soon as I could after prayers, I unrolled the bedding and stretched out on top of it. The room was semi-darkened though external lights penetrated even the heavy canvas, casting the figures in a ghoulish glow. Somehow the Saudi pilgrims seemed more animated than during the day, whereas the rest of us were exhausted. Regardless of their chattering and snacking, I slipped into a deep sleep.

The ground was shaking, then seemingly the tent. Regaining consciousness, a stubby hand shook my shoulder awake.

"Doctora! Doctora!" a voice called to me. Out of habit, I was immediately alert. I rubbed my eyes returning to my surroundings. The tent quaked to a cacophony of snoring. Perhaps it was time for an additional prayer of which I was yet again ignorant. I struggled to see my watch: two a.m. Feeling for my glasses, an anxious face came into view.

"Doctora! Doctora!" The Saudi woman seemed in distress, perhaps she was ill.

"Fi wajja?" (Is there pain?) I asked her, an attempt at the broken Arabic I had learned from Afrikaans-speaking South African nurses in my ICU.

"La, burra, burra." (No, outside, outside.) She responded. Gesturing to me to rise, I had no option but to follow. Rashida appeared from behind. Even more alarming, she had lost all signs of joy. Something must be wrong.

"There is someone in another tent, Doctora Qanta, she needs an injection. Please we need you to do this. Come."

I didn't have time to think how they could have known I was a doctor or how news of someone's distress could travel from tent to tent when cell phones were still rarities in the Kingdom. I slipped on my shoes and pulled on my abbayah. I followed Rashida and the other Saudi woman out of the tent into the night. I had never imagined I would see patients at Hajj. I regretted coming unprepared. I hadn't even packed Band-Aids.

Outside, the night was balmy with a delicious sea breeze. The darkness was impenetrable. We relied on the tiny beam of a flashlight Rashida was carrying. As she hurried, it stabbed a jagged path of light through the velvet night. Like miners, we carved our route forward. We walked past the tent avenues of the morning. I began to recognize some of the turns, but this time we were leaving our section.

Eventually, after fifteen minutes of scurrying, we reached the perimeter of our enclave of tents. I found our section was cordoned off behind steel barred gates, painted deep green. Amazingly they were locked. I couldn't imagine why, when everyone at Hajj was Muslim, engaged in intense worship. As we approached the gate, Rashida pulled out keys, unlocking one. It creaked backward noisily.

We were now on a main road of some kind, running through the Tent City. Vehicles flanked both sides, leaving passage for one vehicle at a time, but none came. The entire complex was asleep. As my eyes adjusted to the darkness, I began to notice details. Many of the vehicles were pickup trucks or heavy goods vehicles. Further on we came across buses much like the ones we had arrived in ourselves.

The quiet was astonishing. In such a congested an area where two and a half million dozed on the eve of Arafat, the most important day of Hajj, there was almost no human activity. A glittering panoply of stars bathed the scalloped rooftops of Tent City. Unlike Mecca, the light pollution was minimal. The night sky at Mina, surrounded by low mountains and devoid of artificial lights, must have looked much like this in the time of the Prophet. I was glad to be awake.

Rashida had stopped, impatiently waiting for me to catch up. I followed her further when suddenly I sensed movement. Stopping for a moment, I searched for the source. Something in my peripheral vision had disturbed me. As I stretched my eyes to see, I began to distinguish first one figure, then dozens, then finally hundreds, surrounding us on both sides of the road. In fact, now that I could see, I spied thousands of squatting black shadows, swaying imperceptibly, stirring around us. They were assembled in uniform rows, stretching for hundreds of yards until they were finally swallowed by the night. Each shifted weight from one tired heel to another. Occasionally a phantom would adjust a black shawl or a headdress. They were under trucks, between vehicles, leaning against tires or peering from behind them. Other specters were fortunate enough to be leaning on gates or propping themselves up against axles or fenders. Everywhere, they huddled in condensed groups which seemed to sway in unison. In the impossible darkness, they were barely visible.

"Rashida, who are all these people? What are they doing here sitting outside so late at night? Why don't they go to their tents and sleep inside?"

"Doctora, they are pilgrims, they are sleeping. They have no tents. They are poor." She pressed on, oblivious of my shock.

While I had been rubbing a sore knee or stretching a knotted back, while I had bemoaned air conditioning that worked poorly or complained about the lavatory, these people had no shelter. They were simply spending the night at the roadside, too crowded with poor pilgrims to allow them even a place to lie down. Armies of shrouded pilgrims were crammed beneath the undercarriages of vehicles, sleeping to a lullaby of ticking engines and exhausts, themselves finally cooling as the heat of the day dissipated from tired turbines. Barely a square meter of tarmac remained empty.

In every direction I looked upon thousands of vagrant pilgrims. Perhaps hundreds of thousands could be here tonight, hiding in the shadows. Yet they were patient, silent, and not the least resentful. They watched me without judgment. Their eyes, glinting in the dark, didn't contain criticism, unlike the hard stares of the unyielding women whom I had offended in my tent. Accepting their hardships, they squatted on lean haunches for hours, waiting for dawn without resentment or question.

This was Hajj.

My heart expanded with love. In the deep darkness of that night, finally I heard a message I specifically needed. Their desperate poverty contained an enormous grace, one which, despite my privilege or perhaps because of it, I sorely lacked. Once again, I was deeply humbled. I had so much to learn, and my lessons were coming thick and fast.

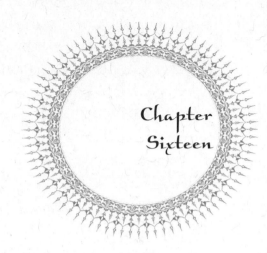

CALLING DOCTORA

ASHIDA WAS DISAPPEARING AROUND A corner. I ran to catch up
for fear of being lost in the labyrinth of Tent City forever. At
last she stopped at a tent exactly like ours. We stepped inside, again
pulling back the canvas curtain. Even this late at night these tents
were open to anyone to enter. They couldn't be locked, and all
pilgrims trusted they would be safe among the millions of pilgrims
at Hajj.

Inside, forty or fifty women were in deep slumber, lips fluttering
with soft snoring, some moaning as they changed position, aching
in their sleep. We followed the beacon of light, careful to tiptoe
between the carpet of bodies. There was almost no room for our
footfalls. In the back of the tent, Rashida led us to one woman who
was still awake. In the dark, I could see she was writhing in pain,
her face furrowed in distress.

Judging by her black abbayah which was still fastened while she was trying to sleep, this woman was Saudi also, though her features looked Palestinian. She was in her late fifties or early sixties, though her obesity was aging. As I kneeled at her bedside, trying not to fall on my own abbayah, the overweight woman looked up at me with pleading eyes. Instantly, her frightened gaze transformed us both. We were now doctor and patient.

I turned to Rashida, asking her to translate when I needed help. Rashida nodded in acquiescence.

"Ana Doctora." (I am the doctor.) I offered to her the Muslim greeting to other Muslims, "Salaam alaikum, Khaala."

"Wa alaikum Salaam Doctora," she replied trying to smile. She winced with an acute onslaught of pain. I noticed she was gripping her back. I was relieved she did not point to her flank. From afar, as she lay writhing, my first impression had been renal colic. For that she would need hospital transfer and who knew how that could be accomplished.

"Fi wajja, hinna?" (Is there pain here?) I asked, placing my hand gently over hers. It felt warm and dry though the knubbly joints of her fingers were deformed with telltale signs of osteoarthritis. At least her chubby hand, alabaster pale, didn't feel febrile to my touch. I was reassured. I didn't have the means to take vital signs.

She directed my hand lower, towards either side of her lumbar spine. I palpated her spine through her thin clothing. I could feel her muscles tensed in spasm on either side of her spinal column; paravertebral muscle spasm, common after hours of back pain. Possibly she had needed pain relief hours earlier, which would have prevented these painful knots. Judging by her weight and the signs in her hands, she probably had arthritis in the vertebral joints as well. The hard, stony floor underneath was doubtless agonizing for her crumbly spinal column.

Rashida talked to the woman and reported to me she did indeed have a history of severe arthritis. She had brought with her usual medications, one of which was an injectable pain reliever, an anti-inflammatory. I raised my brows in surprise. This was not typical at all. There were far better ways to take these drugs. An intramuscular injection was usually reserved for those too ill to swallow tablets, patients who were normally hospitalized for more serious illness. Normally, the woman explained, her daughter would administer the injection for her, but here at Hajj she was traveling only with her husband, who couldn't possibly enter the tent and who didn't know how to inject the medicine anyway. She had made inquiries, but no one in the tent knew how to give an injection either. News had traveled that there was a woman doctor with a group of ladies from Riyadh, and so I had been sent for. I was amazed anyone could know anything here, but here at Hajj, just like everywhere else, women talk and try to find solutions for problems by networking! If only I could speak Arabic, I thought to myself.

The patient struggled to sit up and began searching through her bag. At last, with a flicker of triumph in her hazel eyes, she pulled out a packet of glass vials still encased in their plastic packaging. She also produced a syringe, thankfully still in its sterile packet, and soon a packet of alcohol swabs followed. I smiled. The patient was well-prepared. Looking at the vial, it was a large dose of non-steroidal, just as I had expected. The labeling of the medicine and the dose was in English. I checked the expiration date. It looked fine, though I would have to give it even if it had been outdated. Old habits die hard even when they are impractical.

Without being able to wash my hands immediately before the procedure, I carefully wrapped the tear-dropped tip of the glass vial in the end of my abbayah scarf and, with the familiar satisfying yield of thin glass, I snapped it open at the neck. I unraveled the fractured glass from my scarf, shaking the tiny splinters into the dusty durries where they glinted in the dark. I instructed to Rashida to hold the opened vial still, without spilling any of the precious liquid. Gravely Rashida assisted, while I next readied the syringe. Before drawing up the liquid, I instructed the patient to prepare for the injection. Because the dose was so big, it was best to inject her in the gluteus maximus muscle (in her rear) but the patient, so well-practiced at her role, was already prepared.

When I looked up, she had struggled onto swollen feet and turned to face away from me. Her dimpled right buttock, gleaming white in the dark, was already exposed, waiting patiently for the shot. In her right hand she had gathered her abbayah and dress, lifting them high around her waist, while her left hand clutched at her lower back. She wore no underwear. Perhaps she had removed them for bedtime, or perhaps this was the norm for the hot weather and difficult conditions of Hajj. I didn't know the details, because in Riyadh I had been treating only critically ill patients, who arrived mangled from car wreckages or so gravely ill that they were covered in cloaks of equipment, rendering clothing impossible. I didn't know these details. When I returned to Riyadh, I would have to ask my nurses about the customs of underwear in older matron Kingdom dwellers. For now, I finished aspirating the medicine, squirting a tiny amount out of the needle to avoid injecting any air into the patient. Drops of medicine glinted in the torchlight.

"Bismillah ir-Rahman ir-Rahim! Bismillah ir-Rahman ir-Rahim!" (In the name of God, most Gracious, most Compassionate!) recited my patient, loud enough for both of us to hear.

With my left hand, I gripped her buttock, raising a meaty fold of flesh. The shot had to be intramuscular, not subcutaneous. I would have to dive through a lot of fat to reach the muscle tissue. Satisfied I was finally pinching her muscle rather than the layers of fat encasing it, I briskly plunged the steel needle into a fold. The patient winced but luckily did not move. Drawing back for a moment to check for the absence of blood, I emptied the syringe. The drug was in. Removing the needle, I wiped over the tiny puncture wound with an alcohol swab that Rashida had torn open in anticipation. We had no Band-Aid, so after it dried in a few seconds, I touched the patient's hand, and she allowed her clothing to fall, covering herself once more. She turned around. Her face was tired, but the relief was already evident. She hugged me tight and thanked me.

"Alhumdullilah! Alhumdullilah! Shukran Doctora! Shukran!" (Thanks to God, thanks to God! Thank you doctor! Thank you!) I struggled to emerge from her heavy embrace. I was embarrassed at her profuse thanks and blessings, which Rashida excitedly translated. All tension among the three of us was instantly gone, leaving us with euphoria.

Taking responsibility for a woman who wasn't my patient, administering a drug I had not prescribed, trusting the patient who guided me to give her this medicine, all this was novel for me, and scary. But I was glad I could still be useful at Hajj, where so far I had felt woefully incompetent.

We bid farewell to the patient who was already relaxing back onto her bedroll, easing herself into a much-needed sleep after many restless hours. Retreating the way we came, we returned to our own tent-home. I nodded to the sleeping, squatting army of pilgrims who lined our route, still swaying on their haunches. I couldn't be sure how long we had been gone. Inside, the women remained unrousable. Rashida retreated to her separate tent where she slept with the other maids, leaving with her flashlight. The Saudi woman who had guided us to the patient returned to her bedroll against the near corner of the tent and I went back to my spot, slumping against my suitcase. Covering myself with my angora cardigan (the only warm clothing I had) I lay down, sinking into a deep sleep myself. Looking at my watch, it was 3:45 a.m. Soon I would be waking up for Fajr (morning prayer).

* * *

"Salaat! Salaat!"

I opened my eyes, heavy with fatigue. It was the same woman who had cried Haram. Now she peered at me intently, bending her arthritic back low, to see if I was awake. Today her eyes had lost their hostility. I almost detected affection. I wondered why. Seeing I was awake, she began to straighten up. Before she left, gruffly, she greeted me with salaams. This was a first! I quickly got to my feet, pulled on my abbayah, and hurried to make my ablutions.

Returning to the tent I prayed, this time (following the custom of the women surrounding me) I covered my ears. There were no catcalls of "Haram." I was pleased. I was learning to be a better Muslim and perhaps, maybe because of my eagerness to improve, so too were others. As I sat counting off my "Alhumdullilahs," my "Allah hu Akbars," and my "Subhan'allahs," a Saudi woman passing by corrected me, signaling me to keep count on my right hand, not my left, which in my distraction I had forgotten. This time I didn't take offense but accepted the corrections. This was part of Hajj, to be allowed to improve and develop one's skills of worship. I finished my prayer and readied myself for breakfast, which was already in progress.

I noticed Randa walking in from her morning ablutions. As she wandered the tent, she dried her hair with sporadic rubs from her towel, leaving her damp red locks standing awry. She returned to her place in the tent and waved a friendly hello.

As I returned the greeting, I couldn't help noticing all eyes were on me. A line of teenage Saudi girls followed my every movement. In a silent row, still wrapped in their full-length scarves which they wore, as though mummified, while praying earlier in the morning, they tracked me with their dark eyes. Each smiled at me shyly. One bespectacled girl even called, "Salaam alaikum, Qanta!" I responded, unsure how she could know my name. Elsewhere, older Saudi matrons nodded to me in acknowledgment, showing signs of actual approval. Overnight, something had triggered a volte-face.

"Salaams, Doctora Qanta!" Rashida sang, beaming even more than usual.

Randa grinned, explaining. "We all heard about your midnight rounds, Qanta," Randa called out, "Rashida told us. Everyone has been talking about it since early this morning! News travels fast. They are impressed you are a doctor!"

"Once you have finished your breakfast, Doctora, there are some other ladies who need you. They are waiting for your help. You are so kind. I told them you would know what to do for their pains." Rashida gestured to a row of Saudi women patiently awaiting the end of my breakfast.

I couldn't help but smile at the age-old appeal of a doctor. The orthodox Saudi women sharing my tent valued the woman doctor and didn't want to miss an opportunity for an opinion. Somehow my failings as a Muslim, one who in their rigid opinions wasn't even expert in the execution of her prayers, were more than compensated by an ability to treat patients.

Islam places a great emphasis on easing suffering and the privilege of being a doctor. The Quran says it best in chapter 5:32: "If you save one life it is as though you have saved all mankind," explaining the universally high regard Muslim doctors are held in by their fellow Muslims. Perhaps these women were not able to consult women doctors themselves. Unlike the grandmothers and mothers of Saudi Arabian National Guard military personnel who presented at my hospital in Riyadh, most of these women would have to rely on the local facilities, where fewer personnel were Western and even less likely to be female. I knew the lack of a female doctor was a deterrent to seeking medical care for Saudi women, just as it is in Pakistan or Afghanistan. No wonder they were so excited about sharing a tent with a woman doctor.

Randa had a different explanation, however, "They are impressed with you, Qanta, because you are a doctor. Until they found out about last night, they thought you were just a Pakistani maid." She went on, even more bluntly. "They look at your dark skin, Qanta, dark as an Indian, and they noticed your friendliness to Rashida and Haneefa, the Hijazi maids, and assumed like those black girls, you were also a servant. They probably think you serve a family in Riyadh. They looked down on you because of your Pakistani blood and the fact that as a servant they didn't think you belonged in this tent. Don't worry, Sherief, my husband, gets this all the time too. He is dark-skinned and he is constantly mistaken for a Pakistani or Indian too. When they find out he is Egyptian, it's not much better, though.

"You know the Saudis hate the Egyptians the most and vice versa. It's to do with the economic inequality in our countries. Most Egyptians come to work in the Gulf countries like the Kingdom for economic reasons so Saudis regard them as poor. And on the other hand, the Saudis like to vacation in Egypt, where they unfairly get a reputation of womanizing and drinking, so the Egyptians look down on them, very unhealthy.[15] But in your case, you being with Qudsia doesn't help much either. Because she's black, I mean. I think most women here don't know that she is a nurse, and anyway she is very difficult to talk to."

Randa went on. "Last night when they heard about your trip to the other tent they were quite shocked to discover you are a doctor. But they are pleased about that now! Now you will find they will all want to talk with you! They don't care about your race!" She laughed, returning to apply more unscented lotion to her drying limbs.

I was shocked. I had indeed noticed that while I felt terrible about Rashida and her helpers waiting on us in the tent, like maids, retrieving cutlery, serving food, tidying up, serving drinks, preparing our beds, no one else expressed the same concern. I tried to be as helpful as possible, unused to being waited upon. After eating I always returned my plate and utensils to the bucket in which everything was collected and taken away for washing, and would just get up to retrieve my own cold drink from the refrigerator cabinet in the corner of the tent, rather than ask a maid to fetch me one. I had noticed the Saudis dropping half-empty, crumpled cans on the floor of the tent, leaving their litter for the maids to remove. Or worse, signaling to the maids to bring them another soda with a contemptuous and dismissive wave, not even articulating the words, let alone pleasantries like "please" and "thank you."

This arrogant behavior made me feel uncomfortable and seemed unnecessarily unkind, especially by pilgrims at Hajj towards fellow Muslims who were trying to ease their Hajj. I had wondered why no one else in my tent seemed eager to help the overworked maids to clear away each meal; and now I understood: it was beneath my fellow pilgrims, who had paid top dollar for this "VIP Hajj."

To me "VIP Hajj" meant I was able to travel in buses between the holy sites and stay in air-conditioned comfort in Mina, but to these other Saudi women it meant being waited on hand and foot and enjoying a sense of superiority over these dark-skinned maids from Mecca, poor women who had to work for a living and chose to make a few extra riyals in Hajj season. I felt disgusted. The entire point of Hajj was to remind Muslims of our equal status in the eyes of God and that only God determines if one Muslim is superior to another in matters of the purity of His believers' hearts. Hajj was not an exercise in dominating the weak because of some form of economic power which, unlike each maid attending us, few other women in this tent actually earned for themselves. Worse than this, these women in my tent were feeling racially superior, to the maids and perhaps even to me.

I shouldn't have been stunned. I had already uncovered some racism during my time in the Kingdom. I knew Randa was probably

right. Skin color, previously something I had never considered in my
years of living in the United States or England, had somehow invited
discomfort to me in Riyadh already. It was while I worked among
the Wahabis that I first noticed how some Saudis discriminated, first
among themselves and then among the expatriates. Discrimination
in fact is how many of the Saudis define themselves. Saudi Arabia is
about separation of gender, race, tribe, fiefdoms. I had developed a
theory based on my crude observations, which explained the Wahabi
Saudi ecosystem surrounding me in Riyadh. Perhaps it reached here
too, in a tent full of Saudi orthodox Wahabi women from Riyadh.

The highest position in the Kingdom's racial food chain was
occupied by the "pure" Saudi who was from the Najd, the central
region, the province of which Riyadh was the first city (and therefore the nation's capital). The Najd was also the historical, geograph-
ical, and political node to the current powerbase: the rabidly orthodox
Wahabi clergy. I use the word pure as they, the pure Saudis did. I
had never heard anyone describe themselves as Pure English, Pure
French, Pure Nigerian, Pure Indian, or any such. "Pure American"
of course was an oxymoron, an impossibility which endeared America
so much to me. "Pure Saudi," however, I heard repeatedly; first when
I stumbled across a gorgeous Saudi woman, settling a check at my
beauty salon and "undercover" luxury gym in Riyadh, al-Multaqa.

Ahead of me in line, I had watched the extraordinarily beautiful Saudi woman at the counter. Her creamy skin, enormous eyes,
regal stature, and slim, muscular figure were a breath-taking combination, even for another woman to behold. I surmised her to be of
Palestinian origin. By now in Riyadh, I was learning Palestinians
are a physically beautiful race. I couldn't wait to tell her this and
triumphantly expose her origin, a testament to my growing sophistication and insight in this unusual world.

She signed her bill with an elegant twist of her slim wrist, weighed
down by the obligatory Chopard "Happy Diamonds" watch, *de*

rigueur for the cultivated Saudi lady. She placed her gleaming red cell phone, shiny like nail polish, into an oversized Fendi handbag, and started to fasten her elegant, tailor-made abbayah. She covered her eyes with Dolce and Gabbana shades. Her languid, lean, perfectly manicured, unpolished fingers quickly fastened the jeweled cords to her costly abbayah. Elegant heels, probably Balenciaga, completed the ensemble. I was bewitched by this beautiful creature. I had never seen anything more elegant.

"Are you Palestinian?" I remembered blurting out to her. "You are so beautiful," I told her, simply. She smiled a self-possessed smile, which slowly curved open, revealing a mouthful of pristine teeth, made perfect with expensive West London orthodontics. It was a dazzling smile. Compliments on her beauty were evidently commonplace, even here in a veiled Kingdom. She responded coolly, "No, I am Pure Saudi. I am not a Palestinian."

Brushing past me, she exited, leaving me puzzled.

At the time I barely gave it a thought, watching the rich woman leaving in a cloud of fragrance. This was hardly so very different than many Western societies, I thought, recalling frosty, pooch-carrying, anorexic cadavers scuttling up and down Madison Avenue. So Saudi Arabia had a similar culture of frosty exclusion, a claim to superiority based on economics and tribal origins. The purity that the mysterious woman mentioned was actually an expression of Saudi aristocracy.

Later I realized this was my introduction to the Saudi self-perception of purity. Purity (and the froideur that usually accompanied it) was, in a few short months, already a powerful, recurrent theme in my time in the Kingdom: either one had it or one didn't. I even learned this was a problem for Saudi men, who were forever seen as hybrid races, doomed forever to be migrants because of grandmothers from elsewhere in the Arab world where three generations in the country was "off the boat." This hybrid breeding would actually limit their ascent in organizations. Men, while Saudi nationals by birth, were of "impure" blood, their races were mixed, and they were excluded from the highest positions of power. "Oh yes, but he is an Iraqi Saudi," would be a common lament.

I would discover my observations were not unusual. Ziauddin Sardar observed something similar about racial hierarchy in the Saudi philanthropic culture when he wrote about the "Saudi Sandwich" in 2006.[16] He had noted deep seated preferences based on race as well. I realized the algorithm of racism I had encountered in Riyadh had intruded even the Hajj.

Here at Hajj, I was experiencing a taste of the same poison. While the women in my tent weren't nearly as wealthy or polished as the bewitching woman at al-Multaqa, they subscribed to the same view, deciding (based on skin color and ethnicity) that I surely must be a handmaid or at best nanny to a poor Saudi family who couldn't afford the much better Filipina maids, having instead to resort to Pakistani or worse, Bengali help. In fact I did remember one Saudi woman in the tent asking me if I was Bengali.

Yet I couldn't connect this racial purity with the warmth of the toothless, lined Bedouin women who showed me such affection in the hospital. I thought about the Bedouin patients I had attended in Riyadh and what they had taught me of acceptance. Surely these Bedouin were the purest Saudis of all, Daughters of Arabia, borne of tribal forebears who had roamed Arabia before the slick of oil wealth suffocated their culture, washing them up like half-dead seagulls into the new urban metropolis of modern Saudi Arabia. I decided it had to be wealth which made the stark difference. All I had to do was think back to the "real" Saudis I had met in Riyadh, so different than the women sharing this tent with me.

Chapter Seventeen

DAUGHTERS OF THE DESERT

IT WAS THE EXCEPTIONAL WARMTH that I had encountered in the Bedouin women which so drew me to them. Even in my first few weeks in the Kingdom I quickly began to look forward to caring for them.

Saudi Arabia is the most urbanized country in the entire Arab world and only seven percent of the population of the Kingdom remains nomadic. Nonetheless, we had many Bedouin patients at the King Fahad hospital. I knew I wanted to know more patients like my first, Mrs. al-Otaibi. Their relatives fascinated me too. Few of them were Bedouins in the real sense, wandering and nomadic, most recently settled to Riyadh within a single generation. But when these elders became ill, their sons or grandsons would bring them in for treatment, often the whole family keeping vigil. Occasionally families would pitch tents outside the compound as they waited for the health of their loved one to be restored. And while doing so they cast a cozy umbra of reverence and affection for all those who cared for their kin.

I quickly discovered the Bedouin families were invariably grateful and compliant. No family, indeed no Saudi patient, male or female, ever objected to me, a woman, examining. They did not express even this fundamental discrimination that elsewhere seemed intrinsic to Kingdom life. Bedouin families welcomed women doctors. When I cared for their sons or fathers or husbands or brothers or grandfathers, the very patriarchs of these noble ancient families, even the most orthodox families never objected. In two years not a single Bedouin family ever asked for a male doctor to replace me. Not a single Bedouin objected to my unveiled status.

To the contrary, unlike the wealthy women who surrounded me at Hajj, they accepted me. I was constantly surprised and always gratified when the many families whose relative I did attend expressed open admiration that I was a woman, sentiments they transmitted with intense smiles, with deep, kohl-ringed gazes of emotion, or simply with a clumsy brush of fragrant attar (Arabic essential oil) smeared on the back of my snatched hand, clasped between the roughened, sun-blasted fingers of their senior sons. I blushed deeply when this happened the first time, amazed that a Saudi Bedouin man dared to reach for my unmarried hand and do so publicly. Their warmth was unmistakable and immediately transported me to the Arabia that had so bewitched Lawrence.

Families generally kept vigil either at the ICU bedside of their relative or, during times of intense treatment activity, outside in the hallways, in the visitors' prayer area of the ICU. Any women (if allowed by their male relatives to visit) usually gathered in one corner of the room and squatted tirelessly for hours, a line of black bundles along one wall. In a fiercely protective role of their womenfolk, most families would not permit their female family members to visit during the critical illness of their relative, even a son or husband. They feared overwhelming the women (should they be allowed to see the extent of illness), preferring them to visit once the stormy course of the illness had settled. Of course sometimes this meant that women would enter only as the patient was at the verge of irretrievable death, leading to a sudden heap of fainting bundles at the bedside, but this was clearly a cultural gesture to protect the weaker, frailer womenfolk. I always viewed this as a manifestation of the menfolk's love for their women relatives and not an oppressive behavior.

Meanwhile, the menfolk could never stop in one place, pacing through the ICU and greeting other family members in courtly succession. Once, feeling bad for one family of women whose patriarch was deathly ill, I started collecting chairs from the nurses' station to at least relieve some of them from sitting on the floor where they had been settled for hours. A Saudi colleague asked me what I was doing, and I explained.

"Please don't worry, Qanta. They are Bedouins. Really, they prefer the floor, truly."

I doubted it, but when I handed them the chairs, I looked on, growing even more alarmed to see the bundles mounting the chairs, suddenly precarious on wheels. Distinctly ill at ease in the revolving chairs, these women really did prefer the floor after all. How I wished I could really talk with them and understand them more.

Returned to terra firma, they followed me with kohl-lined eyes, silently locking their sights on me, so many tracking devices. I wondered what they could be thinking as they assessed me. What did my white coat, my Western clothing, my short, unveiled hair, my bright red lipstick, and my Muslim name emblazed across my chest communicate to them? Then I remembered they couldn't read English, so perhaps they didn't know I bore a Muslim name.

Eventually, they began to speak to me. Ultimately, it was the Bedouins who took the initiative. The Bedouins were even more curious than I was!

The conversations usually went something like this. Shyly, they always began by asking me from where I had come, most often making their surreptitious inquiries as I finished off some notes or stored away X rays. This furtive inquiry while I was occupied obviated the need for us to make eye contact, which many Bedouins, even women, did not wish to do. Caught unaware, I would explain, America; after all that was where I had moved from. (It would prove far too convoluted to explain my precise origins as a British-born Muslim woman of Pakistani origin derived of parents transplanted there from a post-Partition India who had herself migrated in adulthood to the United States.)

"America," I would say, bracing for their reaction.

"Amreeka!" they would exclaim, inexplicably delighted. They repeated "Amreeka!" to one another, in affirmation, as if they had guessed as much. For a time, the bundles would babble among themselves:

"Amreeka?"

"Na-am, Amreeka." (Yes, America.) I would confirm.

"Umma, wa Bu-ey?" (And Mom and Dad?) They would inevitably inquire, emboldened. They would ask because tribal genealogy was so important for a woman, especially an unchaperoned female in a foreign country. They wanted to know of my stock.

"Pakistan," I would say.

"Bakistan," they would repeat, smiling widely, being unable to pronounce P (there is no P in Arabic). Thrilled, they would then gather courage to ask finally if I was indeed a Muslim. This, of course, had been the whole point of the interrogation. I would confirm and their veiled faces beamed.

"Mashallah!" (Praise God!) they would cry and let me go about my work, clearly delighted.

"Mashallah, Mashallah, Mashallah!" resonated throughout the bundles. "Musalmaan, Musalmaan," (Muslim) they would say to each other, delighted they had found me to be a fellow believer.

Their curiosity was sated. They asked me nothing further and would always stop at this point, satisfied, pleased, possibly even relieved. Their dark eyes followed me with renewed interest and a genuine sense of pride, because they knew that the woman doctor caring for their family member was a Muslim too. Their ailing relative was in good hands, they must have decided. Being a Muslim made them feel connected to me. They seemed to be able to put aside my alien qualities much more easily than I was feeling. I remembered how very warm these Bedouin were.

This extraordinary approval was repeated countless times; many of the women admiring me probably couldn't read or write and yet looked at me with untold genuine pride. The older women seemed most enthralled by the discovery that I was a Muslim. I was always touched but also so puzzled by how these Bedouin seemed to have so much affection for America. How could this be, when only few of them could have been there and most certainly none of them knew any Americans personally? What was it that infused their voices which such admiration for my origins from "Amreeka," which they revered almost as much as my Muslim pedigree?

NEXT STOP: ABSOLUTION

THE TENT WAS ALREADY IN full swing when I awoke. Today, after an intense day of supplication at the Valley of Arafat, we would be spending the night outdoors on the plain of Muzdullifah. This was the pinnacle of Hajj: Arafat—the Day of Standing. All pilgrims would stand in worship en masse.

Soon the tent was vacated, the air conditioner was switched off, the refrigerator emptied and disconnected. We filed out toward our bus, weaving a route through the city of fifty thousand tents. Outside, Tent City already seemed desolate, thousands of pilgrims setting out for Arafat on foot where today all two and a half million of us would stand before God.

The fifty to one hundred thousand vehicles snarled into impassable traffic. Pilgrims on foot made faster progress. Some were power-walking, weaving through traffic at a rigorous pace.

Even the disabled hobbled faster, such was the urgency to worship. Young steeds pushed wheelchairs over bumpy tarmac while the disabled pilgrims, weak already from effort, prayed aloud. I could see their lips moving to the same Labbaik prayer I was reciting, which literally means "Here I am, Lord, hear me!" It is the Muslim's expression to answer the invitation to perform Hajj.

Tendinous hands clung to Qurans heavy enough to snap their osteoporotic wrists. Even though the glass pane between us silenced our shared Labbaik anthem, I knew we were singing it in unison. Alone, a one-legged African jauntily limped on a homemade crutch, strapped together with rope and elastic, yet he was managing his flowing Hajj robes well and passing many able-bodied pilgrims who struggled behind him. The dynamism of Hajj was astonishing. Not a creature was still. It was as though an entire globe was on the move.

I watched the feet of the millions scurrying by. Many wore sneakers, frequently Nikes! I couldn't imagine a better commercial for Nike than "Just do Hajj!" The American sneakers made an extraordinary contrast in a world of Islam, reminding us that though the Hajj rite was 1,400 years old, we now had modern comforts to ease the process. Many Filipino pilgrims wore plimsolls, their footwear of choice, and I spied a number of Birkenstocks too. Most on foot had to rely on rubber flip-flops. In my tent the teenage girls had shown a penchant for the rubberized platformed sneakers, hideously kitsch, that had seized Riyadh's fashionistas that winter, perhaps because their gargantuan height both eased movement in an abbayah and was the only statement of individuality that female teenagers heavily veiled in public could make in Riyadh at the time. These girls had brought their fashion to Hajj.

Eventually, just before noon, we reached Arafat. The hundred-degree heat was already unbearable, deadeningly hot and humid without any relief of breeze. We were in a giant valley, without shade, and the sun was full-strength at its zenith. Again we were assigned a tent in which to rest and pray.

The older guard heaved themselves against supporting poles of the tents and leaned their weight tiredly. They recited prayers, reading nothing. These were the illiterate Saudi women of a generation earlier. Education was very new to the Kingdom for women other than the highly privileged. Others, who were clearly literate, studied their books intensely.

Fully veiled, I peered out of the tent but saw only a sea of fiberglass. Either everyone had gone to stand at Arafat under the midday sun or actually climbed the Mount of Mercy where the Prophet Muhammad (PBUH) had delivered his final sermon. Most male pilgrims would stand like this all day until sunset, an incredibly arduous task. And most women like us were engaged in intense supplications inside the shade and comfort afforded by tents.

I sat next to the redheaded woman who once more was checking her blood pressure. She had brought her sphygmomanometer even here to Arafat. I saw her measure her pressure, 190/100 mmHg, but she seemed unalarmed at the reading.

"Salaams," I began, wondering if she spoke English.

"Wa alaikum Salaam, Qanta." She knew my name. By now I was unsurprised. She continued in cultured English polished by a colonial Cairo upbringing.

"I am tired and my blood pressure is high. It's the strain, it happens at every Hajj," she went on, smiling patiently. I tried hard to guess how old she was. Somewhere between fifty and sixty-five, I estimated, judging by the fading of her red hair at the temples and her crow's feet on either side of her deep-set blue eyes which sparkled intensely in a sea of freckles. "My name is Yehyia. Most call me Professor Yehyia, but you may call me Yehyia." She popped a pill into her mouth and swallowed water from the plastic bottle she was clutching. In a few minutes she started checking her blood pressure again.

"Where do you teach, Professor Yehyia? And what is your area of expertise?" I asked, anxious to know more. Perhaps like me she was a doctor of medicine.

"I teach in Riyadh. I teach Arabic literature at the King Abdul Aziz University to the Saudi students there. But half of the year I return home to Cairo where I still teach my favorite course, nineteenth century English literature. I teach it at the University in Cairo."

I was amazed. "English literature was my favorite subject at school, Professor Yehyia," I gushed. "I had wanted to study it further, perhaps even at University myself." I babbled on, unable to stop. "Who do you teach, I mean which authors, in your classes?"

"Henry James, among others. I have studied his work in depth, in fact, my PhD was focused on some of his work." She waited for a response.

Feeling ignorant, I confessed, "I have never read any Henry James. Tell me more." And there, surrounded by a tent of orthodox Saudi Wahabis, in a valley eight miles east of Mina, Professor Yehyia instructed me on the finer points of Henry James. We must have talked for at least an hour, probably longer, as her vivid imagination and her perfect command of English led me through a compelling journey of James's contribution to consciousness and morality. I couldn't believe my luck at finding such a brilliant woman amid the confusion of Hajj. As we talked, everything else fell away from our attention. I was bewitched. I wasn't sure if it was proper to talk about Henry James at Hajj but am sure I was allowed a reprieve from the hours of praying. After a while it had become difficult to concentrate.

"So you have attended Hajj before," I finally remembered to ask in between our impromptu seminar in nineteenth century literature.

"Indeed," she responded, "Alhumdullilah, many times," unwilling to divulge how many.

Bluntly I pressed her, "How many times did you make Hajj, Professor Yehyia? Why do you still keep coming?"

"A Muslim is not supposed to announce how many times he has been to Hajj, so I cannot tell you. But, Mashallah, it is many, and most times I have come like this, in a group, because I am alone. I have one son who remains in Egypt and my husband is dead many years now, but still I manage to come. Like you, I come without a man!" She threw back her head laughing with abandon. Some of the orthodox Saudis around us looked up, squinting sharply at the blasphemy of laughter, but they didn't intervene.

"Inshallah, I shall keep coming as long as I can walk, as long as I have strength, and as long as God invites me," she rested back, rubbing her swollen ankle, glinting her charming smile of pearly teeth worn low and uneven through years of bruxism. "You will have to visit me in Riyadh, Qanta. I invite you! We will have dinner!" she decided, terminating our conversation. I quickly made a mental note to obtain her details when we returned to Mina. I had no pen or paper with me here at Arafat. Unwilling to leave her side lest my incredible discovery of such a brilliant Muslim woman vanish into the ether, I stayed next to her and returned to my prayer book. I squeezed her cool, freckled hand in mine, expressing my joy at discovering her. What a journey I was on!

PRAYER UNDER THE STARS

I AWOKE OUTDOORS TO THE sounds of Swahili. Around me on the hessian mat, the women in my group slept. Across the way, on a similar mat the men in our group dozed. We were separated only by a makeshift aisle in the dust.

Latecomers to the plain of Muzdullifah (where we were to spend the night in prayer and rest under a starlit sky) were still arriving, hours after we had reached there by bus. Many pilgrims, tired after their almost twenty-four-hour-long foot journeys, now searched for a place to rest and water to drink. These tall Africans were among the latecomers. In the dark, luminous African smiles ripped incandescent rents of white in the velvet of night.

I watched as one leaned over the water samovar placed in the center of our sleeping group and, with his calloused, arachnoid fingers, carefully poured cups of ZamZam. Balancing the water, he passed the precious liquid down a long, silent line of patient Africans stretching into the black shadows of night. Centipede-like, the waiting Africans reached forward with their sinewy right arms to receive the refreshing drink. There must have been three hundred men at least. Quiet as church mice, so as not to disturb our rest, they had edged toward our water tank in an attempt to slake their thirst. I lay still, enthralled by the amazing scene. My watch said 1:30 a.m. We were only a few hours away from water and eventually, back at Mina, we would have ice cold Pepsi to drink. I hoped there was enough for all of them.

I noticed how different these African pilgrims were from the Saudi cohort I was traveling with. Firstly, they were unaccompanied by women, unlike the Saudi couples I was traveling with, who brought wives with them to Hajj (almost every woman in my tent was married). These men were thinner than the men in our group and sported short wispy facial hair. Most had thinned ribcages, scraggy from lifetimes of hunger, and while at Hajj they had continued to lose weight. Distinctly they looked poorer, with no glints of watches or steel-rimmed glasses. In fact in the whole line I couldn't make out a single wristwatch. Here and there on their feet they wore dusty sandals, but many were in broken or torn flip-flops, and quite a few were barefoot.

I clutched my cardigan around my throat to keep out the cool night air. As I snuggled back to rest I realized the African pilgrims had not even clothing like this to keep them warm, relying only on their thin, worn Hajj garments. Many simply wore threadbare sheets rather than the heavy toweling material sold as Hajj robes widely throughout the Kingdom.

The water was reviving the crowd and true to form, the tired Africans were rejuvenated by the magical ZamZam water. They began to laugh, their Swahili rising into excited bubbles of laughter. Here and there, the hubbub was punctuated by a lone phlegmatic cough.

Suddenly, the Imam leader of our group sat bolt upright, his beard almost standing on end when he saw what was happening.

Like Yosemite Sam, hopping from one blistered foot to another, the desperate Imam began snatching the cups of water from the thirsty Africans and roughly handed them to the sleepy men behind him, men from our group. They started at the spray of ZamZam as the Imam, in his agitation, inadvertently flung precious holy water all over the place.

The line of three hundred Africans stood patiently, continuing to wait in turn, calmly assuming someone else's thirst had become more pressing. I could see the line now stretched even further and more were assembling. These samovars could well be the only source of drinking water for miles around. Incensed by the Africans' failure to comprehend, the Imam resorted to dramatic measures. In fury and exasperation he signaled to two of the younger male pilgrims and ordered them to carry the orange samovars to safety.

Obediently, they followed the Imam's demands. Struggling under the weight, the Saudi pilgrims hauled the huge containers and placed them in the middle of the men's matting instead of in the aisle between us. The men would now guard the water all night long, preventing anyone except our group to drink it. At last the poor Africans understood, and without protest they began turning around, heading back into the darkness of Muzdullifah. Thirsty like the Masai, they made no scene, preferring to conserve their energy for a continued search for water. They even bid warm salaams to the Imam, disappearing back into the night.

I was outraged. At Hajj we were supposedly equal and God was watching every action, and yet our own Imam refused to share water with thirsty pilgrims. Looking at the pilgrims around me I doubted very much any of us would be suffering from serious thirst even if we didn't get another drink of water until we reached Mina in the morning, yet none of us had intervened. Instead we had enabled the panicking Imam and failed our fellow Muslims in need at Hajj. I was ashamed of my group and I was ashamed of myself for not taking a stance. Calmly, Randa and Sherief rationalized the events for me.

"Qanta, they couldn't drink our water. There were hundreds of them. We have to keep it to ourselves. Every group has to be self-sufficient in supplies. You know that. Don't worry so much about it." Randa stared at me hard, as though seeking some kind of approval.

"And the Africans are notorious for being disorganized at every Hajj!" added a pilgrim next to Sherief, thoroughly irritated at the interruption of his sleep. Randa and Sherief were silent. I wondered if the pilgrim knew how racist he sounded. Rolling over and away from Randa, I tried to sleep, but disturbed by the plight of thirsty Africans, it took some time before I dozed off. As I lay thinking about them I could hear the satisfied snoring of the angry Imam. His conscience was evidently clear.

I couldn't help noticing how nationalities even here at Hajj were distinct in their behaviors: the patient yet irrepressibly joyful Africans; the superior, judgmental Saudis secure in their self-appointed supremacy; the unassuming East Londoner Pakistanis with their curiously charming recitation of Quranic verses in heavy cockney accents; the chatty and cultured Egyptians; the friendly, outgoing Americans who, if they had a chance, would be exchanging business contacts inside the al-Haram (so effective were they at connecting); most recently, the noisy, coughing Bengalis. Of all nationalities, however, the most distinctive by far were the Malaysians.

In *Guests of God*, Robert Bianchi explains that female pilgrims had long dominated the Malaysian Hajj, always exceeding fifty-three percent of all Malay pilgrims. They were notably younger, many in their thirties, forties, or fifties, and less than ten percent over seventy years of age. Most of these women were housewives, but many actually earned a second income outside their homes while describing themselves as "housewives." They were the antithesis to most female Muslims in the world who would never have an opportunity to reach Hajj because of economic hardships or male oppression, or more often both reasons.

I had noticed the Malaysians on the first night at Hajj as I watched missiles of Malayan women, arms linked, surge forward through the crowds around the Ka'aba, completing their revolutions around the House of God with the greatest efficiency. Entire cohorts of Malays seemed female, save for their single Imams at the head of each group leading the way with a Quran and a megaphone. Each woman was exactly the same mesomorphic build and none of them exceeded five feet in height. Together, they formed a stocky and satisfyingly dense Hajj organism that coursed through the rites independent of the rest of us, almost unhindered by the huge crowd. They came through each stage like Hajj-express trains, arms linked, faces fixed and firmed in determination, and heads bowed slightly forward as though seeking an actual aerodynamic advantage against fictional headwinds.

These Malaysian bullets of worship were uniform in dress, down to the last detail. As they steamed past, I noticed on every woman, tightly wrapped at the back of the head, identical Malaysian flags methodically sewn onto every veil. These women were a monumental, moving organization eliciting envy and admiration in any pilgrim I spoke to. When they prayed, they lined up immediately in a perfect, precise geometry, while nearby, the rest of us rummaged around, struggling to exit our disorganization. After prayer, they re-formed into their pilgrim-juggernauts and continued their tremendous, unassailable pace. And at last, when they finished their rites, they sat like so many bowling pins in perfectly aligned rows, identical to the last gesture.

So, even without opening my eyes tonight, I had known the spitting and coughing could not have been Malaysian pilgrims. Malaysians were simply not relaxed at Hajj. They had a mission to accomplish and they did so with military precision, year after year with a minimum of fuss. All energies were conserved only for worship. Even spitting, joking, or coughing seemed superfluous to the Malaysian at worship; such was their discipline.

While many Muslims regard Hajj as a farewell and final Islamic obligation to be done toward the end of one's life, the Malaysian women, like me, were already discovering what I was finding to be true: Hajj, while a beautiful closure to life and a gateway to the next life, can also be the threshold to a new life in this world. I was already glad to be experiencing Hajj at thirty-one, and I hadn't even finished yet. I couldn't imagine waiting another forty years for this privilege.

BETWEEN THE DEVIL
AND THE RED SEA

MORNING CAME, AND WE HAD returned to Mina, preparing for the final rites of Hajj. Refreshments had just been served. Haneefa, the shyest maid of all, stood to the side, uncomfortable to be the center of the conversation.

"You know, Doctora," began Rashida excitedly, "Haneefa is a Hafiz! Hafiz-al-Quran, no less!" I was amazed. Hafiz is the title given to one who has memorized the Quran perfectly. The entire book is committed to memory and was so transmitted for many years at the dawn of Islam. Memorization was the only way the revealed word of God was preserved and transmitted unchanged, before scribes began to record the words verbatim which remained, unchanged now, more than 1,400 years later.

"How old are you, Haneefa?" I asked, guessing she couldn't be older than twenty.

Rashida translated for both of us as we talked. "I am fifteen, Doctora Qanta, going to be sixteen next month, Inshallah," she responded.

"So how did you become Hafiz at such a young age?" I asked, puzzled. The only Hafiz I had ever known was my own ninety-year-old grandfather, though I was unsure at what age he had mastered the holy book.

"I studied here in Mecca, at the Madrassah (Islamic school). My father is an Imam there, and he taught me to read. It was easy for me, Alhumdullilah, and with the Grace of God, I became a Hafiz one year ago!" She was unable to conceal her pure joy at her sole but rather staggering accomplishment.

"Prove it to me, Haneefa," I challenged rudely, unable to believe what I was hearing.

Rashida said, "Here, Doctora, take this Quran and read any passage. Haneefa can recite the words which follow without looking. We do this to her all the time, to see if she ever makes a mistake, but she doesn't! She is amazing!"

In disbelief, I opened the Quran at a random page and chose a verse which was at least unknown to me (and of these there are many). I began reading, hoping my Arabic didn't sound too uneducated.

"Mashallah, you read Arabic well," encouraged Rashida generously. Now I knew I must be sounding dreadful, but the words nevertheless were beautiful. Mid-sentence, without warning, I stopped and looked up.

Haneefa had been following me intently, mouthing the words in time to my spoken ones. As soon as I stopped enunciating, she took over and began to recite aloud. My fingers followed the words in the Quran. Haneefa's eyes were closed in concentration by now, and even so there was no way even with eyes open that she could have made out the tiny print from which I was reading. I knew she recited from memory. For pages and pages she recited the Quran perfectly—every word, accent, pause, emphasis, and punctuation. I allowed her to continue for fifteen minutes. I was incredulous.

"Mashallah, Mashallah, Haneefa please stop. You are indeed a Hafiz. I should never have questioned you," and I went on apologizing. "But this is fantastic," I went on. "You are such a scholar so learned. What will you do with this knowledge?"

"Be a better Muslim, Doctora Qanta," she responded without hesitation.

"And marry a very good man, Doctora!" boomed Rashida, roaring with laughter.

I looked at Rashida quizzically.

"It is very desirable to marry a woman who has memorized the Quran. This will help Haneefa in a match." Haneefa was now shrinking in embarrassment, burying her chin into her chest and hiding her eyes from all of us. "You know we are all very poor ladies, Doctora. We cannot be like you, independent, earning money, making our own destinies. We admire you, truly Doctora, but this is not our destiny; Allah did not choose this for us," explained Rashida practically, not the least inflection of self-pity in her voice.

Haneefa and I were worlds apart, yet somehow in Saudi Arabia she did not deserve what I had accepted as a birthright—the freedom to seek an education. I was learning a surprising amount about the Kingdom by being at Hajj. The women I worked with in Riyadh clearly were the privileged and moneyed. These women in Mecca were more representative of the growing underbelly of the lower classes in the Kingdom, the poor strata where oil wealth passed them by. In a society where connections and pedigree are everything, nothing could ever draw them out of their circumstances.

In the afternoon I would find myself quite literally between the Devil and the Red Sea. The most hazardous of the Hajj rites was later today. Soon the time came for the ritual stoning of the three stone pillars at Jamaraat. Muslims believe in good and evil and recognize Satan to be Iblis, the fallen one of God's angels who was too defiant to bow to Adam in acknowledgment of mankind's inherent ability to distinguish good from evil. This defiance earned him expulsion from heaven, doomed to perpetual scorn, which fuels his wickedness further. Muslims must be vigilant of the temptations the Devil may place in efforts to impede sincere progress toward spending a life in good works and worship of the Devil's nemesis: the Creator. The stoning rituals at Jamaraat (where pilgrims symbolically throw tiny stones at three pillars representing the devil) are an opportunity to enact this active repulsion of evil that all Muslims must exercise in their daily jihad of self-improvement.[10]

I approached the pillars on an enormous causeway that split into a two-level road bearing a million men on each level. Underfoot I walked on a river of human hair discarded from newly shorn Hajjis who had completed this ritual earlier that afternoon. Hajji is an honorific title for a man who has completed Hajj, which he can use for the rest of his life. Females who have completed Hajj are called Hajjas. Along the roadside, pilgrim-barbers squatted, shearing scalps of hair, symbolizing the spiritual rebirth of each male Muslim who had completed Hajj.

Clutching my tiny stones, which I had collected in Mina, I approached the maelstrom. The crowds were terrible, focused on the giant pillars; behind me people bore down with incredible

---

[10] This ritual is considered one of the most dangerous and has been the site of many tragedies, most notably in 1998 and 2000. In 1998, 118 pilgrims were crushed to death around these same Jamaraat pillars. One injury can multiply into hundreds before authorities are able to hold back the intense crowds who cannot know what is coming ahead, precipitating deadly stampedes. Brilliant Hajj engineers have recognized that dangerous forces in dense crowds are best dissipated by elliptical shapes, and now the barriers around the pillars and the pillars themselves have been changed to an elliptical shape, allowing a wider surface for stoning, which avoids concentrating dense crowds in one tiny area.

force. I raised my arm to throw a stone. To my side, a short Afghani pilgrim suddenly bent down, grabbing his shoe and, leaning backward at a crazy angle, tossed it with all his force. In doing so, he promptly poked me in my forehead with his sharp elbow. I was a little stunned, almost seeing stars. He proceeded to remove his other shoe and throw that too, all the while shouting vicious "Allah hu Akbars!" full of scorn at the Devil, redoubling the intensity of his efforts. It seemed he had finished his stones and both his shoes but was not done with his scorn. After standing around in a minor daze himself, he turned around. A little deflated, he pushed passed me, transiently locking my gaze with his brilliantly green eyes.

I tried to throw my stones again. This time a small Indonesian woman shrieking at full volume knocked my sunglasses hard at the side of my face with the recoil of her swing. I touched my smarting nose, which was now bleeding from the bump. I wondered if the bleeding had violated my Ihram, but as it was an accident, I hoped not. Gripping my eyeglasses with one hand and my stones in the other, I began. My throws were most certainly gestures; barely any of them actually reached the pockmarked stone pillar, testament to my feeble bat-and-ball skills. Still, as I counted the throws, I couldn't believe the pandemonium around me. I wanted to get out as soon as possible.

For one, the pillar seemed to be soaking in rain. I looked hard, noting the brilliant sunshine beyond the covered asphalt. In the sunlight, the bulldozers were rumbling away moving some form of debris. There was no sign of rain but when I looked at the pillar it was covered in an incessant gray drizzle. Upward, the pillar was disappearing in a black sky of fine spray. Finally I realized this was the downpour of stones! A monsoon of pebbles was raining through the upper circular hole where another ten thousand or so pilgrims were now pressed forward, just like us, striving to complete their rituals. Intermittently the monsoon released bursts of footwear that flew through the stone torrent.

I moved closer to the waist-high wall encircling the pillar, which guarded pilgrims from falling in. Below, a huge mountain of pebbles rose up, almost to the edge of the wall. If I had been fool enough to lean in, I could probably grab a handful of the stones from here. They were collected around the base of the pillar and spilling into a funnel-shaped basin that was being scooped out by more heavy machinery. As we moved away in the distance toward the next two pillars, I could see more bulldozers pushing the pebbles into giant mountains of stones. The millions of stones (each no bigger than a large pea) thrown by the pilgrims had formed a staggering collection.

At last we completed the stoning at all three pillars and we turned back triumphantly to the tent. I began to allow myself the euphoria of a completed Hajj. On the way back with Rashida and Haneefa who had accompanied me to ensure our safety, Randa and I argued about who would cut locks from each other's hair. Returning to the tent, Rula (the youngest Saudi teenager in our group) announced my arrival to the others.

"Hajja Qanta, mabrook!" (Congratulations!) She smiled, the first to bestow the honorific title of Hajja on me. She and I burst out with laughter, and the Saudi matrons nodded a warm approval. Randa rushed up to me and, lifting the veil from my head, eased out my very short hair from the nape of my neck. With sewing scissors made in Sheffield, she sliced away a lock, wishing me "Mabrook!" Now we could celebrate Eid: Eid Ul Addha, the major festival on the Islamic calendar that celebrates the end of Hajj. It was time for sheep shopping!

In Mina, over a million head of cattle: camel, Australian sheep, and goats were already being slaughtered in the giant abattoirs specially built for this purpose. This was in memory of the original sacrifice of the ram by Abraham. Nowadays, the colossal volumes of meat are immediately frozen and loaded into hundreds of jets idling on Jeddah runways that transport the meat to share with the poorest Muslims around the world. Rashida would be preparing goat or lamb today for sure.

Rula handed me a piece of paper from a pile she had been distributing throughout the tent. I read it carefully and realized this was my receipt for the proxy sacrifice of a sheep in my name. The sacrifice had to be by proxy because only Muslim men can sacrifice animals, women being excused from this difficult task. Most Muslims at Hajj, because of its sheer scale, have to relinquish this task to the hundreds of professional Saudi butchers who were specially flown in from all over the Kingdom for the final days of the religious event.

Decades earlier, Muslims came complete with convoys of animals they would later sacrifice, but the proximity of animals and dense crowds had produced tremendous health hazards, and the practice had been stopped. In place, a monumental operation of choreographed sacrificial killing now occurs in clean, refrigerated factories. Here, with industrial precision, male animals, whether camel or sheep or goats, are lain on their sides by a Muslim butcher and immediately sacrificed with one swipe of a very sharp blade to the animal's throat as the butcher calls "Allah hu Akbar!" All blood must drain immediately from the animal for the meat to be considered halal.

I studied the receipt. It documented my name and the date of my Hajj. Meat from a whole sheep had been distributed to someone who needed this assistance. I had probably fed several families for $100. I placed it carefully in my bag and for many months would keep it on a notice board at my home, more proud of this certification than any other credential.

Now that Hajj was over, I could finally take a full shower, something I had been looking forward to for days. I gathered my items, leaving my smiling companions, and went straight to the showers to refresh myself. But inside I already felt new!

Later that evening I made the final visit to the Ka'aba before I would leave Mecca. After completing the penultimate ritual of Hajj, the Sai'e which entailed rushing seven times between the hills of al-Safa and al-Marwa which symbolized Hagar's desperate search for water, it was time to make the final Tawafs. Tearing myself away from these final prayers in the Masjid al-Haram, I drank in the view of the mysterious Ka'aba and prayed for a speedy return.

It was enormously difficult to turn my back on the House of God and leave where I felt most happy. But without leaving there could be no return, and tonight I was leaving the city of Mecca without delay. Pilgrims are instructed to return to their homes immediately after a final farewell to the Ka'aba. I was filled with an intense and purified spirituality, forming concentrated distillations of hope and beginnings.

I left the Hajj complex and scurried toward our waiting bus, which was rumbling just outside the center of the Mosque complex. I had time to grab several prayer mats, which I wanted to gift to friends and family on my return. The markets of Mecca are famed, but I could have no chance to see them. I had to exit the city rapidly.

I ran into Qudsia, the nurse from my hospital who had also traveled with my group. She was munching away on an eight-piece bucket of Kentucky Fried Chicken. Colonel Sanders had made it to Mecca too. She washed her chicken down with a giant cup of soda from Dunkin' Donuts, which had a strong following among Meccans. I directed her to the bus which would take us to the King Abdul Aziz Airport in Jeddah and from there, home. The rest was a blur of exchanged addresses, scribbled phone numbers, and sincere embraces. In no time I was aboard a Saudia flight and then I landed in Riyadh. In my few days away, Riyadh had transformed. For the first time, it felt like home.

I unlocked the door to my apartment, greeted by my bewildered cat who was wondering if I would ever be back. I stroked her until she soothed, and after a long hot shower in my own bathroom, I dressed in my pajamas. As I got into my inviting bed, I put on my cozy cotton socks and crawled under my goose-down comforter. The air-conditioning was already glacial. Surrounded by the comforts of my home to which I had returned with new and genuine appreciation, I fell into a luxurious, deep sleep.

I felt pure.

Chapter
Twenty-One

MUTAWAEEN:
THE MEN IN BROWN

I WOKE UP TO A coughing spasm so severe it ended in a bout of vomiting. I had been back from Hajj for a day and was lying in the on-call room trying to snatch a few hours of sleep. I was physically exhausted. I understood now why Hajj is prescribed only for the able-bodied. In the morning, I stayed on to review new chest X rays with the daytime team of doctors. Mobeen and Imtiaz were recently arrived from Mecca, and like me, freshly minted Hajjis. Shy at their new baldness, they each had covered their nicked, stubbly scalps with Balauchi caps Imtiaz had brought from Pakistan especially for his post-Hajj hair.

I had not veiled after Hajj, though many believe that completion of Hajj warrants a woman permanently to veil herself in public. I had no intention of that, needing to address a number of more fundamental concerns regarding my performance as a Muslim, much more important to me than who could see my hair. As a result I had returned to the ICU much as I had left it, except for the racking cough and a suddenly thinner frame.

"Salaam alaikum wa rahmat-allah wa barakata hu!"

Dramatically, the full-scale formal greeting of Muslim salaams was repeated again in precise Najdi Arabic, first to Mobeen and then to Imtiaz. It was Wadid, the surgeon-cum-terrifyingly-rigid-Muttawa.

There were a number of hybrid clergy-physicians working at the hospital. On one end of the spectrum was Faris, a friendly, easy-going, Canadian-trained Saudi pulmonologist who, rumor had it, had once been a Muttawa before he became a medical man; and, at the other end of the spectrum, infrared in his orthodoxy, was this man: Wadid.

A brilliantly facile surgeon, Wadid was famed for his narrow views which definitely did not include allowing the satanic temptation of unchaperoned women at the workplace (a matter on which he delivered speeches within the hospital in the presence of his Saudi female physician colleagues, even if they were multiply boarded, American-trained specialists).

Toward me, therefore, Wadid took specific and very visceral umbrage. He recoiled from the disgrace of my unmarried, Western Muslim status crowned by my offending short and quite clearly visible hair. We loathed one another with a mutual intensity. Today I felt extra-repelled, encountering him after experiencing such loving Muslims in Mecca. I especially thought of Haneefa.

In profile, his gaunt cheeks sunk into hollows directly beneath the flat obsidian of his eyes. His eyes were emotionally dead, conferring an inanimate appearance. As usual, he had appeared to the ICU in his customary monastic attire. He was dressed like the "Men in Brown," as I called them; identical to the Mutawaeen who hounded women in the mall or who had patrolled the 129 gates to the Holy Mosque.

He wore a brown Muslim overcoat edged with a thin strip of gold thread. Under it, his white thobe ended high above his bare calves. On his feet he wore the de rigueur sandals. Most days, Wadid didn't wear a white coat. He was a fanatical Wahabi and wanted to be seen as such even (or perhaps especially) by his patients, who were probably just as scared of him as I sometimes felt.

Naturally, Wadid made no attempt to even feign any greeting to me, let alone warrant me a greeting as a Muslim. He hardly interpreted me as a Muslim. Doubtless he considered me a Westernized heretic. To resolve the dilemma between reality and his distorted perception, conveniently for him, he merely pretended he didn't see me. For him, I didn't exist.

"Mabrook on your Hajj!" began Wadid, expressing some distant, embryonic memory of joy. Like most überorthodox Wahabis, Wadid expressed two emotions only: ascetic patience and fire-breathing intolerance. There was nothing in between. Reptilian eyes widened imperceptibly as he held Mobeen and Imtiaz's unabashed joy in view, eliciting his distaste. He viewed as profanity their redundant displays of happy self-congratulation.

Unaware of their offending emotional incontinence which was becoming increasingly uncomfortable for the Wahabi, Mobeen and Imtiaz thanked him, accepting his felicitations graciously. Wadid's eyes had by now turned back to stone, the fetal joy within them stillborn. There was a pregnant pause. Ever sensitive, pained at my very public neglect, my colleagues felt compelled to say something,

"Qanta has also completed Hajj, Mashallah," they both offered, clearly excited about my accomplishment.

Wadid did not even move to look in my direction. He said nothing, withholding even a phony "Mabrook" from issuing between lips worn thin with hate. Choosing not to respond, he began reviewing the X rays of a patient I had admitted a few hours before. Mobeen and Imtiaz shifted nervously, glancing toward me, fearing my customary eruption of rage.

I swallowed my venom, ignoring the insult. Instead, I did what pained the misogynistic Wahabi most: practiced medicine. I barked through the patient history, all the while making blazing eye contact at his superciliously half-closed eyelids shielding his eyes, which were unable to behold my offensive person.

Emphatically, I moved around Mobeen and stood directly next to Wadid. A week at Hajj and I had forgotten about the poisonous ways of the Wahabi Kingdom. I had also forgotten all my exercises in patience, self-control, and resolve in the face of ignorance, but I didn't care about any of that now. My blood was boiling. Any feelings of belonging among other Muslims had evaporated in two minutes in front of this creature. I had been rudely reminded of my nihilistic and rather repugnant status in Riyadh in the eyes of men like Wadid.

After presenting the problems of my patient, I excused myself. Pointedly, like a child, tit for tat, I refused to acknowledge Wadid. I stamped off, clicking my shoes noisily on the floor, another no-no for women in Riyadh because female footsteps are thought to be an invitation for sexual admiration. The magic of Mecca had dissipated in my all-too-familiar clash with the male of the Wahabi species. Wadid had rudely reminded me of the realities of everyday life in Riyadh and the Men in Brown.

I had first glimpsed a Muttawa while abbayah shopping with Maurag, my assistant. Since then I had encountered these religious policemen in the glossy malls of Riyadh, or scurrying in the depths of the jewelry market in Deera, or even once at an outdoor market, buying groceries from the security of a car.

At my instruction, my driver had pulled up close to a bank of zucchini. I stared hard through the glass to assess their freshness, ignoring my headscarf puddling around my shoulders. A wooden nightstick rapped on the car window, startling me. Cover your hair, he mouthed through the tinted glass.

The Men in Brown were stealthy. As I grew bolder and shopped alone in the mall, examining Orrefors crystal at a boutique inside the al-Faisaliyah Mall, I was again unaware my head was suddenly exposed (the perils of cheap polyester). A Muttawa appeared silently, looming up immediately behind me. I almost dropped the costly goblet in shock.

Their omnipresence in Saudi life was physically and psychologically oppressive. The Muttawa are part of the Committee of Promotion of Virtue and Prevention of Vice. They operate under command of the Saudi King and are empowered to arrest or apprehend individuals if accompanied by Saudi police, with whom they usually patrol. There are naturally no female Mutawaeen; only males have this authority, which they gain after specifically training at Wahabi clerical school, the center of which is in the Deera area of Riyadh where jewelry shoppers and jihadists collide.

Riyadh, I had soon discovered, was a hornets' nest of Mutawaeen. I had spied the Men in Brown patrolling in squadrons of brownness as they drummed shoppers into the mosque in Deera at prayer time. Salaat (praying) was mandatory! Banging their staffs on the railings of shops or the glass counters of display cabinets, they swarmed into shops, malls, and the labyrinthine jewelry market to ensure all business was closed to observe prayer. Nowhere was out of their corrective reach.

Under the shadow of towering Mutawaeen, shopkeepers bustled to worship under compulsion, leaving behind acres of unsecured gold jewelry. I never saw anyone set a burglar alarm before leaving the glittering jewelry cabinets unattended. In a country where theft can be punished with amputation, the necklaces and bracelets twinkled in a safe silence, assured that none would dare steal them.

Thus, in a few short minutes, even before the Azaan was over, the shops were desolate. All browsers were gone from sight, men scrambling out of their shoes and into the mosque and women scuttling to pray in discrete areas set aside for ladies' prayer (usually subterranean, screened alcoves down a single flight of steps). Other women were sitting out their prayers on low walls around the shopping center, excused by way of menstruation.

Thankfully the Mutawaeen never demanded proof of their periods, but still the women huddled, nervous and exposed, wishing prayer time would pass uneventfully and squirming as they waited for the termination of their public embarrassment. Christians cowered alongside them, hoping the Muttawa would leave them alone. Tasked with preserving virtue and prosecuting vice, the Mutawaeen moved fast. In the field, the Mutawaeen dissipated into individual islands of enforcers. Most hunted for offenders alone, save the companionship of a single Saudi police officer who was authorized to apprehend anyone to whom the Muttawa objected. Nowhere was off limits for either man, even entering sections of restaurants restricted to women. I already knew their intrusions were frightening. I remember one event in particular.

Zubaidah and I were shopping in the Sahara Mall in central Riyadh. Hungry, we settled on one restaurant in the food court. Our shopping bags rested next to us on empty chairs. Around us women, almost all of them orthodox Saudi, were already eating. Most managed to devour their food, without ever removing their facial coverings to eat, simply just lifting the cloth away from their mouths and scrupulously inserting food underneath. Food disappeared into invisible mouths shielded by the black curtains covering their mysterious mouths. I watched several veils slurping on rapidly declining milkshakes.

Zubaidah wore her customary hijab and could eat without removing her scarf. Even so, she allowed the folds of the cloth to

loosen, exposing some of her honey-flaxen hair. In segregated quarters, this discreet relaxation of silent cloth sliding off hair (like men
releasing neckties) was a feeling that always signaled the easing of
the noose that is public Riyadh life. Behind the screened area, I also
allowed my polyester headscarf to expose my hair completely, sick
of wearing it even on the short journey to the mall. We had ordered
food through a filigree screen beyond which a male silhouette took
our requests. Later, perhaps the same man whisked the food to the
table. I began to eat with appetite. Zubaidah sipped her trademark
mint tea. A noisy rustle, a tubercular cough, and then a hasty
scraping of chairs stopped the room abruptly. The diners were
immediately silenced.

I looked up and saw two Mutawaeen enter our strictly female
section. Everywhere, women quickly flung their head covers into
place. I turned to question Zubaidah but she had already disappeared
behind the end of her veil which now covered her entire face.
Sensing safety in mimicry, I rushed to do the same, my fingers
thick and clumsy with fear. One Muttawa approached and, horrif-
ically, stopped directly at our table. He scanned the room like an
ominous Dalek turning his entire body the length and breadth of
the restaurant. Myopic eyes assessed the diners, rich in our evil-
doing. I found I was holding my breath.

A constricted exhalation grew into a sharp pain of anxiety under
my left breast. I wished to sigh but was too afraid to make even that
sound. He was dangerously close. From here, I could see his nose
hairs and the beginnings of gum recession. My eyes followed his
fat fingers as they raced through his unadorned rosary, counting the
wooden beads in a blurred frenzy. Maybe he was counting expletives. I noted his nails were flattened in the characteristic spoon
shape of anemia. For all his corpulence he was malnourished. His
skin was sallow, a combination of inadequate sun exposure and
jaundice. Icteric eyes scoured the room with their milky gaze. His

distaste at the sight of so many unaccompanied women engaging in such profane and public pleasure was palpable. The disgrace of economically independent women exposing themselves by eating in public (instead of within the security of high-walled homes) pained him.

To our horror, from the rostrum of our table, he planted his sandaled feet widely apart and launched an impassioned speech. He sandblasted the room with a rabid onslaught of threats that Zubaidah was unable to translate simultaneously because of his extraordinary proximity. He was allowed to continue his diatribe uninterrupted. No one dared challenge him or even his right to be in the ladies' area, a fundamentally segregated section. Minutes turned to hours; diners turned to stone. I felt myself leaning forward as if taking cover under his stream of hate. I fixed my eye at his widened waist and wished for an end.

Darting my eyes to my left, I spied a quaking line of Bengali waiters behind the filigree screen. Like terracotta figures frozen in grimace, their expressions plead for the departure of the despotic Muttawa. The restaurant manager never came to ask him to leave, aware that his business could practice only in this atmosphere of constant monitoring and chastisement. We were all powerless in the face of the authority of a single abusive man. This time, a Saudi police officer did not appear with the Muttawa, who so boldly exercised his authority without even state sanction.

After an impassioned tirade that rained his actual spittle onto our table, disgusted, he turned on his heel and with a withering look at the Western debauchery of the restaurant-going Saudi public, he left, trailing a wake of Wahabi fear. I stared at the froth of saliva that had discreetly spattered near my table mat. It was a few seconds before anyone dared touch food again. I had lost my appetite.

Zubaidah uncovered her face. Her gorgeous skin was reddened with fury, her gray eyes glinting coals, shining with bright anger.

"Qanta, he has no right to enter here! No right! These women here like us do not have to pray. We are excused because of the time of the month. I am so upset! I wish I was in Amman or Beirut! There it is so much more civilized. I hate these Mutawaeen; they make me hate Riyadh. They ruin my home." She spluttered into a smoldering silence, choking on her rage.

"What was he saying, Zubaidah?"

"He was saying we should not be eating, we should be praying." (Outside the Azaan had just been called for evening prayer.) "'Salaat, Salaat!' was all he could say and then he went on to talk of the evils of women in public. We should be locked in our homes in isolation! In public he says all we represent is danger and risk, encouraging men to sin. So ignorant! So un-Islamic!"

From time to time Zubaidah was almost incoherent in her fury. I sank into a silence finding no words with which to salve her temper. She was right. This was an abominable way to live and one which Riyadh bore uniquely. I was glad she felt the same as I did. I knew she wasn't the only Saudi woman who shared these views. We promptly paid our bill and left.

On other occasions we saw the Mutawaeen in action more remotely. During evenings and weekends the Mutawaeen searched the malls for suspect single men who might be loitering simply to cruise (in futility and very illegally) for women. At designated times the mall was allowed only for families and single women, but brigades of bored bachelors with no other place to go persisted despite these regulations.

The Mutawaeen had cultivated very sharp vision that saw only deviancy. Quickly they flushed out the beleaguered bachelors, chasing the men away with their reprimands and threats. Terrified, the young men retreated like frightened puppies from spectral hounds.

The emasculation of the Saudi male was, in this way, a very public affair. For all their strutting and peacock displays of masculinity, ogling or even harassing women, they were quickly humiliated by corpulent mountains of myopic clergy. Young men colored in shame as they were chased out, banished behind the glass sliding doors of the glossy mall they encircled, so many adolescent sharks, detecting the scent of female blood. Periodically, they peered through the glass at the veiled beauties crossing automated thresholds and trailing a wisp of fragrance behind them, only to suddenly bump their noses against the cool of the steel and glass doors that quickly closed behind the women.

Outside, the boldest boys of all cruised in lipstick-red Ferraris or sunflower-yellow Lamborghinis, astonishing rents of color in the blackness of modern Saudi. They circled the malls with music blaring, engines revving, rubber screeching, and the men themselves roaring at the crowds, alternating between raucous laughter and what seemed like cat-calls. A hot smell of octane and rubber perfused the air with action and a forgotten excitement that spoke more of South Beach than Saudi Arabia.

One evening, I watched a caravan of Ferraris shrieking around Olleya. A red Ferrari overflowed with heavily muscled Saudi jocks in tight white T-shirts revealing hard, sculpted physiques. The car reverberated with gangster hip-hop. These twenty-somethings were having a whale of a time spinning the vehicle into tight loops and fast stops, a calligraphic hell-raising of rubber burn and rumbling, double-barreled exhausts.

One man in particular caught my eye. Across his chest, the Guess logo emblazoned his Western affinity. On his head, a red baseball cap married him to the scarlet car with jaunty panache. A freshly barbered beard in perfectly executed designer stubble delineated a handsome jaw. Feet dressed in $600 Guccis rested on butterscotch Connolly bucket seats. Casually, he sat on the roll bar, periodically hanging out of the vehicle at crazy angles as the muscle car veered in impossible bends. Hurled by the centripetal torque, he swung his chiseled frame outward, flexing his muscles to lean into the night, a gorgeous yachtsman on a supercharged catamaran.

In the staid pace of Riyadh, the man cut a dashing figure of machismo. I watched him for some time. He moved well and seemed aware of the striking beauty of his body. I glanced to either side and sensed the satisfaction of many female onlookers. The night breeze carried murmurs of admiration and perhaps even desire from the women. Like me, they gazed unabashedly and largely unseen through gauzy prisons, captivated by the heady circus of testosterone and Testarossa.

In contrast, to a man, the Mutawaeen were corpulent and hostile. These were unrefined men, using intimidation as the primary means of persuasion. There was nothing gentle about these men who were supposedly schooled in Islam. Something about their indoctrination rendered them professional, fire-breathing fanatics. Battalions of these Men in Brown graduated every year from the Muttawa school for clerics in Riyadh, located in Decra (ironically exactly opposite to the infamous "Chop Chop" square where offenders and criminals were executed on Fridays at noon). A rigid training nurtured intolerance deep within their hearts. Considered holy, I found them instead hard and haughty; supposedly enlightened, they were pitched in an ignorance of impenetrable darkness. Claiming to be Muslim, they were uniformly intolerant of most aspects of Islam accepted by liberal Muslims to be incontrovertible truths. They couldn't be further removed from the Saudi studs, a perfect example of the schizophrenic Kingdom I was discovering.

Wherever they appeared, the Mutawaeen struck chords of fear within Muslims and non-Muslims alike, whether men or women. Saudis feared them too. One could never be sure if one was safe from their machinations or, worse, their incarcerations. They even patrolled Riyadh in their own vehicles, scouring the city for any who dared behave counter to the accepted norms of Wahabiism.

Until one lives in the Kingdom, it is difficult to understand just how much power the Mutawaeen could wield. Outside of Riyadh they stopped drivers to check if their car stereos were playing music. Men quickly learned to turn off the music, which the Muttawa considered Haram. Even Saudi men were forbidden from this debased pleasure, where listening to music could induce a state of Khmair (disconnecting the Muslim from his Maker by allowing him to lose himself in a trance). Whether Khmair was due to music or drugs or alcohol, it was a fatal flaw to be corrected and, foremost, punished.

In Riyadh the clerics could not impose such restrictions, perhaps because the city was so big and the roads mostly urban expressways too fast to be inspected for offenders listening to music. Instead in the city, they contented themselves by prohibiting women from purchasing music. The few shops that sold some form of music in Riyadh banned women from entering. Instead they stood outside, hovering nervously in their veils while they waited for their brothers or husbands to return with the CDs in hand. The insanity of the Mutawaeen knew no bounds. No rule was too petty to be unenforced. As a woman, I immediately hated them and often feared them, but never more so than when I experienced a Muttawa raid. Unknown to me it would follow in the months to come.

Chapter
Twenty-Two

SINGLE SAUDI MALE

W E GATHERED IN THE CONFERENCE room adjoining the ICU for the weekly case conference. There must have been ten of us that morning. Like an O'Keefe painting, sun-blanched light poured through the floor to ceiling windows. We arranged ourselves in our customary semicircle, with me at the farthest edge of the circle. Saraway, my loyal friend (and the ICU pharmacist), came to sit next to me. We waited for Imad to signal the start of the meeting.

Imad had conducted these meetings each week for months, but somehow it was not until this moment that he finally caught my eye. As he spoke, my eyes took in his tall, mesomorphic figure, noting the drape of expensive slacks on long, elegant, heavily muscled legs. On his feet, Italian brogues with hand-stitched soles revealed a man of taste. Now and again the costly leather creaked on the linoleum floor, separating him from the squeaking sneakers and Birkenstocks of the others. His white coat was buttoned up, his name and titles emblazoned in cursive embroidery on his left breast in a traditional American manner, speaking to an academic training beyond Riyadh. A chic, colored tie anchored and separated the elegant chimera from the men around him—a desirable Western man in a desert full of Saudi men.

I listened to his voice, lulled by the sedate, even tone, not hearing the words: soft, cultured, and distinctly North American. I wondered if he was Canadian.

Imad carried his authority comfortably and without fanfare. His voice was low but even, naturally commanding attention as we leaned forward to catch his soft-spoken comments. A silver-gray mane of lush hair, cropped very short, capped a broad, unlined forehead. Wide, darker eyebrows arched above guarded, deep-blue eyes, a sole indicator of expression. Salt and pepper stubble was the briefest of nods to the requirement of facial hair for the observant Muslim male. It only enhanced the striking fairness of his Caucasian-colored skin. Sunlight glinted in reflection from rimless eyeglasses, the blued lenses veiling his expression. He smiled rarely, yet somehow still seemed pleasant. I liked him immediately.

I tried to decipher this man. His first name, Imad, gave him away as a Muslim; his last name was unfamiliar to me and distinctly un-Saudi. I couldn't place his ethnicity. His age was suspended some-where between thirty and forty. His Western dress, his Caucasian skin, and his accent refuted a Saudi nationality pointing to a much more Westernized man than those surrounding him. I wondered if he could be my male counterpart—a Westernized Muslim. Certainly he seemed educated overseas. A quick glance showed that his hand was absent of any silver ring, the customary indicator of marriage in a Muslim man. And it happened like that; under fluorescent lights in a sea-green conference room ten thousand miles from New York. I found my attraction once more ignited. For the first time in Riyadh,

I was glad to be the only woman in a meeting. In fact, for the first time in the Kingdom, I was actually glad to be a woman!

We presented our cases, discussing the differential diagnoses and informing him of relevant diagnostic data. Intermittently, Imad conferred with others for information, always respectfully and always in his hypnotic, low voice. After reviewing these details, Imad advised. Sometimes I could almost hear a sigh of relief when Imad made decisions. He brought comfort to all those around him. At last it was my turn to discuss my patients.

I looked at him as he listened to me respectfully. His legs remained crossed, his arms folded in his lap, perfectly at ease. He was still. As I spoke, he engaged in eye contact with me, meeting my gaze with unblinking blue eyes. To this man, I was not invisible. His polite acquiescence to my clinical recommendations for our patient belied a man who respected women, or even better, just respected clinical ability. I peered at him more closely.

His alabaster skin was a blank canvas to blend with all cultures. His clear eyes (the bluest I had seen in Riyadh) concealed a safe of secrets to which I wanted the combination. I had to know more of the depths within. He could be Canadian or American, possibly Lebanese or Jordanian. I was still confused when the meeting concluded. Finishing off some final documentation, Saraway was working at the nurse's station in the ICU after the meeting.

I went to join him, swinging on the revolving chair at the station next to Saraway. I watched Imad leave the ICU, walking alone, straight backed, with a slight forward tilt of his head. He greeted almost no one and never stopped to chat. He seemed to be a man of purpose. In a few short paces he was gone, the automated ICU doors clanging shut behind him. Immediately I wanted to know more. Saraway had worked with Imad for years. What luck, I thought. Saraway was my friend. Now Saraway would become my informant.

"Who was that guy, Saraway? Is he Canadian? I have seen him before. Is he the director of pharmacy?" Saraway chuckled and paused to answer his pager. I found I was on tenterhooks.

"He sounds Canadian," I persisted.

"No, no, Qanta, everyone thinks that." Saraway continued typing in a screen. "Imad is a Saudi. I think he trained in Canada. But he is definitely a born-and-bred Saudi, for sure. And he is not a pharmacist." Saraway laughed out loud at what was evidently a preposterous suggestion. "He is the Executive Director of Quality Assurance and Chairman of Academic Affairs. He is a very powerful man, Qanta."

I was astounded. A Saudi who looked non-Saudi? A Saudi man who wore Gucci instead of shemaghs? A Saudi man more Brioni than Bedouin? A Saudi man who was white, and most amazing of all, a Saudi Muslim who was understated yet somehow sexy? My head was reeling. I pressed Saraway for more information.

"Does he have a family, Saraway? Is he married?"

"No, Qanta, Imad is single. He is definitely a bachelor." And Saraway chuckled, refusing to say more.

The desirable was also available. But on what pretext could I be allowed more access? How could I learn more about this man in this country where dating was illegal, where mixing with members of the opposite sex was punishable, with house arrest for women, the possibility of deportation and jailing for the courting male. I would have to be very imaginative indeed. I began to plot a map to bring me closer to this new species: the single Saudi male. Perhaps, along the way, it could become a map into his mysterious heart.

The Calm before the Storm

We had spent the day with international visiting faculty who were attending a scientific symposium in the Kingdom. I was granted a minor role as a speaker and had delivered a lecture earlier in the day. As part of scheduled activities for the visiting speakers, dinner at a local Saudi restaurant in Riyadh was planned for later that evening. I was also invited along.

When the time came, I was ferried from the hospital compound with other participants. Imad, as the chairman of the meeting, was hosting the dinner. I was pleased he had invited me to participate. Perhaps I would have a chance to get to know this intriguing man a little more.

The European and American faculty who traveled from Johns Hopkins and the University of Geneva among other places were transported in motor coaches from the Hotel Intercontinental where they had been accommodated during their brief visit.

I stepped out of the hospital bus which had woven its way into an unfamiliar area of Riyadh. As usual, veering off a familiar route left me disoriented in the city. I followed others down a narrow, crudely cemented path, thinking how easily one could be lost in this city. Without the umbilical connection to my hospital, I was completely vulnerable. My abbayah trailed in the pervasive dust, leaving swirling patterns behind me. Tonight my feet were encased in vertiginous Badgley Mischka heels; Bergdorf booty that I had thrown into my case at the last moment before leaving New York. I had to admit, a beautiful pair of shoes transformed my loathsome veil and abbayah into a floating folly. Tonight, I felt almost feminine.

Inside, the restaurant owner was personally greeting the foreign dignitaries. Broad smiles welcomed the white males among us. Visiting female American faculty arrived in borrowed abbayahs. Their gauche veils hung clumsily from their broad shoulders made solid from American summers spent swimming. As I watched their gangly progress, I measured my own adjustment to the alien accoutrements that had now become routine for me.

We entered a carpeted room. The walls were mud-baked. Maroon and orange durries lined the floor. Cylindrical, colored cushions made of nubby cotton lined the perimeter of the covered area. This was our dining area. Like Romans, we would eat, elbows bolstered on pillows, semi-recumbent. We were in a private dining room where men and women would eat together. Behind us a wooden carved door closed. Metallic lanterns showered a fluttering, colored light as though we were ensconced in a Bedouin's tent.

We settled into place. I loosened my abbayah and ultimately removed it. Underneath, I was wearing a black tuxedo, purchased in a now unbelievably remote Dallas. I straightened the ribbon trimmed trousers as I carefully crossed my legs, unwilling to crease the press, and loosened the button on the single breasted jacket. A diamond broach on my lapel was the sole adornment. At last, I could be chic in Riyadh. For a time I kept the impossible heels on, but following others, I finally unbuckled them and placed them to the side so that footwear would not offend the dining space.

On my left sat Hamid, one of my favorite colleagues. I greeted him. He responded with his characteristic generous and extremely handsome white-toothed smile. He was one of the first male colleagues I had met at the hospital, and I had learned to discern him from the others despite his identical thobe and checkered red-and-white ghutra, which never varied either from the other men or from within his own wardrobe. He dressed identically every day. In the dim light his smile dazzled a little more than usual. His perfect teeth were accentuated by his elegant and very short graying beard which covered most of his handsome face. His eyes were hazel and spilled warmth. Hamid was always good-tempered, and his voice was a mixture of velvet and vermouth, rich and dry at the same time. Hamid was attractive in the very tantalizing way men who don't know their own appeal are, powerfully so.

Others were engaged in deep conversation with U.S. counter-parts. Imad had accomplished some landmark research in the Middle East. His work, I was learning, was already celebrated state-side. I was puzzled that I hadn't learned of his accolades from my Saudi colleagues. It was the visiting faculty who had mentioned these achievements to me, perhaps explained by institutional envy.

I watched Imad as he held court, host to this glittering inter-national faculty. Though only in his mid-thirties, and by far the youngest academic at the meeting, his influence, or (in Arabic) wasta, was clearly global. He had spent months assembling this meeting to launch the first research meeting in the region. The strain had been showing in his normally patient demeanor. Tonight he looked tired, but perhaps, in the unfurrowing of his smooth brow, Imad was almost on the verge of happiness.

He was dressed in his trademark khaki chinos and Ralph Lauren blue checked shirt: the consummate Saudi Westerner. A white undershirt peeked out of the collar, a single button released at the throat, attempting (in this subtle exposure) to convey a worldly man at ease. His open collar revealed a clean-shaven, cologned neck. Traces of black stubble were already puncturing pale white skin stretched tight over a generous but fleshy Adams apple which urged his collar forward. The stolen glimpse of throat was surprisingly sexual. My eyes dilated with attraction, magnified in a sterile world where all sexuality was permanently concealed. I hurried to conceal desire, lowering my gaze.

A heavy, riveted, blue-rimmed Rolex glinted under his left shirt cuff. It was probably a diving watch, watertight to one hundred meters. Yet I doubted he could swim; he didn't seem an outdoorsman. Meaty alabaster hands twirled an expensive Motorola cell phone with surprising delicacy. The black cellular and the steel watch flashed eddies of reflected light across the mud-baked ceiling of the room. Idly, he extended and retracted an aerial. Intermittently he made calls, all the while blue eyes darting, scanning from side to side.

Imad was never seen without his phone and was noted for constantly upgrading to a new model every few weeks. Even though he was enormously educated and privileged, he shared the same anxiety as the restless teens in Riyadh. He needed the latest toy to feel *au courant*. Though Imad was dressed a picture of Kennebunkport relaxation, something about him remained taut, alert, and fundamentally tense. I stared hard. I couldn't distinguish what held him back.

"Qanta, you must try this," Hamid urged. I looked up and noticed that a tablecloth had been spread across the durries. Food was now unfurled in every direction. There were no appetizers or aperitifs. The entire feast had been served. Saudi men in full regalia waited to the side like bearers. Others were already loading their plates with rice, goat meat, breads, olives, cheeses, and other delicacies. Hamid held out a plate of rice towards me. I served myself.

"Where did you grow up, Hamid?" I asked, realizing I knew very little about my colleagues even after months working together.

"I was born in a small village outside of Jeddah. We are Hijazi!" He flashed a wry smile at me. "My father was a fisherman, Qanta. He would go in his small fishing boat into the Red Sea and catch food for all of us. The rest that we didn't need, he would sell. I would help my father drag the nets and sometimes mend them."

I studied his starched cuffs and the perfectly pressed collar on his thobe which was completely buttoned up. It was hard to imagine the hands of a fisherman's son as I looked at his cultivated digits, now more accustomed to stethoscopes than fishing lines. A silver Waterman pen with a blue cap twinkled in his single breast pocket. Doubtless his forebears were illiterate. On his wrist, a plain Swiss watch was framed in the soft black hair of his forearm. His father kept time with the rise of the sun and the fall of the tide, perhaps even praying moored at sea. This family had gone from fishermen to physicians in the brief space of half a generation.

"My father still fishes, but of course he doesn't need to. He enjoys it. He is in his seventies now and we have bought him a better boat, Mashallah, but he loves the sea. He wanted me to have an education, Qanta, it was very important. You see, my father cannot read."

I had guessed correctly. Even so, Hamid had studied overseas. Like many of the doctors at the King Fahad Hospital, he was a graduate of Hamilton (Ontario) and later of a University in Toronto. Hamid was a multiply certified specialist and, from what I had seen, a very capable one.

"When the National Guard announced they wanted to sponsor doctors to travel to the West to gain education (only if they returned after their training to our country) my father pushed me to do it. I was the first one in our family to leave the country in many generations. You know the Hijazi are heavily derived of migrating pilgrims who used to come to make Hajj decades earlier and never left the country afterward. Hijazis are famous for being worldly and of mixed blood, very different to the Najdi here in Riyadh. Anyway, I attended medical school in Canada on a government scholarship from the Saudi Arabian National Guard. Then they sponsored my residency and my fellowship. I came back one of the first Saudi nationals with that training, in the whole Kingdom and of course, they gave me a job."

In a rare moment of pride, Hamid leaned back and smiled at his achievement. I wondered if he saw the influence of racial aristocracy as a Saudi national (who would naturally be chosen over Western contemporaries for the best, most senior appointments) rather than an actual meritocracy of his achievements as the main driver for his early administrative seniority. I couldn't bring myself to ask Hamid these deeper questions. I didn't want to offend a kind and generous man.

A waiter proffered me a meat dish which was newly arrived. A pungent odor drove me away from it. Unsure if this was the smell of the meat or of Hamid's stockinged feet, I was repelled but accepted anyway, unwilling to offend my Saudi hosts. My nostrils strained to separate the offending scent, tracing it to the dish after all. I forced myself to eat some of the fibrous meat drenched in a thick sauce of some kind. It tasted even worse than it smelled. Hamid looked on, highly amused.

"So, you like camel flesh, Qanta?"

I promptly stopped mid-mastication and before I could be embarrassed by my retching, I struggled to swallow the remainder

with minimal fuss. Working fast, I gobbled some plain pita bread
to dilute the strong, leathery taste. I was reminded of sweaty camel
sellers who came to the ICU in search of injured friends. The ICU
would smell for hours after their visits. Trying to salvage a fragment
of decorum, I looked at Hamid and began to formulate a satirical
response. His head was thrown back in a gale of laughter at my
predicament, especially when he saw my eyes were tearing from the
repugnant taste. I began to laugh a little myself, my lips curving
helplessly into a smile. I was having fun.

Suddenly, we were quickly silenced by the sounds of intrusion.
In a startling moment, fishermen and camel sellers were forgotten.
Looking at Hamid, I discovered his eyes were now widened in
terror. We could hear angry shouts and loud banging. Even dining
in a private room in a discreet restaurant, we had been discovered.

The Mutawaeen were here.

WAHABI WRATH

EVERYONE STOPPED EATING. THE AIR was pregnant with fear. Across from me, I watched Alon, a visiting professor from Johns Hopkins, turn sallow as all color drained from his face. The door flung open revealing a single, glowering Muttawa. We were in the company of our deepest fears.

The Muttawa entered the room triumphantly, pushing through our cross-legged ranks. He stood in the middle of the durries laid with food, sandaled feet abutting salad trays. From our seated position he towered over us. His lean, sharp carriage emanated a mean, rigid spirit. Narrowed eyes shone with the triumph of his catch: over a dozen men and women, seated at dinner without segregation or veiling. His bisht, a material of thin brown muslin worn over a white robe, trembled with excitement. Swelling with a ripe, turgid rage he prepared to ejaculate his fury upon us. He moistened his full, purple lips with a fat pink tongue. His sour mouth was fringed with coarse facial hair. Around him we retreated into impotence, actually shrinking. He radiated evil.

Beyond the dining room we could hear his colleagues apprehending the restaurateur, several waiters, and one woman from our party (who had been unfortunate enough to be returning from the restroom when she encountered the Muttawa raid). For the first time, I noticed the room had only one exit, now blocked by a Wahabi Muttawa, and then glanced at my stilettos, useless in a getaway. We were trapped. A sharp scream rang out. Alarm rippled through the gathering. We were really in danger.

"Let me go! You are hurting me! Ow!" It was Diana's voice, sounding more indignant than afraid. "You have no right to touch me! How dare you lay a finger on me, a Muslim woman! My husband will file a complaint! I am a married Muslim woman. You will regret this!"

Diana was defying the Mutawaeen. An American, she had lived in the Kingdom for more than a decade and was married to a Saudi man by whom she had two children. She had accompanied us to dinner in her role as the events manager. Her blonde hair and her white skin hid her conversion to the Muslim faith, fooling most who crossed her path. Even ten years of living in the Kingdom had not lessened her leonine, if foolish, courage. She especially detested the religious police.

Thick retorts in pharyngeal Arabic rose in objection to her protests. The Mutawaeen sounded even angrier. My fears began to grow. When the lone Muttawa sentry had turned his back, I signaled to Sami (an Egyptian toxicologist sitting diagonally across from me) to hand me my shoes. I sidled my stockinged foot from under me and began strapping the glittering stilettos in place. My fingers fumbled in fear.

Friends had warned me of the Gestapo-like raids of the

Mutawaeen. Just before I had arrived, a Western secretary to the ICU chairman had been repatriated after her relationship with a fellow Westerner had been discovered at a restaurant in Riyadh where she had dined with her then-boyfriend. He had been deported immediately, she placed under house arrest. Finally she was advised by her home consulate (Australian) that a return to Sydney would probably be best.

Warnings were not issued only to expatriates. The Saudis feared the Muttawa too, both at their indiscriminate use of force (beatings in their custody were well-described) as well as the slur on one's reputation that followed questioning and incarceration. The prowling Muttawa patrols were one reason why even innocent romance in the Kingdom was such a secret and illicit affair. Even husbands and wives out in public in Riyadh never left their homes without their marriage licenses in tow. Mutawaeen could demand legal proof of marital status of both Saudis and non-Saudis alike.

Nowhere in the Kingdom was immune. Even individuals' homes had been raided when private gatherings were suspected. This of course was now increasingly difficult when the homes were provided by powerful agencies who employed expatriates as a matter of course, explaining why at the National Guard Hospital the Muttawa were never seen on the grounds; the Saudi National Guard were too powerful by dint of their Royal patronage. In fact, the Saudi National Guard force had been created precisely to counter the Mutawaeen threats to the monarchy.

Other safe harbors in Riyadh (free from their monitoring) were believed to exist on certain, very costly properties belonging to the famed heroic "free prince," known simply as al-Waleed. There, in chic eateries where one was surrounded by powerful princes and members of the Royal glitterati, the state-employed Mutawaeen did not dare enter, let alone arrest or harass any influential guests. Upsetting the wrong prince could upset the delicate symbiotic relationship between the clergy and the monarchy. But the influence of Prince al-Waleed, nephew to the King and the fifth richest man in the world, a wealth he had generated by his own wits rather than simply siphoning off oil money, was simply too powerful. So perhaps it was not so shocking that tonight, in a private restaurant in an unknown suburb of central Riyadh, we were at the mercy of the Mutawaeen. I wondered how, or indeed if, we could reach home at all.

One by one, the Muttawa demanded to know our nationalities.

"Egyptian."

"American."

"Canadian."

"Bahraini."

"Yemeni."

"Omani."

He stopped at Imad, pausing.

"Qatari," he lied, squirming uncomfortably. None of the Saudi men with us was prepared to admit his Saudi nationality; not even our host. Even Hamid, the salt of the earth Hijazi Saudi, didn't present himself as that, seeking shelter behind a feigned Kuwaiti citizenship. I was agog. These men were truly afraid. After a few minutes, the situation deteriorated.

The Muttawa then began confronting Manaal, who had just returned from UCLA where she had finished a fellowship. They were locked in an escalating crescendo of Arabic. She carried dual nationality, both American and Saudi. Unlike the men, she was defiant, puzzling the dull Muttawa. I held my breath, fearing the worst.

Manaal's transplantation from UCLA to Riyadh had been exceptionally difficult for such an intelligent and confident Saudi woman. We had often shared notes over our difficulties as professional

women in the Kingdom. Sometimes her Saudi husband's indignation on her behalf toward her dilemmas was even stronger than ours.
Manaal was the product of a liberated Saudi father and a very
modern and supportive Saudi husband. She was enormously proud
of the influence these men had been in her life. I remembered her
saying only days earlier:

"Oh Qanta, my father is incredible! He takes special pride in
'taking down' arrogant men. He loves to hear them rant on about
how inferior women are, only to then embarrass them by saying,
'Mashallah my daughters, one a pediatrician, the other a cardiologist, are far more brilliant than the men in our family. They inher-
ited all the smart genes from their mother's side!' That usually
shuts them up." And she laughed out loud. "He calls himself 'The
Feminist Nazi.' He is so irrationally and fanatically pro-Women!"

Now returned to Riyadh, she had begun encountering the
antithesis of her father's philosophy. For her, back in the Kingdom
for only a few weeks, the Muttawa were excruciatingly offensive.
Even I was more accustomed to them now than Manaal, navigating
them with circumspection rather than at the full-speed ahead
conflict with which Manaal seemed to surge. She would have to
relearn the rules of engagement here. Manaal's voice began to rise,
spilling over into blatant anger. I asked Sami to translate.

"She is saying the Muttawa is a disgrace to the Kingdom,"
he whispered. "That he is embarrassing all the international dele-
gates visiting our institution. She even adds he has no Islamic basis
for his investigations. She is adding that he is humiliating the
Saudi hosts who are trying to show the world how advanced we
are in science and medicine. Does he realize we have Christian
visitors here who are being introduced to Islam for the first time
in this meeting?"

I cringed. Could Manaal have said anything more infuriating
to them? Sami continued his running commentary. "Instead, you,

the Muttawa, are showing the reality of Riyadh. Still a very backward and primitive society where only Wahabi Islam rules!"

Sami stopped translating, silenced by the critical mass of rage Manaal and the Muttawa had reached. By now, the Muttawa was leaning down toward Manaal's upturned face, flushed with evident fury. She was a force. Her anger was frightening. Her creamy cheeks were suffused with a pink afterglow, framing coal-black eyes that blazed dangerously. They were almost butting chins as they collided in conflict; hers cleft, his receding. The Wahabi cleric and the Saudi academic were equally intense in their defiance. It was hard to decide who was more dogmatic in their beliefs. Riyadh's überorthodox climate, a pressure cooker of conflict, transformed even moderates into fanatics. There could be no middle ground here.

"Manaal, please stop. That is enough. You are making things worse." Imad's calm voice broke through the impasse between the cleric and the clinician. "Please, Manaal, it's no use arguing with him. You are only making him angrier."

I looked at Imad, pale from the strain of the proceedings. His perspiring brow glittered under the lamplight. Yet despite the ordeal, Imad still managed to be calm. He was a master of self-control. Manaal was humiliated by this public chastisement by an academic senior. Furthermore, Imad had made the reprimand very public by expressing it in English. Now all of us understood; Manaal's hot temper was a liability, endangering us further. I was just deciding whether the Muttawa could understand this exchange when he headed straight toward me. I was immobilized in his bloodless stare. All eyes were on me.

He addressed me in incomprehensible Arabic. I stared at him nonplussed as he spewed his speech. Sensing danger in his venom, I grasped my handbag closer to me and zipped it carefully shut. By strange chance (in preparation of forthcoming travel) it contained my passport tonight. I didn't want him to see the telltale British insignia stamped on maroon leather. I suspected even an illiterate would recognize this to be British. It was possible he reserved special malice for expatriate Muslims who mixed with Westerners. Unexpectedly, the Muttawa stopped speaking, staring at me pugnaciously. He must have asked a question. No one offered to translate, so I responded.

"I don't understand Arabic." Resorting to the colonial origins of my forebears, I enunciated the words in cut-glass English, an accent I reserved for particularly difficult moments. My emerging voice surprised me; constricted by fear, it sounded several octaves higher than normal.

"You—don't—speak—Arabic," he taunted, mimicking me dangerously. I was shocked that he knew any English at all. He had probably heard everything Imad had said to Manaal and understood it. Our fear was giving him considerable satisfaction and now we couldn't even hide behind interchanges in English. He leaned in, even more closely.

"I am British!" I answered, through gritted teeth, barely able to contain the coiling cobra of fury inside me.

"Oh, you are British?" he taunted. "Show me your passport! Where is it? Show me!"

Everyone was silent. I was in a dilemma. If I proved to him my status, there was a real danger he would impound my passport and I would be in custody at the mercy of the Mutawaeen. But if I refused, perhaps I would be punished as a Saudi. I was unsure which of these was likely to be a worse fate. I looked around me for clues but my colleagues were paralyzed in their own fears. They waited for my response with baited breath. Even Sami had stopped smiling, an especially ominous sign. Imad, poker-faced, was a blank canvas. I glanced a final time to him for direction but he stared back, impassive, a Saudi sphinx, something in which I had learned he was masterfully practiced. Positions of authority in the Kingdom demanded an inhuman ability to conceal one's authentic opinions. Perhaps this was why he had risen to such starry heights at such a young age.

"Show me your passport!" The Muttawa was insistent. I wondered if he had glimpsed Her Majesty's crest peeping out of a pocket in my handbag where I had casually slipped it earlier in the evening. I decided to be honest. I had already come to my senses and realized the Muttawa was operating without a Saudi police officer. To my knowledge without the authority of the police force, he had no grounds for harassing us.

"I don't think I should show you my passport." I tried hard to sound firm.

"You don't think you should show it to me?" he mimicked spitefully. If we hadn't been so afraid, the situation was approaching a bizarre, almost Pythonian comedy. I had a sudden desire to laugh: nerves.

"No, I think not," I answered, almost haughty. I was beginning to feel marginally more confident. Scuffles outside distracted the Muttawa. In a quick spin of bisht and thobe, he left the room.

From the vestibule we could hear anxious Bengali protestations. The voices faded away into futility. We heard a vehicle pulling up to the restaurant and driving away. The waiters had been apprehended for serving a mixed crowd and were now en route to the Mutawaeen's custody. The restaurateur was still being interrogated. With the Muttawa out of the room, we all turned to Imad to salvage the situation. Alon looked frankly nauseated. He was loosening his necktie and wiped sweat away from his brow with a linen napkin. His perspiration did not abate.

"Imad! You have to do something!" demanded Manaal, angry at both the Muttawa for imprisoning us and Imad for chastising her.

"Calm down, Manaal," he answered controlling his irritation.

"I have made some calls. The National Guard will be here soon to transport the ladies back to the compound and the men will be released." We stared at him blankly. Reluctantly, Imad explained.

"As soon as we heard them entering, I called the CEO," Imad told us. The newly appointed CEO must be powerful, I guessed. I didn't know the reach of his wasta (influence). "He phoned Dr. Fahad," continued Imad. "He was our prior CEO, now a senior Royal advisor to the Crown Prince," explained Imad to the few who didn't already know. "He then activated the Crown Prince's office. They called the Crown Prince himself at the palace and he ordered the Governor of Riyadh to call the Mutawaeen off. It is just a matter of time."

We stared at him in disbelief. Our rescue required maneuvering at the very apex of the Saudi monarchy. "Don't worry," he continued matter-of-factly. "Just be calm. We will get out of here shortly." Imad came to a halt. So Imad's fidgeting and endless phone calls had been a negotiating mission to get us out. Even under the height of pressure, he had risen to the occasion.

I studied him. I was relieved we had access to the Saudi supreme authorities. Yet these machinations, this dance which Imad had had to engage in to rescue us, was intensely emasculating. He couldn't just lead his group out of here; he had to rely on a network of Princes and courtiers to secure us safe egress. Though it was obvious he had wasta (after all he had known all the correct numbers to dial), and while wasta is highly valued in Arab and specifically Saudi culture, his lack of *personal* wasta, personal influence, demonstrated by his need to rely on the wasta of others, only documented his impotence, both as a man and a leader, in painful clarity. As an individual, or even as a senior administrator at the pinnacle of Saudi medicine, he didn't have sufficient influence to avert the Mutawaeen himself.

I watched him loosen his collar under tension. He seemed at once influential and fatally weak. His authority was a mirage, his manhood manifested only through a mobile phone. Like the privileged racer-boys in lipstick-red Ferraris, he too had been publicly emasculated by the Mutawaeen. I realized this wasn't the first time Imad had been stripped of his masculinity. His wasta would never be greater than a collection of telephone numbers. He was a minion in a world ruled by monster-sized monarchies and monstrous Mutawaeen.

We lapsed into an uncomfortable silence. Around us, congealed rice and hardened bread reminded us of the evening's abject failure. Imad, more than anyone else, had been humiliated by the raid. As host, he had led us into danger. The Muttawa returned to the room but something had changed. All relish had left his vicious face. He stared at each of us in turn and, saving a particularly nasty look for me, turned on his splayed heel to exit. Like a wizard, he disappeared behind the cover of his billowing brown cloak.

Minutes later, a National Guard driver entered the room, informing us that several buses were outside ready to ship the women back to safety. Quickly we stood, sealing ourselves shut in our abbayahs. Manaal led the way, covering her face in addition to her usual hijab, but even the swathes of cloth couldn't stifle her temper. I merely covered my hair and followed the line of four other women. As we left the men behind, wondering about their fate, they watched, locked in silence. They looked uncomfortable and worried. At their center, Imad was a mixture of humiliation and relief. At least the women in his party would reach their homes safely.

Outside the dining room, in the vestibule of the restaurant, we found ourselves flanked by ranks of men in brown. There were a dozen Mutawaeen standing on either side of us. Astonishingly, an entire brigade of Mutawaeen had been dispatched to disband the debauchery of our evening. At their head was the malignant Muttawa who had held us hostage for over an hour. En masse they were even more frightening, but leashed back by the authority of the Crown Prince and the Governor of Riyadh, like wild dogs, they had been muzzled.

Recoiling from us in disgust, they allowed us to pass. They smoldered, almost crackling with contempt. We hurried out into the street, which strangely was still as deserted as when we arrived. It was a dead-end, one-way lane where no through traffic could pass, leading only to the discreet side entrance of the restaurant. It wasn't until we were secure inside the bus, with doors slammed shut and the driver pulled away, that any of us dared speak. Diana was bursting to tell us her ordeal.

"Those Mutawaeen are unbelievable. Wait until my husband hears about this!" It never ceased to amaze me how women always referred to male authority for validation. "He started pulling on my arm, grabbing me! I couldn't believe it. So that's why I screamed. Remember when I shouted 'ow'?" she said. "I did it really to frighten him. He could be in trouble for manhandling a woman! He was scared, the coward. He didn't hurt me at all." And laughing loudly, she pulled up the sleeve to her abbayah revealing a plump, creamy arm. She fingered her gold bracelets with obvious pleasure. "See, no bruises!" She laughed, coquettishly.

I was puzzled at my anger toward her. She evidently had played the situation like a game. Didn't she understand matters could be far worse had the Mutawaeen reacted to her contrived hysteria differently? As she was the events manager for our international guests, I was even more offended. Her antics had only made our time more difficult. She had shown no insight for our collective safety.

The other women (two of whom were U.S. visiting faculty) were stony silent and relieved to be safe. One of them began, "But I felt ill for Alon. Did you see how pale he turned when the Muttawa entered? His wife was very upset that he had agreed to be visiting faculty to the meeting at all. She called me to talk him out of the trip. She worried that his religion would be discovered, that it would endanger him. She was furious that he decided to attend."

I had to turn around, compelled to express my astonishment, "You mean Alon is Jewish? And he entered the Kingdom?"

"Of course," responded an American woman, also a visitor from Hopkins. "Imad invited him. He knew he is Jewish. Everyone here knows. He simply labeled himself Christian on his visa documents, of course. But Imad guaranteed his safety as long as he stayed with the meeting congress at all times. You can imagine what a nightmare tonight was for him. If those Mutawaeen had discovered there was a Jew among us, who knows what could have happened?" I shuddered at the thought. Who knew what could happen in Riyadh where Wahabis were in state-authorized power?

"What a fool," I said. "How could he even agree to attend here? He should know how dangerous the climate is at the moment. His selfish decision to come, even against his common sense and his wife's warnings, was foolish. Tonight could have been much worse! Doesn't he know Jews are never admitted to the Kingdom? Imad is certainly senior but he doesn't have *that* kind of influence." At least, I didn't think so and, by his dependence on the chain of remote power accessed by cell phones, it was clear he was at the bureaucratically lower end of the Saudi food chain. He could no more guarantee Alon's safety than I could. We fell into an awkward silence.

I had heard rumors of Jewish communities in the Kingdom, small clusters of them living a life of subterfuge under the shelter of prominent royal families. One heard tales of eminent Jewish physicians expressly employed to attend members of the royal family. These Jews were granted permission and protection while they and their families lived hermetic existences in Riyadh. I didn't know how much of this could be true, but I did remember accounts of

Jewish children studying at the international school where my friend Katherine had taught for years. Their parents were professionals, all working in the Kingdom. Some were here for brief stays of a few months while their expertise was authorized by a senior Royal allowing them to work. Others were here for very short visits, while they offered their opinions on medical conditions to senior royalty. This I could confirm from direct experience.

At least one senior pulmonologist, a brilliant American Jewish physician from the Cleveland Clinic, had been flown to Riyadh because of his world-renowned expertise. The doctor had been requested to attend a very senior prince. In a hospital canteen stateside, he recounted the incident to me over lunch.

A Prince had developed a difficult pneumonia which was not improving satisfactorily. Part of his assessment was a telescope exam of the lungs under sedation, a bronchoscopy. In the Kingdom, however, when the professor explained the procedure, the Prince refused to accept even the routine minimal risk of death attached to the procedure, effectively invalidating informed consent. Instead, he demanded an unreasonable guarantee that he would survive the procedure under any circumstances. Very uncomfortably, without much choice, the clinician did perform the procedure which, as was anticipated, went uneventfully. After a day or two he returned back to the clinic. Even in the canteen, he shuddered to consider the consequences he might have faced if the Prince had died during the procedure. During his stay in the Kingdom the physician had remained in a palatial compound, seeing nothing of the medical facilities or wider city. Instead, a treatment facility was provided for him inside the palace.

Others had told me stories about Jewish rabbis arriving in the Kingdom during the Gulf War. I remembered my Canadian friend, a maxillofacial surgeon at the hospital, recount one incident in particular.

"In the late summer and early fall of 1990, as the build up to attacking Iraq proceeded, there was a huge influx of U.S. military personnel into the Kingdom. Here, our hospital was designated to receive (what was expected to be many hundreds, but became a few dozen) orthopedic trauma and burns. Two complete military reserve medical units (from Georgia and Pennsylvania) came to the hospital and were integrated into the staff. These units consisted of various professionals including surgeons, nurses, pharmacists. Of course they were of all religions, including many Christian denominations, and also Jewish Americans too." David thought for a moment. "Now that I think, I can even remember one nurse who was an American Muslim. Anyway, one of the Americans became my tennis partner. He was Jewish. He told me he had been ordered stateside to leave his religious designation off his dog tags. Even so, the forces came with all their various clergy represented, since there were thousands of military in Riyadh and all over KSA. These included Catholic priests, protestant ministers, and rabbis. They were all officially listed as 'Morale Officers,' so as not to cause any offense to the Saudis."

I knew that even the U.S. army couldn't allow it to be known that Jews were entering the Kingdom. Jews entering the Kingdom was not a minor matter. Alon's predicament as a visitor arrived without personal authorization by a royal patron was far more tenuous than a Morale Officer with the might of the U.S. army behind him. I also knew a number of prominent Jewish American academics who had declined invitations to speak at meetings in the Kingdom because of their fears for personal safety. The danger was most certainly not virtual. At the hands of rabid Mutawaeen, it was real.

The bus pulled into the compound. Seeing the National Guard soldiers wave us in, lowering the barriers behind us and closing the Mutawaeen out, was gratifying. I finally felt safe. At last I noticed how much my shoes were now pinching, as though I had finally returned to my senses. I felt drained from the evening. I climbed out of the bus and arrived at the threshold of my apartment.

I flung my keys on the credenza and dialed Imad's number. He answered immediately.

"Imad, are you alright? Where are you?" I asked him.

"I am at home at the villa. We are all fine. The Muttawa left immediately after you all did. I paid the bill and then drove the others back to their hotel. Alon was a bit shaken but no damage done. I was worried about Diana. How is she?"

"Oh, she is fine!" I answered, annoyed. "She was just pretending she was hurt to frighten the Mutawaeen. Silly woman." Imad responded with silence, infuriating me further. "It was horrible. I had heard about Muttawa raids but I had never believed I would experience one. Can you believe he thought I was Saudi, when he tried to speak to me in Arabic?"

"I know," he answered lamely, "but what is really disturbing me, Qanta, is how could they know that we were there? I mean, no one knew about that event except the symposium organizers. You do realize, someone tipped off the Mutawaeen?" My eyes widened in slow comprehension.

"But you have such enemies, Imad?" I countered. "People from inside the National Guard hospital would want to hurt you in such a public way? Who do you think it could be?"

"I do have a lot of enemies, as you know, Qanta." He chuckled, clearly satisfied at his notoriety. We had talked of this before. Imad's extraordinary academic and administrative successes were hotly envied around the institution. Even my obtuse view as a non-Arabic-speaking woman could see the hostility which constantly haunted him. "Personally I think it could be Qasim. I have always suspected he doesn't like me."

"Qasim, but he is such a minor employee. He just books the

venues and arranges transport…"

"Exactly, Qanta," Imad interrupted. "He is the only one other than Malea, my secretary, who knew where we were going tonight. And you know Malea could never do such a thing." Internally I agreed. Malea, a Filipina woman, had intense loyalty, almost protective, toward her overworked boss. She would never have done this to him.

"And Qanta, I assure you, I personally checked out the location last week. I deliberately chose this place because the Mutawaeen do not usually come here and it was very discreet. This is off the beaten track. Did you notice the side entrance? No one can even see anyone enter that way. Only an informer could have led the Mutawaeen here. This raid was planned. Qasim was probably paid off. But by whom, I don't know."

I had no answer for what Imad told me. Imad was one of the few figures at the hospital capable of organizing an international meeting on the basis of his well-deserved scientific reputation. That someone would hurt him in this manner and endanger visitors to the country was unthinkable.

"Who knew that Alon was Jewish?"

"Oh, you heard that too, Qanta." He sounded surprised. "Of course, Alon told me when we were at a meeting in the States. He really wanted to come, and of course, I wanted him to see our work here. I cleared it with the CEO. He guaranteed his safety. But Alon was never allowed to leave the visiting faculty and go into the city alone. I told him I couldn't protect him outside of our events, but tonight I could barely do that."

"Did anyone else know he was Jewish, Imad? Think carefully."

Imad paused, "No, Qanta, I didn't even tell you." Hesitating, he added, "And we talk about everything lately," referring to our shy friendship which was blossoming recently. I allowed myself a first smile. "I deliberately mentioned it to no one so that the secret couldn't accidentally get out. I don't think even his U.S. colleagues knew, unless Alon told people himself, but his wife was so scared I am sure he kept it very quiet. She actually called me about that."

"Well, what are we going to do tomorrow? Where is dinner arranged for the faculty tomorrow night? How can you be sure it is safe to move as a group with this informer, whoever he is?"

"That's no problem, Qanta; we are having it in the Officer's Mess in the National Guard Military Base itself. The Mutawaeen cannot enter there. We will be very safe. You are coming, aren't you? The son of the Crown Prince, Prince Salman, will be there. You must meet him."

Wishing each other good night, I clicked the phone and pondered the events. My latest brush with the Mutawaeen had been the most uncomfortable. Everything friends and colleagues had warned me about them was just as unpleasant as they had led me to believe. There was no exaggeration of their frightening power. Only echelons of the monarchy could shelter privileged or connected individuals in this manner. Had we been less so, as women we would have been languishing under house arrest now and the men would be pleading their cases in a Mutawaeen garrison, negotiating through their relevant embassies for a safe deportation. Alon's fate would have been anyone's guess, especially in the intense period of anti-Western feeling which seemed to be circulating lately.

As a part of Saudi culture, the Mutawaeen were both notorious and opaque. Rumors that the modern Mutawaeen were actually reformed convicts who had won their freedom by memorizing the Quran and endorsing an intense Wahabi indoctrination circulated in Riyadh all the time. Supposedly, the prisoners became fire-breathing preachers. This was a very commonly held belief among expatriates, but I had heard no confirmation of this from the Saudis I knew. I couldn't understand which crimes could have been abrogated in this manner under the harsh interpretation of Sharia law that was practiced in Riyadh. But without question, the Mutawaeen carried a checkered history of complicated and conflicting roles. I finally began to understand why I feared them so.

The Men in Brown who had terrorized us tonight belonged to the League for the Promotion of Virtue and the Eradication of Vice (Ha'iya li-l'amr bi-l'ma'ruf wa-l-nahy an al-Minkar) also commonly referred to as the Mutawaeen.[17] They had been appointed in this role early in the twentieth century, by King Abdul Aziz himself, the founding ruler of the Kingdom. He founded the committee of Mutawaeen to control the zeal of the Ikhwan (the brotherhood), which was an armed body of religiously indoctrinated radical men of Bedouin origin, the force with which the al-Sauds conquered huge territories of desolate Arabia. Because of the Ikhwan, the al-Sauds were able to gain tribal and military supremacy over vast tracts of the Arabian Peninsula. Doing so ironically facilitated their goals of absolute power by using groups of Bedouin origin to eradicate the Bedouin way of life which had existed until they exerted their extraordinary ambition to rule.

At the time, the religious flavor of the Ikhwan was a useful excuse to convince otherwise disparate clans to unify their goals of "cleansing" and eradicating "ignorance," also known as *Jahiliya* in Arabic (literally meaning "ignorance," it is actually a namesake for "spiritual darkness"). The efforts of the Ikhwan would replace this primitive culture with the clarity of their furious Islam. A convenient military strategy was therefore cloaked in a righteous enforcement.

Thus, al-Saud, through the Ikhwan, exerted his influences all over the peninsula by forming settlements of Ikhwan-led communities, or hijras, in initially punctate areas of the now Kingdom. Eventually these settlements spread rapidly and coalesced into the skeletons of future conurbations of modern-day Saudi Arabia. There, in these hijras, with the aid of intense and fervent preaching and the use of violent, intimidating force, local nomadic populations were subdued and encouraged to follow the path of The Prophet, even if it was recommended to them under compulsion! Religious zealotry therefore became the anchoring fabric weaving fractious fiefdoms together into a Kingdom.

By 1929, the Ikhwan under the leadership of Abdul Aziz had established 120 settlements. In this manner they settled huge communities of nomadic Bedouins into sedentary peoples, effectively terminating their liberated, free-spirited lives on the Saudi steppes. The Ikhwan were terrifyingly violent to most people and for a time they bloodied the landscape, becoming enormously feared. At the time, parts of the peninsula were under British protectorates and when the British resident in Jeddah threatened to oppose the encroaching Ikhwan in 1918, Abdul Aziz muzzled them to maintain his useful alliances with the British. The Ikhwan were growing too powerful; dangerously autonomous.

This love-hate relationship between the clerical forces and an impotent monarchy would become a pattern which would be mimicked repetitively in modern day Saudi Arabia. Ignominiously reined in by their ruler, the Ikhwan became deeply offended, especially as they considered themselves the religious Army of God. The rude rebuff drove them to question their unwavering loyalty for their King. Thus the first crisis of clergy and King was conceived.

Eventually, an open confrontation between the King and the army would follow, and in 1929, with the help of British armaments and soldiers, the King was secured. Treasonous Ikhwan leaders were rounded up and garrisoned in Riyadh, and this quickly precipitated the creation of the League for the Promotion of Virtue and the Eradication of Vice as an essential curb of a monster devised initially to meet the King's ambitious goals of conquering Arabia.

The Mutawaeen who had intimidated us tonight were an

impotent relic of their voracious forebears because they remained muzzled in the costly, decorated bridle of the Saudi monarchy. The origins of the Mutawaeen therefore were never to be an anti-Western mine-sweeping tool, rather a means of policing the state for the security of the precarious monarchy that had conquered it.

It was the 1979 Iranian revolution that radically infected the Mutawaeen with a new zeal for Islamization and a novel obsession with harassing Westerners. It was not surprising that we needed monarchic intervention to rescue us that evening because I was realizing that, effectively, the monarchy was on the same side as we were.[18]

Some believed it would only be a matter of time before the Wahabi clergy of the Mutawaeen was sufficiently emboldened to take on the monarchy itself. Many of their ranks watched the arrival of an Ayatollah in supreme power with animated relish. I knew what they must have thought: how much they preferred a turbaned coronet to a jeweled one.

Chapter
Twenty-Five

DOCTOR ZHIVAGO OF ARABIA

I T HAD BEEN SEVERAL MONTHS since my unexpected enchantment
with Imad. Since he was Saudi and I an expatriate Muslim, it was
impossible to openly pursue him in anything resembling standard,
Western dating. My reticence, together with my inability to unravel
the ways of the Kingdom, left me very much at a personal stale-
mate in the approach to the object of my desire.

Instead I decided to increase my professional contact with him,
hoping that would lead me to know him better. I invited him to write
with me. I finally found my hospital email of use. Though most
employees had access to the internal email system, it was notori-
ously unreliable; servers would go down for days at end and most
had quickly set up web mail accounts to bypass this irritation.

One day I searched for his address, finding it quickly. In a short
note, I asked him to collaborate on a paper that I was already

publishing with another colleague. In a few hours, he had taken the bait, expressing delight in the invitation. Now I had a reason to contact him. I was surprised at my cunning. At least one female trait had not deserted me here.

"I would like to see your resume, Imad," I emailed. "I want to see what you have published."

His documents revealed his age, thirty-four, and his marital status, single. I was amused to note the date of his birthday. Tomorrow he would turn thirty-five. He was born in Mecca. So Imad was definitely a Saudi national, even though his appearance was so very North American. I went on to read his publications. The resume extended for dozens of pages. His credentials were amazing. He was far more than met the eye. Imad was an international authority in his field and at such an impossibly young age. He had been incredibly industrious. I was curious to know more about this handsome, intelligent man. I paged him the next day.

"Allo?" he answered.

"First of all, happy birthday, Imad!" I told him daringly.

"How did you know today is my birthday?" He sounded alarmed.

"Because you sent me your resume! I noticed the birth date. How are you celebrating? Perhaps some shopping downtown, in Olleyah, or perhaps some cake maybe?" I paused.

"Oh no, nothing like that." He sounded intensely bashful, quickly trailing off into an awkward silence.

"That's too bad. You should have some fun on your birthday." I giggled to hide my mounting shyness. Recognizing the topic was now extinct (especially in a community where observing birthdays for adults was a pagan, Western behavior contaminating the peninsula) I decided to talk about the real reason I had wanted to call: to arrange a meeting. He listened politely.

After further emails he had agreed to write the paper with me. A few days later, I took a pile of references and marched off to his office, where we had planned to meet.

The Internet had only arrived in the Kingdom in 1998 and at the National Guard hospital in 1999. Without this new technology it would have been impossible to contact the single Saudi male. Thank God for the Web!

Along the way to his office, I detected butterflies inside me and a long forgotten excitement of anticipation that took me back to my girlhood. I hadn't had a crush of these dimensions for a long time. I smiled, enjoying the delicious sensations of forgotten frisson. I hurried toward the building where I would find his office.

The sun warmed my hair. I felt the perpetual Riyadh breeze ruffle my short crop. It was always marvelous to come out into the open, and here on the medical compound I could always exit without an abbayah or veil. I was perfectly at ease, though doubtless many eyes were watching my unusual progress, which generated surprise wherever I went. Saraway, my pharmacist friend, told me about this, condensing my diaphanous vapors of suspicion that I was being observed into a very concrete reality.

"Qanta, you know when you first started inviting me to have lunch in the canteen, I felt really strange. I wasn't sure if I should go. I mean it was unheard of for a woman to eat with a male colleague at work." I was surprised, remembering my natural invitation of Saraway to eat with me as soon as we had finished making our first rounds together. Because he was American, we became friends immediately. I hadn't realized I had distressed the Ethiopian American Coptic Christian quite so much. I listened.

"I mean, you cannot know how startling it was to see you arrive in the ICU, Qanta. We had never had a woman there before. Even for me as an American it was hard because after five years in Riyadh, you kind of get used to the segregation."

"What did you notice, Saraway?" I asked, out of genuine curiosity. I had been so overwhelmed by adjusting to the strange society around me that I had been unaware that I myself was a source of any consternation.

"Well, one day you were discussing some CT scans with a group of doctors, all men. I watched from a distance and even from there I could see your body language was different. You were leaning against the monitor with one hand in your trouser pocket, just like a guy."

Saraway stopped to demonstrate. He had captured one of my favorite postures when deep in thought. Like most women, I especially enjoyed trousers that had pockets in them.

"Just how you were standing, so comfortable in a ring of men, completely unaware of the division between men and women, well, it was really shocking, for men and women," Saraway continued. "I mean, the nurses always worked with the male doctors, but because of their role, the men never considered them their equals and always managed to be apart. No woman could stand with them the way you do.

"At first, every time I came back from lunch with you, the other pharmacists would always say, 'So, did you have lunch with your *friend* again?'" Saraway laughed, actually uncomfortable in recollection. I was astonished.

"What were they implying about us, Saraway?"

"Well, the guys used to tease me about you, suggesting we were engaged in something illicit."

"Like an affair?" I asked, incredulous.

"Yes," he answered bluntly. I looked at him in disbelief. I was also amazed that I had sensed none of the ripples of shock that clearly just my presence had elicited. Working in a man's world (which much of medicine still remains) had been a way of life for me for almost a decade at the point I arrived in Riyadh. I hadn't realized that I had absorbed any of the masculine traits that Saraway had identified in the eyes of locals as scandalous: confidence, authority, physical ease around men, and above all, a will unbent by the conjecture and speculation of the society around me. Evidently, I was a chimera to my Saudi and Arab colleagues. I was a man in a woman's body, a Westerner with a Muslim name. I was impossible to place.

Finally I found Imad's office and walked toward it. Just as I turned into the small corridor leading there, I came across lines of footwear encroaching onto the hallway. His office, it emerged, was immediately next to the building's private mosque, where the administrators worshipped. I was startled to confront a mosque on the threshold of my attraction. I hurried past, glimpsing a lone Saudi man prostrate in prayer. I was beginning to feel guilty about my feelings.

Hoping there was no lipstick on my teeth, I knocked at the door. Imad's soft voice called out, "Come in."

I hesitated for a moment, wondering how I had arrived at such a point. Acutely, I felt shy and girlish. Inside he was ensconced at a large desk that wrapped around him, piled high with papers. He peered into a computer screen and alternately glanced at his laptop. As soon as I entered he stood up and greeted me with a formal handshake. His hands were soft and cool. In this single gesture he had recognized the Westerner and the peer within me. It was the first time a Saudi man had shook hands with me. I was touched and broke into a smile.

I looked at his face and noted an imperceptible curve of his full, pink lips. A glint of perfect teeth appeared under his neatly groomed moustache. He quickly bundled the smile away, indicating I should sit. Obediently I did so, careful to leave the door ajar behind me. I wasn't sure of the proper decorum of a woman meeting a Saudi man unchaperoned in the institute. Outside the door I could hear his Filipina secretary, Malea, diligently typing. I felt intensely uncomfortable and guilty. I wondered if my foolish, gaping smile gave away my secret attraction. I was glad Imad chose not to notice anything. His rimless eyewear cast a bluish reflection over his eyes as though veiling them. From time to time, when we accidentally locked glances, I couldn't be sure what I could know in his eyes.

I chose to sit in the low-slung, black leather settee in the Le Corbusier style. His basement office had a distinctly masculine appeal to it. With the leather and chrome furniture, there was a distinct air of Hugh Heffner about the room. I suppressed a secret smile. Overhead, sandaled footsteps echoed from outside a window which peered onto the sidewalk above us. We were in a secret and very hidden place.

Just as I was relaxing and responding to Imad's initial pleasantries inquiring of caseload and patient outcome in the ICU, the Azaan rang out: afternoon prayer. I stopped mid-sentence, unsure what to do. It was not my custom to observe prayer in the middle of my working day, preferring to condense my prayers in the early morning and before bedtime. I stared at Imad, expecting him to rush off to pray. He remained motionless and apparently intent on my next words.

"Do you need to pray, Imad?" I asked shyly, wondering if the question embarrassed him. "I didn't realize your office is next to the mosque," I added, trying to inject some levity into the air of mounting sexual tension.

"No, Qanta, I don't." And, without explanation, he left it at that. "Now let's talk about our paper." Moving from his desk, he came to sit near me in an armchair to my left. I was surprised. This soft-spoken and powerful Saudi man did not appear to worry who would see him missing from the ranks of his praying colleagues. I wondered if he observed prayer at all.

He settled into his chair comfortably. He must have been six foot four at least. From this proximity he seemed even larger. I was intimidated by his manliness. He crossed one leg over the other and seemed to be relaxing in anticipation of a long conversation. Around the office his phones were blinking, calls on hold being diverted by Malea. A fax machine furled out endless communiqués and his email notification system was beeping intermittently. He responded to none of it, fixing his open and disarming stare on me.

Avoiding his eyes, I noticed the fine silk tie he was wearing over a crisply pressed shirt. As usual, his white coat was buttoned up and the lapels perfectly pressed. Now I was close enough to read his name emblazoned on his chest. Mounted on the wall I counted multiple framed diplomas and soon realized his middle initial shared the same as my father's name. I was surprised by my appetite for these details. Already I was bewitched. From this proximity he was even more attractive to me.

His coloration was fascinatingly Caucasian, and the blue eyes were startlingly deep, a navy-violet color almost; sometimes they appeared black and sometimes blue. His neatly barbered, vigorous gray hair was thickly waved. Flecked with silver, his manicured beard was beginning to turn fully white. I curbed a sudden desire to ruffle his mane, imagining its plush, thick pile.

After a brief conversation outlining the paper I had sketched, we fell into an awkward silence. Unusually for me, I was tongue-tied. Just as I was trying hard to think of something witty, an unexpected sound startled me, the sound of a very loud cricket. I jumped out of my seat, thinking there was an insect loose in the room. Imad roared with laughter, his eyes crinkling, creased in giggles.

"Qanta, don't worry, there is nothing here, that is just my screen saver!" We both giggled with nervous relief. For some time, he leaned back in his chair and smiled at me with genuine glee. His twinkling eyes revealed amusement. The ice was finally broken. This Saudi man had a sense of humor. We fell into a chat about writing and medicine. I was now on familiar territory. Imad was very engaged. He seemed to want to tell me a lot. I questioned. He talked.

"I went to medical school residency and fellowship in DC, Qanta. I loved it there. I lived there with my mother and father and my sister. My father had business interests there for many years. In all, I spent ten years there. After residency, I did two fellowships."

"So you are triple-boarded, Imad?"

"Yes," he confirmed, sounding not the least ostentatious. He seemed a modest man.

"I had great mentors there, Qanta. I had a terrific time in residency. I loved the States, still do."

"Why did you come back here, Imad?"

"It's been about ten years since I came home. My education was sponsored by the Saudi Arabian National Guard, so I had to return here to work for them in exchange for a free education. When I arrived, they made me chair immediately. I was a chair in a department of one—me!"

He stopped, chuckling. He was extremely attractive when he laughed. I continued listening. "Since then, I hired everyone you know today. We are a department of seven at the moment and of course a fantastic team of nurses. They are really loyal to me."

"What about your writing? How did you become so published so quickly, Imad?"

"I always enjoyed it. I had a wonderful mentor at Georgetown. We wrote a lot together. He developed a habit of observing and publishing in me which served me well. I created the first research database here and of course that generated publications. Everything else followed."

"But you seem to write a lot on your own, Imad. You don't have any residents or fellows who would like to write with you?"

"No, Qanta, we don't have these programs yet, but Inshallah I will build one." He paused, focusing on a distant future.

We began to work intently on several documents I had brought with me. He leaned in toward me as we digested a particularly obtuse paragraph. His immaculately dressed thigh was millimeters away from mine. He was powerfully muscular. I followed the perfect crease of his trousers upward until it disappeared under the fold of his coat. I could feel the electricity between us. We disappeared into an engulfing silence, neither of us daring to look up from the paragraph, frightened of what our locked gaze might reveal.

Instead, I followed the inside of his wrist as he pointed something out on the document. The skin peeping out from under his starched cuff was blue-veined and delicate. A fat Rolex sank backward a fraction, dragged by its weight. I imagined kissing the tantalizing skin. His body seemed untouched, whether by sunlight or sex.

By this stage, I couldn't even hear Imad's observations about the paper. Even Malea's typing seemed to have retreated into the background. Imad and I were locked in a bubble of connection. As he bowed his head over the paper, locks of his gray, wiry hair brushed his shirt collar, creating a tiny rustle. Now and again he stroked his beard in deep thought. I was intensely distracted, unable to formulate a single coherent thought. Fortunately Imad was busy reading aloud the manuscript that was propped on his muscular knee. He didn't seem to need any response from me. It was adequate that I listen.

I was glad my coloring rarely gave away the deepening blush that was gathering to the roots of my hair. The heat in my ears was making them itch. Staggered by the intensity of my own attraction, I suddenly felt an intense desire to leave. I stood up abruptly, surprising both of us. I tried hard not to run, barely controlling my exit. He was clearly disappointed. The screen saver rang out with cricket calls once again.

He spoke slowly and softly, very sure of his words.

"You have to leave now, Qanta?" He paused. For a long time, he looked at me, unblinking. Finally, I could escape his gaze no longer. I allowed myself to see his fluid eyes which blazed like fiery brandy on a wintry day. In their blue reflection, I recognized the Doctor Zhivago of Arabia.

"Yes, unfortunately," I lied. "But this was pleasant, Imad. I think this will be fun to work on this project together," I added lamely, unsure how to end the conversation.

"Yes, it will be," he said, leaning back in his chair. He crossed his long lean legs at the ankle as he relaxed backward.

His face relaxed into a smile as he wished me good day. We assured each other that we would remain in contact via email. Uninvited, Imad handed me his card with several numbers. On the back, in spidery writing he scratched his personal mobile number on the reverse. I carried the numbers out like a trophy.

As I turned to exit the door, I waved a final goodbye. Imad looked up, Sphinx-like once more. All traces of animation in his smile or cascading laughter had disappeared. He had returned to his public persona. I struggled to define what accounted for the change. Whatever the manufactured mask he had donned, he now looked at me through the veil of public office.

It was too late, however. I was already ensnared by the man beneath.

LOVE IN THE KINGDOM

WEEKS WENT BY AND BOTH my contact with Imad and my dilemma increased. Imad never suggested lunch or dinner. Following suit, neither did I. It would have been impossible for him to have been seen to have lunch with me in the hospital and as a single man living in Astra (the adjoining residential accommodations for the Saudi employees at our hospital) an invitation for me to visit him at his home would be scandalous and rather public, under the scrutiny of his colleagues who lived and worked with both of us on National Guard properties. I had never considered inviting him to my apartment even though I had a table to seat ten. I just knew he would never feel comfortable agreeing to drive to see me so publicly. There was a very real feeling of being observed in the Kingdom, and a man relating to a woman in any capacity always attracted inordinate attention. As a result we had no option but to continue our electronic relationship through emails and telephone calls. We could meet only in a virtual world.

After weeks of serial emails, some of which would total dozens in a day, Imad informed me he had an account with MSN Messenger. Together with AOL and Yahoo Instant Messenger, these were my links to the world I had left behind. Out of habit, the very first thing I did was open these accounts on my Internet access as soon as I entered my home. At the end of my day in Saudi, morning was dawning on the Eastern Seaboard and my friends could "visit" with me fairly frequently. It was like leaving an open door to my home. I felt less disconnected with the messages that popped up—quite literally; I now had someone with whom to chat.

Imad continued a daily catalogue of emails discussing his family, his friendships, his work, his travels. I had now grown used to our dialogue, which was already peppered with frequent phone calls. Mostly he would call me once I had reached home and often we would chat for several hours. Sometimes we would leave the calls to eat and then return to our conversations after our dinners prepared alone for ourselves in our separate houses. We were on internal numbers so the calls were unbilled, but I wasn't sure if they were unmonitored; without fail, after an hour, the call would be automatically disconnected. I never understood why and no one had any reasonable explanation. Likely the landlines in the Kingdom were still limited and so perhaps this allowed others to place their calls in turn. Either that, or someone was actually recording the conversations and, as we often joked, needed to change tapes. We never examined the matter more deeply, afraid of what we might learn.

Our conversations covered innumerable topics except the reality of what was transpiring in our evolving feelings for one another, feelings of which I was growing more confident. Instead, we exchanged professional opinions about our shared patients as well as our personal histories, family events, and feelings about the

Kingdom and the worlds we both knew beyond here. When he finally met me online, we had been spending several hours a day corresponding via email. I was at my screen yapping to a friend in San Francisco when a message popped up from Indiana Jones.

"Hi, it's me."

"Who is this?" I typed, cautiously, ready to delete the contact instantly.

"It's me, Qanta. It's Imad."

I was surprised that the cautious, introspective Saudi had chosen such a flamboyant screen name. He characterized himself as an academic (yet still smoldering) screen hero! This was a man disconnected from a sense of self, childishly, at that. I kept these observations to myself. And so a real-time dialogue began. I discovered though he was intelligent, his command of written English was actually poor. I took pleasure in introducing him to new words, until on one occasion, he set me straight.

"Qanta, I feel like I am in English class!" followed by an onscreen laugh. In this way, over hours on the Internet, Imad began to come out of his very calcified shell.

In our secrecy, I didn't know we were engaging in the new illicit rage sweeping the Kingdom: online dating. Though I didn't realize at the time, what was normal and unremarkable for me to conduct with friends across the planet, in Riyadh carried serious connotations.

Here, it was the only way for Saudi men and women to really connect in pursuit of their attraction. Even though I was attracted to Imad it wasn't until years later that I fully understood what this virtual connection with me could mean. For him this was the foundation for a full-blown, modern-day Saudi romance. It was the only way he could know more about me. For me, it was a means to learn more about a man who couldn't approach me safely in any other forum, a way to pass time, and something I engaged in with friends as well as those who might become more significant.

Unquestionably, in the Kingdom, the matrix of online chatting was a combustible interface of sexual repression, desegregation, and the dangers of an accelerated, electronic pseudo-intimacy. The Internet allowed socially inhibited, closeted men to finally begin to communicate, in many cases, with equally suppressed women. The combination was flammable and under the veil of these false intimacies, individuals thought they were falling in love.

For men who had never known any women outside of their families, their abilities to discern any woman were severely limited. Anyone who showed attentive interest was alluring and, in a Kingdom where relationships almost always ended in marriage, a prospective wife. It was impossible for me to know what Imad was deriving from our conversations, but I was clear. I was learning more about a delightfully attractive and seemingly available Saudi man. He continued to intrigue me. Perhaps his very inaccessibility made him all the more mysterious. It was hard to know for sure.

Even so, I began to build a fuller picture of him. He had an unmarried younger sister who was training to be a plastic surgeon, a brother who was a colorectal surgeon. His father, once a jet-setting entrepreneur, was now in retirement, an irritable insomniac. Of his mother he revealed very little, other than that she was difficult to please. But he was committed to satisfying his parents, returning to see them most weekends that he was free.

Though I was learning more, I was bursting to spend more time with him personally rather than virtually. No situation seemed to present itself. The very real prospect of facing house arrest and incarceration by Mutawaeen weakened even my bold aspirations of dating this man the way many Westerners were doing in the Kingdom—snatched moments at hotels around the city. I knew that wasn't for me or for Imad, either here or anywhere else. We were far too serious, perhaps even about each other but more importantly, very influenced by our Islamic values.

For others less inhibited, Riyadh offered a varied but very secret night life. Rushed sex in hotel rooms checked-in under anonymous names, or frighteningly risky meetings in sympathetic locations around the city (like the Hotel Intercontinental, where expatriates teemed the lobbies and restaurants) were the only trysts that couples could engage in. At the time hotel rooms could only be booked under male names. No woman was authorized to book under her own aegis, the assumption being she was attempting to stay unchaperoned without permission of a male relative. I remembered Dodi and Abdul Aziz, the young muturjams (translators)[11] who had recently confirmed my suspicions.

"Make no mistake, Doctora, this is a city of four million. You can get anything here, anything! If you have a girlfriend and want to meet her, a guy can rent an apartment. We can get alcohol, drugs, women—you just need to know the right people." Dodi looked at me very hard, perhaps trying to communicate an invitation. I didn't dare express a single question in response.

Alternatives were more pallid. Some lovers persisted developing their relationships under the shelter of sympathetic friends. Frustrated lovers met either on a Western compound which, in our compound, would entail circumnavigating guards who knew not to admit Saudi nationals onto the grounds without express clearance, or at semi-public events limited to Western expatriates, whether a drive into the desert concealed in a procession of real married couples or a dull rendition of a Noel Coward play staged in a private auditorium built inside one of the more exclusive compounds.

Even in these places little privacy remained, and only the generosity of friends who would provide a vacated villa could allow the couple to be together for a few stolen hours. I found

---

[11] Medicine in the Kingdom is widely practiced in English, and with the number of expatriates, the National Guard Hospital provided around the clock translators so that doctors could speak to patients.

the gray-haired Western lovers to be the boldest with one another. Often they openly shopped in malls, the woman exposing her gray hair revealing both her defiance and her age, while she was escorted by her silver-haired squire. Generally speaking the Mutawaeen seemed deferent to age. They were rarely stopped.

* * *

Sometimes relationships reached a frenzy of excitement on the eve of Valentine's Day which always precipitated a raid of florists by the Mutawaeen who would confiscate every red rose, red wrapping, or Valentine teddy. In defiance, a number of us decided to wear red underwear as our subversive retaliation on the "immoral" day. Other more resourceful couples would express their feelings in flurries of exchanged gifts mediated through cooperative secretaries, maids, or drivers.[19] Some would even purchase their roses days in advance, asking for them to be delivered in the middle of the night to avoid the fearful Mutawaeen.[20]

For those lovers with economic power, weekends away over the bridge from Dammam to Bahrain, or a short flight to Dubai, or stolen days in Amman or Beirut were the only alternative. For men this was relatively easy, often being able to drive themselves across borders or book flights. For Saudi women, travel entailed the permission of a male family member or, for a single expatriate female like me, permission from an employer. Most Saudi women couldn't obtain permissions from their male relatives for trysts.

For expatriates like me, entering and leaving the Kingdom required both an exit and re-entry visa. The coveted multiple-exit-re-entry visa was very difficult to obtain, and I didn't have the wherewithal to arrange this for myself. No, in my landlocked state in the Kingdom without the influences Imad enjoyed I was very limited in my options even to have dinner with Imad. I wondered if we would ever meet overseas.

Those that were emboldened enough to actually pursue a relationship beyond an Internet connection or Bluetoothing were constantly under threat of discovery and serious consequences. None of them, however, was ever seen publicly dating a Saudi in Riyadh. In fact, I had seen no cross-cultural relationships of any kind, whether in acquaintances or in the patients and families I attended. Once in a while socially I had come across an occasional American woman who had married a Saudi after a relationship conducted exclusively out of the Kingdom, not returning until marriage deemed them legal partners. Dating in the Kingdom was a very serious and illicit affair.

I found myself remembering Amanda's words well. As an English nurse who was found extremely attractive by many men, her warning was explicit.

"Don't fall in love with a Saudi, Qanta. That's a mistake. Use them for sex, that's all. But whatever you do, don't get attached. They never give up their families, their mothers, their culture." She sounded bitter.

She went on to describe an impassioned affair she was currently engaged in with a young Saudi of twenty-five, some ten years her junior. They had met at a hospital Masalaama (farewell party) on the compound. He had been a junior employee in a minor administrative role. A newly married man, he was in her arms disarmingly charming in his puppyish attraction for her. They began meeting during the day in her deserted villa on compound, when her fellow roommates (also British nurses) would be busy at work. Amanda volunteered for additional night shifts so that her days could be free to pursue her desires.

In turn, her lover left his desk largely unnoticed and in broad daylight drove himself to her apartment, also on the complex. No one had ever stopped him. He had hospital identification and was on hospital property. There they would meet and in a dull back bedroom on a lumpy bed, finding little in common, they would quickly embark on intense and very compressed sex, which satisfied something in both of them. Amanda actually could tell me very few substantial details about him. She knew he was married and lived in Malaaz, a neighborhood close to the hospital and, ironically, very close to the central prison in Riyadh where trespassers of "virtue" were frequently incarcerated.

Zachariah my driver had once pointed out the sinister building as we drove to the stable where I rode horses at a private arena in the same area. It would be years later before I would read in the *Arab News*[21] of what actually transpired inside the Malaaz Prison.

Within the labyrinth of concrete cells the Mutawaeen "questioned" detainees observed by a panel of clerics concealed behind one way glass. After brutal interrogations, offenders were compelled to sign pre-written confessions to nameless crimes with their fingerprints under the mandate of a Sheikh. This is what Amanda's lover would face, were he discovered. The punishment for adultery in the Kingdom was death for a married man and at the very least flogging for an unmarried woman. Amanda herself, still married to a husband overseas, was risking the death penalty. I wondered if she could know this.

Because of its grave nature, a charge of adultery has to be supported by the sworn testimony of four witnesses, according to Islam. Even so, I thought Amanda incredibly reckless to discuss what was essentially a capital crime in open earshot of the bustling ICU. Her lover, already a young father of a son, age two, was expecting another child later in the summer. He had no intention of leaving his wife who, unlike him, spoke no English and was barely literate in Arabic. He felt obliged to remain married to her because she had been chosen for him by his parents. Divorce for him was unthinkable, and the financial obligations to his divorced wife likely too expensive for his small salary. He was trapped.

Amanda had obligations too. She was estranged from her husband in London and over past weeks was gradually negotiating a rapprochement with him over strained phone calls. She had no interest in a future with him either.

"This affair is purely for kicks, Qanta," she said nonchalantly. "He doesn't mean anything to me. I am just having fun." She bowed her head, busying herself with a clipboard. She colored to the roots of her hair at the memory of the sex she had had earlier in the day, but even so she sounded at once cold as she talked about her lover. I looked around to see who might be listening in the ICU but no one was nearby.

"I am very clear about what I am getting from this. He's just meeting a need, Qanta. You see I've been faithful to my husband since we were married, but since I came out here to Riyadh to help save for our house that we are buying in Islington, he confessed he had bedded a woman we both know. So I thought, what the hell. Fuck it! I am going to have some fun myself." Bedding the young Saudi was easy for Amanda. At the Masalaama he had drunk rather a lot of our moonshine, Siddiquie (Arabic for "buddy," which was the name for bootleg homemade beer that was rampant across the compound). With a bit of Dutch courage, he finally responded to her very blatant attentions.

"He wasn't the most experienced, though, Qanta. I had to show him a thing or two," and she trailed off, giggling, leaving me to my own imagination. I shuddered to think how the naïve young Saudi had coped with this raucous nurse raised on a diet of beer and debauchery in London. Even though there was no love involved, I had no doubt they had both gained from each other through this relationship.

In my opinion Imad and I needed an occasion to meet outside the hospital. Though not for the reasons Amanda sought with her lover. I wanted to see whether I was running away with a fantasy or whether my attraction to this delightful Saudi man was real and returned. Daily, I pleaded with my ICU pharmacist friend Saraway to put in a good word for me, to act as a mediator, and perhaps even mention my romantic interest in Imad, but he was mortified by the prospect.

"Qanta, that is ridiculous. I have worked with him, for him, for five years but there is no way that I can speak to him about this. I guarantee you this is absolutely incorrect. You will embarrass both of us, and I assure you he will run for the hills. Imad is a very formal man. He has never had a girlfriend as far as I know. The answer is no!"

Even pleading with Saraway's wife to manipulate her husband's decision was out of the question.

"No, Qanta, Saraway will not do it, though it is a shame. He does seem very nice and I hear you both seem to get along well. We don't know that he has anyone, but then our relationship with him has been very professional. We don't socialize with him or other Saudis in fact. You know how it is here for expatriates. We can't really break out of our parallel worlds."

An unmarried status conferred suspicion on men and women alike in the Kingdom. In me this usually raised questions of a prior divorce. Saudis would come out point blank and ask me if I was divorced. But for a man to be unmarried into his thirties was even more unthinkable. In this, well into his thirties, Imad was extraordinarily controversial. Many were suspicious of Imad because he was such a private, quiet man; very few people really knew him well.

Single men in the Kingdom invited intense scrutiny, though not of the kind I as a single woman had experienced. Unmarried men were constantly defending their sexuality. Homosexuality, a grave sin in the Kingdom, punishable by death, was the most feared rumor of all. Saraway and I both knew several of our Western colleagues were unmistakably gay.

Heath was a very well-known, flamboyant figure. He had an extremely camp inflection to his voice indicating (to any Westerner at least) that he was openly homosexual. Imad was often seen accompanying Heath to various committee meetings. They ate their lunch together in the male section of the doctors' canteen. They seemed to be friendly and at ease with one another, but no more than a decade-old collegiality would breed. Others were probably much more damning in their assessment.

Heath was, however, known to have a parade of young, Saudi, male friends who regularly visited him in his apartments on the compound. He lived in an identical apartment building to mine, just a few blocks away. Saraway and his wife Iman lived in a neighboring block and noted the comings and goings, which were well-known in the neighborhood. We wondered how exactly Heath made these friends and if they ever stayed over. Some of the boys were not old enough to be employees with us, judging only by appearance. The rumors about Heath's sexuality abounded, but it was more taboo in the Kingdom to discuss homosexuality than any other topic. While adultery was discussed within earshot of patients and mutarjums, even discussing an unimaginable fall of the Saudi monarchy was easier to broach than this dangerous subject.

One of the nurse managers who ran the ICU was also overtly gay. An Irish American of part Italian stock, Mark was friendly, efficient, and effective. He did a terrific job. He was also friendly with Heath and together they often discussed their dreams of settling in Sri Lanka, where both had acquired separate properties paid for by long years of work in the Kingdom. I would occasionally enter Mark's small office, interrupting their conversations about Sri Lankan emeralds and the lush landscape, utterly removed from our stark surroundings. Even though I was comfortable talking to Mark about almost any subject (simply because of our experiences of working long nights on call in the setting of a trauma ICU) I never dared endanger him by enquiring about the gay lifestyle in the Kingdom. Questioning him about the "Kingdom in the Closet"[22] was a violent intrusion. Some things were better left unknown.

Nevertheless several factors probably facilitated homosexual tendencies to be embraced by many men in the Kingdom: the severe, same-sex gender divisions in the Kingdom sanctioned by legislation which prevented men from comfortably being with women; the long forays overseas for workers who arrived in cohorts from the Far East and lived in intensely cramped conditions (sometimes six laborers sleeping in a single room on triple bunk beds) where physical proximity inevitably led to homosexual behavior (whether invited or compelled); and simply the climate of repression, suppression, and severe curtailing of even innocent exchanges between the opposite sexes all led to an intensified and completely unmanageable mass of sexual desires, driving some to appease their uncomfortable libido by seeking acquired homosexual behaviors.

Stories of attractive Filipino rent boys were rife; some of the Filipinos were overtly camp and feminine in their voices and deportment. Jeddah was reputed to be more liberal, where these affectations were openly flaunted. Some of the Saudi behaviors among men who observed the very courtly mode of greeting other men with serial kisses and a deferent squeeze to the hand or a brush of lips against a clothed shoulder seemed to linger by miniscule moments, a trace too long. I watched men as they went about their business. My detection of latent homosexuality was probably accurate.

I was finding love in the Kingdom to be a complicated, secretive matter and, like everything else here, thoroughly opaque.

Show Me Your
Marriage License!

O NE EVENING, SARAWAY TELEPHONED ME at home to tell me
the news. He and his wife Iman had finally decided to leave
the Kingdom. They were firm in their decision; it had been something they had been considering for some time. I would be losing
my first close friends in just a few weeks. Of course, immediately
I saw an opportunity: we would have to celebrate by going out for
dinner. Naturally, I could arrange something and include Imad in
the invitation. Iman and Saraway laughed at my determination to
meet him outside of work.

"Well," laughed Iman, "that will be an interesting dinner and
I think Saraway will enjoy it."

I scrabbled to formulate a plan. The first challenge was
persuading Imad to attend between what I was learning was his
routine international and national travel. Few weeks went by when

Imad did not travel either to Jeddah for meetings or to see his aging parents, or out of the Kingdom for his various guises as academic, advisor, consultant, or government inspector. Imad was a very busy man. When I explained to him my plans to arrange a send-off for Saraway, he sounded pleased. I began to feel excited. It looked like I would finally get to see him away from work. The choice of venue was critical.

"Just be very careful, Qanta." Imad said no more, indicating his anxiety in everything left unsaid. I had already decided. We would eat inside the newly opened restaurant which was wowing everyone across the city.

Cristal had been open a few weeks. It was the glittering restaurant inside the al-Faisaliyah Hotel which had sprung up in a few short months, now the tallest building in Riyadh. Even though the isosceles sky scraper (testament to architect Sir Norman Foster's obsession with the triangle) was still unfinished, the building was already breath-taking. The most gorgeous landmark on the Saudi horizon, I had to admit even Manhattan had nothing like it.

Its apex wasn't even finished yet, and the spectacular glass globe suspended at the very tip of the triangle was still unfurnished inside. It would eventually house the first cigar bar for the city's überchic. Changes were afoot in Riyadh.

The astonishing tower itself was the vision of the mysterious Prince known simply in the Kingdom as al-Waleed. Prince al-Waleed bin Talal was one of the first Princes to visibly reinvest his extraordinary wealth back into the Kingdom. While in New York City we knew of his holdings in Citigroup and the Four Seasons, or of the George V in Paris, it wasn't until he built the al-Faisaliyah and, soon after, the even more astonishing al-Mumlaqa Tower, that his fellow countrymen could see evidence of his considerable confidence in Riyadh as an investment. His buildings were exquisitely planned and executed and, to me, my favorite places to escape the realities of

Kingdom life. Dinner at Cristal would be a perfect setting to get to know more about Imad.

The evening arrived. I arrived at the hotel with Saraway and Iman. Imad was to meet us there. We were in a festive mood.

We pulled up under the heated hotel portico studded with thousands of spotlights. Stepping out of the car we were blinded, as though stars caught in snapping flashbulbs. A columnar fountain crashed sheets of white water from a monumental height, creating a cool vapor that drifted on the chilly night.

I shivered with excitement. Around us Saudis, in small aliquots of mysterious veiled and thobed cargo, were decanted discreetly into the hotel lobby. The guests were immediately whisked from sight. The black Benzes and BMWs contained the crème de la crème of Saudi society. This was the venue to be seen at in Riyadh, though ironically that meant to be even more unseen than usual.

We entered through the lobby. Almost everyone within sight was a male Saudi. Two Caucasian businessmen chatted, awaiting their rides to the airport. They discussed their recent business endeavors half within earshot. In their blue blazers and stiff ties they looked inelegant and out-of-place. By their ruddy cheeks and boyish haircuts, I guessed them to be English. In contrast, the Saudi gentlemen around us were all immaculately thobed, mostly in white robes, but one or two still persisted in wearing the deep navy or black thobes that the winter season allowed, some of which were made of the finest suit materials. This combination of dark, masculine gabardines and gray wools in the shape of the ancient medieval male dress was extremely alluring to me; a very sexy cross-dressing of Saville Row and Saudi. Unfailing, the dark thobes made every man appear handsome. I found myself wondering if we would see Imad in his Saudi finery tonight. I very much hoped so.

We stepped into an elevator, climbing several floors to reach the restaurant itself. Our table was waiting and, as instructed, the maitre d' had reserved the best spot at my persuasive request. There were probably only a dozen tables in total, almost all of which were round, perfect for deep conversations. We were seated at one such table, discreetly tucked away toward the back of the wood paneled room.

Around us, clusters of Saudis dined. Tonight we were the only Westerners here. I noticed several veiled women who ate ensconced by Saudi men, sometimes one woman eating in the company of two men. None of the women wore any facial covering but some chose to keep their hair covered even in this inner sanctum of Saudi sophistication.

Time began to pass. I found myself actually wondering if Imad would appear. Just as I was beginning to think he had forgotten, his tall silhouette caught my eye. At his usual brisk pace, he entered the room, scanning for us. I was disappointed to see he had not donned his Saudi thobe. Instead he arrived in a relaxed outfit of slacks and shirt. He appeared in neither tie nor jacket, preferring instead a blue shirt (this time Dior) unbuttoned just once at the throat. He greeted us and took his seat, the empty chair next to mine.

"The meeting at the Ministry seemed to drag on for ages tonight. I thought I was never going to get here," he explained. I remembered on Sunday nights this was his routine. He would go to attend the weekly meetings to discuss matters at a national level. Though Imad was not Minister of Health, I had no doubt he one day would likely be selected for the role. No one else in the Kingdom was more qualified. "And then the traffic, it's really crazy in Riyadh lately. Everything is getting so congested. I was speeding to get here," and he laughed, casting a sidelong glance at me. The evening had begun.

Another dinner guest breezed by our table, trailing a cloud of attar. His thobe brushed our table cloth and as he passed, I noticed a beautiful silver rosary, which he was rotating in his right hand. These men were impossibly elegant. It prompted me to ask, "Imad, why didn't you wear the Saudi dress? I think it looks fantastic!"

He grimaced in disgust, terminating my smile. "I hate wearing that stuff. It's just not me, Qanta. I am more comfortable in khakis and shirts. I have never worn those clothes, except on certain very specific occasions like family weddings. Ugh, I would never come out in those clothes."

I was surprised by his vehemence. He didn't see how elegant his countrymen appeared, even in such a glamorous setting. He leaned back in his chair, his hands on each armrest. The glint of a Ferregamo belt caught the light. He was relaxing. We were almost brushing elbows. The familiar frisson I had fought to suppress returned. Transiently shy, I lowered my head. The blue black dial on his expensive watch read 9:15 p.m. Time was flying fast. Imad continued however. Tonight, he had a lot to say.

"You see, no one ever recognizes my nationality, no one ever guesses I am a Saudi," he smiled with satisfaction.

"What do they think you are, Imad?" I asked, nonplussed.

"Canadian, American, Jordanian, Lebanese. They never believe my nationality is really Saudi." He seemed to take pride in this. I was puzzled. I began to see the self-loathing Imad carried about his identity: eschewing his national clothes, taking pride in an ethnic ambiguity, and here in one of the finest establishments in Riyadh, among his contemporaries, clearly in his dress, a complete misfit. I wonder if his cultural distress extended to his religious beliefs or perhaps his ambitions for a future. I resolved to inquire about this later.

Knowing Imad liked seafood, as many men from coastal Jeddah do, we ordered oysters, which arrived undressed on a spectacular ice platform. A little lemon juice and we had gobbled them up; delicious. Today, on Sunday, they had been freshly flown in from New England only this morning. In fact the lobster was also brought in twice a week from Maine, all the way here to the hotel. The vegetables came from Brussels several times a week. No expense had been spared. Even so, I was not expecting a cuisine of a standard close to London or New York or Paris. I couldn't have been more wrong. The food was equal to Petrus or Jean Georges or any Michelin-starred dining room. We ate in astonishment.

Throughout dinner, I found myself laughing. Always, Imad laughed with me. He was obviously enjoying himself. Tonight he seemed unguarded, actually open. He frequently glanced at me, locking my eyes in his blue-jeweled gaze. His eyes danced and his laugh cascaded, tumbling out of his bearded, brilliant smile into surprisingly infectious giggles. The mask had fallen and the real man was shining through. I had unveiled him. He seemed unconcerned at what he was revealing about himself—a real and rather vibrant attraction for me. Periodically Saraway and Iman were glancing at one another, looking intermittently mortified and alternately genuinely pleased.

"Qanta, my face is hurting from all this laughing. I had no idea you were so funny," Imad told me. I had come to the same conclusion about him. His sense of humor, while a little shy, was wry and droll. "You know I am so glad I came this evening. I almost decided not to show up."

We were all surprised.

"You see, over the years, all kinds of things have happened to friends in Riyadh who go out in mixed groups. I now believe anything is possible. As you know, one can't rule out a raid anywhere." He lowered his voice conspiratorially. Evidently it was time to be serious. "Anything can happen in Riyadh, you know that, don't you? The Muttawa can disrupt any gathering, and question people for being together, especially when the Saudis and non-Saudis mix. They don't look on that kindly, as you know."

"But Imad, we are in the company of a married couple. You do have your marriage license with you, don't you, Saraway?" I looked at Saraway and Iman who nodded in unison at a question which was idiotically naïve to the veteran expat. "So I am sure it is fine that you are here with us," I told Imad, genuinely believing my logic and trying to reassure him. Again he laughed, but this time he sounded callow. There was coldness to his voice.

"No, Qanta, if the Muttawa were to enter here, they would ask you, 'And who is your husband? And where is your marriage license?' And if there was none, I would be arrested, and you would probably be deported. Sometimes the National Guard Hospital is not powerful enough to protect even a British citizen. By eating here tonight, we are certainly at risk." He stopped short, wondering if he was spoiling our relaxed evening. He monitored my reaction. I met his inquiring, kind eyes with a puzzled stare.

Now I recognized Imad's late arrival was more likely a reflection of his internal fear. Even a powerful man in his own nation was fearful. In his Western dress and his North American appearance, Imad was a man caught between two worlds. He was ambivalent, perhaps in more ways than one. Just at that point, a minor hubbub at the threshold of the entrance caught our attention.

In the distance a handful of brown robes condensed into an anxious fluttering deposit. A nidus of Mutawaeen had entered the al-Faisaliyah center, a very rare occurrence. The maitre d' looked up from his rostrum and glanced at us, preparing to muster any necessary action. Discreetly he began dialing a number. I wondered if he had activated a panic button. Perhaps Imad's prediction was about to become manifest. Several of the Saudi men dining at neighboring tables looked up. Yet none other than us seemed alarmed. In fact some, recognizing the disruption as mere Mutawaeen, returned to their meals at once, minimally irritated. There was no fear here. It was such a contrast to the air of menace that the same religious police carried normally here that their power was defused.

For a moment the Mutawaeen were suspended as though flies

in a web, unable to enter or leave. Even though the huge entrance lacked a door, simply being a wide arch, they were repelled by an invisible barrier: the powerful force field of the Free Prince. We were on al-Waleed's turf, a Kingdom Holding Company building. Here, the Mutawaeen couldn't touch us.

Like all good things, the evening ran away before we knew it, and it was time to leave. Imad exited first to retrieve his car from the hotel's garage. He had offered to drive us all home to the compound. We agreed, even though traveling around in the city in this manner was also a risk. It was late at night, and Imad assured us he was confident he could speed us home without being stopped. With Saraway's bald pate and dark complexion which was so often mistaken as Saudi, and his wife in tow, we would probably pass as a reasonable married group. He pulled up in a seven series BMW and ushered us to enter.

Saraway offered me the front seat but as usual I declined. To the sound of Craig David's British R&B we sped off into the night traffic, Imad racing quickly to over a hundred miles per hour. I was shocked both at his recklessness and his taste in music! He didn't wear his seat belt either until finally he gave in to my insistence. (One of my perpetual anxieties in Riyadh as a permanent passenger was injury of whomever was driving me—in recent months my worries were approaching a neurosis.)

"Please, Imad, this is so dangerous." I stopped looking out of the passenger window, which revealed our lightning progress in comparison to the other vehicles on the road. We were passing everyone. He responded with a self-satisfied chuckle. I couldn't wait to get out. I triple checked my seat belt.

In this strange adolescent behavior, Imad revealed yet another male Saudi side of himself—the male appetite for speeding. The expression of his unarticulated masculinity in rubber burn and his evident pleasure at navigating the busy highways in this dangerous manner without regard for the very plain fear of his passengers was juvenile. Unfortunately, this was a commonly expressed characteristic of the bored young men in Riyadh and, I was discovering tonight, not the exclusive provenance of the uneducated.

Imad couldn't have been any other way, despite a long exposure to the West; his culture was simply too strong. Though his guise was extremely Western—German cars, French ties, Swiss watches, Caucasian skin, Italian footwear—it couldn't blot a very Middle Eastern mentality: entitled male authority and sexual boredom compressed in a perpetually trapped playground. This was the Saudi Zhivago I had chosen.

Chapter
Twenty-Eight

AN EYE FOR AN EYE

I HAD RETURNED FROM A brief interlude in New York, arriving only two days earlier into the Kingdom. I couldn't believe what I was hearing. I went immediately to the bedside of the extraordinary patient Imran had just described.

Juliette, one of my favorite Filipina nurses, was busy cleaning him. She paused, visibly perspiring under the weight of the flaccid, dead flesh. Gently, she released the fat buttock that she had been dressing, where a wet pressure sore had developed already. Like a flank of refrigerated meat, the hip slapped heavily onto the bed.

"Doctora! Good evening! Welcome back!" Juliette was eternally pleasant. Her warmth was genuine. I wondered how she remained so graceful even in the most revolting of situations. I answered her pleasantries and then asked her about the patient.

"What's the story, Juliette?"

"He is, I mean, he was fourteen. This is day four of his ICU stay. He arrived after a penetrating stab wound to the heart. After open cardiac massage, they got him beating again. He was pulseless for at least fifty-five minutes. We don't know how long he was out cold after he was stabbed. His brain was already swollen on the first CT scan of the head right after that. We knew he would have anoxic brain injury. He never recovered brain reflexes. He has been declared clinically brain dead for days now. He has never been sedated. They haven't discussed withdrawing life support or the usual assessments for organ harvesting. We can't believe it, Doctora."

Neither could I. I stared at the body. The glossy shock of thick, unruly hair remained the sole, rude reminder that the patient had been a vigorous adolescent until only a few days ago.

The obese teen was in suspended animation, machinery performing all of his bodily functions while the essence of his being, the seat of his consciousness, was already dead. I looked at the patient. His face was swollen to the size of a football. Eyes were sealed shut forever under edematous lids. Protective lubricant conferred a sheen of tears as though he wept for his own fate. A respirator connected to a fresh tracheostomy site was pushing air in and out of dead lungs.

"But this is ridiculous. Why are we doing all this, Juliette? This is medical futility... it's completely unethical."

Huffing with irritation, I resolved to talk to Dr. Faris in the morning. Perhaps there was something I didn't know. Ignoring the ethical maelstrom, Juliette addressed more pragmatic matters.

"Doctora, what do you want to do about Fouad's blood sodium?" She pushed some results into view. I glanced at them. His brain had stopped controlling sodium along with many other minerals in his blood stream. Correcting this would make no difference to the patient's outcome, which had already been decided, and it seemed organ donation wasn't even a consideration (something that would mandate careful control of the serum levels of sodium). I walked away, leaving Juliette with the data. I had no help to give.

"How can you justify this situation continuing?" I challenged Dr. Faris in his office the next morning. Faris shifted uncomfortably in his chair, and finally, exhaling a sigh of contained exasperation, he began to explain the bizarre circumstances.

"Qanta, you must know Sharia law in Saudi Arabia carries the death penalty for all murderers?" I nodded impatiently, wondering how this could be possibly relevant. Faris was often circuitous in his explanations. Aching from a long night on call, I hardly had the energy for another one of his shaggy dog stories.

"Well, this patient was stabbed by another child, a Saudi boy who was also fourteen. They were outside their school. We don't know what the argument was about but the boy who stabbed him— the assaulter—swears he had no intention to kill. If we withdraw care, Fouad will be declared dead and the boy will be convicted for murder. A teenager faces the same consequences as an adult in our country." I looked at him incredulous. There was more.

"So the assailant's family has offered blood money, by way of damages for the wounded child. It is up to Fouad's family to decide if they will forgive the transgression, but so far they are refusing. They want the other child to be executed in retribution. So of course, in desperation, the transgressor's family has appealed to the King himself. There is a delicate discussion going on at the highest levels. So you see, Qanta, while this is all being decided we cannot disconnect care because we do not want to be responsible for bringing a youngster to the death penalty. That is a matter for the higher authorities, for the Sharia courts. And so last week we had instruction, by Royal decree, to continue all care. By order of the King, we cannot discontinue our efforts. Do you understand? It is very important you are clear on this matter, Qanta. There must be no confusion."

He looked at me sharply. I understood perfectly. Sharia law played a huge and very foreboding role in all aspects of life and death in the Kingdom. This was not a matter of medical ethics at all. This was a case for Islamic jurisprudence as interpreted by the Wahabi clerics in Riyadh.

"I understand your dilemma very well, Qanta," he went on. "Like you I was also trained in North America. I withdrew care on many patients who needed that at Hamilton where I trained." He referred to his fellowship years in Ontario. "I understand the end-of-life decision-making and the consequences of brain death very clearly, but this matter is much more serious. It contains consequences that are much broader than the immediate patient. If Fouad is pronounced dead, this could affect an entire family and could result in the death of another teen."

He became pensive, leaving me in a puzzled silence. Medical futility was not the only ethical dilemma in this case. The King had interceded by issuing a royal decree to prevent death from being declared in the hope that clemency would be forthcoming from the victim's family. Even the King couldn't offer clemency on behalf of the parents of a murdered child. That was a decision only the family could make. No one else, not even a monarch, had the right to determine justice on their behalf. What the King had done, however, was buy the families more time, in the hope that hearts would soften and mercy would ensue.

"I hope the victim accepts the diyya (compensation) from Fouad's family," Faris began, referring to the Quranic teaching that the families bereaved as victims of intentional death should seek diyya rather than qisas (retaliation) in the way of equivalent punishment.[23] Faris began to explain. As usual he had identified my near-habitual confusion at more sophisticated Islamic principles and sought to teach me.

"You know Islam teaches compassion in every situation, don't you, Qanta?" I nodded an affirmative. I very much believed this.

"Well, the principle of an eye for an eye is indeed present in Islam, because above all Islam is justice. Islam believes in equality and in infinite justice. The following verse reminds us of this," and Faris quoted the Quran from memory. After he had spoken in Arabic, he translated for me.

"We have prescribed for thee therein a life for a life, and an eye for an eye, and a nose for a nose, and an ear for an ear, and a tooth for a tooth, and for wounds retaliation; but whoso remits it, it is an expiation (atonement) for him, but he whoso will not judge by what God has revealed, these be the unjust."

He went on to explain Islam bestows permission for Muslims to exact justice in very precise and equivalent terms, but never beyond these precisely specified terms. A Muslim cannot punish one crime with a greater crime. Islam discourages vindictive behavior, endorsing only the meting of precise justice. But as Muslims we are also given the option of relief from exacting justice. Instead, retribution is actually preferred to retaliation. In the Kingdom there are even set rules about this. For instance, the death of a Muslim man must be compensated by a fine of SR 100,000, about $26,000, half for a female because in the Kingdom, few women are breadwinners. If the immediate family of the murderer does not have money, any extended family may offer it, even any member of the tribe. Sometimes members of the royal family will ease these difficulties. But this compensation is required. It is up to the family of the victim to accept this in lieu of qisas. I listened to the complex explanation carefully, but there was still the fundamental youth of the assailant which disturbed me.

"But in this case the murderer is a teenager! Can he face decapitation?"

"Unfortunately, Qanta," Faris explained, "once the boy has become an adult, with developed secondary sexual characteristics, he is considered adult in the eyes of the law. Committing an adult crime requires an adult punishment.

"I am afraid that is the way, but even until the last moment the family can forgive him and he will be spared. We pray they show mercy." Faris fell silent. I understood the conversation to be over. I excused myself and left the room, closing the door softly behind me.

I walked through the ICU to exit. I paused by Fouad's room. Fouad, or rather Fouad's body, was still heaving with each shuddering breath of the respirator. His vital signs were more or less normal. Juliette had finished her night shift and now Vicky, a Zulu South African, was tending to his dressings. She sang a ballad softly under her breath, perfectly occupied. Fouad looked like any other patient in the ICU. From this vantage, the illusion of life was maintained in perfect order but easing him into a dignified and final death would be much more difficult. It was not our decision, nor apparently his Maker's. The Sharia courts, the families, and his Monarch would decide. In the meantime we must tinker on, effectively ministering to a cadaver. Deeply disturbed, I left the unit.

The next day I decided to call my friend Jane for more information. I was still troubled by the brain dead patient. Jane, a Kiwi from Auckland, was a physiotherapist and a long-time veteran of expatriate living in the Kingdom. She knew the answers about a lot of things here.

"Oh yes, Qanta, the blood money thing; it's very common here. Everyone who drives a car, all the men I mean," she paused, "have to have car insurance in case they need to pay out blood money. Think of it a bit like life insurance. Interestingly, if an expat is killed, his death is not usually legally required to be compensated in blood money, but lo and behold if you run over a Saudi, you better have that blood money ready." I wasn't sure this was entirely accurate, so I went back to Faris.

We sat in his office, sharing tea while he explained to me the principles of accountability and compensation. As usual I listened in silence, amazed both at the extent of his knowledge and my ignorance.

Any accident in the Kingdom found to be the responsibility of another warrants diyya, compensation, irrespective of Saudi nationality. If the responsible parties cannot pay the blood money, others can step in to meet these costs.

I knew that Faris was correct in this. There were some tremendous examples of unexpected generosity in the Kingdom. Articles were often published in the *Arab News*, the daily national paper. Saraway and Iman had told me about the story, which I now remembered.

"Listen to this Qanta, in the *Arab News* yesterday!" Saraway began partially quoting an article to me over the telephone.

The article described a Saudi man entering a courtroom in Hail, a town in the north of the country. There he publically offered SR 50,000 ($13,000) to the family of an Indian worker who had been killed in a motor vehicle accident partly caused by a Sri Lankan whose family could not afford the compensation. Fortunately, the driver had survived, but still the court ordered blood money to be paid to the Sri Lankan family who had lost their only breadwinner.

Until payment of compensation, the surviving driver, who was partly responsible for the accident (along with the deceased), remained incarcerated. The *Arab News* reported his consulate had appealed to the local Indian community to help raise funds, but no help had been forthcoming. Somehow the anonymous Saudi man learned about the case, not knowing either the driver or the deceased, and wished to relieve the distress of both the driver's family and the victim's widow. He disbursed the monies completely unexpectedly. They were given to the Sri Lankan consulate to be wired to the widow at once.

"Wow, that is generous, Qanta!" Saraway gushed, as he read from the paper. "And they never revealed who donated the money." Saraway paused.

"Why did he do it, Saraway? Did it say anything about the donor?"

"Let me see… yes, here at the end it mentions the donor wanted to give because while he didn't expect any reward in this life, he knew Allah is bountiful and will reward him in the next. That's all it says. He must be one rich guy."

"And a generous one, Saraway." I repeated the tale to Jane later in the evening. Her cynicism was partly alleviated.

"I had never heard of that before, but it does make sense. I have to say the Arabic reputation for generosity is legendary. And for good reason. You know I go to the Palace to do physiotherapy on the Crown Prince and one of his wives? They both have pretty bad osteoarthritis of the knee. Anyway, while I am on my knees working on the Princess, bending down doing the range-of-motion stuff, the courtiers are usually bustling about bringing requests from their subjects to their attention. I think they actually take them seriously. Once in a while she stops me in the middle of our exercises to make a decision. I have heard some even get to have an audience with the CP himself."

I looked at her blankly. "Crown Prince," she explained. "I guess think of it as town hall meetings. The princes meet with their local 'constituencies' as it were (can't think of a better term, Qanta), and they hold a weekly Majlis, which means a kind of conference, literally a place of sitting. People tell him their troubles. The Prince helps solve them. Sometimes he mediates disputes over the amounts of diyya demanding which seem to be climbing to astronomical levels here.[24] People come to the Prince as a final court of appeal. The monarchy is very alive here, Qanta, and very involved with their people, make no mistake!"

Ultimately the heaving adolescent cadaver was transferred out of the ICU to a chronic respiratory ward where his body continued to be supported by artificial means. He remained suspended there for some time until finally even artificial life support could not keep his organs functioning. After the death of the teenager his family, with careful persuasion from local elders and the encouragement of their Monarch, accepted blood money in lieu of the death penalty. The juvenile assaulter got to live.

So, while it was Fouad who was condemned at the moment of the stabbing in this life, the surviving teen lived to be condemned in the next.

Princes, Polygamists, and Paupers

JANE HAD MADE ME THINK about monarchy more deeply. As a British citizen I understood the unique affection a subject can have for a monarch, particularly one who has ruled for more than half a century. But in Saudi Arabia the monarch and his monarchy were not as remote from everyday Kingdom life as perhaps might be so in other countries. Working in a hospital, it was not uncommon for them to minister to the sick or to open a building. Sometimes they came to the hospital for their own treatment, though often they chose to receive care at international institutions of renowned status. Other times they came for private fly-by-night visits on business that I could not fully understand.

On one such an evening, I had just finished assessing the patients in the ICU. It was close to midnight. As I closed a heavy file, the charge nurse reminded me that a senior member of the royal family might appear in the ICU. I disregarded the nurse's fussing. Everyone was making their patient space even tidier than usual. Emma, a gorgeous Filipina, was once again applying her already-perfect lipstick. I caught her checking her enviable ruby pout in a pocket mirror. She fixed a stray hair into place. An excitement was in the air and just at that moment the automated steel door of the ICU flung open.

A tiny figure, veiled in an abbayah, entered the ICU. About ten steps behind her, I recognized one of the hospital administrators looking very much the worse for wear, being up so late at night. Evidently he was escorting our much anticipated royal guest. All the nurses stood up, acknowledging the dignitary. They paused in their work for a moment, before continuing in their duties. Mark, the night ICU manager, sidled up to me explaining who she was.

"She is actually one of King Fahad's wives," he whispered, awestruck himself.

I was shocked at her youth, she could be no more than thirty-two; and the King, we all knew, was a debilitated man, a stroke patient, already in his advanced eighties. We followed the figure's progress as she moved through the ICU. Her footsteps clicked discreetly with the sound of costly couture. She took small, careful steps on the shiny floor; measured, mincing. As she wandered past the patients, she approached no one. In response no one dared to address her directly. Unschooled in royal protocol, I was unsure what was proper. How could she understand what she was seeing if no one explained the patients to her, I wondered, watching her circuit the unit.

Nervously she peered through the glass windows of each patient cubicle. She seemed naïve of the critical care environment in the way that most lay-people tend to be. I wondered if she was actually alarmed at the graphic illness here. Her face was revealed as her veil fluttered slightly with her motion. She looked a little pale and drawn. The administrative escort tarried even further behind when he saw her approaching a cubicle directly. He was obviously queasy as the young Queen stopped to gaze at a man with limp, fractured limbs patched together with steel fixtures. The patient, sunk deeply in an air mattress, lay atop a snake's pit of intravenous and dialysis lines that pulsed with his recycled blood. He looked like a corpse in a casket. Surprisingly, the Queen seemed undisturbed—impressive for a lay-visitor.

She continued walking around the perimeter of the unit, finally turning toward my direction. Spying my white coat, which distinguished me from all other women in the room, she recognized I must be the physician on call. She paused, locking her almond-shaped, hazel eyes with mine. Even surrounded by a headscarf, she was ravishing. Her skin was a perfect shade of pale nutmeg, her nose subtly aquiline. Arched brows, refined and slim, elevated imperceptibly into a subtle inquiry. A flicker of smile appeared on glossed lips.

"Salaam alaikum," I volunteered, inexplicably finding myself compulsively bowing from my head and shoulders. She responded in cut-glass, classical Arabic.

She studied me in silence, as did I her. No one moved. The administrator was flummoxed as though not knowing how to manage such a breach of the Queen's personal space that my address had created. I was equally motionless. I was caught in the fiery light of magnificent diamonds that glittered on her person. Her delicate ear lobes were heavy with carats of Graff diamonds. They radiated a brilliance that pierced the gossamer blackness of her muslin veil. As she adjusted her veil, her slim fingers on both hands sparkled, laden with glittering stones, their radiance reflecting in the polished tips of her manicured nails. A Cellini wristwatch glittered with gems, beaming like headlamps in the dark. Her whole personage was illuminated, other worldly. I was intimidated.

"Welcome to the ICU, your Highness," was all I could offer. Immediately I wondered if I should have used "Majesty." She nodded a smiling acknowledgment in return. A moment of connection passed between us in a shared gaze. And then, with a downward flutter of her kohl-lashed lids, I was dismissed. The moment had passed and the Queen had moved on. In a few seconds she had disappeared through the steel doors, the administrator scurrying behind her. The silence, which had contracted opaquely around the mysterious Queen, began to dissipate, dissolving back into the edges of the humming unit. I regretted my reticence.

The young Queen who came to visit the hospital that day was one of many wives of the elderly King. No one knew exactly how many he had taken. The monarchy had traditionally strengthened its ranks through polygamy, a means of transferring and even consolidating power through women. Polygamy was not encountered solely among the royals; many of my Saudi colleagues were children of polygamous families, though none of them were participants in polygamous marriages. The working-class ranks of Saudi professionals, among them physicians, had the same economic challenges as monogamous couples in the West: polygamy was expensive. One wife was quite enough purse to muster for the male Saudi breadwinner.

The practice of polygamy in the Kingdom is a remnant of pre-Islamic Arab tribalism, though Islam certainly grants a man permission to have up to four wives simultaneously. A specific verse in the Quran discusses the possibility of polygamy for men in Islam which, while clearly permissible, is far from actually ordained.

And if you fear that you cannot act equitably toward orphans, then marry such women as seem good to you, two, three, and four; but if you fear that you may not do justice to them, then (marry) only one.
(Quran 4:3)

Scholars mention always that this particular verse was revealed to the Prophet after a battle in which many Muslim fathers and husbands were slain, leaving orphaned children and widowed wives behind. At the time, carefully institutionalized polygamy was suggested as a solution of social welfare for the surviving unattended and unsupported women and children. The critical observation to make, however, is that Allah recommends polygamy only for those who can actually dispense equal and impartial affection, circumstances, lifestyles, and homes for each wife.

The Quran then goes on to mention that this kind of fairness is unlikely to be possible for a mere mortal, preference being human nature and that therefore (because partiality is likely to result) polygamy is effectively invalidated. Preferential treatment for one wife over another or one set of offspring over another is considered completely un-Islamic.

In Saudi Arabia, however, polygamy at an unprecedented level was integral to the cementing together of disparate fiefdoms into al-Saud's early empire. The al-Saud dynasty was conceived and nurtured by a power base possible only through polygamy. Unquestionably, this practice of polygamy upon which the Kingdom was built flouts Islamic teachings, if only through the sheer numbers of marriages men entered.

Pascal Ménoret describes this phenomenon best in his seminal work, *The Saudi Enigma*.[25] Abdul Aziz al-Saud, the Kingdom's first king, was reputed to have married 135 virgins and one hundred other women in addition, far in excess of the maximum prescribed four wives for a single Muslim man. The King chose brides from among the greatest Bedouin tribes and through his marriages melded partnerships and contracts throughout his Kingdom. His wives were among the daughters of eminent Bedouins or the aristocracy of settled sedentary communities holding power in the Najd. Others were apparently daughters of more-popular clans and less-exclusive stock. Some women were even daughters of the enslaved.

With this astonishing policy of institutional matrimony, King Abdul Aziz al-Saud pieced together a staggering dynastic network; one that extended across all geographic regions of the Kingdom. By intermarrying across tribal boundaries of families, clans, and even across classes of his future subjects, he knitted together the beginnings of a Kingdom. Ménoret suggests this was not merely to forge alliances through marriage, which he correctly notes could not be a secure means of building a Kingdom, because (since divorce was allowed in the Kingdom as prescribed in Islam), merely marrying and then replacing wives at whim would likely alienate various parties, paradoxically weakening his Kingdom-building.

Instead, it was the subjugation, the very taming of a rolling, nomadic nation, that Abdul Aziz accomplished through his voracious and determined appetite for polygamy, which he fueled with enormous wealth and indomitable ambition. He used the wealth he had amassed through progressive control of settlements in the Kingdom secured by his fierce Army of God and his strategic conquering of vast expanses of land. Soon after, oil wealth served to consolidate his power into an unassailable supremacy which, far from perpetuating tribal links, actually superseded them precisely because he had married across and through various influential tribes. His collective influence now exceeded that of any single prominent tribe. His power was best described (as termed by Ménoret) to be "supra-tribal." Without polygamy, Abdul Aziz al-Saud could never have accomplished this dominion, and the Kingdom likely would have remained fragmented into fractious fiefdoms.

Thus, like overarching swathes of canopied canvas in a Bedouin tent, Abdul Aziz swept up each of the prominent tribes in the Kingdom under his rule. As a result, ordinary members of each individual tribe were forever ensured access to a sympathetic ear in this diverse parquetry of monarchy because the King had married representatives from all. Each subject therefore (through intermediaries and community bureaucrats) could take their concerns to their own tribal component of royalty within these intricate, recessed eaves of the House of Saud.

Today, his progeny, the Saudi ruling class, is now estimated to number anywhere from seven to twelve thousand strong; a vast, shifting network of interrelated überaristocracy full of intrigue, conflicts, competing interests, and competitive ascendancy. The young Queen who had floated into our ICU one night was merely one of many figures at the helm of the apical echelons of this extraordinary family.

One morning, as I was being driven to work by the trusty Zachariah, I watched the scene through the car window. The hospital grounds were abuzz with activity. New palm trees were being unloaded from endless flatbed trucks. The bald, stiff trees were being planted in symmetrical lines on either side of my usual route to work. It was pleasant to see that the hospital was finally landscaping what was, until then, an eyesore of ripped up earth and desolate building lots awaiting construction. In the matter of a few months an entire building had arisen from the dusty embers of the desiccated land. The new building gleamed white in the morning light. A huge insignia denoted this to be the Cardiac Surgery Building. This was where Ghadah's husband would now operate.

My image of monarchy in the Kingdom was molded after that of my Saudi friends. Zubaidah and Ghadah, even Jane, who had actually met the highest levels of Saudi monarchy, saw the Crown Prince Abdullah as a benevolent and indulgent prince who had a fondness for all in his Kingdom. He was adored especially as a champion of women. In time, listening to the Saudi women who had lived in the Kingdom all their lives, I had conjured an image of a powerful yet avuncular man.

As I studied a huge banner being applied to the building, something completely different came into view. Next to the gargantuan canvas, dozens of thin, sun-burned workers were rendered Lilliputian in size. In the image I was reminded of dictatorship. Something about the scale of the picture—its gray and white palette; its elevated vantage; its monumental supremacy—was distinctly pharonic.

I watched the Bengali laborers. They tied the canvas tight with ropes, ensnaring a fluttering Gulliver. I was deeply disturbed by the iconography. In the Kingdom, the rulers were revered almost to the point of idolatry. I thought about my own short Queen, a Sovereign in humdrum hats and handbags. There was something ordinary and mundane about her stature. Somehow she remained of us, rather than apart from us, even though she was the undisputed monarch. I could recall no image of her of the same stature as the one at which I gazed. In a country ruled by iconoclastic Wahabiism where followers refused even to display their facial photographs on their ID badges and any art other than geometry was scorned upon, I couldn't tally the contrasts of the towering image above. The Islamic ideals I understood to be universal and the reality of living in the Kingdom seemed again to clash. I stood gazing into the gray, blind, canvas eye of the Prince overhead. It revealed nothing.

The next morning, once more on the way to work, I noticed all the unrolled grass had already been neatly turfed. The bald palm trees, slowly relaxing their scant, tall leaves, were now surrounded by an undulating landscape of rolling greens. Overnight the avenue leading to the hospital had morphed into a Jack Nicklaus golf course. Here and there, gardeners worked on trimming the edges of the lawn with diligent precision. Only one problem remained: without rain for more than twelve months, the grass, transported from elsewhere in the Kingdom, was a dull, inanimate brown.

The workers hurled water at it through myriad hoses and a new sprinkler system, but still it remained a resistant bronze. A South Indian foreman was screaming at the workers. They cowered under the shower of his verbal abuse but even the best gardener was powerless against the prevailing four percent humidity of Riyadh, where annual rainfall rarely exceeds four inches. I severely doubted the grass would be green for the Prince's entourage of black S-Class Benzes, which was due to roll by this avenue in the late morning of the next day. I had underestimated the landscapers' ingenuity.

On Wednesday morning, again Zachariah drove me to work. It was seven a.m. The Crown Prince was due in at eleven. Overnight the transformation had continued. Isolated gardeners were evening out the final ripples in the now lovely and verdant vista. Even the trees seemed a little more settled in their new roots. One worker, trailing a damp towel tucked into the rear hip pocket of his blue boiler suit, sprayed what looked to be pesticide with a motorized pump. He sprayed the now green lawn evenly and consistently. I was puzzled. I had never noticed mosquitoes in Riyadh, and pesticide in February was distinctly unusual. The city was perched on an arid plateau. Now that I considered it, I had never seen the grass being sprayed before. But as I took in the lush scene, perhaps all the watering had paid off. The lawn looked sumptuous, a perfect green, no traces of the dull brown grass remained.

I commented to Zachariah that the green grass looked wonderful. Months since I had ventured out of the Kingdom, I found myself craving greenery. The smell of fresh-cut grass, the universal marker since my English childhood of the onset of summer, had long escaped my memory here in the sterile Kingdom. And that's when it struck me: though I could see grass, I couldn't smell it.

The men were not watering the grass; they were spraying it an emerald green. This was Ireland in an atomizer. The workers were coloring the dead, hurrying to finish before the Crown Prince's gaze would zoom by, perhaps peering through the bullet-proofed, tinted, heavily armored glass of his German car.

So much about the Kingdom concerned outward appearances. Veneer was as important as substance, perhaps more so. The Crown Prince's entourage would arrive in moments, so the vista must appear perfect. Climate was hardly an excuse. I was astonished at the efforts, seemingly wasteful, to welcome royalty. As the Bengali workers toiled in prostrate dignity, I was struck by the futility of their efforts. They had slaved for days to create an illusion that may or may not elicit royal note. If the Prince was studying his speech as he passed by in muted luxury, he might miss the entire scene, invalidating their days of underpaid effort.

A few hours later, the royal party arrived in a fleet of two dozen racing Mercedes. They rushed through the barriers, not stopping until they reached the steps of the building. The motorcade had sped past the newly minted avenue at fifty miles per hour. I doubted the Prince had even glimpsed the greened grass. The aging Regent stepped out of his vehicle and slowly greeted a waiting reception line of carefully selected Caucasian nurses.

Less than an hour later the motorcade left, halogen headlights blazing, brilliant even in mid-morning sunlight. As they screeched around the corner onto the Khuraij Road, a tiny Saudi beggar boy, perhaps no more than six, looked at the gleaming cars racing, blasting away. His torn thobe fluttered in the rip currents of powerful German exhausts. He coughed a little and shifted his shoeless feet on the rapidly heating asphalt. In a Kingdom of princes, paupers could only watch.

Chapter
Thirty

DIVORCE, SAUDI-STYLE

I HAD HEARD OF FARIS'S divorce some weeks earlier. Recently he had also been hospitalized. One evening, I mentioned this to Zubaidah.

"Yes, Qanta, we heard. Someone had heard from the mosque that he was not there on Jumma (Friday prayer). But of course, we think it is a reaction to his divorce." She fixed her hair matter-of-factly, securing it back with a final pin. We were in the women's room.

"I didn't know he was divorced, Zubaidah. In fact I didn't know he was married. I never asked him about that."

"Oh Qanta, everyone in the Kingdom is married. It's most unusual to be like us, single and unmarried." She cast me a side-long, droll glance. She refused to expound. My curiosity was piqued.

A few days later, I decided to ask my colleague Imran. He was the chosen confidante of every nurse in the ICU. He always knew the latest gossip.

"Oh gosh, that's old news." I waited for him to explain. "You must know his wife. I mean his ex-wife, Fatima? You know, she comes to our conferences. She was at the last conference we had for that patient that turned out to have vasculitis?" I did indeed remember.

I began forming a picture of Fatima. She was the extremely soft-spoken Saudi woman who was practically buried up to her nose in her veil. She always seemed to smile at me when I was in the same meetings, but being unable to see even her crow's feet, I couldn't ever be sure, and often met her with my blank, puzzled stare. She usually went on to discuss the biopsy specimens. Her advice was always pertinent. We all considered her an excellent clinician, but I didn't know anything else about her.

"So what happened, Imran? Why did they divorce?"

Imran began chuckling to himself, wheezing a little. He obviously thought something was funny. "Poor guy. It seems he fell in love with another Saudi woman, the nuclear cardiologist. Maybe you know who I mean? The one in the white veil? Anyway, it seemed he suddenly decided to take her as his second wife, because his love was so passionate for her." Imran was obviously exercising poetic license with the story. He giggled, "You know, he even followed her to California, settling her in to her fellowship at UCSF, and planned to marry her when she returned after her training. They say he actually escorted her during her emigration, flying with her all the way. Unbelievable. Anyway, when he told Fatima, his wife, she said 'Forget it! I am not agreeing to that.' And she promptly asked for a divorce. Of course now the children are divided. I think they live on the same compound but now in different villas."

"What happened to the woman he loved, the young cardiologist?" I asked, struggling to keep Imran focused on the details.

"Oh, her. Well, when she told her family that she was considering marrying a married man, they absolutely forbade it, plus it turns out she was from a different tribe and her family didn't allow inter-tribal marriages. I think she is still single." Imran returned to some X rays and began to make a phone call.

I was suddenly reminded of the woman in question. Nameless, she always caught my eye because of the intense wrapping of her white linen veil, which covered her entire face except for her eyelids. But this woman, being particularly orthodox, was even more cautious, securing her layers of head covering with visible safety pins which she applied just next to her right eye, as though she was worried about a sudden gust of wind which might tear her precarious veil away.

The safety pin really disturbed me. I hadn't seen anything like it in the Kingdom. She peered through a tiny rent of the white linen, her quiet, blank eyes darting around, mostly in fear. Now I wondered whether she was worried about running into Fatima, who also worked at the same hospital, though I doubted that, enveloped in their veilings, they could actually recognize each other. What a mystery Faris was. I wondered how he had wooed the young doctor. In the Kingdom, a man's desire must have been particularly arduous to find its way through all these veils.

I hadn't known of anyone who intended to be divorced during my stay in the Kingdom. In a country where tribal and endogamous marriages were common and the stigma of divorce both culturally and theologically enormous, I wondered how commonly divorces could occur. I referred the question once again to Zubaidah, carefully steering myself away from the reasons she, at thirty-six, continued to remain single.

"Oh Qanta, it is becoming terribly common. We don't know why. In my opinion the women are becoming very educated and independent, and finding suitable marriage partners becomes more and more difficult for the girl's family. You know that marriage is very important for Muslims, Qanta, don't you?" I nodded. "Allah has written for us in his book there is someone for each of us. Let me remind you." She opened the Holy Quran which she kept at her small, neat desk, searching for a passage. After a few moments, she read to me in Arabic. I waited for the translation.

"I read you the translation, Qanta," and she glanced up at me with her gray eyes to check I was listening. In this late-afternoon light they seemed almost green.

Among His signs is [the fact] that He has created spouses for you from among yourselves so that you may console yourselves with them. He has planted affection and mercy between you; in that are signs for people who think things over. (based on Quran 30:21)

"That sounds lovely, Zubaidah. So maybe he has created one such for me. I would like someone to 'console' me!" For a time we both laughed.

"Families here are afraid of divorce. After divorce it is hard for a Saudi woman to remarry, and anyway marriage is very expensive for the man and his family. You must have heard of the mahr, the bridal price, which must be paid to the bride (to her, not to her family, Qanta). It's due when the wedding occurs. Well, a lot of men don't have that money or have to earn for years to save it. Things are becoming difficult. We want our Saudi men to marry Saudi women, because we are a small race, but nowadays they are going overseas to marry ladies from Jordan and Lebanon and of course, sometimes Americans and Europeans, because for them the mahr isn't really enforced. So, we are left with more and more Saudi women waiting to be married.

"When they do marry, because they have waited so long, it is too much of a strain for the older Saudi woman to adjust. I think it's OK if you are like Ghadah, who got married at 19. She got to grow up with her husband, but otherwise it becomes very difficult. And while women have been waiting, in the more educated classes, they become working women, like us. Adjusting to a marriage with a man who then only wants you to be at home or to cook and raise children is a big shock. Lots of women cannot do it."

"So women are asking for divorce, Zubaidah?"

"Of course, Qanta!" Zubaidah always became invigorated whenever she discussed Islam. "Islam permits it on several bases. The woman has just as many rights to divorce as a man; she has the right to leave if the marriage is not working. Remember always, Islam is justice, if nothing else!

"For example, if a man wants to take a second wife, that cannot happen without the first wife's permission. And if he insists, that is grounds for her asking for divorce. Islam allows additional wives to a man, up to a maximum of four on very special circumstances, let's say if the first wife cannot bear children or if she is mentally sick. Then instead of just discarding his wife, Islam allows the man to take a second wife while keeping the first. However, the Quran is very specific: the man must provide for both women equally and allow them independent living quarters of equal economic status. He has to love them equally. And right after this verse the Quran adds another restriction." She paused to say emphatically, "The Quran says, 'And for you as a human being this will be very difficult,' because partiality is a natural human tendency and therefore you will not be able to fulfill the recommendations in this way."

"In my interpretation it means that really it isn't possible for men to behave so perfectly, Qanta. So yes, Allah gives them the option, but it is not easy to meet the requirements. So polygamy is not required, it is only an allowed possibility that God expects most men will not be able to handle either spiritually, emotionally, or economically—wives are expensive, my dear!"

Zubaidah had a way of explaining everything with such clarity. It was a pleasure to learn about my religion from her knee, so to speak. What basis could Faris have had to ask for a second wife, from his wife who had borne him four children, and after such a flagrantly pursued romance of which even Imran seemed to have gleaned every detail?

I made plans to meet with Fatima and investigate. Doubtless she was feeling abandoned; perhaps she could use an inquisitive friend. Though I was single for entirely different reasons, I was astounded by the excellent company I was keeping among dozens of single, never-married women in the Kingdom—many of them extremely well-educated. By 2002 an estimated one and a half million Saudi women were estimated to be never married. Simultaneously, divorce rates have risen astronomically, to one in three Saudi marriages ending in divorce by 2002. This has met with pressure to reduce the oppressive mahr sums that Zubaidah referred to, to more affordable levels, permitting remarriage and encouraging marriage at earlier ages.[26]

The mahr is paid either in total at the time of the marriage and may come in the form of cash, jewels, property, or a combination of all three, or if acceptable to the bride, a certain amount is paid at the beginning of marriage and the remainder deferred until after death or if the marriage is terminated based on divorce.

These mahr, properties, for instance, or sums of money, cannot be divided as assets of the marriage after divorce. The mahr is expressly for the bride and none other. In fact, if the woman does bring other assets and wealth, perhaps of her own earnings or inheritance, into a marriage of her own, Islam demands that these remain categorically hers and cannot be settled when a marriage ends, unless she chooses to share with her husband.

According to Muslim family law, always the financial obligations of the divorced wife, the nafqa, are borne by the divorced husband, but never the other way around. A wife's status is a precious, serious, and very protected one in the eyes of Islam, and Islamic law as translated by Sharia in the Kingdom is closely integrated with these beliefs, in contrast to the hypocrisy of some of the other cultural practices that are somehow sanctioned in the Kingdom.

Some women plan their marriages with a great deal of foresight, considering possibilities like polygamy. These women, in a display of Islamic feminism, consult with religious sheikhs from their local community to insert protective clauses in their marriage contracts to hold husbands accountable to certain indisputable Islamic rights for the wives they plan to marry. These documents can be effectively thought of as prenuptial agreements.[27]

The women ask the sheikhs to insert clauses, known as Shurut (conditions)[28] that are binding to the husband and that will protect her status after marriage; for instance, clauses that enable the woman to travel freely, the freedom to travel abroad to study, to take employment, and other liberating privileges. In order to exercise their social autonomies after marriage, these women are citing Islamic references, which in an ultraconservative world actually affirm women's rights. Sometimes the wives can specify whether or not they would permit the husband to take a second wife, and if not, they can stipulate grounds for divorce. Often the women can record in the clause that they are unsure of their possible response to the arrival of a new wife in the marriage and hold reservations permitting them to divorce on this basis if that becomes their final response.

The Prophet Muhammad (PBUH) said that of all things permissible for Muslims, divorce was most detestable. I couldn't help imagining Faris's humiliation. For many Muslims divorce carries terrible shame and a sense of failure. Faris, being a deeply religious if bumbling man, must have been devastated by what seemed like an unexpected response of divorce from his wife.

One thing was clear: like all people everywhere, Saudis longed for meaningful and intimate connection. Their behaviors spoke to trapped isolation among people who just knew no other ways to intimately connect with the opposite sex. In this hermetically-sealed, sterile environment of intense Wahabi intrusion into day-to-day living, people became desperate. Men, locked in depression and unable to communicate, sought solace in affairs, returning to their wives with second wives in tow. And what of the fate of the divorced women left behind? I made plans to meet with Fatima. I wanted to know more.

Chapter
Thirty-One

THE SAUDI DIVORCÉE

A COUPLE OF DAYS LATER, I ran into Fatima in the hallway. At least
I was pretty sure it was her. This time I stopped to talk.

"Salaam alaikum, Fatima. How are you?"

Her eyes crinkled with pleasure. "Salaam alaikum, Qanta!
Mashallah you look so well. Your hair looks great! You got it cut!"
In a world where almost everyone was veiled, this was an unusual
compliment in public. I thanked her.

"Alhumdullilah, Qanta. I am very well, and you?"

"Of course, fine, Fatima, but I have been worried about Dr.
Faris. He didn't look very well yesterday. I worry he may be
depressed. I am encouraging him to see his doctor." Fatima paused,
pensive, saying nothing. "And I am so sorry to hear the news of your
divorce," I continued. "That is very upsetting, Fatima. I didn't
know. Actually I didn't even know you were married to each other."

For the first time it occurred to me that I had never realized the two doctors, Fatima and Faris, had any connection to one another, even after spending so many meetings in the same room with both of them. They never acknowledged one another in public, not even with the most minimal of salaams. Usually Fatima slipped in discreetly after the meeting began, which Faris often chaired, yet somehow always left moments before the end, avoiding greeting anyone. I had always considered her a very private person. Perhaps now in my inquiries, I was being intrusive.

"Thank you, Qanta. Thank you for being concerned about Faris. Yes, we are very sad to be divorced, Qanta. But Alhumdullilah I am getting stronger every day, and Allah guides me."

"Is there anything I can do for you, Fatima? Can I assist with anything?"

"No, my dear," she responded warmly, "but I would like you to come to my house and take tea with me. I will give you my address and my numbers. Perhaps you can visit soon. You know where the Astra compound is? Let's arrange it soon." And handing me her details, she floated off, surging ahead through the black waterfall of her abbayah. She sounded quite excited to invite me home. I wondered what I would learn about divorced women in this Kingdom of Strangers.

The day of the visit I had been especially busy at the hospital. Running late, I rushed home and readied myself for my small outing. Astra was just a few minutes away from the compound where I lived but I would have to go there with Zachariah, the driver. I dialed the number, and quickly, securing my abbayah in one hand, a small house gift in the other, I hurried down the unlit steps to wait for him outside.

The familiar night breeze fluttered around my abbayah. I waited for the taxi headlights to materialize out of darkness. Behind me, I could feel the apartment building radiating heat, each wave of hotness pushing me farther into the cooler night. Even the ground pulsed underfoot. It was almost nine p.m. but it was still over 100°F.

Zachariah bumped into view. I got into the cab, and to the filtering sounds of an unknown symphony on a crackling radio station, we rode into the night. When we arrived at the Astra compound gate, a soldier asked for our identification. I showed my hospital badge which seemed to be enough, though I had my Iqama (national ID) at the ready. He quickly waved us through and we lurched over the speed bumps.

The compound looked different than mine. It was landscaped into wide avenues that were surrounded by large, low bungalows and two-story homes on either side. Neatly maintained lawns fronted most properties. Each avenue led, it seemed, to many others. Thousands of Saudi citizens made their homes here. Finally we approached a dimly lit cul-de-sac. A solitary street lamp buzzed in the darkness. As we rolled up to our destination I spotted Faris's white Cadillac a few houses away. So the rumors were true: husband and wife now lived in separate villas just a few homes apart.

Zachariah dropped me off and, waving him away, I walked up a tidy path. I spied a tricycle lying on its side where a child must have just flung it. A flaccid garden hose lay curled over the still-damp lawn. Inside, the lights were on. I rang the doorbell and waited.

The door opened, and a diminutive figure stood just to one side of the heavy wooden paneling. At once I could smell cardamom. Fatima must be preparing coffee. The headlamps of the taxi swept past the doorway and then faded into the dark, just as a tiny and very fair hand pulled me inwards by the sleeve of my abbayah. As the door closed behind me, I turned around and found myself looking at Fatima.

In the bright lights of her home, after the thick darkness of the Riyadh night, I was dazzled. My eyes were smarting with black spots. Fatima smiled at me shyly and after a few moments, her face curved into a wide, cerise bow. Her lipsticked smile was giant, and her pink lips over white teeth reminded me of a Cover Girl commercial. She was gorgeous in a pristine way. I was momentarily taken aback, trying to tally this image with the mumbling, shapeless figure that I knew to be her in the hospital. After an awkward pause, we greeted each other as Muslim women do, with a series of embraces. A delicate scent of jasmine rose up from her smooth, white neck. Her hair was neatly styled in a short bob that jostled from side to side with her every animation. She was slim and sporty in build. Dressed in slacks and a pretty sweater she looked like an attractive soccer mom. She was definitely an older "hottie."

Excitedly, she bustled me into a sitting room just off her kitchen. I couldn't take my eyes off this beauty. How could Faris have wanted anything more than this woman, I caught myself thinking. I began to recognize the veiled Fatima in this, her unveiled persona. She was smiling the same mysterious Mona Lisa smile that I had always suspected she was reflecting back at me through the shadows of her veil.

Now that I could see her crow's feet, I could in fact confirm Fatima was a woman who smiled, and now I could hear, also laughed often. She was positively jolly. Her teeth were perfectly even and unusually long. She laughed a crisp, cultivated peal. Her skin was palest Caucasian, and on her hands, delicate blue veins were easily visible. Her beauty was translucent. I saw she wore no rings, at least not this evening.

"I am so glad you agreed to come for a visit, Qanta," she started, obviously pleased.

"Me too, Fatima! Thank you for inviting me. Where are the children?" I asked immediately noticing the silence.

"Oh, tonight they visit their father, but they will be home soon. Inshallah, I wanted you to come when I had time to be free of distractions." She giggled. As I faced her on the sofa, my eye was drawn to the gingham curtains hanging over a window in the kitchen, by the sink. Carefully tied back with ribbon, they revealed a pretty domesticity that somehow I hadn't expected. I felt suddenly sad, knowing this had not been enough for her husband. Though the view was nothing but a concrete wall (expected of course in the Kingdom where privacy is so intensely guarded) Fatima obviously wanted to make a home out of her drab surroundings. Rubbermaid gloves on the faucet were drying. Someone had just finished doing the dishes. Fatima was a house-proud Saudi. She was trying hard to make a home out of an anonymous villa. Faris had left this cozy picture. Having put his wife in an unbearable position, he had no choice but to move out.

"So how are you doing, Fatima?" I asked as she busied herself making coffee for us. She laid a plate of my favorite cookies on the table: ma'moul (flour-covered cookies stuffed with dates). I reached out to eat one.

"Alhumdullilah I am in much better shape now, but these have been some very difficult months, Qanta, I can't tell you." I waited for her, munching on the delicious ma'moul that was melting in my mouth.

Unable to speak, Fatima allowed herself to express some of her sorrow. "You know Faris and I were married for a long time. Mashallah we have three children." She drew me to pictures of the children that were scattered around the room. I looked into the faces of two sons and a daughter, wondering what their lives were like.

"Faris was chosen for me by my father. We knew his family. It was a very good match. We knew he was from Mecca, a Hijazi, and perhaps with a different outlook from our family. We are from the interior, the Najd," she explained. "But I think even after all these years I didn't really know him. He is difficult, he is changeable, he has some terrible moods. I think you are right, he may suffer from depression." She paused, looking at me for a moment. Nearby, the kettle puttered to a boil. I watched the steam rise into swirling patterns which then condensed into a fog on the nearby windowpane.

"Qanta, let me make the coffee. I gave the house maid her evening off tonight. I wanted us to be alone so we can speak freely." I watched as she mixed the coffee, bringing it to a boil, scenting it with cardamom which she had freshly ground in a mortar and pestle. Finally she poured the concoction into a special thermos to keep it piping hot.

"Faris's family life was unstable growing up. I don't think his mother and father had a good relationship, and his father had more than one wife." She looked at me, almost triumphantly. "So you see I was very shocked when he came to me seeking my permission for him to marry Noura." This must be the name of the cardiologist. "I mean, like all marriages we had our good times and bad times, but I never saw this coming. I think they met at work, and you know Faris. He is very kind-hearted, to a fault. I think he just felt like helping her and perhaps he became too involved. I don't know. I cannot bear to really hear the details, but he did make it clear to her he already had a wife and children. She still was prepared to be with him and so I think he had decided in his brain he was going to marry her, and that she would be wife number two!" She puffed with incredulity.

"Well, for me that was totally unacceptable. I could never allow it. I told him that if he insisted, I would divorce him. He continued to insist on his rights as a man, the right to have more than one wife. I didn't agree with this and so I divorced him at once. It was a matter of days. We didn't even go through mediation. For me it was clear: I didn't ask for divorce, I demanded it. He was violating my rights as a wife. I had told him from the start of the marriage I would not tolerate this. I am an educated woman. I am fellowship-trained from Cleveland Clinic, Qanta. I am the only

Saudi woman with these credentials."

Her voice was climbing into an unsteady crescendo. I was worried that she would start to cry, but rather her high color, and the rare streaks of anger she allowed herself, began to show in her eyes and her white, high-boned cheeks. She was furious, not tearful.

"I thought I was marrying an educated man, and you know Faris is a trained scholar in Islam. He should know better the proper reasons for taking another wife, and you know he cannot really afford that either. After all, I am a working mom! He attended the clerical school here in Riyadh where he was studying Islam in detail before attending to his medical school. He should know better than to behave like this."

"I understand, Fatima. It must be very difficult to consider sharing a husband," I offered clumsily. "How are the kids doing?" I decided to change the subject, unsure how much more candid Fatima might become about my chairman.

"Oh Qanta, that is the worst part. They are crying constantly. They miss seeing their mom and dad together, and you know the two eldest go and live with their father. I had no options about that; it is the way. The little one is with me now. But in a few years he can also decide to be with his father if he wishes. I may possibly be living alone a few years from now."

Her beauty finally crumpled as she wept for her loss into a bundle of tissues. After a while, twisting the tissues into a soggy rope in her elegant fingers, she settled down and continued.

"You must know Islam has provided guidance on where and how the children of the divorced must live?" I indicated my lack of knowledge. I had no idea on the rulings of custody in Islam. I had barely any knowledge about marriage in Islam let alone the death of one.

"OK, let me teach you." She flashed me a dazzling smile. I was always struck at how eager the Muslims in the Kingdom were to educate me on matters of religious scholarship. It was a reflection of their passionate belief.

Over the next several hours Fatima explained to me how families resolved divorce, always with the interests of the children as the foremost consideration. Islamic teachings demarcate three stages in childhood: the age of weaning, the age of discretion, and the age of sexual maturity. Weaning usually means until about the age of two, and discretion until about the age of seven or nine (when a child can express his or her free will and understand the choices). In between, the child matures until he or she reaches the age of sexual maturity and is an adult. These stages determine custody of children in the event of a divorce. Fatima explained the custody of her children in these terms:

"My eldest son is fourteen and my daughter is twelve. The littlest has just turned five years old. Faris and I decided that the eldest boy would be better served in the company of his father now that he is becoming a man, and in fact at his age the custody usually goes to the father anyway. My daughter expressed a desire to live with Faris, so she is with him. She has reached the age of discretion so she is allowed to choose where she will live." Fatima looked wistful and after a short pause, explained further.

"She is a very caring soul and I think was very worried about how her father would cope without me. I of course supported her choice to live with him and I see her all the time. She is not far from me. You know, Faris's house is that one over there." She drew back the curtain pointing to a house across the cul-de-sac. "So of course they play together all day, the kids. The little one is still not at the age of discretion and Islam favors his custody to me, the mother. He will stay with me until, like his sister and brother, he is old enough to make his own choices."

I already knew Riyadh was ruled according to Sharia law determined by the Riyadh clergy. In the Kingdom, a Saudi mother is allowed to maintain custody of sons until the age of nine, and female children until age seven after which the father's custodial rights take precedence. Most importantly, Sharia courts always dictate that the child go to the home most likely to foster the purest Islamic environment. In Fatima's case, both the father and mother could provide this, so in the court's eyes this wasn't a dilemma.

Saudi fathers always maintain legal custody even when the mother is Saudi herself. By law he retains all rights over where his children live and travel. My eyes widened as Fatima reassured me.

"Thank God Faris and I have a good relationship that we can still communicate respectfully. He would never take the children away from me, and he knows I provide them stability and support, which is hard for him to do. You know about his nighttime duties at the King's Majlis, I assume?" I nodded, remembering his sleep-deprived weariness, which greeted us so often in morning report in the ICU. She wanted to explain more. I asked her what would prevail if she married outside her religion.

"The custody is also affected if I decide to marry a non-Muslim after divorce, which of course I will never do." Fatima giggled at such a preposterous possibility. "If I did, I would lose custody by remarrying a non-Muslim, or if I decided to live in a home of nonrelatives. Do you see, Qanta, our customs seek to preserve families even when the marriage is broken? Our laws guarantee that the child's religious upbringing is not compromised. God forbid if something happens to Faris, even if he knows my wishes to keep the children together, Sharia law allows custody of children to be awarded to the closest male relative of a Saudi father. That might be a difficult one to fight. I don't know. Inshallah, I hope it never comes to that."

I was stunned. A divorce here truly meant the destruction of a family. Not only parents separating but brothers and sisters too. And where was the emphasis on motherhood which I had learned from the tiniest age, from my father: "first comes your mother, your mother, your mother, then your father," in a paraphrase of The Prophet's words[12] when asked to determine which parent is most revered in Islam. In a society where family was the base-unit kernel to every community, divorce was atomizing societies into particles that could never consolidate together in the same way. What had been once an indisputable sense of unity in community—the basic nuclear family—was just as fractured and damaged as in suburban America. The Saudis were struggling with the same issues we did in the States. I had more questions.

"But Fatima, tell me more about divorce. How do you know it is time to end a marriage? What is this mediation process, designed to put the brakes on an angry couple? What were the negotiations that you refused really to consider?"

Fatima locked her clear gaze onto me, pausing to consider her response. "You are right. There are several stages that have to pass when either the husband or the wife has decided to seek divorce." Her face had become grave. The smiling bow was transiently unfolded into a firmed jaw. I concentrated to follow her detailed explanations.

Fatima explained that if a man did inform his wife of the desire to divorce, using the word "Talaq," and he uttered it serially, three times, after that the marriage can only be dissolved after three months and not in that instant, a commonly held misperception. Muslims must continue to live in their married home under the same roof but retreat from sexual relations during that time. In fact the wait is determined by three cycles of the woman's period. In this way the wife will discover if she may be unknowingly

---

[12] In al-Bakhari Kitab al-Adab (Cairo, Matba'at al-Sha'b). Hadith describing the Prophet's response when asked by a man: "And who among people is most deserving of my good companionship?" And the Prophet responded, "Your mother," "And who deserves it next?" "Your mother," "And who after that?" "Your mother," "And after that?" "Your father."

pregnant and if so, the divorcing husband will be required to meet his responsibilities for the new baby. But equally important, however, is that these three months can be a useful cooling-off period in which they hopefully seek a reconciliation, which is also permitted in Islam. If the husband and wife do reconcile, at any time during this period they are permitted to re-enter the marriage without a need for a new contract or a new ceremony or even a new mahr. I glanced at the ticking clock. It was growing late.

"In fact," Fatima continued, "this three-cycle waiting period can be repeated, but if there is mention or demand of divorce a third time, then it cannot be avoided. It becomes permanent, irrevocable. For me it became very clear Faris and I could not agree on this central issue. There was no other solution but to dissolve our fifteen-year marriage."

I wanted to know more. "In the States some couples do re-marry even after divorce. Is this allowed according to Islam?"

"Yes, Qanta, a man is allowed to re-marry the same woman twice. After the third divorce she becomes haram for him to marry. Forbidden."

"So perhaps you and Faris will reconcile one day?" I asked hopefully.

She threw her head back in disbelief. "No chance, Qanta. This is for good." She offered me more coffee, which I accepted. I watched her pour the thin, golden liquid into the small cup. She poured herself some more too and curled her legs up onto the sofa, kicking off her sandals.

"So Fatima, what about you? If not Faris, will you think of marrying again? Or are you done?"

She smiled indulgently to herself and finally in a peal of giggles, looked up at me, quite girlish for a woman of forty-seven.

"Oh yes, Qanta. This time I will marry for romance, for love, for passion! I don't want any more children. Alhumdullilah I have three, Mashallah, long may they live. No, this time I will be completely selfish. I want to be with a man who will take me to Paris and Geneva. I want to have flowers and chocolates and see movies. I want to be courted and cherished!" She hugged her knees tight like a teenager dreaming about her high school crush.

"Wow, that sounds great, Fatima. Where will you find that? What kind of man will he be? Will he be a Saudi?"

"Of course he will, Qanta. I am going to marry a man who is already married. I don't want to marry a naïve bachelor. I want to marry a man whose primary needs are already met." I was nonplussed. She had just denied her husband the opportunity of a second wife, but she was willing to adopt that very role herself?

"I couldn't imagine anything more undesirable, Fatima, than to be with an unavailable man. Where is the fun in that? You would always be second best. Please, I don't understand, can you explain this more clearly? I have never met a woman who wanted to marry a married man. I mean, that's the worst nightmare of every single woman in America."

"Well, Qanta, I have my busy career, my professional conferences, my meetings. My career demands a lot of time. And then I also raise my children. I don't have energy to do this again for another man. I don't want to, in fact. I am not a young girl anymore. I am a forty-seven-year-old woman of the world." I severely doubted her "of the world" statement, but I couldn't deny that she had already raised a family. She was bubbling on in excitement, oblivious to my reaction.

"And most Saudi men would not accept a Saudi wife dedicating so much time to her work. Sometimes I must come in and read emergency biopsies at inconvenient or very late times. You know that." I nodded in confirmation. "But if I married a man who already had one wife, perhaps even two, then there would obviously be evenings when he didn't require me, nights that would be my own, when I can do whatever I chose, whether work at the hospital or take a bubble bath at home. I would have freedom!"

"Marrying a man who is married means freedom to you?"

"Yes, Qanta, of course." And again she giggled.

I was dumbfounded. This was actually something she wanted. "But why didn't you want Faris to have the same freedom?"

"That is completely different! It was not my wish. He was doing that for his own comfort, not for mine."

She sounded bitter. I wondered if she had been uncherished in her marriage to a limited, possibly depressed man. Although Faris was universally accepted to be extremely kind, perhaps meaningful intimacy truly eluded him.

"No, now it is time for me to think of myself. After fifteen years of marriage I want to be selfish. I want something for me, a man who comes to me because he desires me, wants me, wants to spoil me and make me laugh. He is under no obligations to be with me for children. He just wants me for myself. I tell you, that is what I want, and what I will seek! Khalaas!" With the familiar Saudi vernacular for "that's it" or "that's the end of it" she bustled up to the kitchen to make more coffee. She had said the final word on the matter.

I sipped my coffee in puzzled silence. There was something sad and incredibly deprived about Fatima's juvenile aspirations, as though she was planning to finally live her teenage dreams in her later years. Where would her children fit into this scenario with a polygamous man? Did she really believe she would have the care-free, globetrotting trysts of a girlish imagination in a marriage to a married Saudi man? Perhaps I was mistaken. Perhaps that could be possible. But as I watched her slipping her hands into the Rubbermaid gloves to clean out the dregs from the coffee thermos, I severely doubted it. Her life was already half-gone in a marriage cemented around children, not passion. A brilliantly intelligent woman, these years had muted, eroded her blossoming passion, and now I doubted she would ever find sincere partnership in a man in her society. From what I had seen it was highly unlikely. Fatima was a Saudi divorcée and likely to always remain so.

Today she remains without a partner. She never remarried, though Faris eventually did. Her whirlwind romance with a Saudi polygamist never did arrive. But Fatima remains hopeful. Despite her weakening sight, she can still see her dreams clearly.

Chapter Thirty-Two

DESPERATE HOUSEWIVES

I HAD ARRIVED ALONE AT the hotel. Hurrying through the lobby in my abbayah, fearful of the omnipresent Muttawa who could appear without warning, I scurried toward the ladies' hall. Finding it at last by following my nose (there was a cloying smell of heavy scent), I stepped into a ballroom, joining the other ladies. I allowed myself out of my abbayah, comfortable in a room full of women. We were in segregated company. Filipina waitresses circulated with Arabic coffee and sweets. Following the others' lead, I allowed my abbayah to hang from my chair. I chose a spot toward the back of the room.

It was a wintry evening. In anticipation for the cold return journey later that evening, I had come warmly dressed. I quickly discovered I was the most covered woman in the wedding hall, but my itching turtleneck and hot feet were quickly forgotten as I watched the spectacle unfold.

Nadija adjusted her veil in the final moments before she stepped into the blazing spotlights. She stood just a couple of yards from where I sat. I studied the young Saudi bride.

She stood alone. Behind her, two female relatives, bustling in jewel-colored evening gowns, coaxed her toward the staged platform where she would be on display. Nadija was a member of the lower middle class. Unlike her colleague, Zubaidah, she really needed her small salary. Nevertheless, her family had pulled out all the stops at her wedding.

She was dressed exactly like an American bride. She wore a huge, white bridal gown complete with a lace veil that draped over her face, reaching almost to her knees. The dress was pure 1950s Hollywood; all hoop and lace. I was reminded of a young Grace Kelly without the restraining elegance. Everything about the gown and the bride was overdone. The sweetheart neckline was cut low, exposing a young and unblemished cleavage. Her décolletage shuddered under the glacial air conditioning showering from high ceilings. She shivered. Goose-bumped arms were smoothly outlined in shimmering sleeves of jeweled lace, the wrists reaching to the middle of her hand and looping over the middle finger to secure them in place. She rustled as she moved nervously to her destiny.

I looked at her heavily made-up face, studying her profile. Her eyes were deeply lined, her complexion rouged into a vibrant plum, and around her eyes, layers of glitter shone above arched, long brow bones. Unfortunately the makeup conferred a preternaturally startled look on her pretty face. Liquid brown eyes shot brief glances around the room, fearful and nervous as a puppy. Even so, I could still detect ephemeral flutters of excitement behind the carefully painted mask of makeup. Periodically, she broke into a nervous, deeply dimpled smile, exposing a single chip in an upper incisor. This slight, charming imperfection of her toothy grin was the only genuine beauty resilient under the thick dunes of an airbrushed foundation. I watched as she fluttered in her steps, tremulous with circulating adrenaline. I wondered if she thought of her groom.

She clutched a bouquet of creamy white Columbian roses handed to her. Frigid petals trembled with her mounting bridal anxiety. The lovely flowers lacked fragrance, obliterated by hours in the icy hold of cargo planes that had left South America days earlier. Like the beauty surrounding me, the flowers were sterile and lifeless. At last, following final moments of encouragement from women around her, she took a single step forward, revealing a strappy, spiraling, silver stiletto: very Vegas. Her women friends retreated, releasing an audible sigh of relief, easing the pressure of boned bodices barely containing their rippling, already-married bosoms.

She stepped out toward the stage, where a pair of wedding thrones awaited the crowning moment of marriage that was to be recorded in a family album forever. A ginger first step revealed toenails manicured a deep burgundy, matching her hands. She must be menstruating, I decided, by now knowing the Kingdom women's practice of painting nails only during their periods. The orthodox Saudi women believed that proper cleansing before prayers could not be accomplished with nail polish and so they avoided manicures and pedicures during the month when they were not bleeding, when prayer is allowed. When menstruating, Muslim women are not permitted to pray, so at that time, most orthodox and even less-orthodox Saudi women would splurge on their nails. Even Zubaidah followed this practice. Her friend Nadija was probably no different.

Inadvertently I had selected a seat close to the sentinel subwoofer fueling the roar which passed as music. Hungry, because I hadn't eaten since lunch, my head was already beginning to throb and food was hours away. I hadn't been aware; weddings in Riyadh were distinctly late-night affairs. Still, from here, I had a terrific view.

I watched as the bride began to walk. Like so many Saudi women desperate to become wives, this was the moment she had been waiting for since childhood. She was steps away from life as a wife.

The rows were packed; there were at least six hundred women present, the largest gathering I had yet attended in Riyadh, and easily the most dazzling. It was at least forty minutes before I noticed Zubaidah entering the room. She had spotted me, waving at once, but there were other people she had to greet first. I followed her with my gaze, agog.

Zubaidah had exchanged her demure baby-blue daytime shades of chiffon and linen for the svelte lines of a Saudi siren. Regal in a maroon, charmeuse silk gown with oversized diamante buttons, she was utterly dazzling in her womanhood. Her flaxen hair was exquisitely coiffed into glossy, voluminous flounces. Her makeup, though heavy and dated, eyes almost obliterated by dark eye shadow, added to her a new mystique. She looked like a Beiruti chanteuse from the 1950s. Impossibly black eyeliner was seeping into her already red, stinging eyes, as she gazed at onlooking guests with molten allure. Heavy lashes, obviously prosthetic, dragged her hooded lids downward, conferring an even more doe-eyed look than usual. Her ample bust was beautifully captured in a tasteful, ruched neckline. As she extended a long-sleeved, elegant, but definitely plump arm to elderly dowagers who ringed the stage in circles of crooked sentries, she cut a dashing but still conservative figure. Zubaidah was the model prospective bride-to-be.

In comparison, other women had clearly lost the plot entirely. Their fleshy desperation was on full display, either to forget the misery of their marriages for a few hours or to somehow scrabble into the mystery of marriages they were desperate to enter. The amount of exposed flesh was unbelievable. I had never seen this much leg, breast, and thigh in New York City. I couldn't believe this was Riyadh. I couldn't believe these women were Muslim.

In my dumpy outfit, I had already attracted disapproving looks. I was inappropriately dressed for such an important occasion. I wore no jewels. My clothes had no shine, glitter, or polish. The other women had evidently spent hours, some even days, in preparation. Around me almost all women were in sleeveless dresses; in this instance Zubaidah was an exception. I spied colossal jewels: Cellini, Di Grisogono, Kwiat, and Damiani, to name a few. These were jewels one only ever saw in magazines, but at a dietician's wedding, they were common currency.

The jewels lay on bared expanses of creamy skin, though one or two women may have been as dark complexioned as I was. Most wore dresses a couple of sizes too small, accentuating fulsome breasts, some still lactating, others clearly lifted and augmented. The plump circular outlines of hardened silicon implants were dead giveaways of a visit to the plastic surgeon, likely in Jordan or Beirut. Perhaps some of them had even been revised by Mu'ayyad, my plastic surgery colleague who often salvaged the worst breast jobs from around the Persian Gulf.

Coolly he once mentioned the commonest indication for breast implants in the Kingdom was a bored husband pondering the assumption of a second wife. Desperate to avoid this, women rushed to him in droves for plastic surgery, pleading with him for revisions or further augmentations. Mu'ayyad calmly explained that breast implants would never be a salve to a wounded relationship, sending them away without the silicone breastplates they craved to protect failing loves. He turned many of these desperate housewives away, leaving them to find a less-scrupulous surgeon who would agree to carve away their mounting fears of wife number two.

But tonight, whether silicon or adipose, the high domes of breasts were scaffolding to gravity-defying gowns. Too-narrow dresses cut viciously into the once-small waists of several-babies-ago. Merciless satin spilled ugly panniculi of lumpy fat unhinged by the cruel seams. The scene was an anarchic Oscar night without stylists to hold back the poor-tasted, petulant appetites of the diva army.

Many women wore backless dresses, some forgoing efforts to hide cumbersome brassieres in the process. I studied the layers of flab cascading down the back of a woman who was already dancing to the unbearably loud music. Her black bra strap crushed her back into a bizarre reverse cleavage—fascinatingly ugly.

The bride wasn't the only one exposing fledgling cleavage. Far more brazen, her guests were competing with one another in plunging necklines and dresses slit to reveal plump and newly waxed legs that had never seen a StairMaster. The draconian makeup was reminiscent of an Egyptian soap opera. Nothing was left to the imagination. Every feature was intensified; lips, eyes, and cheeks all were emphasized until the women resembled Pharonic masks. Rather like Carnivale, I was attending a masked ball in Riyadh. The garish makeup ensured I couldn't distinguish anyone's expression. Somehow the women were still veiled, even when so exposed. And funnier still, they all seemed to have been to the same makeup artist.

Like actresses in a Saudi Mikado, high and hard eye shadow was heavy, dragged upward into a near-Japanese altitude at the edges of the eyes to make the eyes appear even wider apart. They looked like transsexual Geishas. Faces were whitened with dense foundations, enhancing even naturally light-colored skin to a further extreme. In the middle of the smoothed, unlined canvas, collagen-injected mouths were rubied into hard, garish gashes that moved relentlessly over yellowed, lipstick-flecked teeth as they mouthed mummified pleasantries, repeated on endless loops.

The only women unaffected by the desire to compete in this display of bosoms and behinds and Botox were an inner circle of older matrons. They dressed conservatively, many of them remaining in their abbayahs, or else revealing their dour, glum, tent-like dresses that swept loosely over robust, often obese figures. Invariably they wore clothes patterned in burnt-orange-and-brown paisleys, tiny patterns magnifying their heaviness. A sickly sweet scent of attar floated from the grand dame army, hovering just above in thick clouds of rose vapor. The matrons didn't depend on jewels or satin or expensive updos for their status. Their breasts were unaugmented expanses of flattened flesh long abandoned by overstretched brassieres. Instead their bosoms sagged on ligaments stretched loose by endless pregnancies and relentless decades of breast-feeding. These women were exalted. Their status was codified in the generations of sons and daughters they had birthed and the grandsons which had followed.

Like a ring of Mafia mothers, they held court, slowly lifting their thick, turkey-necked, weighty heads in appraisal of prospective brides like Zubaidah. They peered at the younger women with reptilian eyes surmounted by balding eyebrows, giving away the prevalent underlying hypothyroidism. They scratched their thinning scalps with unjewelled fingers, tipped in fresh orange henna. Now and again a solitary gold bangle caught the light, but otherwise they remained unadorned.

Matchmaking, however, was feverishly unfolding as I watched, and ever-hopeful, over-bearing mothers clucked their daughters forward to the paisley-clad, stumpy matrons, hoping perhaps to ensnare a potential son-in-law by the end of the evening. A beady-eyed once-over had the potential to make the eager single woman into the much-sought-after housewife that so many women in this city desperately dreamed of becoming.

I watched Zubaidah's pearly smile crinkle repeatedly under pressure. She had been going through this with her avant-garde mother for years. Tonight her own mother didn't even attend, bored by the dull proceedings that every winter wedding circuit seemed to bring. Still, out of respect, Zubaidah called on the other mothers, most of whom knew her and seemed genuinely happy to see her. Inside, I was certain Zubaidah hated every minute of the proceedings, but she was too gracious to admit as much, even to herself. Rather than stay home yet another evening, she compelled herself to engage in the social duties of attending a colleague's wedding. Being at this wedding surely reminded her that as a single woman over twenty-five in the Kingdom, others believed she should by now be desperate to be a housewife. At her age she was no longer in a position to choose; her best years were already behind her.

The bride walked up a central aisle, unaccompanied, to the stage. No one gave her away. She proceeded to the stage in a slow march in time to the garish music. Clutching her fluttering bouquet under an unforgiving glare of flashbulbs and fluorescent lights, she continued on her path forward. As the female Saudi photographer captured wedding moments on film, women around the room scurried to veil or duck, avoiding incriminating photography of their cleavages and dimpled, satin-wrapped rears. Performing a strange Mexican wave, in choreographed synchrony, the women lifted their arms into abbayahs, draping their heads and shoulders into the blackness as the searchlight of the photographers' flashbulb swept across the room.

From the far left of the stage, the wedding singers began their ceremonial renditions. An all-female, ebony-skinned, svelte-limbed Sudanese drumming quartet released the high-pitched, ululating soprano cries, the hallmark of marriage in the Kingdom. In the face of cameras, only the bride remained unveiled, her glittered eyes creasing deeply as she smiled and blinked back tears of emotion. Finally, she reached the stage and perched, head high and still unveiled, on an overstuffed white brocade sofa-throne, surrounded by arrangements of white roses and sweeping palm fronds. She surveyed the kitsch tableau of her entry into married life with evident pride. I had no doubt she felt queen-like. Unlike the arranged brides at weddings I had seen in my childhood, she was clearly glowing with excitement and did not fear marriage. She was relishing the prospect of becoming a wife to the unseen groom who was presently celebrating with menfolk in an adjoining ballroom.

By midnight the men had not appeared and, exhausted from waiting for refreshments or further spectacle, I took my leave. I rubbed my breastbone to soothe the racing heart caused by hours of cardamom-laced Arabic coffee.

As I turned to exit, Zubaidah was still ensconced in a circle of dancing women who had wrapped scarves around their hips and were sedately gyrating to thumping music. The lighting remained mercilessly bright, but the women were undeterred, shifting their weight from side to side, briefly encircling the bravest wedding guests of all, those who dared dance a solo in the center of the circle. Zubaidah was firmly situated in the safety amid the ranks of satin and chiffon. She didn't see me leave.

As I moved through the lobby I could hear the rising roar of men chanting in song. The sounds were coming from the adjoining ballroom where men were locking arms and performing a choreographed sword dance, likely the brothers and uncles and father of the groom. The groom was not likely to join his bride in the women's room until the early hours of the morning or later the next day.

Later, Zubaidah would confirm he didn't arrive until after 2 a.m. Notice of course was provided and the women who were not family could fully veil in preparation for the influx of men. Only after he entered and took his seat on the upholstered wedding throne next to his bride (who by then was crumpled with exhaustion from a dizzying vapor of excitement, stress, and hunger) was dinner finally served. I had made the right decision to leave early. By the time the groom looked woodenly at his nervous new wife, I was already deeply asleep. Even my hunger had been unable to keep me awake.

Several days later I described my experiences of the wedding to Zubaidah, explaining that I had left before seeing the men enter.

"Qanta, I looked to see where you were but I couldn't see you. I was searching for you around one a.m." Zubaidah paused, awaiting my explanation, far too polite to explain just quite how insulting my behavior was as a guest who left before dinner was served.

"Zubaidah, it was so late! I was starving. I felt as though I had to wait for dinner as long as I have to wait to find my own husband!" and we both laughed in unison.

"What about you, Zubaidah, will you have a wedding like this? Is that what you want, Zubaidah?"

"Wa Allah, Qanta, that is a difficult question." Zubaidah cocked her head to the side, considering her response. "Of course, I would like to be married, but I pray Allah finds me the right man. I am not desperate to be married. My family is educated, they are liberal. They would like to see me settled, but there is no requirement for me to do this in a rush. Alhumdullilah, my father is very understanding, and so too my mother." She went on to explain the conundrum her unmarried state continued to present, both for herself and her family.

Periodically her mother and father invited prospective suitors. They would arrive at their elegant family home and take tea with both parents and Zubaidah. In these strained and highly choreographed events Zubaidah would perhaps have a very short conversation with the suitor while the parents waited discreetly in another living room in the home. Zubaidah had been through these events on many occasions. She was accustomed to the tedium of receiving and graciously declining a number of proposals.

"Wa Allah, Qanta, we just don't find anyone suitable." I waited for her to continue.

"Recently I was introduced to a man from Damascus. He was much older—widowed, but he had no children. He was OK, Qanta, but I didn't feel anything, and I suspected he was not very educated.

He was not very good-looking either. I know he had wealth, but that is not enough for me. I can't explain it. I just did not have a good feeling and I am not sure if he was really serious about Islam, the way I am.

"You have to understand my father, my brothers, Mourad and Haroon, are very educated. I cannot be with anyone less. Everyone agrees on this. I suppose I will be married only when Allah chooses. I have stopped worrying."

"But don't you wish to seek independence, Zubaidah? I mean while you are waiting, why not travel, work overseas, just have some independence and fun. Have you thought about that?" I was unsatisfied with her response. Surely she wanted more than to simply wait.

"No, Qanta, I have no desires like you to live alone, or to have my own apartment or to be financially independent. I have never wanted what you want. I love to be with my family. Alhumdullilah I am very comfortable in my father's home. You see I have my own suite here. I couldn't bear to be away, thousands of miles from them, like you. I should be terribly lonely. I just don't have the same desire to be apart from my family as you. I never will." I just stared at Zubaidah, wondering how she could be so different, to the point that her fire of independence, which surely burns deeply in all women, vanished?

Little by little I realized she had never needed to rebel. She accepted her lifestyle and her family's expectations and had fully embraced them as her own. Unlike me, she was not in conflict with her cultural expectations; rather she was cocooned by them. She had no need to surge with rebellion and overcome restrictions she didn't even identify as such; she was cozy and comfortable amid convention. Here lay our difference: in my family I was an anomaly; in my culture an outcast. In hers, she was accepted, the conformist; and was, in fact, most fulfilled being nothing else.

While the Southeast Asian and Saudi cultures were undoubtedly similar in the pursuit of marriage (which was arranged and often endogamous), Zubaidah's relationship to her culture was diametrically opposite to mine. What I resented, she welcomed. What I rebelled from, she embraced. What I dreaded, she longed for. I looked at her across the table, preoccupied in unknown thoughts, stirring the foam in a creamy cappuccino, her hooded eyes casting heavy, crescent shadows of long lashes over her porcelain skin. She seemed content, not despondent. She was patient; she was not desperate. She would become a wife only if Allah willed it and until then she was content to wait. She wanted little more.

Nadija's wedding prompted me to wonder more about the dreams my Saudi women friends held for themselves. There were several women I wanted to know more about; perhaps I would find they too were desperate housewives themselves. I had so much to learn about the female Saudi psyche. As I learned more, I was finding that it was often both partly familiar and partly alien.

I set off to speak to the Saudi Jackie Onassis look-alike, as I liked to think of Ghadah. I wondered if her life of marriage to a surgeon and mother to three daughters was the romantic dream it appeared from the outside. At the same time I decided to compare notes with Reem who, like me, was still single into her early thirties, and, a talented surgeon, hell-bent on pursuing a vascular fellowship in Canada. I wanted to know more about the Kingdom's women, whether already desperate housewives or desperate to become such.

THE MAKING OF A FEMALE SAUDI SURGEON

REEM'S REPUTATION PRECEDED HER. SHE was beloved by nurses, widely respected by her Saudi and Western colleagues, and clearly held in awe by the sprawling sandaled troops of male Saudi surgeons (many of whom were military officers in the Saudi Arabian National Guard) whom she trained in her role as senior surgical resident. They followed her on rounds very much like chicks following a mother hen. Deferent, they waited for her to opine and reveal her knowledge to them. They hung on her every soft-spoken word, carefully drawn maps, and detailed instruction as she gently taught them the science of surgery both within the operating room and outside it. She executed all of her duties without ever wavering from Islamic ideals.

She was already a familiar sight at the National Guard Hospital as she scurried from patient to patient whether long before dawn or late into the lonely night. Her hair was never exposed, even by accident, because she always secured her headscarf with small safety pins, tucking the ends into her V-necked, green surgical scrubs which themselves were covered by a white coat buttoned up to the throat. She moved through her work effortlessly and unencumbered by her restrictions required of her expression of Islam.

Whenever I saw her I knew she must have been uncomfortably hot even within the air-conditioned marble wards and hallways of the ICU, surgical wards, or the sterile finality of the operating room. She would sweat with effort at securing a line, finishing meticulous sutures, or cleansing a purulent wound, yet still she did everything with grace, patience, and evident pleasure. Sometimes she emerged from the operating room sprayed with blood, but always her gown closed, her hair covered, and her soft voice gently reassuring the worried families who had been awaiting the outcome. She was a paragon of the female Muslim professional. Reem was the archetypal Saudi female surgeon.

Even in crises or when she had reason to be provoked, she never raised her voice, she never displayed her frustrations. I had been watching her for some time, noticing her go about her duties whenever she entered the ICU to write surgical orders on my patients. As she moved silently and efficiently she often cast a pleasant smile in my direction.

Yet for a time she remained an enigma to me. I was inhibited by her decorous behavior, which somehow spotlighted the deficiencies in my own conduct. While I could see I was crashing into fury and anger several times a day, unable to navigate conflicts with even remote diplomacy, Reem remained perfectly in control of herself. With so much turmoil in my own behavior and such tranquility in hers, I was deeply puzzled and suddenly shy to know such a woman. How did she glide through her life when I was forever stumbling? I wanted to know more about her.

I already knew that the salient qualities of an ideal Muslim are encompassed in valuing self-control—control of one's actions, one's body, one's tongue and ultimately one's soul. As Muslims age and engage in the practice of Islam with greater understanding and insight through their lifetimes, their ultimate goal of emulating the Prophet Muhammad (PBUH) in excellence of compassionate behaviors drives them to seek to become more God-like. They strive toward tolerance and patience and perseverance. These are perhaps the finest aspirations Muslims can express and to me, it seemed that at thirty-one, Reem had virtually arrived at this stage already. I couldn't be further removed from these ideals with my mouthy New York City aphorisms that dropped from me at the slightest irritation. I was ugly; she was pure. Against the turbulent backdrop of the fast-paced, high-octane ICU, Reem shimmered, a lake of tranquility. She was unaffected by pandemonium surrounding her, whether required to attend several traumas at once or to seek resolution among an arguing cabal of clinicians competing to impose their self-important opinions. She seemed angelic. I was just pondering this very thought yet again, when Reem marched directly toward me.

"Dr. Ahmed, I am the senior surgical resident, Reem Jumma." It seemed she didn't realize I knew who she was. "I wanted to let you know I have written the transfer orders for the patient in bed nine. He can go to the ward anytime you choose." Quietly, she waited for me to respond.

"Thank you, Dr. Jumma." Without pausing, I found myself spilling my tirade. "I have been calling for these orders all morning. It's unbelievable it has taken so long to get them done! So frustrating!" I noted her patient eyes calmly absorbing my irritation. I was somewhat subdued by her gaze. "Well," I continued, "it's very kind of you to come and write them, but can you tell me how to avoid these delays in the future? The ER is constantly calling to move patients from their holding area here, and until I have orders, I can't transfer patients out to make room for new admissions." I had begun to sound lame, as though I was still complaining at the delay in orders that Reem had just resolved.

Unperturbed she responded, "I am very sorry that my residents caused you to wait. I will address the matter myself but in the future please just call me. I will be happy to assist." I was firmly but gently defused. She was offering her services above and beyond the call of duty and seemed not the least bit bothered by my plaintive bleating. Just as she turned around to leave the ICU, I touched her arm.

"Reem, it would be lovely to meet when we are not at work. Let me give you my numbers." She burst into an unrestrained and very wide smile revealing small, even teeth. Her grin briefly rectified the asymmetrical plainness of her face that somehow accorded her the pathos that struck me as her hallmark. Her voice rose in excitement as she confirmed our plans to meet, displaying raw emotion for the first time. As she scribbled her numbers on a scrap of paper, her eyes twinkled joyfully. In that moment I knew we had commenced a friendship that would last well beyond my time in the Kingdom.

We met a few weeks later. After an evening of window-shopping we settled in a favorite café.

"Tell me, Reem, how did you decide to pursue surgery as your career? How does a woman become a surgeon in the Kingdom, a Saudi woman at that? What are your plans after residency here?"

Reem stirred the crystallized-sugar swizzle stick in her foamy café latte. We were at a table at Jawad's coffeehouse on Thalia Street, one of my favorite spots in Riyadh. We had found a secure place behind a screened section for women. Reem had undone her scarf, allowing me to see her luscious, thick, black hair. The glossy locks transformed her from a surgical nun to a very attractive woman. I wondered if Reem knew how beautiful she was. Even though she was continually devoid of makeup and her eyebrows were ungroomed, she was lovely looking. The plainness of her open features merely added to her charm.

"Well, Qanta, I am from a very educated family. My father is a professor of economics. He lectures at a university in Jeddah. He always believed it was very important I get an education, and we all agreed medicine was a noble and fine career choice. Alhumdullilah, I was able to find a place at the King Abdul Aziz Medical School in Riyadh and I won a National Guard scholarship to sponsor my residency in surgery. That's when I switched to our hospital at the National Guard. I have been there four years. This is my last year."

"What are you planning on next, Reem?" She released a clumsy gale of high-spirited peals. I was surprised by the volume of her laughter. She seemed suddenly and totally uninhibited.

"Oh Qanta, I want to be a vascular surgeon! That's my passion. I can't tell you how much I love repairing the circulation and watching limbs re-perfuse again. That's my greatest joy. My dream is to have a vascular surgery practice. I am working toward that."

I was astonished; vascular surgery is one of the most blood-sucking, soul-destroying, pride-swallowing surgical areas to pursue. One needs the patience of a saint to be a good vascular surgeon, to constantly rebuild and bypass clogged arteries and dying veins only to see one's painstaking handiwork destroyed by a patient's addiction to tobacco or the inexorable course of diabetes. The surgeries are invariably long, backbreaking, and infinitely humbling exercises in surgical fortitude. What an interesting choice for Reem. She was a glutton for punishment in my estimation, but perhaps her preference spoke to her evident talents for resilience, compassion, and tolerance.

"Will your fellowship be here, Reem? I didn't know they had a vascular surgery fellowship in Riyadh."

"Well, Qanta, they don't have a fellowship yet, but Inshallah they will someday soon. In the meantime, my mentor Dr. Saud al-Turki is encouraging me to apply for fellowship in vascular surgery at the University of Toronto."

I had to interrupt, "Toronto, Reem? That's incredible news. You must go. How exciting Reem!" She gave in to her own excitement in another smile and spilled her coffee while she allowed herself another full-throttled laugh of pure pleasure.

"Well, Dr. al-Turki has been amazing, Qanta. He is such an incredible mentor. He is always encouraging me. He treats me and the other female residents with incredible respect and consideration. He is the perfect Saudi gentleman, and he really does believe women are worthy of pursuing the most advanced studies available. Plus he allows me opportunities to publish and speak; he helped me prepare my first case report as a second-year resident. He even encouraged my parents to think about allowing me to move to Toronto. I couldn't ask for a better teacher." Her voice deepened with sincerity at the dedication of her teacher who sounded to me like a model mentor.

"Do you think you are influenced by Dr. al-Turki? I mean, because he is so compassionate and such an elegant and intelligent Muslim. Do you think that's why you want to do vascular? Perhaps your aspiration is to somehow become him?" Reem paused to give this some thought.

I knew from my own experience the relationship between academic mentor and the mentored could be a heady mix of nurturing, idealism, and unquestionably (if the relationship is rewarding) a lasting, deep love. Perhaps she had found the same experience too.

"It is quite possible, Qanta." She cocked her head to one side trying to focus on a deeper answer. "I do wish to succeed and I have no doubt that I am drawn to his specialty because, of all the surgeons in the OR, he was the one who taught me with real compassion and dignity. The others did what they could, but I often felt they didn't believe I should be in the operating room with so many men there. Dr. al-Turki made me feel only like a surgeon. It was immaterial to him whether I was male or female. We just had a common goal, to perform surgery in the best way. And I think that's why I naturally gravitated toward emulating him."

She paused and sipped her coffee. "It is possible, Qanta. Perhaps he has really influenced me in the choice of specialty I wish to cultivate for my own career. I agree, I must concede you that, at least."

She stopped speaking, following her own train of thought in silence. Among everything else I was also startled at her flawless command of English. Like most of my Saudi colleagues, she had schooled within the Kingdom yet learned the Queen's English. Even so, she spoke perfect colloquial Arabic, could discuss and prescribe medicine in English and Arabic, and had enough command of her native tongue to understand the exalted classical Arabic in which the Quran is written. I soon discovered in Reem a repository of knowledge in matters of Islamic jurisprudence. Whether I wanted an explanation of Islamic teachings on divorce or inheritance or the Islamic ideals of observing Ramadan, Reem seemed to have acquired enormous knowledge beyond medicine.

I asked about her astonishing knowledge of Islam.

"Well, Qanta, I went to school in Jeddah at a state school. Islamic studies were mandatory. We took classes for five years in several disciplines. Quranic studies, the history of Islam, Islamic jurisprudence, the life of the Prophet, and also Islamic theology. Every child who goes to school in the Kingdom has to attend these classes. But the reality is my father is an incredible scholar, so anything especially difficult we could always go and ask him. My mother, too, is very learned, though she has never worked outside of the home. They love poetry and the history of Islam and my father also knows Farsi, so we have also read a great deal about the Persian culture.

"All of us children were raised in the Kingdom. This is my country, our home. I do understand that to be a vascular surgeon— the first woman vascular surgeon in the Kingdom—would help my countrymen a lot, Qanta. There are women who have ischemic leg ulcers and do not want to seek treatment because all the physicians and surgeons are usually male. They need the skills of women like me." She studied me earnestly, checking to see if I had absorbed the full import of her commitment.

I had met this sincere commitment to improving the Kingdom time and time again, whether issuing from curved, moustached lips of aristocratic Saudi academics, or the bare, unglossed lips of earnest Saudi female clinicians. They revealed an affection for their nation of enormous and very sincere dimensions. I had no doubt that doctors like Reem, al-Turki, and Mu'ayyad were very much driven by a deep desire to improve medicine for the average Saudi national. I was struck by Reem's altruism and searched for signs of the same within myself. I wasn't sure when I had lost my ideals of serving the needy and seamlessly replaced them with an insatiable hunger for reward. I had definitely lost something along the way that Reem, like so many of the pioneering Saudi clinicians I knew, clearly had not.

They worked not only for the patients in their immediate charge but, through these actions and choices, by striving for a role of public service in their country, also for the wider community. There was no doubt in their minds that what they chose to do and how they exercised their skills and privilege was moving their country forward in tiny degrees; like a bloated oil tanker changing direction, every miniscule and unseen effort helped moved the behemoth Kingdom toward modernity and advancement. Reem, like many of the Saudis I met, was a die-hard idealist, willing to direct her career to serve that calling. Like all of her Saudi colleagues, she had the credentials and clout to pursue a fine medical career outside of the Kingdom, but instead she wished to invest her expertise within her native land.

We were finishing our coffee that had since grown cold. Outside, Thalia Street was illuminated with glossy boutique stores selling precious dates, fine culinary items, and the ubiquitous, exclusive jewelry. We noticed that our driver had appeared, waiting to take us both back to the compound. As a single working woman, like me, Reem had an identical apartment on compound where she preferred to live rather than stay as a perpetual houseguest at her sister's married home, which was also in Riyadh. Reem's family trusted her implicitly and allowed her an unusual degree of independence.

In so many ways, Reem thought, acted, and lived exactly like me. Within this Kingdom I was discovering some very liberated, independent, powerful, and highly intellectual women. Interestingly, I was beginning to discern the glimmers of a new insight. I began that evening to realize most of these extraordinary women had arrived in these circumstances by dint of progressive fathers and nurturing male mentors. In the Kingdom, women were gaining their opportunities with the encouragement and often unabashed support of their male Saudi counterparts. This was a complex tapestry of inter-gender cooperation that was finally coming into view, antithetical to the rabid preachings of the state-sponsored Wahabi clergy who wished women voiceless, invisible, and socially inert.

After months of feeling, seeing, and experiencing male supremacy, I was discovering the most fervent supporters and enablers of women's liberation in the Kingdom often came in the form of enlightened men, whether through fatherhood, marriages, or professional mentorships. The Saudi male was much more than I had realized, and Reem, without discounting her own personal efforts or minimizing her own determination and appetite for development, was a product of exactly these forces. I felt myself warming to the Saudi male. I had sorely underestimated him. But there was more to Reem than met the eye. A week later she called me for an evening of conversation.

"Qanta, I have news!" Reem's voice was pressured and tense with excitement.

"What is it?" I asked, rousing myself from the void of a nap that had found me painfully curled up on my eternally lumpy sofa. I patted around to find my eyeglasses that I had cast off in a foggy doze some hours earlier. Reem was jabbering at high speed. It took me a while to understand exactly what she was telling me.

"I got accepted! University of Toronto! I have the fellowship! I can't believe it, Qanta! I am going to be a vascular surgeon!"

"Congratulations, Reem, when did you hear? Mashallah that is terrific. You will be the first female vascular surgeon in the Kingdom! I am so proud of you. You deserve this. Quickly, I want to know first, what did Dr. al-Turki say when you told him?"

"Oh Qanta, *he* told *me*! He was ecstatic. He called me at home and then he called my parents to congratulate them. He heard from the program director in Toronto that I matched. I am so excited, I cannot tell you. This is a dream come true for me. It's hard to believe it is actually happening." She released a gale of laughter which I couldn't help sharing. We giggled for a while, clutching our telephones.

Still holding the phone, I slipped my feet into slippers and started to open the windows in the apartment, hoping for the evening breeze to sweep through the musty apartment. Reem was rattling off more news, without pausing even for breath. As I listened to her animated voice, I poured myself some water. The day had been unusually hot and, as the top apartment of the block, my apartment took hours for the superheated ceilings to cool down.

Outside, the Maghreb (evening) Azaan sounded. A scraggly flock of pigeons rose into the air, startled by a stray cat.

"When do you leave, Reem?" I asked, thinking already how much I would miss my lovely friend and colleague. In the past months we had solved so many clinical problems together. I had discovered she was a brilliant clinician and she often helped me turn over difficult problems in the patients we shared.

"Well, Qanta the fellowship starts in July, like all programs over there." I already knew this but still waited to hear her plans. "But I need permission from my father first. You know I can't travel without his consent and it's going to be difficult for my family…" she trailed off. I detected the first tones of uncertainty.

"But Reem," I caught myself defending her, already adopting sides of an invisible argument, "you have lived away from them for years in Riyadh. You live alone here. They know how seriously you take your career. Of course it will be terrible in the beginning. All the homesickness in Canada, the horrible winters. But I have confidence you, and they, will get over it. I am sure they will and of course, two years are going to fly by so fast, you won't even know you are gone before it's time to come back!" I ended on a triumphant note; what was there to discuss? She had to go. Anything else was clearly out of the question.

Reem responded slowly, carefully, "My father is a conservative man, Qanta."

"But you mentioned he is so educated, a professor," I hastened to interrupt, not understanding where Reem was leading.

"Yes, Qanta, he is indeed highly educated, but he still is concerned about me as his only unmarried daughter. He didn't allow me to attend a surgical conference at the European Vascular Course in Marseilles last year. Here in the Kingdom an unmarried woman has to have the written permission of her male guardian in order to travel outside to meetings or to study. My father did not grant that."

"Why not, Reem? All you would be doing is anastomosis work-shops and attending some lectures. So what if it was in beautiful Marseilles?" I could feel my indignation rising.

"It's difficult for him, Qanta. Saudi society, even in more-relaxed Jeddah, is still very conservative. If he is seen to be too liberal with his daughter, there could be consequences to my reputation."

"But that's rubbish, Reem. You are the most honorable woman I know. You would never violate their trust, and you are old enough to choose your own path. Allah knows your inner intentions. Tell your father to stop worrying about this and trust in the fine daughter he has raised." Then I added, "Honestly, Reem, that's ridiculous." I couldn't help voicing my anger. Her concerns reminded me of women in my own family raised within the confines of expatriate Pakistani culture. I couldn't believe what I was hearing this young surgeon tell me.

"So," she continued guardedly now that she sensed my concern about her decisions, "I am well aware that if I insist on assuming my place in the fellowship, I will only be allowed to go as a married or engaged woman. Without that it will be impossible for me to migrate." I was speechless.

"My father mentioned this to me when I was applying. He didn't prevent me at all—far from it, he encouraged me—but he made it clear he could never allow me overseas without being spoken for."

It was as simple as that. Reem would not be allowed the chance to pursue fellowship unless she had given herself away in a commit-ment to marriage. I was amazed. Reem had never mentioned any aspirations for married life. I suspected, like me, she would pursue a career first and then worry about those matters much later. In her case this path wasn't an option. Career could only come at the price of marriage whether or not this was an aspiration. This was not a desperate housewife scenario, this was a desperate surgeon scenario;

a surgeon who would attain her credentials only through marriage rather than in spite of or without marriage.

"What about your mother? Surely she doesn't think this is a good idea, compelling marriage just so that you get to study a little more? I can't believe she supports this, Reem."

"My mother says nothing. It is up to Father, but she is very concerned about my solitude in Toronto. I think privately she prefers I have a fiancé. That would reassure her."

"So you have agreed, Reem? Are you actually telling me that you have decided to marry so you can attend a fellowship?"

My voice was filled with undisguised anger. I couldn't believe a woman so intelligent could be so stupid and so weak. Why couldn't she defy her family, like I had been able to? Why were women so spineless? And why were our own mothers so eternally silent? To where in the world had all the maternal indignation gone? I could tell from my trembling voice there was more feeling in me than just about her situation. I was thinking about every snatched opportunity I had to claw back toward myself, always fending off the specter of arranged marriage with a pitchfork of determination and defiance.

"Of course, I agreed. I have no options, Qanta. If I don't agree, my father will not approve my exit visa applications, and I cannot enter Canada. I have wanted to pursue vascular surgery for years now, and I am not going to be stubborn about it. If I have to marry, I have to marry. I see no problem with that." She was suddenly firm in her authority.

"Have they selected anyone for you yet?" I asked sheepishly.

"Yes, Qanta, a Saudi from Jeddah. He is in IT. The oldest son, he is responsible for his retired parents; his name is Sultan. We met last weekend in my parents' house. Qanta, I really like him!" This last remark shocked me. Reem had just met a stranger and was contemplating marriage and actually sounded excited. And I had thought her my alter ego!

"We are going to be engaged, Qanta! I can't wait for you to meet him!"

"Will Sultan accompany you to Canada, Reem, perhaps after the wedding ceremony?" I asked, completely confused. Perhaps that had been the point of the engagement, so that he would be able to chaperone her around Toronto. Better still, as a husband he could live with her and be her protection, guarding her honor from whatever her parents and their community feared.

"Oh no, Qanta, he will remain in Jeddah working and saving for the wedding. We will communicate by telephone and Internet. I can't believe how many hours we spend on MSN Messenger already. I am not sure, but I could be falling in love."

I had nothing further to say. From my vantage, the cool calm surgeon was gripped in a demented delirium that I had seen affect so many Muslim women who had no contact with the opposite sex outside their immediate relatives. They thought themselves in love in a matter of weeks. They made decisions to commit their lives to strange men without even a pause or hesitation. It was such a polar opposite to the values I had absorbed in the West, the values that had subsumed those of my parents' culture.

What earthly protection could her fiancé on the other end of a dial-up connection in the Hijaz offer her in wintry Toronto? Who in Toronto would care whether the vascular surgical fellow was a married woman or not? Reem had already informed me she planned to continue wearing her headscarf in Canada, so I couldn't imagine she would be accosted by curious Canadian men. The headscarf alone was deterrent enough in my opinion, particularly in Canada, where sensitivities to foreign cultures in cities like Toronto were fairly pervasive. And how could Jeddah society be placated and Reem's honor preserved by her cyber-betrothal? I had a million logical questions.

Inside I knew the answers already. It came down to the age-old enemy of independence: what people will think. Like my family,

Reem's family feared what other people would think if they allowed her to leave the Kingdom unattached. This fear outweighed any other decision for the family as a whole, irrespective of the fact that Reem had secured the only scholarship for vascular surgery in the Kingdom and that she was making history by becoming the first Saudi female to train in this discipline. That was immaterial. What really mattered for Saudi daughters, like Pakistani ones, was what other people thought.

In the weeks that followed, Reem quickly became formally engaged and began to return to Jeddah on weekends more often than her custom prior to engagement. There she would meet her fiancé in her family home, or sometimes his, always chaperoned. It was clear she would soon be a married woman but first she would begin her fellowship in Canada as an engaged woman. In the weeks leading up to her June departure, she asked me to be part of her farewell party, which some female surgeons were busy planning. There would be a soiree at her apartment on the compound. Recently returned from a few weeks out of the Kingdom myself, I was excited to attend and give Reem a proper send-off.

As I arrived at her apartment, I found myself in the middle of a scurrying throng of Saudi women. They were all dressed in pretty daytime ensembles, mostly long skirts and long-sleeved blouses. The air was thick with perfume and heavy with hair spray. Every woman was long-haired and none other than Reem and I were raven-haired. Most were dyed reddish in pretty shades that complemented their warm skin tones. The women laughed and giggled, occasionally leaning on chairs to ease a stitch caused by so much giggling. Most of the conversations were in Arabic, so I was left to watch the scene in puzzled silence.

Glasses were filled with sparkling apple juice, known widely in the Kingdom as "Saudi Champagne." Reeme, a junior surgical resident and one of Reem's closest friends, was busy arranging fresh mint leaves inside long flutes readied for the sparkling juice. Another friend, Leila, a medicine intern, was scooping ice out of the ice maker, occasionally spilling cubes onto the marble floor.

Next to me I knew this was Mai, also a young surgeon. Though she had been at the National Guard only a year, she already had a well-earned reputation as a defiant wild child more at home in South Kensington than Saudi Arabia. She was already whipping up a storm of controversy with accounts of her antics in Europe the previous summer. She was fun.

I glanced at Reem. In the midst of this joyous party I noticed she looked overwhelmed and a little bit awkward at the sight of so much revelry in her name. She was uncomfortable with the genuine warmth that so many women surgeons and physicians at the hospital clearly held for her. We gathered our plates, filling them with delicacies, and settled in the sitting room, a sewing circle of Saudi surgeons.

Mai was laughing raucously about a quip she had just cracked. The others were in stitches.

Mai and I talked about how much we liked the gym where we both worked out, a welcome relief from the daily drudgery of Riyadh life. The al-Multaqa was always a glossy, cosseted, and very satisfying experience. A women-only venue, we could allow our abbayahs to fall away and move through the high, opaque-glass atriums and saunter toward aerobics classes or browse the Internet in a downstairs café or study the latest fashions imported from Paris and London. The architecture was airy and Scandinavian with a touch of Vegas about it.

Mostly we loved it because there was no need to veil inside where everyone, the cleaners, the waitresses, and the instructors were women. On this we agreed and as we discussed our weekly routine I realized why we had never really spoken inside the club. By the time I arrived, Mai was usually huffing and puffing as she did her crunches and reps on the StairMaster. Sometimes she stretched out her tired muscles on the yoga mats next to the ballet bar, eyeing herself critically in the floor-to-ceiling mirrors. Ruddy-faced, we usually nodded a brisk hello to each other before going our separate ways, she ending her workout as I began mine. I had no idea until today that she was a friend of Reem.

"So how did you like London, Mai? You were telling me…" I prompted her to continue, "You mentioned you lived in South Kensington?"

"Yes, Qanta, or 'Saudi Kensington' as I like to call it. London is fabulous. The restaurants, the shopping, the movies, the bookstores, it's all great except that, like Geneva or Marbella, half of Riyadh is there at the same time. Even London can get to be a bit suffocating."

Mai paused while I tried to think of something diplomatic to say. She had a very staccato mode of communicating, leaving me forever unprepared for the ends of her sentences. We struggled to find a rhythm in our conversation.

"Did you have many Saudi friends there in London too?" I offered, already fearing the question was a weak attempt to paper-over awkward spaces in our conversation.

"A few, but mostly I hung out with the Barts crowd. Most of my friends are English. But I often ran into a circle of Saudi girls, more my older sister's age than mine."

"What were they doing in London, apart from perhaps decompressing from the cabin fever of being in Riyadh year-round?" I added, hoping she would not be offended.

She rolled her eyes dramatically.

"I know!" Mai exclaimed, "Tell me about it! Riyadh drives me stir crazy, especially my hideous veil. I am not one of the new generation that has bought into this veiling craze. I am like my mother, a rebel." She tossed her head back releasing a fabulous laugh, embracing her own defiance. I liked her; she was spunky.

"But to answer your question, Qanta, a lot of the Saudi women were in London having medical procedures performed during convenient short breaks." I looked up peering at her closely. Mai wasn't joking.

"You mean plastic surgery surely. Let me guess: breast jobs? Rhinoplasties? Liposuction? Botox?"

"Yeah, yeah, Qanta, all of that, except we have some terrific surgeons in Riyadh now who do that right here and relatively less expensively than flying to London and staying at, say, the Dorchester. No, they go for something rather more exotic."

"Well, what else, Mai? What's the rage right now in elective procedures?"

"Hymen reconstruction, of course, haven't you heard? It's the latest craze at the moment. Women from here are going over in droves for the awfully convenient repairs!" She looked around triumphantly, revealing a downwardly curved smile immediately betraying an insatiable appetite for attention seeking. I stared at her blankly. She explained.

"Qanta, in our society, a woman's honor is her virginity. It must be preserved at all costs and kept intact until marriage. There is simply no negotiation about this matter." I nodded, aware this was true in my culture too. She continued, "In Saudi, of course, some girls are risk-takers, rule-breakers, like anywhere else. They perhaps are pursued by men who desire them, maybe they are caught up in their immediate desires. We are human after all. We are not perfect, we are not frigid, we feel!" She searched the sewing circle for a response. The crowd began to separate a little from us, safeguarding themselves from even talking about such a diabolical taboo. Mai was undeterred.

"So some girls, not only Saudis, but also from the other Gulf countries, are determined not to let a little matter like lost virginity land them into disaster. A woman whose virginity is lost could

never be marriageable in our society, unless of course she is divorced
and then everyone knows she is 'used goods' or a 'hand-me-down.'
For the rest of us unmarrieds, it all depends on the contiguity of
the hymen. In our society the anatomy of the hymen carries a
medico-legal value, Qanta. This is a very serious matter."

"So where do these women go? What is the procedure?" I
asked, curious to know more.

"A lot of this is done on Harley Street and in the surrounding
exclusive clinics in London. It's a minor matter, I hear, perhaps
just a few days' recovery. Sometimes they can place tiny stitches
and repair the defect; nowadays I think they can even fix it with
a laser. Ouch."[29]

I shifted, uncomfortable at imagining the procedure but more
so at something imperceptibly vulgar in Mai's demeanor. As a physician, no subject was ever truly taboo, but something about her
audacity and her insensitivity in such a cloistered community made
me uneasy. I wondered exactly how she could know what she did
and immediately pushed my uncharitable suspicions about her away.

Mai continued, relentless, "Other women need a more extensive reconstruction. They might need to be fitted with a biodegrad-
able implant of a membrane that can simulate the whole thing…
and our habibis can never know." She descended into an orgasm
of laughter.

I was astonished. In all my years of attending patients I had
never read of hymenoplasty as a past surgical procedure. Over a
decade of history-taking and I hadn't come across a patient who
admitted to undergoing hymen repair. Staggering too was the value
the Kingdom placed on virginity. For Saudi families, like most
Muslim cultures, a woman's chastity was a family honor, a property to be prized. If she lost her chastity, her intactness, whether
by choice or by assault, the family's honor became irreplaceable.
This terrible burden on young women, some of whom were perhaps

lost between two privileged cultures, or far worse, prey to predators, drove them to seek out solutions including the hymenoplasty that Mai described.

The rising number of these procedures being performed elsewhere in the Persian Gulf is well-documented and the subject of a number of reviews including publications in both *The Lancet* and the *British Medical Journal*. I knew Mai was not making this up; I had seen the articles myself. Quite sure that the procedure was illegal in the Kingdom, I didn't dare ask anyone about this, not even my closest medical colleagues. After Mai's very public allusion to the subject, I never heard it discussed again, but the data was clear. Women were desperate to present themselves as virgins in a climate where suspicion was cast even by family members, or perhaps especially by family members. I was well aware of the consequences— divorce, often—if on the wedding night a bride was found not to bleed after intercourse, raising suspicions that she was not pristine after all. A single word and her honor was dismantled forever, based on the unquestioned word of her husband.

Women were learning to retaliate, however, threatening to countercharge the man's sexual inexperience or worst of all denouncing him as impotent, the threat of which forced some men to continue their marriages in an uneasy truce of resentment and clouded suspicion. In other circumstances, women could risk death if determined not to be virgins. Honor killings are widely reported among Pakistani, Jordanian, and other Muslim communities, but I had heard nothing of this nature during my stay in the Kingdom. I had no doubt, however, that in tribal and closed communities, such a violation of the family's honor could well cost a young woman her life.

As a result, women who had means flew out of the Kingdom (presumably under the aegis of a male relative) to secure the skilled repair of the hymen as a preparation for marriage. Many are operated on in Egypt, while others opt for Mai's leafy and expensive stomping ground in West London. Data suggest the rising numbers of procedures in Egypt has significantly curtailed honor killings in that country, encouraging the surgeons that they are certainly relieving distress and extending life by performing the secret reconstructions. Some surgeons are able to repair the membrane and insert a viscous, red-colored gel that mimics blood flow after rupture, a procedure called hymenorraphy. This technique satisfies both partners by providing the sought after physical evidence that a virgin has been penetrated (even though this is not definitive medical confirmation of virginity). This procedure also protects actual virgin athletes, who may have bled without notice in their youth and are thus unable to provide the tell-tale stain on their wedding night.

My head was spinning from Mai's unwelcome assault of sexual practices in the Kingdom. I returned to the fray and joined the circle of women who were by now swaying with laughter. At the center, Reem actually looked to be holding court, thoroughly enjoying the proceedings. I returned to sit next to my friend in the middle of the sofa and I noticed Mai smirked uncomfortably to the outside edges of the gathering. For the first time I finally realized that she looked less at home even than I did. There was something barely tolerated about her. She was an outcast in her own community.

Disregarding my uncomfortable observations, I turned to Reem, "Translate for me! What is so funny that has you laughing hysterically? I want to know!" Reem waited until she caught her breath and then turned toward me.

"My goodness, Sameera is hysterical." Reem pointed toward one of her guests who was obviously regaling a tale to the rest, tears streaming down her face with laughter. In the tumult of Arabic, I recognized a name I knew: Thunayan. He was the extremely tall surgeon whom I had seen from time to time in the ICU. A dour man, not at all attractive to me, I always thought him aloof; perhaps because of his extreme reserve, and especially so when compared to the alternative and friendly Mu'ayyad whom even I had to admit was incredibly sexy. What could they be talking about?

"She's talking about her attraction for Thunayan. Apparently he is not married yet. He just returned from Canada, Qanta." Reem was simultaneously translating and giggling. "Well, Sameera has got a major crush on him. When she operates alongside him she says she can't remember the answers to any of his questions, so she feels like a fool, but she hopes her eyes look bigger as she glances at him over her mask." Reem collapsed into more side-splitting laughter.

I looked at Sameera, who was flushed as she shared her innocent crush with the surrounding women, many of whom were still unmarried into their late twenties and early thirties. Like me, almost all of these women had selected career over and in place of marriage. Other than Qudsia, who seemed older, Reem would be the first among us to be married.

"And so she says every time she sees Thunayan, she loses her trail of thought—" Reem broke off, crippled by waves of hysteria that had seized the whole group. I was puzzled. They were adolescent in their appetite for details about Sameera's crush. I suddenly felt I was at a sweet sixteen rather than a farewell soiree for a surgeon.

They giggled coquettishly and girlishly. The atmosphere was at once innocent and deeply saddening. The women, starved for meaningful contact with the opposite sex, fell into two camps before marriage; panicked promiscuity on threat of dishonor or even worse, and adolescent, girlish fantasies that would never lead to a real relationship. I failed to see my own fantasy weaving in my daydreams about Imad. I was no more immune to the artificial climate of Riyadh myself, no matter how Westernized I thought myself to be.

I sank back into silence, thinking of hymens and hysteria. Around me the women chattered on unrestrained in Arabic and soon I returned to my customary role as silent observer. Only Mai noticed my dismay. I wondered how Reem would fare in Toronto. Would she really be able to stand up to the expectations her culture had placed on womanhood? To cackling laughter yet again about the lanky surgeon, I quietly excused myself and left the room, leaving their girlish desperations resonating behind closed doors.

Chapter
Thirty-four

THE HOT MAMMA

⁜—⁜—⁜—⁜—⁜—⁜—⁜

BALANCING ONE DAUGHTER ON HER slim hip, Ghadah was scrambling eggs for my breakfast. I felt nurtured, a feeling I realized I had been missing for a very long time. She had invited me over for brunch at her villa, which was just adjacent to my apartment. Post-call from the ICU with the whole day ahead of me, I had dragged myself over. Being in her kitchen was soothing. Ignoring my sleep deprivation, I was already glad to have come. I soon forgot I was sleepy.

"I want to make you something nutritious, Qanta. You seem to be losing weight! And you know as a dietician I like my guests to eat well!" Ghadah chortled at herself while she handed her child to her Filipina nanny and busied herself chopping spring onions and tomatoes to add to my omelet. I was growing hungrier by the minute.

Though Ghadah was several years younger than I, she was evidently the consummate mother. She had been married for more than a decade, from the tender age of nineteen, was already mother to two young daughters, and now pregnant with a third child. She was lush in her beauty, a dead ringer for Jackie Onassis, with the same wide-set, beguiling eyes and long, curved brows that were the envy of every woman who knew her.

Her hair was casually cut into medium length which tumbled onto her wide, sculpted shoulders rising out of a boat-necked Pucci shirt. The tunic stylishly encased her growing belly. As she heated the pan and melted some butter, I noticed how relaxed Ghadah was within herself. Her comfortable, faded jeans outlined long, athletic legs perfectly, lean and muscular, even in advanced pregnancy. On her feet she wore platform slides in white patent leather revealing a chipped, purple pedicure. There was something warm and casual about Ghadah. Though astonishingly gorgeous, Ghadah would never be a prisoner to her beauty; even with hair displaced by the grasping toddler in her arms, a trace of flour smudged over her button nose, and her fractured nail polish, Ghadah was one hot mamma.

"Would you like toast, Qanta? And do you prefer coffee or tea? Tell me, I want to make you your favorite breakfast!" She was beaming, her lipstick (a pale sixties' pink applied too thickly) highlighted her crooked, rather uneven teeth, which nevertheless still dazzled in her fabulous smile. I was enchanted by Ghadah. Her beauty was so powerful I was constantly distracted. She looked at me for a moment waiting to hear my preference.

"Toast, Ghadah, and coffee. That would be wonderful."

She went about laying the table, pouring coffee grounds in the coffeemaker, all the while briefly instructing the Filipina maid who stood close by to assist. Ghadah spoke gently but quickly in staccato Arabic while waving the maid away. Ghadah was determined to prepare everything for me personally; I was her guest, not her maid's. She gently sat her child down in one chair, tucking her in and watching the child begin to tear pieces of pita bread and dip them into the hummus and thick, creamy yogurt laid in a plate before her.

Shyly, Ghadah's older daughter, Nada, just turned seven, approached the table. Soon I was flanked by the two small Saudi girls who watched me as intently as I did them. Her children were peach-complexioned with long, curly, light brown hair which stretched in thick ropes of ponytails down to their small waists. They were dressed in pink and white and adorned with pretty hair grips and ribbons. Ghadah's daughters were cherished and decorated. These were loved children who sparkled with health and vivacity. Ghadah was raising confident children, daughters who would grow up to be confident Saudi women, just like their magnificent mother.

"So Qanta, how do you like Riyadh?" Ghadah shot me a piercing look, twisting her wide lips into a knot as she suppressed laughter. At once I knew I could speak frankly.

"It's not always fun, Ghadah," I began cautiously, "but what about you? How do you like it?" Ghadah approached the table with the sizzling omelet and, sitting down, began serving us.

"I can't tell you, Qanta. This has been the most difficult year for me. You know I was in Canada for years while Haydar was training in Ottawa? He did his surgical residency and then cardio-thoracic fellowship there. My girls were raised there, and that's where I did my training as a nutritionist. I loved Canada. We had a great time. Now it seems like over there I got to be with my husband so much more, even though he was often operating or on call. Every weekend we could do things as a family, without the distraction of so many relatives. And then of course the independence! I could drive myself and my daughters anywhere. We could see movies. We could go to restaurants, the mall, anywhere. No one cared what you we were wearing. No Muttawa in Canada, you know, Qanta." We both laughed out loud. She continued. "Riyadh was unbearable for me in the beginning. I cried a lot, Qanta, I have to tell you. Haydar was really worried I wouldn't be able to make the adjustment." She stopped to chomp on some toast, a little breathless. I was surprised that, as a Saudi who had been born and raised in Riyadh, she found her own country suffocating.

"It's hard when you have a family, Qanta. Things change. The first married years we lived in Canada, we didn't have children immediately. You know, I was very young so we were just getting used to each other.

"Haydar and I had an arranged marriage. He says he selected me from among his cousins but I didn't know it. My mother and father asked me to marry him, so I agreed, and I was very pleased when we met each other. We did spend time together going out before we were wed—we went out to dinner and cafés in Riyadh right after we were engaged, so I was already falling in love with him before the wedding. We are very advanced, Qanta! Even though we risked harassment from the Mutawaeen."

Again she laughed in delight. "Anyway, it was great to be able to develop our relationship further in Canada. We had a lot of fun, and then in his second year of residency we got pregnant, and right after that the children followed, and we have even more fun now, don't we Habibti?" She turned to wipe yogurt from her toddler's mouth.

"Now that we are back in Riyadh, every weekend is the same: Thursday we meet his relatives, Friday, mine. They usually gather at our house because Haydar and I are the eldest in our families so it's nonstop entertaining for me. We have no time as a family alone. No time! Sometimes I want to scream. I mean, I love my parents, my family, but really, a marriage, a family needs its own private time, its own private space. Here I feel we have none, we belong to other people.

"Canada was so carefree. What a contrast! I could meet my husband at the hospital for lunch in Ottawa if he was between cases, but now we are just too busy, and any time we do have has to be spent attending to our family commitments. And our families are big, Qanta!

"And then during the week, you know, I am a working woman. It's a race to get everyone to work and get the kids to school and be fully present at my own job five days a week at the hospital and make sure I am doing as dedicated a job as all the single Saudi women who have none of these responsibilities." I was beginning to understand Ghadah's multiple pressures.

She had stopped smiling. Ghadah was mourning the loss of her privacy, not so much because of the oppressive official régimes or even the lack of driving, for instance. Rather she was craving a retreat from the culture of extended family that is the hallmark of Saudi society. I didn't know what to say. I just listened while she continued talking.

"My husband is a wonderful man. I love him very much, I mean, I am glad to be married. I wouldn't want it any other way. We have a very full life, Alhumdullilah. After breakfast I am going to show you our family album, especially the pictures from our honeymoon."

She bowed her head smiling at a private memory. "I am so proud of Haydar. He is a very talented surgeon, Qanta. He is so dedicated, and he works incredibly hard. He is always at the hospital before seven, every day. He even rounds on his patients when he is not on call. You know it was all his decision to come back to Riyadh. I fought it for a long time. I told him I didn't want my daughters to grow up with such restrictions, but he was intent on serving our country. I knew inside he was right. He said I could provide the girls with the right environments in our home, I mean we both could, no matter the difficult public life here. There aren't any other men in our country who can do what Haydar does. If he didn't come back we wouldn't have the cardiac program we do now. I really admire him for that, Qanta."

"What about you, Ghadah? Do you have the same feelings about serving the country?"

"Not really to the same extent, but I do like to help other Saudi nationals. Like any mother, my first priority is to serve my family. Make no mistake, I love my job and I know many Saudi women don't get the opportunities to work that they should have. I really enjoy being a nutritionist, and of course you must know I am applying to be the nutritionist for the cardiac program. We have to make a lot of improvements in our dietary habits for our people. You must know that pediatric obesity is becoming a major problem here?"

I did indeed know this by watching Saudi families with multiple children in tow hauling huge carts of soda and candy from the local warehouse superstore The Max (the equivalent of Costco). Their shopping patterns were much like most of America and just as disordered, especially when the native diet of dates and olives, yogurt and lentils, and unleavened bread was so much healthier than Snickers and Coke.

"Our people need information. Like Haydar, I am in a position to provide it. I am making it my mission." She had raised her chiseled chin as she made her point. I had no doubt she would. Ghadah was a force.

Brought up in an affluent Saudi Palestinian family, Ghadah moved in the same sets as Zubaidah. Her father had made his money in business after exile from Palestine in 1948 and made a point of educating all of his children, both sons and daughters. He wanted his children to be independent. While Ghadah's mother was not educated, all her daughters were professionals in health care and each was married to a highly educated man. Ghadah had the same plans for her daughters too.

"It's very important for a woman to have education, Qanta. My family believes that, especially Haydar. It is actually a valued prize in Islam. The Prophet said that the man who educates the women-folk in his family is most beloved to Allah. We live by that. Haydar is the biggest feminist thinker of all of us! I am amazed at my husband. He is unusual. He loves his daughters. He never once complained that we didn't have sons, though perhaps this last child will be our boy." Pensive, she rubbed her belly.

"To Haydar it's not important what sex our children are. The only thing that matters is that his children, our children, whether daughters or sons, have choices and a voice. That is where they will always have power." I couldn't agree more, but before I could inter-ject, Ghadah swiftly changed the subject. "Let me show you the house!

"You have to excuse the mess, Qanta. We only moved a year ago from Canada and all my furniture is still arriving. Eventually we have to leave the compound and move to a new house Haydar is having built for us. This place becomes so crowded at our family gatherings. There isn't room to move. You try preparing food for forty in this tiny kitchen! It's a challenge even for a nutritionist."

To me it was spacious, especially compared to my tiny dwelling, but imagining Ghadah and Haydar's extended families rolling up weekend after weekend, their vehicles clogging the whole street outside, I had to agree she probably did need more space.

We walked out of the kitchen into a pretty sitting room that was the family room. The furniture dwarfed everything in sight, leaving almost no space to walk. I bumped into the coffee table.

"Sorry about that table. Don't worry, you should see me, Qanta. I am the klutz! I am always doing that!" She giggled at her clum-siness while I giggled at a Saudi using idiomatic Yiddish. Ghadah had obviously a lot of experience living in North America.

We crossed a marble hallway, entering Ghadah's drawing room. Huge, it looked like a furniture warehouse. The room was scattered with oversized Louis XV armchairs upholstered in garish pony, leopard, and zebra skins. Heavy, plate-glass tables cluttered the room, their bronze pedestals sinking deep into piled carpet that still smelled freshly installed. Tiny, high windows were draped in heavy curtains and (even though it was brilliantly sunny outside) Ghadah scurried around the room switching on the heavy crystal table lamps. Soon the room was dappled with thick umbras of fluttering yellow light perforating the gloom. This formality didn't seem to go with Ghadah's casual outlook at all, but perhaps she entertained here.

I looked at a series of cushions perfectly arranged on a long, low sofa that looked suspiciously like a Beidermeier. They were white silk, surrounded by thick black borders that framed a central leonine design in raised gold thread. I peered a bit more closely.

"Ghadah, this reminds me of Versace. The designs are very similar. I saw them in New York when I was last there."

"It's all Versace, Qanta! I am so glad you recognized it!" Ghadah was flushed with pleasure.

"All Versace, Ghadah?" She nodded, rather surprised at the question. I was astonished. Slowly it dawned on me that Ghadah did not rely on her nutritionist salary or indeed that of her hard-working heart surgeon husband's. Like much of the merchant Palestinian community that had taken sanctuary in the Kingdom in the 1950s, theirs was family money. They were very wealthy indeed.

As I was preparing to leave, Haydar arrived home from work. He greeted me graciously, shaking my hand and inquiring after my health and that of my family. Even though he or indeed any of my Saudi friends would never be likely to meet my family, it was a common courtesy to inquire about one's family, parents particularly. Haydar smiled his dazzling grin, genuinely pleased to see me. He was extremely handsome, fairer than Ghadah, and dashing in a streamlined beard. They were a glittering couple, even on the weekend.

"Please, Qanta, stay a while! Ghadah, bring some more tea for our guest!" Without a murmur Ghadah scuttled off to put the kettle on. "Please, Qanta, take a seat." I was a little embarrassed. I had come in a short-sleeved T-shirt, and my abbayah was of course hanging up in a closet where Ghadah had placed it. Perhaps my bare arms would offend Haydar.

I began apologizing. "Nonsense, Qanta! These things are not important to us. You are dressed perfectly well. We are not like that at all. Please don't feel uncomfortable. Consider yourself in your own home." My anxieties thus assuaged, he effortlessly began to converse about patients we shared, about his return to Riyadh and life for his wife and daughters.

"Mrs. Tarfa has made an amazing recovery, Haydar," I began, remarking on a Saudi woman who had survived a horrific fire at a wedding party some months earlier. Haydar had just replaced two of her heart valves.

Haydar replied, "Thank you, Qanta, Alhumdullilah, looking after that woman really affected me. It makes me feel worthwhile here to help patients like her."

With the incredibly advanced care we could provide here and thanks to aggressive surgeons like Haydar and Mu'ayyad, she was actually going to live and perhaps even eventually be well enough for prosthetic limbs.

"So, do you yearn for Canada, or are you settled here now, Haydar?" I asked, curious to see if his answer would merge with Ghadah's.

"Alhumdullilah, Qanta, we have returned to the Kingdom at a very good time. We are grateful the mood here is changing, and things are becoming more open. The radical clerics are weakening, and our country is finally moving ahead in the right direction. The National Guard Hospital is very progressive, Qanta. Soon we will be performing the Kingdom's leading transplant program.

Mashallah, the Crown Prince Abdullah himself is very, very supportive to us here. We are fortunate because he is heavily invested in progress and development. None of this would really be possible without his patronage and his actions. He diverts a lot of funding to us here at the National Guard. That's why we are the premier center in the Kingdom. And we will soon be training our own surgeons right here, instead of constantly sending them to Canada or the States. It's why I came back."

"Don't you miss Canada, Haydar?" I asked, comfortable addressing him by his first name. "Ghadah seems to very much."

He smiled at his wife who, true to form, had just stubbed her toe on the credenza.

"Careful, Habibti," he told her, leaping up to take the heavy tray from his pregnant wife. He caressed her arm gently and pulled her down toward the sofa near him. Clearly they were still very much in love. Haydar poured me my tea while Ghadah and I watched, equally enchanted by this marvelous Saudi man.

"Sure, I miss Canada. I had great mentors there. The clinical experience was incredible, but to be honest we see more pathology here. There are fewer heart surgeons here so of course I get a very broad surgical experience. It's good for me to be here, and I am sure you have talked to Mu'ayyad. I just feel I have to do this for my country. The least I can do is return to serve my people."

As I watched Haydar's clear, green eyes burning with commitment, a light radiated from his beautiful face. There was nothing contrived or insincere about his feelings for his country. This wasn't the immature nationalism of an angry young man. Haydar was a member of the intellectual glitterati who really wanted to enable change. All over the Kingdom, couples like Ghadah and Haydar raised progressive families while they pursued the very real task of developing their nation, which found itself strangling in the suffocating slick of extraordinary wealth that had paralyzed so many.

Haydar and Ghadah were the New Generation of Saudis: the ideal-ists, the community activists, the servants of the masses, the intellectual gluttons, the progressives, the liberals.

"Here, Qanta, my album!" Ghadah pushed the heavy, leather-bound volume onto my knee, turning the pages herself.

"Oh, Qanta, you will be here another three hours! My wife loves to show her photographs." Haydar watched her fondly as she showed me the beginning of their story.

"And this one was taken in Thailand, where we went on our honeymoon." Shyly Ghadah pointed out a picture of her with her husband obviously on the way to a special dinner. He was dressed in slacks and a white shirt, she in a lace, long-sleeved dress which revealed surprisingly stumpy ankles! Like many Saudis, they veiled only in Riyadh for social propriety, not for orthodox attachments to more extreme beliefs. Ghadah was still very modestly dressed, revealing only her ankles, but her husband's relaxed posture toward her both in the picture and now as they looked at it together with me years later belied progressive Muslims who were more attached to actions than appearances. Ghadah was completely absorbed in her album, showing me the images of her marriage, complete with the archetypal wedding thrones that had graced the late-night wedding I had attended last week. In many ways, Ghadah and Haydar were bread-and-butter Saudi and in other ways completely alternative.

As I watched them talk about their future, as I saw Haydar intently listening to Ghadah about her plans to enroll in a PhD program in London after the birth of her third child, and saw him beaming with pride at her academic dreams (dreams that she did indeed fulfill several years later), I realized I had significantly under-estimated the Saudis I was working with. They didn't work to pass time, though certainly a number of them truly did not need the salary in the way that I did. Rather, they preferred to work to accomplish change. They worked as a team in their very forward and healthy marriages, which in turn influenced the circles around them and their society overall.

Ghadah was far from a desperate housewife, even if her home already looked like it was straight off the ABC set. Instead, Ghadah was a fulfilled woman with ambitious goals and the unwavering support of an equally brilliant husband, one who took enormous pride in the progress of his wife and daughters and in that of his country. Realizing that he had married Ghadah at nineteen when he was in his mid-twenties, I did agree that Haydar was perhaps as influential in her life as her broad-minded father. Ghadah was the product of nurturing men, whether in her childhood home or in the marital home. A woman like Ghadah would not be possible were it not for the confident, loving, supportive, and empathic men surrounding her.

I had a lot to learn from Ghadah and Haydar. Their relationship was a microcosm of all the good that was unfolding in the Kingdom, just like this, inside family homes, in the soft, safe recesses of loving marriages, in the indulgent connections of fathers to their daughters, and finally in the hopes that confident, valued mothers pinned on their children. The Kingdom of Loss was becoming one of beauty.

Chapter
Thirty-Five

THE GLORIA STEINEM OF ARABIA

I FOUND MYSELF IN THE neonatal ICU early one afternoon. On Dr. Fahad's recommendation, I was seeking out Dr. Maha al-Muneef. Incubators, full of premature babies in varying stages of growth, hummed in unison. A primal current of life surged through the unit, dense with young beginnings of future Saudis. Nurses worked intently on their tiny patients, reaching toward frail limbs still covered in a glossy pelage of lanugo. Giant latexed fingers pushed through the Perspex hatches, tending to the delicate needs of the youngest patients at the National Guard Hospital. Through a glass pane, a veiled Saudi mother, clearly limping from the pain of recent childbirth, scanned the scene until her visored gaze spied her baby. She gazed at the neonate through an opaque cloud of blackness.

Maha was conducting rounds. She was dressed in a disposable sterile gown, the yellow paper cloth covering her doctor's coat which dwarfed a tiny frame. She looked no more than five feet tall. On her head she wore a black scarf which constantly slipped backward, sometimes exposing the crown of her hair, occasionally exposing a fraction of her neck. Her dynamic gestures and the energy that inhabited her made for an annoyingly mobile veil that she tolerated without irritation. She stood in a flurry of gesticulations, holding court amid her Saudi residents and Western nurses, explaining her decision-making with patience and precision.

In the midst of prescribing and teaching, she adjusted her scarf constantly, covering unruly hair. She made eye contact with everyone around her to determine their level of understanding. Satisfied the issues were resolved, she briskly stripped off her gloves with a snap, casting them into the receptacle, and moved to the next patient. Periodically, she laughed with her colleagues, emitting an audible peal that was surprisingly infectious. In turn, her colleagues laughed with her, evidently comfortable with their female Saudi senior. She was a woman very much at ease within herself. Her confident body language unextinguished even by a mandated head-scarf, a relaxed candor, and a natural authority belied a powerful, secure woman.

Catching my eye, she smiled a wide, toothy grin, flashing her gorgeous teeth. Her cheeks dimpled in sincerity and the smile infused her almond-shaped, hazel eyes framed by a ray of crow's feet. Without makeup, dressed in the sterile yellow gown, her beauty remained unquashed. I studied her for a time, searching for the source of familiarity in my attraction to ineluctable good looks. After a few moments, I found it: the squared-off jaw leading to a subtly cleft chin; the perfectly symmetrical nasolabial folds, deep lines stretched across full, high cheeks flanking the wide, warm smile; and finally, the endearing yet slightly imperfect alignment between her incisors peeping between wide bow-shaped lips were all very familiar. She was a Saudi Gloria Steinem.

She finished her last assessment and at once came to greet me, holding a tiny outstretched hand in greeting.

"Salaam alaikum, Dr. Qanta! Dr. Fahad mentioned you would visit me!" She gripped my hand in a surprisingly steely handshake. I found myself smiling at her vigor.

"Wa alaikum Salaam, Dr. al-Muneef! I am delighted to meet with you. Dr. Fahad mentioned you would be a wonderful guide for me. I want to hear all about your work." We walked out of the ICU together to return to her office.

Maha was a pediatric infectious disease specialist and the Deputy Chairman of the Department of Pediatrics. She consulted in the hospital on all varieties of infectious diseases. A widely published academic, she was trained at Ivy League programs in the U.S. I also was beginning to recognize that Maha was very busy as an activist. She was a proponent of human rights for women and children in the Kingdom.

"Please, come in, make yourself comfortable, Qanta." Closing the door, she removed her scarf from her hair. Without it she was even more beautiful, and her softly colored hair curled up above her shoulders in a very stylishly cut bob. Under the light, subtle highlights warmed her thick head of hair with flecks of burgundy.

Her office was in the basement of the administration buildings. Small, high windows shielded with Venetian blinds that remained closed still allowed sunlight into the room without affording a view of the interior, a contrast from Faris's office, which was walled with thick panes of glass looking out over lush swathes of manicured lawns; or Dr. Fahad's office, which revealed pretty dappled sunlight filtering through the young plane trees outside the window. Maha, as a woman, couldn't allow herself a clear view of the outside, even if she wasn't in a basement office, because women must not be seen in Saudi Arabia. Women spent lifetimes incarcerated in guarded privacy and secrecy. A woman working at her desk in clear view of a large window would be unacceptable in this society which wasn't yet ready to receive women in the public arena.

She settled herself in a giant swivel chair that only magnified her petite frame. Her desk was cluttered in a corner of the room and was mainly occupied by a tall CPU that dwarfed its user. On top of the CPU a yellow silken prayer mat, much worn from use, was casually folded up, obviously placed there since the noon prayer that took place earlier that day. Pinned on the notice board were candid snaps of her children, daughters and sons, who were dressed in casual clothing, relaxing in a garden. A photocopied newspaper article in Arabic was taped to the window. A Nokia Sidekick intermittently vibrated with missed calls and new emails. A bookshelf was filled to the brim with texts and journals and the occasional framed photograph. She took me at once to a framed picture that was perched in pride of place at the top of the shelf. It was a picture of Maha with Barbara Walters.

"You may have seen this interview in New York while you were there recently. Barbara Walters came here with her 20/20 team and asked to interview me.[30] They followed me around at work and at home to learn about professional Saudi women. It was fantastic, Qanta. She is a great lady." She looked at the picture with affection, before placing it carefully on the top-most shelf.

"Gosh, Maha, that's a picture I would keep on my desk for everyone to see!" I gushed, impressed.

"No, Qanta, it's not like that here. You can see my relaxed scarf on my head there, and of course not everyone here is a fan of this famous American journalist. It's better to keep this picture somewhere where people can't see it unless I show them. Unfortunately in my society people are limited and not always open to my position on matters." I looked at her, pressing for her to reveal more.

"You know, Qanta, you probably already are aware our society does not like outspoken persons, whether men or women."

I was immediately reminded of a conversation I had already shared with Imad, when I was surprised to see as a man, he had made the exact same observation. I was learning that it wasn't only women who were oppressed by the puritanical dictates that determined life in the Kingdom; the autonomy of moderate men was shackled too. Even someone as powerful as our CEO, Dr. Fahad, had to constantly fend off pressures from the Wahabi clergy, for instance, in seeking to justify his employment policies. I suddenly remembered him crumpling up faxed fatwas from the Mutawaeen, threatening him for employing so many women, women like myself and Maha. At the time I wasn't sure if I was more shocked at the fatwas which included one forbidding women from wearing seat belts because of the resulting defined cleavage, or the fact that the clergy had fax machines. Rabid orthodoxy was a lot more high tech than I had ever imagined. Maha continued unaware of the racing thoughts she had triggered inside me.

"As a Saudi woman who has chosen to speak out for the weakest in society, the children and women, I face a lot of pressure. I have to be very careful to try and be a model citizen, while I work for progress in a private and professional manner. This is a complex society where there are many rules and rituals and cultural expectations. I have learned how to accomplish things here, within our framework which can be restrictive. I have learned how to accomplish a lot, Alhumdullilah, but much work needs to be done."

Over the next several hours she began to explain her work and her passion in the Kingdom with an energy that blazed through her small frame. I was entranced to hear Maha talk about the progress she was making in exposing child abuse and protecting battered women throughout the Kingdom. I knew there was a need for this work from several patients either I or my friends had attended in months past. Two children in particular stood out in mind.

It was winter in Riyàdh, and this had been an especially long week of difficult admissions. The ICU nurses and many among our physician ranks were demoralized. We had lost several young patients despite our best efforts. I had started my evening on call a little deflated.

"Dr. Qanta!" It was chirpy Juliette. "The emergency room on the phone, they want to know do you have a bed for acute respiratory failure?" Without taking any details, I nodded assent. Juliette relayed the information into the phone. "We are getting an admission," she announced after a few moments. "A vent," indicating the patient was on a respirator, which was doing the breathing for the patient.

"Fine, just page me when the patient arrives," I called out and continued writing.

Some time later, I received the relevant call and arrived to see my new patient. As I entered the patient cubicle, buttoning up my coat and reaching for fresh gloves, I gently pushed the flurry of nurses to one side in order to reach the bedside. I found the nurses clustering around a tiny body.

"This is my patient?" I asked, flummoxed at the sight of a child. "We are not a pediatric ICU. I have no pediatric critical care training! Why are we receiving him?" Annoyed, I failed to recall it was my fault for not inquiring of the details of the patient.

"Doctora, he is an adult, here. Any child who displays even one pubic hair is classified as adult here. We have to receive him. He is to be admitted here." And, while she was inserting a Foley catheter to drain the patient's bladder and measure the urine output, Nurse Rita pulled back the patient's gown to show me the offending wisp of pubic hair that accompanied the penis of a child. The child was clearly Tanner stage 1, the first step of pubertal development.

"How old is he?"

"Nine, Doctora, last month."

"And his weight?"

"Forty-eight pounds, Doctora. He seems really underweight. I would guess he is perhaps four feet tall. I don't know, we have to measure."

I studied the thin frame, examining my tiny patient. His ribs were showing through his sallow skin. His hands were wizened, without the normal fullness of youth. His eyes were sunken hollows, closed under the deep sedation administered in the emergency room. They were studded with gorgeous, long, lush lashes that touched his joyless cheeks. His thick, tousled hair was dirty and had not been washed in days, possibly weeks. The nurses covered his head with a surgical hat, keeping it apart from our peering heads to avoid the inadvertent transmission of lice, which could be a potential risk. Later they would shampoo and brush his hair, after I had finished my assessment.

I examined his heart, beating rapidly and easily audible through his thin rib cage despite the rushing wind of mechanical breaths underneath. His lungs were clear. His belly was scaphoid and hollow and sank into the narrow pelvis of a child. Little legs were underweight and lay flaccid in their knock-kneed stance typical of many children at this age. I noticed a healing scab from when he must have fallen playing. His feet were caked in dirt and roughened already with young callous. Perhaps he was one of the boys who kicked a dusty soccer ball around in the vacant lots awaiting development. His hands were flaccid and open-palmed. I noticed the fingernails were bitten to the quick and some of the hangnails recently bloody. His crumpled thobe, stained and worn, lay soiled on the floor. A smell of stale urine pervaded the air and then my eyes finally saw the precipitant of admission.

As I moved in to examine the head and review the airway, his thin T-shirt, torn and now partly cut by the nurses in order to attach EKG leads, fell from his throat. A series of ringed marks appeared at the front of his neck, like the coiling of something tight. They encircled his small throat. The bruises were easily visible once I moved the cloth away. I adjusted an angle poise lamp on the wall to eliminate the shadow cast under his small chin. I was sure; these were ligature marks.

I learned from a quick call to the emergency room that the child indeed had been a victim of strangulation. The nine-year-old Saudi boy had been found hanging from a noose in a bathroom at his family home. Discovering the curtains to the shower closed but no water flowing, his siblings had stumbled across the child suspended from the shower head. A thin noose of plastic cord was tightening around his neck. They managed to cut him down at once and rush him to the emergency room in the back of the family car. His fourteen-year-old brother had driven him here. In the emergency room he was ashen and barely breathing. With difficulty he was placed on the respirator, the doctor struggling with a tiny tube to gain entry beyond the vocal cords swollen and engorged by the strangulation. Had his family been any later, he would have been dead at the scene. As I surveyed his frail body, I wondered if indeed he had been lucky to survive, after all.

Deeply distressed, the nurses were whispering soothing words to the unconscious child, examining his body for bruises and cuts. We found some nondescript marks on his flank that could have been there from the tiled wall in the shower. No parents came to see him in the unit as long as he was admitted to us. I ordered some high-dose steroids and inhalational treatments to improve his breathing. Conferring with another colleague, we made careful adjustments to the ventilator so it would breathe for the tiny, sparrow-like boy.

"I guarantee it." Nurse Mama Mary was agitated. Her steel eyes flashed. "This child is a victim of abuse. Either he was trying to end his life to escape a horrible fate or his abuser was worried he would squeal and wanted to silence him forever. Those kids bringing him in, they were brave. But we're never going to know. Mark my words. We never do find out. This isn't the first child who has come in like this." I looked at her, unable to conceal my shock. "Please, Dr. Qanta, when you have been here as long as I have, you get to see a lot of things. It's a disgrace." She bustled off to finish her tasks, grumbling her anger all the way.

I stared at the unconscious child for a long time, knowing his secret pains, the ones I couldn't see, would remain insoluble. His spirit was desolate and abandoned. I could feel a void of sadness emanating from his malnourished frame. Even sedation couldn't obliterate the horrors his short years had brought him.

A couple of days later, we inspected his vocal cords with a fiber-optic camera. The swelling was much better; the steroids appeared to have worked. Slowly we decreased the sedative medications and the child began to breathe independently of the machine. At last, we were able to remove him from the respirator. He was weakened, but alive. Most importantly, and to our surprise, he survived without any damage to his brain. After a period of careful observation, he was returned to the pediatric ward service, and shortly thereafter, sent back to the home in which he had been hung.

There was no investigation or recourse. Social services were limited at the time, and what comes from families remains in families for the most part. No children's homes existed, no basis existed to cast suspicion on his parents. We could never prove his abuse, merely powerlessly know that he was likely to face the same abuses in the future.

I spoke to David. As an emergency room attending for at least a dozen years in the Kingdom, he was very familiar with my patient's case and began to share another story of his own.

"Oh Qanta, it is heartbreaking. We do see these children from time to time, often enough that one is not surprised by it. I guess it's like any other society. We saw abuse in North America. Why wouldn't we see it here? Families have the same sicknesses wherever you go. In some common denominators, man is universally consistent, however much we don't want to see that. The Saudis are not unusual in that respect, nor are they immune from these societal diseases. It's just a lot less reported here. People are afraid, and the networks to report it in order to take action don't really exist right now."

"So tell me if you have seen a case of child abuse recently," I asked, always curious to learn from my knowledgeable friend.

"A kid was brought into the ER on a busy Thursday night some time ago. He was a scoop and run. By that I mean they had just piled him into the back of the pickup and dumped him onto a gurney in the ER. At the time we didn't have the Red Crescent ambulance services which we have now, Qanta. We worked hard for those ambulances here at the National Guard."

I knew this; David had been a major reformer of EMS services in Riyadh. Adequate first-responder service was one of his over-arching passions.

"Anyway, I was right there and noticed the kid looked really flat, just languid and really in a desperate condition. Nearby a Saudi man, who said he was his guardian, but probably his owner, was standing to one side looking remarkably unconcerned. He was making calls on a cell phone. Disengaged. I knew at once something was wrong." David looked at me to emphasize his point. I knew exactly what he meant. His sixth sense as an experienced clinician had been alerted.

"The kid was a ragamuffin, a little Saudi boy. I was told he was twelve but he looked more like seven years of age to me. His skin was anemic, his hair was falling out. He had lost most of his teeth. They told me he had been a camel jockey that week, you know, Qanta, those kids who are trained to ride camels in races. They have to be tiny so that they don't slow the animals down because of their weight. Anyway, they said they found him like this, in his bed at the Camel Souq (market).

"Come to think of it, it must have been the time for the al-Jenadriyah Festival. You know, Qanta, it's every March. So that's how I just knew. I knew the kid must have been racing every day. They have camel races there specially for the festival, right outside the city." I nodded.

David's patient must have worked long and unpaid hours, alternately grooming and riding the camels with his tiny legs tucked up high underneath him.

Perhaps the little boy had to shepherd and corral a flock. Maybe he felt bonded in his servitude to these creatures. The camels were likely the only beauty he had known. I was afraid to hear what David would say next. "So here I was," he said, "about to examine this kid, when I realized he wasn't breathing. Literally he had just rolled in. Not even a minute had passed. I called a cardiac arrest code and started CPR but he was already dead. Actually he was cold. He had obviously been dead for some time." He paused.

"They said that's how they found him…" he continued.

"But why would they bring him to the ER?" I asked, puzzled.

"Well, Qanta, the owner or whatever he was got scared. He didn't know what to do with a child's body. The easiest thing to do was bring him to the hospital. Obviously this child had been living without his family for who knows how long. They were done with him; they didn't want to answer any awkward questions and start explaining things to the police, even if they would have investigated, which I doubt."

"So what did you do?"

"Well I knew CPR was futile. But I started it because I felt compelled. I think it was just an emotional reflex on my part. Poor kid. To think he probably spent his whole life in the camel market…" David trailed off. We were left to our own thoughts for a time. After a few moments, he began again.

"Even though he was dead, I examined him in detail and took photographs for my digital library. I figured they might be useful for a court case if this could ever be reported. I took pictures of his skin wounds. His skin was like putty, really dehydrated for a long time prior to death. On his arms I noticed marks on both wrists. He had obviously been tied up, again, for a very long time. They were encircling and pretty deep, Qanta, kind of in a spiral. Very much like ligature marks. They couldn't have been anything else. When I showed the slave owner, because that was what I decided he must be, he didn't seem to know or even care. He didn't even look like he was afraid that I had discovered the injuries. He was unmoved when I told him the kid was dead. He actually looked relieved to have me confirm this.

"I examined the rest of his body very closely. He was covered in welts and bruises. I noticed he had a displaced fracture of a collar bone that had healed badly. I think he also had an ankle fracture that had never been set. It was sickening." David looked queasy even retelling the story years later.

"How old were your sons at the time?" I asked, gently, helping David expose the source of his deep distress.

"Well, my youngest, Frank, was the same age. He had just turned five."

"But you said the patient was twelve."

"No, Qanta, that's what the heavy said. I did a skeletal series, looking for evidence of abuse, and I deliberately X-rayed the epiphyses, his wrists actually, to determine radiographic age. The radiology techs arrived after I had pronounced him, but I had them image him posthumously anyway, again in case we could ever bring the perpetrator to justice. The films showed he had terrible osteoporosis, from his poor diet and the lack of vitamin D. It's very common here because people are so shielded from the sun, but this kid probably didn't have any type of healthy nutrition anyway."

"What else did the X rays show?"

"Oh, the usual, old broken ribs that had healed, a nasty break of the forearm that seemed to have been set, but badly, certainly not by one of our surgeons. And his age, the radiologist confirmed it. He could not have been older than five, at the most. I was sick. Someone had abused this child for his whole short life and he wound up dead on a gurney on a Thursday night. We never knew his real name." David stopped speaking. I didn't have the appetite for any more pain. I knew without asking that no one had been brought to justice and no one ever would.[31]

I realized Maha spoke for all the silenced Saudi children; she was their champion.

CHAMPION OF CHILDREN

I WAS DEEPLY DISTURBED BY David's tale. I wanted to know what Maha thought of this story and more of her activism. We spoke a few days later.

"Yes, Qanta, you are probably right, these children were both victims of abuse. No question. We had very limited resources then, even now, and you know like in any country there are ignorant, cruel people here too. It's our women and children who suffer most at their hands. I have seen many cases like this. I am trying to change this. Our sponsors, both of them Saudi princesses, are very concerned to improve the conditions of our country. They are really supportive." She looked at me earnestly, willing me to understand her efforts.

"I want to hear more, Maha." She sipped a cup of sweetened mint tea, relaxing her abbayah a little. We were in a private home, chatting on a breezy veranda. She wore a stylish silk blouse with a high throat tied in a bow over some fashionable boot-cut jeans. Maha was incredibly hip. The contrast of denim and abbayah was marvelous.

"You must have seen the news. It was on the BBC, about our newsreader here in Riyadh, Rania al-Baz. She is the presenter of *The Kingdom This Morning*, a show on state TV." I nodded in acknowledgment. Even though I didn't know the show, I had heard of the newsreader's story. Maha recounted the painful details.

It had been an awful incident. Everyone had heard the story. She was beaten by her Saudi husband until she was so disfigured she had needed plastic surgical intervention. Reports were he had banged her head on the marble floor of their home, and when he went to dispose of her body thinking she was dead, in fact she stirred a little. Panicking, he had brought her to Bughshan hospital. He lied of course, saying she had been in a car accident and ran off to "rescue others."

Maha's lips curved in disgust as she continued.

"They didn't know if she would survive. Can you imagine, he had inflicted over a dozen fractures, I think thirteen perhaps, and she had horrific injuries and bruises on her head. She was admitted like a rag doll, nearly dead. I don't know how she survived without brain damage, but Alhumdullilah she was saved in the end. While she was in ICU and recovering, it was her Saudi father who recorded her injuries in the photographs to be able to show her later what had happened. When she got better and had thought about it, she decided to release the pictures to the media. It was her choice; no one else's."

I had read some accounts myself. Her husband, it was clear, had been especially inflamed by his wife's growing success because she had become a symbol for women all over the Kingdom. A newsreader, she appeared on air with her head covered, but instead of sticking to regulation limp black scarves, she wore colorful silk scarves, often Hermes squares. On camera she was always perfectly made up. The headscarves framed her powerful beauty. She wasn't extinguished by veiling. Rather, somehow her beauty was enhanced because of veiling. The veil was merely a tool that she used in order to interface in the public arena. She was, judging by photographs, like the many Saudi women I knew: gorgeous. But as an icon, however, her significance transcended even her beauty. She represented the future, a future of possibilities for many women in the Kingdom where women on television were still a novelty. I couldn't help thinking how symbolic her husband's violence was, revealing a deep desire to destroy her, quite literally by crushing her beautiful face.

"Anyway, she came on television with her fresh bruises and her swollen face as well as allowing the world to see her when she was critically injured. It was really painful to watch, but it did a lot for the awareness of women's abuse and that of children in our country." Maha continued explaining, "I think that was our turning point, Qanta. I mean, it was terrible for her to have to go through that, but you know, she turned it into an opportunity to help millions in a way we hadn't imagined before.

"You know she, Alhumdullilah, sought divorce and won custody of the children. The courts for once supported a wronged woman. One of our princesses paid her medical bills. Her husband was sentenced to three hundred lashes, but this was halved because she pardoned him publicly in order to secure custody of the kids. Of course, she was given the children, even though it is very unusual in the Kingdom. There was no way they couldn't. The public mood was outraged.

"Her story is a sad one, Qanta. She is not from the lower classes; she was the daughter of a wealthy man, an hotelier. Remember, you know from your medical background that abuse affects all demographic profiles. No segment of society is immune.

"Through her father's connections she was offered a spot in the media where, until then, the females (if any) had been mostly fully veiled and older. She broke the mold at the time and that voice, her voice, was really attractive to listeners.

"As a young woman in media, she fell in love with the singer Fallata who just swept her off her feet. They married quickly. It was a love match, very unusual in our society at the time. But soon she had become a victim of regular violence at his hands, even after bearing him three children. I read in the paper, she had even complained to her grandmother about it, saying that she felt like his maid. And you know what?" Maha sputtered, choking on fury. I found myself holding my breath in tension.

"The grandmother said, 'Correct, you are his maid!' I mean, this is a big part of the problem in our community. Generations of women are ignorant, ignorant of the Quran and its teachings. If we don't inform ourselves as women, we don't know about the rights we can exercise, which are empowering to women actually, because Islam is such an egalitarian religion, Qanta! Islam gave women inheritance rights and property rights and the rights to divorce and to choose a marriage partner. Servitude never enters the equation. Beatings are Haram."

Maha was burning with an inner energy. She continued, "Since Rania came back to her work, even though her colleagues supported her to go public with the story, she found herself unwelcome at the station. She was encouraged to quit by colleagues. She found that by speaking out she had lost her livelihood. I think she is writing her memoirs now, to be published in France, in Arabic. I cannot wait to read them."

Nor could I. I hoped for an English translation.

"It's very typical that when women speak out, they become ostracized in our society. Can you believe because of her, the first research study on abused wives was published by the King Saud specialist Medical Center and it found ninety percent of the women in the study had seen their mothers go through the same abuse? Ninety percent! So they are brainwashed. They think it's normal. They cannot betray their husbands because they might lose their children; in fact, their homes, their reputations, everything."

I also knew of the terrible culture of secrecy in the Kingdom. I believed it must be linked to shame. In the Kingdom, like many Muslim and Arab societies, matters were weighed between shame and honor. Either something brings honor or it brings shame. And families in the Kingdom appeared to bind all their honor in their womenfolk. Shame was so powerful that everything, even atrocities, must be buried.

We sat in silence for a while. Maha paused for a breath, sipping her mint tea in an agitated state. She stirred the crystalline sugar stick maniacally for a few moments, banging it harshly against the Limoges porcelain. I was reminded of another female colleague, Dr. Sameera al-Tuwaijri, an obstetrician who had specialized in public health policy and long since left the Kingdom to work at the UN.

"Qanta, the mandated veiling and the prevention of women driving in the Kingdom are not the disease itself; they are merely symptoms of the very serious illness at the center of our country. They are merely clinical signs of a much more significant syndrome." I was beginning to see what she meant. She had added a further, much more ominous comment.

"Qanta, I am from among the elite. I don't mean money. Alhumdullilah we have always had that. But from among the intellectual elite. I eventually realized I was as suffocated and oppressed as the illiterate women I was treating in my clinics. My country lacks any civil or human rights. I had to abandon living in the Kingdom. I hope the life I offer my daughter will be a healthier beginning, and that she will avoid the suffering I had to go through."

In effect, she was explaining to me that she couldn't stand the cultural oppression of being a working woman in Saudi who was not accepted by her elite family.

Preventing women from driving or working in the public sphere was another way of oppressing those who would choose to pursue that otherwise. This society was wholly tipped against women. By removing the ability to drive themselves anywhere, women were at the mercy of male authority, compelled always to inform men of their destinations and returns, and in a country where women could not travel without prior authorization by men, they were effectively hostage to their male relatives.

Rania al-Baz, the battered newsreader, explained this perfectly in her October 2005 interview in *The Guardian*:[32]

"The structure of society—the fact that a woman cannot drive or travel without authorization, for example, gives a special sense of strength to the man. And this strength is directly connected to the violence. It creates a sense of immunity; that he can do whatever he wants, without sanction. The core issue is not the violence itself. It is this immunity for men, the idea that men can do what they like. It is the society of which the violence is an expression."

Rania al-Baz's observation of male impunity and links to violence and entitlement rang true. It accounted for some of the unbelievable crashes caused by bored and very spoiled Saudi youths who pushed their luxury sports cars beyond the limits of their reckless handling. The Porsches, the Lamborghinis, or sometimes even the mundane Japanese luxury sedans careened into a violent spiraling carnage of Connolly leather and roadkill. Those who survived were admitted to my ICU. Most evenings we had at least one crash victim who made it to the ICU, perhaps a half-dozen who were less critically wounded, and an occasional patient who was dead on arrival.

But I couldn't help wondering how this ban on operating motor vehicles could possibly tally with the rest of Islamic history, when women were previously so empowered that they could even be Islamic jurists teaching hundreds of scholars in mosques in Damascus and Istanbul, or even earlier, when the first Muslim for instance, Hazrat Khadija, was herself a wealthy merchant trader who rode her own camels, made and managed her own wealth, and actually chose her own husband, the Prophet, inviting him to marry her. How had we reached here, where all women were banned from driving from such auspicious beginnings? I thought about David who was a mine of amazing anecdotes when he recounted an especially bizarre phobia of women and driving.

"One funny little story comes to mind, Qanta," David chuckled to himself in anticipation of the tale, "My wife attended a talk at the embassy given by a young woman, a member of the US Air Force, who piloted one of those huge tanker planes that do mid-air refueling during the Gulf War. She told us a story about her first flight into Riyadh, which even I couldn't believe. As she reached the Arabian Peninsula, she radioed the control tower to ask for clearance to land in Saudi Airspace. She was met by complete silence. There was absolutely no reply at all. She began to think her radio was faulty but continued to no avail.

"Luckily her second officer was male. He tried and since his voice had the *proper timbre*," and David guffawed, "He was answered in the usual protocol. The landing proceeded. After all, since women are incapable of driving a car here, the first request couldn't possibly have happened, Qanta. The apparent female voice from the aircraft must have been a djinn!"

* * *

I had no doubt David was telling the truth. The degree of social restrictions on the movement of women was unparalleled here. The beginnings of our religion glorified powerful, autonomous women and now State sanctioned Wahabi extremism denied even the existence of empowered women even when they piloted jets. Feminism is a fundamental right and expectation of all Muslim women. I already knew, as in early Islamic periods, feminist rights would have to be demanded by women for other women. The Kingdom would be no different than any other stage in the formative history of Islam.

Maha was pressing on. She still had a lot more to say.

*　*　*

"This problem is much bigger than I realized," Maha said. "We are trying to change our culture here, a culture of silence. Women are finally finding the confidence to speak out. Look at the newsreader, she has status, wealth, prestige, and she didn't mention it for years.

"But it will take time. It's hard for our country to allow itself some introspection; even harder if it is introspection in a public forum. But I am still optimistic, Qanta! Mashallah, the Kingdom is moving at an incredible pace. I think our brainchild, the National Family Safety Program, is going to help a lot of Saudi families.[33] The Saudi government has started to work against this violence. We even formed a human rights society that has as a major focus domestic violence. Now we have domestic violence courts, and finally we may have women to stand at the bar and defend cases. Inshallah, change is coming, change is coming!"

Maha went on to explain that the Saudi monarchy had been instrumental in enabling her to accomplish such tremendous change.

"We now have official approval of His Majesty the King through royal decree for our efforts. Our honorary president for our agency is Her Highness Princess Sita Bint Abdul-Aziz ibn Saud, who is the King's sister. Believe me, Qanta, she is not just a figurehead, she is an action woman! We have her support in both addressing the problem and finding solutions. This program, which I formed under the umbrella of our hospital which is a government agency, can now function as a nonprofit organization with royal patronage. This is critical because of the influence and access that brings to us in our society. We have wasta!

"I have been very fortunate. The Princess has been so welcoming to these ideas and has had the courage to take on these challenging and very painful problems our countrywomen face. You probably read about the arrival of Saudi women who will be practicing law in our own country pioneered by the Ahmed Zaki Yamani law. They just decided to start hiring women.

"Please, there is more to Saudi women than driving and abbayahs! We are much more complicated than that!"

Again, I noticed the resonance with early Islamic feminism. Women first had to exercise their rights, voice their demands for freedom and privilege, and recover some of their autonomy from men. Along the way, Saudi women, just as in my experience in the Kingdom, would indeed encounter supportive and benevolent men who aided their efforts, but clearly Saudi women would have to make considerable effort by and for themselves. Perhaps women were finally beginning to gain the confidence of becoming a palpable entity in society, a social advocacy group, a force for change, on their terms, and at their pace, not that of their menfolk.

I understood Maha's dilemma to want controlled change, change that had powerful royal sponsors to foster it to success, which she had to balance with an intense impatience for justice for the weakest in her society. So much about Saudi Arabia was sliced into unintelligible sound bytes that ultimately didn't explain anything and somehow demeaned the sincere efforts of the modern intellectual glitterati, as I liked to think of my friends in the Kingdom.

Trivialization was exactly the right word to describe the dangers of assessing events as an outsider. The West preferred to see the

Kingdom as a caricature, its realities were unfamiliar, and to many, simply unbelievable.

Exhausted by her own passion, Maha was finally silent. She quivered with energy. Her face shone with noor, the light that is said to emerge from the truly good. The woman was a tour de force in a pint-sized abbayah.

"And do you know what Qanta? We just put the first offender in prison. Can you believe we changed the law? These were crimes that were not punishable by imprisonment. Well we, a group of veiled Saudi women, we have changed this!

"Believe me, Saudi women are going to finally have their day! We are learning, we are becoming braver, and we are finding men like Dr. Fahad, who supports all my efforts at the National Guard and has fostered an environment where I could create these agencies; and men like our King, who lends influence so I can accomplish these things. Alhumdullilah, we have every thing in the Kingdom we need to solve our own problems. We just have to have courage. And Allah grants us that. It is said Allah will help those who help themselves, and that God does not change a people unless they change themselves first. I give you the citation, check it my dear! This is a very important point. Islam values progress and self-improvement in its followers. We have a responsibility to live up to that.

"Make no mistake, Qanta my dear, we are changing!"

I had no doubt. Maha, the Gloria Steinem of Arabia, was ensuring it.

Chapter Thirty-Seven

9/11 IN SAUDI ARABIA

A T FOUR IN THE AFTERNOON on a Tuesday, I was home early. I filled the kettle with the sun-warmed, desalinated water. I allowed myself a rare moment of joy. My resignation was tendered. Finally I would return to New York. After two years, I would be leaving the Kingdom. I would be returning to the real, free world, where I could be valued as a woman once more. I felt a warm sense of satisfaction.

Outside, the vapid, midafternoon heat strangled the rooftop apartment. This was now to be my last Saudi September, my last month of buffeting desert breezes, my last dusty days shrouded, suffocating in black polyester.

Downloading email, I savored the anticipation of contact with the real world. The television was on. The nostalgic sound of Katie Couric soothed me. NBC seemed to be running the same news item. Staccato sirens insistently pulled me to the screen and I glanced at the image of a single smoldering tower.

Moments later, any nostalgia drowned in swirling currents of horror. Scrambling to the phone, I began dialing numbers to reach friends in New York City. For me, 9/11, moments before, had been a day of freedom and beginnings. Instead, my American future was now supplanted by the fearful vacuum arrived in plane-shaped arrowheads that sheared our world in two. The terror had come like an arrow through its quarry. I was reminded of the chilling hadith which now in these moments seemed prophetic. It was ascribed as the words of the Prophet when asked what he feared most for his followers:

They recite the Quran and consider it in their favor but
it is against them
They transpose Quranic verses meant to refer to unbelievers and make
them refer to the believers
What I fear most for my Ummah is a man who interprets verses of the
Quran out of context[13]
They will pass through Islam as an arrow passes through its quarry.
Wherever you meet them, kill them!
The one who kills them or is killed by them is blessed
They are the dogs of the People of Hell

The deadly attacks were looped on endless replay. I watched the digital currents of debris sweeping over the monitor and surging through Lower Manhattan, sending reverberations of destruction rippling across the globe. I could already feel them here. I called Imad at once.

---

[13] The Prophet is referring to imposters who will commit destruction in the name of Islam. He mentions the gravest enemies of Islam will emerge from within it.

"I know, Qanta, we are watching it now in the administration office. It's unbelievable." Imad sounded engrossed. Yet his voice was somehow cold. We were yet to discover the nationality of the perpetrators. Finding myself reluctant to explore his reaction, we agreed to talk later.

Compelled to dart between speed dial and satellite TV through sleepless hours, I arrived at work the next morning drained. Around me, in the Intensive Care Unit, glossy with the rich patina of U.S. tax dollars, the air was pregnant with muted exaltation. I recalled a similar, palpable excitement when Governor George W. Bush was announced president in 2000. Then, Saudi Arabia breathed an anguished sigh of relief. My puzzlement at the time was singular in its naïve stupidity. Didn't I know that if Gore had been elected, the U.S. presidency would have been "one heartbeat away from a Jew," colleagues had irritably explained, referring to Senator Lieberman. Shocked, I had recoiled at the effortless anti-Semitism rampant among my educated peers.

Months later, I found myself once more flummoxed. In a crucible of silence, punctuated only by mechanized breaths of the patients around me, I condensed my searing anxieties. Distracted, I studied colleagues through plate glass as I examined my patients.

No one approached me to express concern about New York, even though it was the place I still called home. As I ventured beyond my ruminations, I was increasingly aware of excitement. Inside the hermetic world of the ICU, I detected the unmistakable fetor of relish in the face of destruction.

I watched through the glass. Majeed studied an X ray, his ivory brow furrowed in concentration. His fair, veined skin glowed blue-white against the light box. An Omani national, and a brilliant, U.S.-educated physician whose work was published in the best American journals of medicine, he was a valued, experienced colleague.

This morning, his cool, blue eyes glinted with unusual energy. Normally a man of little emotion, he was clearly excited. I didn't dare ask him why, remembering his staggering outburst at my Polish colleagues months earlier contesting the realities of the Shoah. Radek and Jan had looked at each other in disbelief, Radek especially amazed since his friend ran historic tours for Israelis visiting Kraków. Majeed was a self-confessed Holocaust denier. I had witnessed his indignant nihilism about the six million condemned to be extinguished infinitely in countless narrow minds like his. Despite his intelligence, he possessed capacities I had never previously encountered.

I was, however, alone in my naïveté. Jan and Radek were, in contrast, more than familiar with virulent anti-Semitism in the Kingdom. One incident stood out in particular. Jan and his wife Yola were visiting a stadium on a guided tour arranged by the National Guard Hospital. The Palestinian guide, excited to spy the national Polish emblem on Jan's T-shirt, singled out the friendly couple. He treated them to a special, very attentive tour; afterward, Jan mentioned how surprised he was that a Palestinian could recognize the Polish insignia.

"Oh, Dr. Adamski, the Palestinians *love* the Polish! Didn't you know? Because of the way you took care of the Jewish problem so effectively. We adore you!" Jan and Yola crumpled, paling with nausea. The friendly Palestinian looked on, beaming—he earnestly admired the Polish couple.

I had long been a painful oddity within the sophisticated medical circles of Riyadh. My relationships with Jewish friends in America in particular were at best a puzzlement (prompting one Saudi woman to ask, "And what do Jews eat?") and at worst (in the eyes of the orthodox) an immoral deviancy only confirming my heresy. In the eyes of many of my colleagues and Saudi friends, these friendships made me someone who was apart, other, outcast.

I turned to my Pakistani friends, hoping to seek shelter. Imran, the brilliant, Manhattan-trained intensivist who had embraced me in his family, was a handsome man, a dead ringer for Dylan McDermott. I could always rely on his wit and humor to cheer the dullest of days. Today, he was in no mood for jokes, yet he seemed strangely infused with energy. Mobeen, a more orthodox Muslim and benevolent Pakistani, was actually laughing, fascinated by the news reports. Only Imtiaz, who could barely tear himself away from his beloved Persian poetry to attend patients, seemed remotely concerned.

He said, "These are terrible times for America. Dark days have arrived for that country." I scrutinized his expression, unsure if he felt compassion. Before I could decide, Imran clarified any doubts I might have about popular sentiment.

"So, they lost thousands of Americans. They are guessing three thousand right now. Do you have any idea how many people die in Palestine every day, Qanta? The loss of these lives is hardly equal to the daily losses of life in the Muslim world in past years. Don't you know about the carnage we faced working in Karachi, at our alma mater hospitals?" Imtiaz nodded his assent.

"God, those bomb blasts that go off so often in Karachi were terrible. I remember them from my medical student days. Those were some of the first patients I ever attended," Imtiaz volunteered, referring to the years of violence that had troubled the city for so long.

I glanced up at Imran. We were attending a patient with a badly infected limb. I was surprised to meet his angry stare. He was angry at my sorrow. I gazed at the fetid wound we were inspecting. We had worked on this patient for weeks. Somehow, in the eyes of the doctors around me, our efforts on a single Muslim were worthier than the three thousand souls who had perished ten thousand miles west of here. I was stupefied.

"What happened, Qanta? You look terrible!" blurted out another Beiruti colleague who rarely entered conversation. "Are you ill? What's the matter?" His face was genuinely blank.

"What do you mean?" I snapped. "Didn't you see the news? Don't you know how many Americans died yesterday? Of course I look terrible. I was trying to reach my friends all night on the phone. It's just unbelievable." I actually began to express some of my mounting anger. Imran laughed hollowly.

"Qanta, where have you been? You are so naïve. We always thought that. But we figured, she can't know because she doesn't follow politics, so we excused you. It's time you realized, America has been doing this to people all over the planet. Murder. It was their turn. They deserved this..." I was already moving away, I didn't hear the rest. I couldn't be around my colleagues, men whom I had considered friends. My final distinction from my surroundings had become clear. I was not of these Muslims. I was something other.

My brain shrieked with echoes of their self-righteous insanity. They were treating patients in the wealthiest Arab state in the world only by dint of their American credentials; credentials they had acquired in years of patient mentoring from Americans, often-times from Jewish Americans. These men had accomplished all this, arriving from impoverished schools in other countries to travel to America, only because they had been invited on generous visas by the American government. I was sick. Of all Muslims, these American-trained Pakistani nationals, men who had made homes in New York City, men who were physicians, should know better, feel more, and experience shame at their own reactions.

Stumbling away from these men I no longer understood, I didn't know where to put my sadness. No one wanted my foolish sentiments of loss. As physicians, guarding life was the keystone of our life-purpose. This calculating mathematics of hatred, a hunger for blood, from physician colleagues, professing to be Muslim, stunned me. Irrespective of the men's roles as healers, sworn to first do no harm, to preserve life, to ease suffering, they brandished their badges of hatred openly, proudly, immediately. They almost chastised me for not sharing their sentiments. Thankfully, something about me curbed them. We had already divided.

Later, making evening rounds, huddling in the darkness of the ICU, amid beeping monitors and muted telephones, my nurses asked to speak to me.

"What is it, ladies?" I asked, weary and ready to end the ward round. It was well past midnight.

"Not here, Doctora, not here," Mama Mary looked grave. Vicky, the Zululander, recently widowed, actually looked afraid. "In here, this should be OK. We can't be heard in here."

They pulled me into a vacant isolation room, normally reserved for transplant recipients. The double doors sealed behind us. The shades were lowered. Laminar airflow rushed a quiet hiss. Tonight the silence wasn't soothing. My nurses surrounded me. In our circle we were a world of nationalities ourselves, each a woman from a different continent: Swedes, South Africans, Indians, Filipinas, Canadians, and myself. Mama Mary haltingly told me of the events of 9/11 during the day. While I had been glued to my television, they had been on duty. The Scandinavian was already crying.

"Doctora, on the maternity wards, and on the general medical and surgical wards, the patients were watching TV when the towers crumbled. Patients, Saudis, actually clapped."

Normally timid, Juliette interrupted, impassioned.

"One of my nursing friends, an American, was there on the ward doing her medication rounds. When the patients started clapping she told them, 'I am an American.' They laughed. They still clapped. She started crying while she was trying to give them their medicines."

"But the worst—it's a disgrace!" Sputtering, Mama Mary's Afrikaans-inflected voice cut through us all, thickened with outrage. "Those bloody obstetricians, two Saudi women—women for Christ's sake—ordered cakes!"

"Cakes? You cannot be sure!" I cut her off in disbelief.

"Cakes, Doctora Qanta! Cakes! Yes, yes. I am not exaggerating. They ordered not one but two cakes, as soon as the towers crumbled. They had them delivered from the Diplomat Bakery. They were dialing right away, as they watched the towers fall. And they sliced them up and fed them to other staff, as a form of mabrook (congratulations). They even sent the cakes over to the cheering patients, the same wards where the American and other Western nurses were on duty."

"How do you know? Did you see this?" I pressed, quizzing her intensely, refusing to accept the possibility this could be true.

"So you didn't see the memo? Dr. Fahad sent a hospital-wide memo as soon as he found out, condemning their behavior. I don't think they were disciplined. We don't know. But he wrote and had it put up in every unit in the hospital reminding us we are an institution with fifty-three nationalities in our ranks, many of whom have family or homes in America, and he expressed sorrow for the events in New York City. He added, 'Any other response is unacceptable as a member of the organization.'"

I knew then that this was not a figment of an overactive imagination or vicious rumor. This was real. A few meters away from us, Saudi women, women who were obstetricians, women who delivered new life in their highly skilled hands every day, had commemorated murder with angel food cake and butter icing.

For a time we whispered our muzzled outrage amidst the beeping canvas of cardiac monitors and hissing ventilators, our sense of loss secure in isolation. I was relieved that my patients were comatose, powerless to hurt me. After a while, stunned, we fell into silence, not wishing to leave the safety of unmonitored privacy. I felt comfortable among the Westerners, the Africans, the Filipinas. Every woman around me was a Christian compelled to hide her religion. Yet here at the epicenter of Islam I was alone amid Muslims who alienated me in their hatreds. I couldn't see a place among them. I no longer belonged here.

Within days, the terrorists were identified as Saudi. The world now rotated around a new axis. Overnight, I had found myself at the wrong pole. I found myself paralyzed in the frightening aftermath that many expatriates sensed.

"I have been eating a lot of chocolate, Qanta." Jane and I were chatting a couple of evenings later. We discussed my discoveries of the last few days. She had heard the same stories. She paused to munch on a snack as we talked on the phone. "And I haven't really talked to any of the Saudis in the department. It's not really a subject we can open with them. I have been sticking to my British and Kiwi friends. We're pretty much keeping to ourselves."

"Me too, Jane," I said, realizing how quickly we had become demarcated from the Saudi nationals we knew. We were too afraid to engage in dialogue, even moving in the educated sector. Visiting the grocery store on the compound confirmed the prevalent hate.

The South Indian check-out boy scanned my shopping. Always chatty, he wanted to talk. He spoke in his native Hindi, which I answered in Urdu. He was eager to discuss the news.

"This news in New York has been very good, Doctora! The Americans deserved it." I looked up from my wallet, disgusted. A man of only twenty-two, perhaps, he had until now, always impressed me with his friendliness and warmth. There had been a certain curiosity about him that belied promise. Instead he proved himself ignorant and hateful.

"New York City is my home!" I barked. "My friends and my family are there. Don't ever say that again. You call yourself Muslim and you celebrate death! Don't you know life is the most sacred thing in Islam? That the right to human life overrides even the rights of God?" The young man cowered under my blistering attack. Shamed, he immediately began to apologize. I snatched my goods from him, threw a handful of notes in payment and pushed my way past other shoppers. I wanted to get away.

In the days following 9/11, I bore witness to an extraordinary fabric, uniting the most educated and elite of Muslims to the weakest and least educated in shared hatreds. As I stumbled upon rancid hates and crude appetites, I was reminded of what I had chosen to forget: the deep-rooted currents of anti-Americanism and anti-Semitism that here often seemed to run together. An instance flashed into recall.

A few months earlier, in the compound video store, I was about to leave when I noticed a Saudi couple. The woman was wearing a hijab with her face uncovered, standing with her thobe-clad husband. They were renting a movie; planning their Thursday night as a family. A daughter, perhaps ten at most, stood between them. She was unveiled. Her curly hair cascaded into a lush mane. Clinging on to her mother's hand with slim fingers decorated with plastic jewelry, she waited for them silently. Ribboned hair indicated she was cherished, adorned. Warming at the sight of a valued daughter, I was surprised to notice the mother clutched an Al Pacino movie, *The Devil's Advocate*. I had seen the film and knew it to be inappropriate for a ten-year-old. I had to say something.

"Excuse me, but some of the film is a little explicit. It's not what you should be allowing your young daughter to see. I have seen it. I think you won't be able to have your little girl watch it."

"We know exactly what it is like. We know the ratings," said the mother brightly, as though I had underestimated her. "That's why we want our daughter to see it!"

I was shocked. The movie imagined a world in which Pacino plays Satan. Group sexuality peppers the film, conveying Satanic evil. The violence in it is extreme, and ironically, it's portrayed against a sleek, glossy interpretation of modern-day New York City.

"Are you sure you wish her to see it?" I looked at the mother, unable to know quite how to tell her she would be exposing her daughter to sexually graphic images without completely embarrassing her in the tiny shop.

"Yes, we want our daughter to understand all the things which are so bad about the West, and especially America. We want our daughter to be aware of all the bad things that come out of there, for her own protection. I don't believe in sheltering my daughter. We believe we should expose her to the true reflection of that corrupt and debased world! I want to inform my daughter. She needs to be prepared." I was amazed, both at her ignorance and the highly articulated English with which she expressed it. I couldn't let this go.

"Rubbish! You couldn't be more wrong. I am a product of New York City. This movie is no reflection of that. It is fantasy. You are not telling your daughter the truth; you will be lying to her. And as a British Muslim woman myself, I take offense personally at what you have said. I have lived in New York City and I can assure you, my morals are intact, like those of many New Yorkers and Americans. You are cultivating ignorance in your daughter."

I looked hard, first at the woman barricaded within her cozy prejudice, and then at her soft-haired daughter who remained still innocent of discrimination. The spineless father shifted uneasily from side to side, unwilling to engage in the melee, unsure of how to react. I left the store not knowing if they changed their minds about the movie. I was beginning to realize some mothers inculcated hatred in the way others did love. Privilege and foreign training, an excellent command of English, and opportunity were still no panacea for hate.

As a result, even if I had denied it as time went on, I was well-acquainted with hate in the Kingdom. In the days after 9/11, anxious friends urged me to get out. Unsolicited, Jewish friends were the first to offer practical help.

"Get out now!" urged Stuart when we spoke on the phone, my dear friend and research mentor. "There is an incredible cry for blood here. It's not safe. There is a talk of a strike. I don't know if you are secure here. Do you need a ticket? Money? Tell us!"

"Will help to get you out! Get out now!" read Alan's message. "Tell me what you need! We are waiting!" I could feel his concern in his staccato emails, which, usually a rarity, were now persistent.

"Come home now, we are worried for you," from Ronna, my mentor's wife.

In a roiling Muslim sea, my lifelines were cast by Jewish hands. I was grateful for their solidarity toward me and felt glad that Allah had blessed me with such Jewish goodness in my life. I felt no shame for my allegiances with Jews in the way so many Muslims around the world are wrongly raised to express, especially after 9/11. I felt deep shame only for the ignorance and hatred I had now witnessed among Muslims.

In the difficult weeks following, I quickly discovered that anti-Semitism infected many of my Muslim circles. Both Saudi and non-Saudi Muslims felt free to express their hate to me, even as some planned to flee to their Virginia homes with blue passports in hand. Somehow, my Muslim calling card announced (in their eyes) a tolerance and permission to express hatred, some of it particularly virulent. The worst incident I had encountered was perhaps the most crushing disappointment of all.

Mu'ayyad had finally invited me for dinner. Newly married, he wanted to introduce me to his young wife, Najwa. After years as a playboy, racing speedboats on Lake Cuomo during long summer vacations, of growing his hair long and resisting his culture,

Mu'ayyad had bought into the traditional role prescribed him as a Saudi male. He had married a Saudi Muslim woman, albeit one who was exceptionally beautiful.

"I saw her at a wedding in Aqaba, and I just knew I was going to marry her. She hated me. She thought I was arrogant." Mu'ayyad flushed at the memory of his first ardor while his stunning wife looked on in adoration. We were in their living room decorated with French antiques. Heavy damask draperies cosseted the room in a musty perfumed silence. His wife handed me a stemmed Baccarat glass of freshly squeezed juice. Her slim, creamy arms showed through the chiffon sleeves of a stylish tunic, probably Gucci couture. It accented her Earl jeans perfectly.

"I did!" she laughed. "He was so confident, so full of himself!"

"And then we fell in love! I had to marry her, right, habibti?" Squeezing her waist, he used her endearing nickname, in reference to her gorgeous skin. Mu'ayyad was evidently still entranced with his young wife nine months after the birth of their first child, a son, called Mohammed.

They described their whirlwind international romance, conducted like that of so many Saudis, outside the country's borders, in the widespread phenomenon of transnational dating.[34] In response to the restrictive social climate inside the Kingdom, many Saudis courted overseas, often traveling with family members in tow, to pursue important social networking during their long summer vacations, often falling in love in the process.

I looked at the family. I was happy for Mu'ayyad. A chain-smoking, highly strung, hypertensive surgeon of exceptional brilliance, Mu'ayyad had trouble winding down. Najwa seemed to have helped him relax. But he was still a workaholic. Even my clinical neuroticism attending his critically ill patients was not up to his exacting obsession with the care of his patients. Often he worked days without a break, operating around the clock with limited relief. A sub-specialized surgeon, he was unique in his country. No one else possessed his skills, and patients came from across the wider Arab region to benefit from his expertise. Many of his patients were indigent and poor, some with very serious congenital defects, a result of generations of intermarriage, defects he could repair. He operated on anyone whom he could help. Whether operating on rare defects or simply the humdrum routine of debriding scarred wounds, Mu'ayyad was the consummate clinician, tireless, dedicated, a perfectionist.

The other quality I liked most about Mu'ayyad was his recognition of women. He was one of the few Saudi men with whom I consulted who treated me exactly as an equal. On many occasions, he actually deferred to my expertise. Whenever I conferred with Mu'ayyad I was instantly transported back in the West. And he also had a profound knowledge of the Quran, able to cite long passages from memory and then dissect them critically with his brilliant mind. Clearly he was a scholar of Islam. I admired him greatly, uncritically.

The elegant couple served me a dinner of Lebanese delicacies including my favorite, a Lebanese fish dish, sayyadieh, which Najwa had prepared herself. We talked of religion and politics. In Riyadh it was impossible to have dinner without discussing either.

"So, Mu'ayyad, I hear congratulations are in order. I heard from Salim that you donated a huge sum, hundreds of thousands of dollars, to your alma mater fellowship in Ohio. Mashallah, you are so generous. What a wonderful gesture." Mu'ayyad flushed with pleasure and seemed awkward at the discovery of his good deed.

"Oh, so you heard?" he began. "Alhumdullilah, Allah has given me much. I wanted to give back. With this money I have created a fund so that each year a single resident from the National Guard could be trained in the States without incurring costs and then return to serve our nation. I want to improve surgery for our country."

"You must be a very wealthy man, Mu'ayyad, Mashallah." He visibly straightened.

"This is not family money, Qanta," Mu'ayyad underlined, anxious to separate his wealth from that of his father's, who was once a senior advisor in the Treasury and a very affluent man. "This is from earnings I have made from my margins trading. I am really good at it, and I wanted to use the money for a good purpose. I am pleased I could do at least this. Inshallah maybe I will be able to do more.

"Last month, I flew over there to present the check. They had a wonderful ceremony. I got to see my professors again. I love my mentor. He has given me everything, Qanta, everything, my credentials, my skills. I will never forget that." Mu'ayyad continued explaining details of the joint academic program he was developing, linking the two institutions.

After a time the conversation turned to Palestine.

"But Qanta, the problem with America is its affiliation with Israel. It is an uncritical supporter of Israel. It never defends the Palestinians' rights. No one does. It's horrific, the conditions out there. Have you seen how they are forced to live in Gaza?" I listened in concern. If I learned anything during my time in the Kingdom, it was how much I didn't know about the Israeli-Palestinian conflict.

But before I could respond, Mu'ayyad was blustering on, "You know Qanta, I have to tell you. I hate Jews. I hate them." I looked at my handsome friend in his elegant home to suddenly find a stranger's face curled into a snarl.

"Well, I can't support that view, Mu'ayyad," I began gently, wondering how to respond to my host in his home without becoming an extremely rude guest. "But everything I have learned," I continued, "everything I have been trained in came to me from Jewish physicians, brilliant ones, who taught me very kindly. I have wonderful friendships with the Jewish physicians as a matter of fact. And I don't agree with hate in any principle."

"Oh Qanta, don't get me wrong. I love my mentor. He is Jewish too. I loved him so much I gave his program a quarter of a million dollars. But that's different, we had a personal relationship. I don't care if he is Jewish, but I will always hate Jews as a whole." I was puzzled. Mu'ayyad bounced his gorgeous son on his knee, unaware of how illogical he was. I gazed at the baby.

"I don't think you should be saying this in front of the baby," I began, realizing how stupid it sounded, because the baby could hardly speak words in Arabic, let alone understand English, but Mu'ayyad's venom seemed toxic for his child.

"It's OK," defended Najwa, locking a gorgeous, kohl-rimmed stare at me.

"What about you, Najwa?" I asked. "Do you hate Jews too?"

"Yes," answered the twenty-four-year-old graduate of a Boston college, without a moment's hesitation. "Of course I hate the Jews. I hate what they do to Palestine."

"But then if you both decide to hate Jews, how will you avoid influencing Mohammed? He is pure now. He has no hate now. How will he be able to make an unbiased choice on relating to Jews?" By now I was unable to hide my distress. My voice came out a little too high-pitched.

"Oh Qanta," responded the mother coolly, bouncing the baby who was cooing. "Our son will grow up to hate Jews too."

I had no response. I was crestfallen. The man I had regarded as a liberal, Westernized, brilliantly trained acolyte, a philanthropist to boot, had emerged a rabid anti-Semite. For all his scholarship of the Quran, I realized it hadn't reached further than his throat. It hadn't touched his heart. Islam guides Muslims to enjoin with all People of the Book, Jews included, to achieve mutual goals in the pursuit of virtue. For him, when convenient, Islam was lip-service.

It took me weeks to recover from my disappointment. I wanted so much to think well of my elite friends, but in the end, I discovered they were little better than the cake-ordering celebrators of murder. Though Mu'ayyad worked long nights and hard days to debride dead flesh on unfortunate patients in an effort to heal them, I realized he would never be able to debride his own devitalized hatreds that encased his glossy world. His hates would never heal. They would only propagate. He had no desire to shed the crusty cocoon of anti-Semitism, impenetrable to the love of a Jewish academic mentor and ultimately unsoftened even by the responsibility to preserve the innocence of his child. I felt hopeless.

These were the darkest weeks in the Kingdom for me. A veil had been lifted. The courtliness and courtesies had been swept aside, allowing coils of nurtured hates to become clear in the most unexpected corners. Whether perpetrating violence or merely condoning it, the Hadith had come true, just as The Prophet had predicted more than 1,400 years earlier: the worst enemies of Islam would come from within. Like arrows in a quarry, they were suddenly in our midst, and some of them wore Gucci and smoked Dunhills.

Chapter Thirty-Eight

Final Moments, Final Days

I WAS LEAVING IN THREE days. I stood in my living room. The cool November night carried the smell of the desert through open windows. My cat, Souhaa, lay napping with a fat, full belly, softly snoring. Around me my humble abode, once an ugly apartment, over time had morphed into a pretty twinkling Saudi home.

Life in Saudi Arabia was perpetually transient for all who worked there. I was no exception in this Kingdom where, for non-Saudis, the only certainty was impermanence. I looked at the containers that had arrived in the living room. They were big enough to hold me. These would return the contents of my home to New York. Two years suddenly had flashed by. Like all departures, I was experiencing mixed emotions of both relief and loss. I couldn't wait for the turmoil of transition to be over.

"Qanta, I would like to arrange a farewell dinner for you," Imad had mentioned during a phone call some days earlier. "I want to give you a send-off." I had flushed with pleasure, surprised.

"Please invite anyone you wish. They will be my guests." He wouldn't hear of anything else. We chose to dine at a restaurant in Olleyah, a place renowned for the freshest seafood from the Red Sea. Lobsters were a particular specialty. For Imad, it was a serious passion.

I considered who else I could invite. Even though he had disappointed me terribly, I couldn't leave without saying goodbye to Mu'ayyad. I wanted to remember him in a positive light. Of course friendly Hamid was a must, along with Ahmed, Imad's best friend. I well knew my Saudi women friends wouldn't think of accompanying me to a mixed gathering, even in a private room in a restaurant in the Kingdom. Such open mixing would wound their family reputation and, further, consorting with men from work would ensure everyone would hear about this scandalous mixing. I didn't bother even asking them. We would meet and have our own farewells. As a result, I found myself invited to dinner with four men.

My relationship with Faris had been strained since my resignation, and somehow my Pakistani colleagues declined to join me as Imad's guests. Even in recognizing my departure, my friendships revealed themselves to be fragmented and disconnected. The men were divided by status as migrant worker or Saudi citizen. I was the lone link between divided factions. Declining politely, the others determined to accord separate occasions for our goodbyes, but this dinner (days from my final exit) would be the last time I would see Imad before returning to New York City. Immediately after, he would leave for a meeting in Jeddah.

On the evening of the dinner, I dressed up in a beautiful Escada suit only for it to be swamped in my horrid black abbayah. I was already counting the days before I could discard my polyester prison forever. My faithful driver, Zachariah, arrived exactly on time. I was looking forward to dinner and rather excited at the prospect of dining with so many men. As we journeyed into central Riyadh, I realized how much of my world, while interfacing with occasional Saudi women, was really the world inhabited by Saudi men.

It was after evening prayer. The religious police would be patrolling restaurants and malls making a nuisance of themselves far from us. As always, there remained a risk of being apprehended, but Imad obviously believed this was manageable and a risk worth taking. I found myself flattered and rather taken aback at his boldness.

Though we had still not discussed our deepening feelings for one another, we had made a habit of speaking to each other on a daily basis. Telephoning, often late into the night, we felt close. I already realized I would miss him enormously and privately I wondered if I would have the courage to declare my feelings to him before I would leave his country for good.

Zachariah dropped me off in a nondescript parking lot outside the restaurant venue. I scurried toward the entrance. Years in the Kingdom had not expunged my intense discomfort of being in public, especially when unaccompanied. A knot of fear gathered in the pit of my stomach, which always happened to me when I left my home and went outdoors in Riyadh. For a single woman, being outside the security of a gated compound, a glass walled ICU, or the privacy of high concrete walls was unsettling, bringing feelings of exposure and vulnerability into sharp focus. I actually felt a guilt of some kind. I was finally beginning to understand the Saudi women whom I had seen scuttling about in Riyadh, whether in veils in malls or in scrubs in hospital corridors. I could understand their intense recoil from public space, where anything could befall them, a place where their vulnerabilities were most visceral. Now, I felt the same.

Inside, the restaurant was dimly lit. Heavily paneled walls of teak shone, glossy with the glow of bonhomie. Instantly I felt glad to be ensconced away from the public space. Almost as soon as I approached the reservation desk, I was flanked by the four men: Mu'ayyad, Hamid, Ahmed, and Imad. We greeted each other with warmth expressed only in handshakes; in itself anathema for Saudi men when greeting Muslim women, but each man here was comfortable with the Western woman within me. To a man, they looked thrilled.

As a group, we raised no eyebrows; behind partitions other dinners were busy enjoying their meals. We passed the screened-off men's section quickly and bypassed the ladies' section. Instead, we were lead by the South Indian waiter to a private cabin inside the family section, where each table was placed inside a room of its own. Behind the wooden panels and the frosted glass, we were relatively secure. It would be difficult for the Muttawa to intrude, unable to tell whether they would be accosting a Saudi family enjoying a private dinner or, like us, surreptitious friends who were flouting the law.

The panels were about seven feet in height; the room like a giant office space divided into cubicles. No ceilings enclosed each dining area. A soft hubbub of conversations in Najdi Arabic, the clink of cutlery, and the sound of ice trickled in from above.

We seated ourselves. Ever thoughtful, Imad had invited his most senior nurse, Lynn, who was already settled. He had asked her along so that I would not feel uncomfortable surrounded by men. I was surprised to see her there but was touched at his clumsy consideration, immediately knowing she was a panacea not for my discomfort but for his. In Saudi Arabia it still remained illegal and brazen to dine with an unrelated, unchaperoned woman in public.

As a man from a conservative traditional and very elite Saudi family, I knew just how far Imad had deviated from his usual customs. A son of a Senior Saudi bureaucrat, Imad was steeped in protocols of religion and culture. While he may well have been comfortable dining in mixed company in the West, in the Kingdom he was violating a social taboo that would offend his closest family members. I was surprised that despite all his inhibitions, Imad had suggested such a public gesture and in the presence of his closest male colleagues. As usual, he transmitted mixed messages. I could never truly know what he felt about me and what he intended for me to feel in turn.

Saturated with heavy cologne, all the men except Imad were dressed in long flowing Saudi thobes. I inhaled their masculinity, realizing how much I had craved mixed company. Imad chose to stick to his customary khakis and open-necked shirt. Among them all, it was Mu'ayyad who looked truly glamorous.

In place of scrubs, his thobe was exceptionally fine, the linen sheen on it perfectly pressed, starched, and glowing blue-white in halogen spot lights. Silver buttons glinted at the throat. A high, starched collar, almost Victorian, framed handsome and very fair Caucasian skin, freshly shaven and dressed in aftershave. His head-dress was subtly elegant and, like many dashing rakes in Riyadh, he had folded the cloth at the front into the low peak of a Stetson-shaped drape. Tonight he was a truly polished Saudi cowboy. The long drapes of his ghutra were tossed behind his broad, chiseled shoulders, sweeping into an elegant mane. I spied a tiny Dunhill logo on a corner of the cloth, revealing the discerning taste of the man within. In slim, blue-veined fingers, with a surgeon's precision, Mu'ayyad twisted a costly silver and lapis lazuli rosary. Nicotine-stained nails gave away his extremely heavy smoking habit. I complimented the men on their national dress. While the others looked uneasy, characteristically Mu'ayyad handled it well.

"Thank you, Qanta. I like to dress up when I go out. Our national dress is so comfortable. I much prefer it to Western clothing." He smiled, laying the expensive rosary on the table. He was extremely dashing. I regretted not getting to know Mu'ayyad sooner. Now that I was leaving I would miss him a lot.

Only Imad was dressed in Western clothing and he squirmed as Mu'ayyad was speaking.

As I watched Imad around his countrymen that evening, I finally began to see how he was as much an outcast in this environment as I was. Trapped in the echelons of power, his nonconformity was even more striking and even more disabling. In his Tommy Hilfiger he was a jarring outcast among the elegant Saudi men surrounding him.

The food arrived. Too salty to eat, I hardly touched my soup while I was busy talking. My Saudi hosts ordered like emperors, the table spread with enough food for ten. Ahmed regaled us with funny stories in a very butchered rendition of Glaswegian. We laughed for hours. Finally the mood became more serious.

"This is not a good thing, that you're leaving," Mu'ayyad began, smiling sincerely. "Are you sure you can't change your mind? Dr. Fahad would easily arrange it."

"Oh that's kind, Mu'ayyad, but I am already packing. The cargo people come the day after tomorrow. And you know it's better for me to plan a move. I have done what I can here." Imad was looking at me intently. I wondered if he wanted to express his reservations about my departure.

"And Imad suggested I consider changing to do less intensive care. Didn't you, Imad? We even thought perhaps I should change departments, but none of it would get me back to my dream of returning to New York. No, Mu'ayyad, it's definitely time to go. I need to return to somewhere where I can be free. You know it's not easy for a woman here, especially for an unmarried one."

None of them looked me in the eye. The nurse busied herself with the breadbasket. I had probably insulted my hosts by pointing out the uncomfortable and ugly realities of Kingdom life, something to which, as men, they were completely immune. In many ways, men were as free here as they were in the West, especially the affluent men who were seated next to me.

When the absence of cinemas or restaurants that were secure from the Muttawa grew too wearing, they could jump in their cars and drive themselves out of the country, reaching Dubai or Oman or Bahrain in a few hours. As men, they could apply and receive multiple entry and exit visas and take as many international trips as they liked without seeking anyone's permission. I discovered that evening that the Saudi employees did not grant their employers possession of their passports in the way I had been compelled to do for these two years. No, their experiences of the Kingdom were very different than mine. Whatever hardships they might perceive they faced, they paled against the plight of even privileged women like me.

"Well, America may not be the same place you left, Qanta, not after 9/11," Ahmed warned, "especially if it continues in this direction in these weeks after 9/11. Look at what they are doing with food parcels and bombs in Afghanistan. It's a disgrace."

"We will flush them out!" someone mocked, remembering President Bush's initial speech post 9/11. The men at the table laughed in scorn.

"And just look at the state of Palestine," Mu'ayyad continued. "America is always allying with Israel, no matter how bad the conditions become because of the occupation. How can you want to live in America, that Israeli ally?" Mu'ayyad was smoldering, impassioned. He tapped a bruised packet of Marlboros, extracting a single cigarette. Lighting his cigarette he snapped his heavy lighter shut with an expensive click. I watched him take a long, sexy drag, struggling to order my thoughts. Nervously, I side-stepped his anti-Semitism. I didn't want to bring that ugliness to the fore again.

"Well, Mu'ayyad," I began gingerly, "I think America is a great country." I hoped my voice didn't sound too plaintive. "It is a country that allows me to be freer than here, a country that is the closest we have to a pure meritocracy. It gave me all my abilities, all my training, and all the opportunities that stemmed from that effort. I am not an expert on the Israeli-Palestinian conflict. I hadn't even met Palestinians until I moved here to Riyadh.

"God has granted the Arab Muslim world unparalleled wealth and what is being done with it? Sometimes I feel the wealth here from oil has just been set ablaze, ignited. Like so many oil rigs aflame, it's just vaporizing. Prince al-Waleed is a leader in reinvesting in his country, one of very few men who do this. For the rest of us, all the GDP we earn travels out of the Kingdom. We don't give back to our countries. But for me, most importantly, in America I get to be a Muslim on my terms, not on those of some illiterate Muttawa! No one tells me how to be a Muslim there, or how to be a woman there, for that matter!"

I stopped, breathless and rather worried.

My fellow dinner guests were silent. I had deeply offended them. For once Mu'ayyad didn't have a pat answer. He blew smoke circles and started biting his ragged nails. Lynn looked up in concern but didn't dare enter the discussion. With nervous laughter, looking up at the open ceiling, Imad broke the awkward silence.

"Well Qanta, if the Mutawaeen enter, we will tell them it was you that said that! We will watch them carry you away." The table dissolved into strained giggles. I laughed the loudest and the tension ebbed. He smiled at me, meeting my gaze warmly.

Like the *People* magazines that arrived in the Kingdom censored, with ripped-out pages and photographs blacked out in thick marker, there were many subjects that could not be discussed outside the barricaded privacy of high-walled homes. In his squirming discomfort, Imad was feeling, like the other men here, some of the same vulnerabilities I sensed as a woman. They were afraid. However, unlike my upbringing in England and America, he and his colleagues had never mastered the freedom of expression that a liberated life in the West truly inculcates. Worse than the defiant women I had encountered in the Kingdom, these men were afraid to stand up for themselves. They had become their own censors to the degree that the governing forces didn't need to actively impose restrictions. The men had censored their own logical dissent and viewed matters, whether women's rights, driving legislation, or the frighteningly passionate subject of Middle Eastern politics, through the same distorted lens of a society that enforced oppression. The men around me, while allowed certain liberties, were no more free than the heavily veiled women who scuttled around them.

The time flew too quickly and soon dinner was over. Imad offered to drive me home, again with the chaperone of the nurse as a cover. Instead, my driver was waiting and so, crestfallen, he escorted us to my car. Discreetly the nurse seated herself into the vehicle, allowing us time alone. Under the Riyadh sky still glowing with light pollution, I finally gazed at Imad. We stood face to face. He was tall and leaning over me slightly, from my vantage, at a perfect height for a kiss. I never felt more attracted to him, but between us, in the short distance which separated us, was a world of traditions, Mutawaeen, restrictions, and cultures that would ultimately separate us forever. On that evening we still believed in each other and the possibility of a shared future. Imad did his best to reassure me.

"You know Qanta, I travel a lot. I am in London and Paris very often. We will see each other soon." He continued to smile at me, all the shyness suddenly gone.

We stood together in silence for a while and then, after chastely shaking hands, I got into the car. I watched his tall figure absorbed into the darkness. The last image I had was of a rangy muscular figure, hands in pockets, locked in a puddle of street lighting. Like a performer on a stage he was spotlit, immobile, watching me leave, until finally I could see him no more.

Detecting my somber mood, the nurse reassured me, "Don't worry Qanta, you will see him again. He travels all the time. This isn't so much a farewell as a 'see you later.'" She beamed at me. I suddenly wondered if she was privy to Imad's feelings.

The next day I resumed the slow task of packing and dismantling. I folded up my prayer mats, purchased in the marketplace outside the mosque in Mecca during Hajj. How I wished I could see the Ka'aba again before I left. I stroked the silken rug, watching the soft pile change color with direction. Just as I was pondering this, the phone rang.

"Qanta, how's the packing going? When do you leave?" It was Randa, my friend who had taken me on the first circuits around the Ka'aba during Hajj.

"Hey Randa! I leave on Thursday night at two a.m. I only have a couple of days left, the containers are here, but you know what, Randa? I want to go to Mecca again. It would be great to perform Umrah at this point of change in my life. I wish I had planned it earlier."

"Why don't you call Saudia?" She was referring to the national airline in the Kingdom. "In fact, let me call my husband—he can probably help you get a return trip to Jeddah. You could leave tonight and come back in the morning. People do it all the time!"

I couldn't believe what I was hearing nor the timing of her call. Randa prattled on, reminding me her husband often did this trip on weekends.

At that moment, completely out of character, I stopped my organized preparations for departure and answered the powerful desire to return to Mecca.

Sure enough, in under half an hour I had a flight to Jeddah for midnight that evening. I would be back at 8 a.m. the next day with an entire day to pack. I still needed a way to get to Mecca from

Jeddah. I remembered Reem's open invitation to visit her family home in Jeddah.

"Reem, I am coming to Jeddah tonight. I want to make Umrah this evening! Can we go together? We always talked about this!"

"That's fantastic, Qanta! I will meet you in Jeddah at the airport. My driver can take us to the al-Haram Mosque. Mashallah, Qanta, this is a wonderful opportunity. Tonight is the night before Ramadan. It will be very auspicious for you on the threshold of a new life. I can't wait! I am so glad you asked me along." She sounded ecstatic.

I traveled to the airport a few hours later, feeling strangely free. All I had with me was my handbag because I needed no luggage at the House of God. I couldn't believe my luck nor the spontaneity of the opportunity. I felt carried on a current back to the epicenter of Islam. This was how I was supposed to leave this world, with a Divine blessing.

My memories of Hajj were still fresh, and I wondered how the short Umrah would feel in comparison. Unperturbed at my ignorance, I knew Reem would show me exactly what to do. I found my fears and apprehensions about resigning and leaving, my uncertainties about Imad, all flowing away. I knew I was on a trajectory prescribed for me by destiny. I busied myself preparing for my spontaneous journey.

After a short flight, I arrived in Jeddah. Even in late November the air was sodden with humidity from the Red Sea. Reem was waiting for me, standing outside the burgundy Cadillac that would take us to the Ka'aba. The fat American car glided along the highway, following exits marked for Muslims only.

We talked nonstop along the way until, spying the mountains that surround the holy city, we were lulled into silence. The night was beautiful, a low glow emanating from the Holy Mosque. I couldn't wait to see the Ka'aba again.

The driver parked the car in a multistory parking lot, and Reem and I strolled to the Grand Mosque. I was full of joy as I approached the huge marble forecourt. It was close to 2:30 a.m., but the mosque was illuminated as bright as day. Fellow worshipers sauntered to the entrance. There was an air of relaxation and joy about the Mosque. The fearful tension of Hajj, the feelings of reckoning that had accompanied that trip, were absent. This was a different experience altogether.

We crossed the enormous forecourt. Walking through one of the large gateways in the mosque, we were waved in by a sole veiled sentry. Beyond her I gazed on an unimpeded view of the Ka'aba.

It was there exactly as I had left it months earlier, still reverberating with an invisible, eternal energy. Suddenly massive in proximity, it surged with a palpable force. It had grown in size since my memory, calling me closer. I followed the call, unable to break my stare from the black and gold Kisweh that glowed in the night air. My face was already wide in a reflex smile that came from deep within my core. My joy spilled over into my happy, clumsy footsteps that hastily carried me further into the heart of Islam.

I was at home again.

Reem and I immediately went to the station of Abraham and proceeded to begin our seven counterclockwise circumnavigations of the Ka'aba. This time, unlike Hajj, we could do so on the ground level, rather than on the aerial roof. With so few people in the Mosque, we could approach the Ka'aba directly and walk immediately around its perimeter. We could even touch the walls of the house of God, walk next to it with none other separating us, but something about its sanctity was awesome. I wanted to see it from a slight distance, so that the whole was not obscured by my tiny view. I found myself unable to concentrate on my prayer book, the same one given me for Hajj by Nadir the Saudi surgeon.

Reem was praying aloud for both us from her extensive memo-rized knowledge of the Quran. I merely basked in the shadow of my Maker, unable to take my eyes from the place that represented my belief in Him. Just as at Hajj, I felt Him galloping toward me with outstretched arms. In a few short steps into the Haram I was ensconced, engulfed, and embraced by God. Gladness, light, and joy filled me from within.

Reem made sure to point out the Black Stone, the footprints of Abraham, and the details of the Kisweh to me. I was almost unable to hear her. I couldn't stop comparing my experiences at Hajj to my feelings now.

Where once I had been frightened and overwhelmed and awed by the House of God during the confusion and crush of Hajj, all was clarity.

Where once I had been restricted, confined, and pulled by the current of humanity at Hajj, I was unencumbered, liberated, light, and able to decide which directions I should take.

Where once I was astonished at my Maker's acceptance in the face of my shame, now I found my shame replaced with honor.

Where once I was uncertain, now I was secure.

Where once I felt alien, now I belonged.

The Umrah was a metaphor for my recent transitions. I had arrived in this Kingdom a stranger to Islam and I was leaving it as a citizen of my faith. In this Kingdom of extremes, in the sharp shadow of intolerant orthodoxy, I had pried open the seams of my faith and snatched the gemstone of belonging. Glittering and bril-liant, it was mine forever. Though I was soon to leave this extraor-dinary oyster-Kingdom and, at its core, the luminous pearl of Islam, I was taking something within me forever, something from which I could never be separated.

I took with me my place in my faith, my place as a Muslim.

Reem indicated we settle on a spot to pray. She chose a place directly opposite the Ka'aba. As I kneeled and prostrated along-side her, I found myself unable to bow my gaze. The hypnotic Ka'aba was too mesmerizing, too alive, too compelling. Constantly I lost my place in my repetitions. Finally I abandoned any attempts to pray conventionally.

My eye was drawn upward to the sky above, where angels circled the Throne of God. Sparrows circled the Ka'aba, strangely coun-terclockwise. I watched them unblinking. They were utterly free, happy in song, even at three a.m. I never saw a single bird fly across the Ka'aba or perch on its roof. They were engaged in their own tiny, pure worships. Like me, they were His creatures.

After a time I resumed prayer. With each prostration my bounding blood rushed to my head, beating in my ears. I felt myself heady on the wine of Divine love, almost completely forgetting the mantra of my prayers. Instead, I found myself communing with my Maker, in a language known only to my fluttering spirit. My soul pushed the very boundaries of my flesh, forward, forward, forward, trying to rejoin the essence from whence it had once come and to which it would surely one day return.

Afterwards, I sat and stared and stared at the Ka'aba. I viewed the beautiful blackness. It seemed to expand and shrink, as though a gentle, giant respiration or a heart pulsating with life. For me, Islam had changed from an abstract affiliation to a living organism, and I had experienced this transition against the backdrop of a desiccated desert Kingdom. In a Kingdom where, over centuries, culture had been distilled into salty, harsh, unyielding condensates, my senses had been sharpened and my drink of Islam made sweeter against the bitter aftertaste of extreme orthodoxy. Savoring the sweetness of epiphany, in sands bloodied with Wahabiism, my struggles were validated, worthy, and rewarded. I could not have accomplished this insight without experiencing the hardships of Kingdom life and the scars of my self-inflicted exile from Islam which was now ended.

I thought about all the people who had brought me to this point. My parents who gave me my faith and my education. My mentors, Americans who had trained me to a level where my skills had served the Kingdom dwellers. Many of my teachers I remembered were Jewish. In that too-short night, I realized that I had come to meet Allah through the efforts of dedicated Jews who had shared their knowledge and love with me. I prayed for them all and for each Muslim to whom they had led me.

Zubaidah's beaming smile came into view, morphing into Ghadah's impish Onassis grin. I saw Imad's clear eyes and patient, handsome brow. I remembered Mu'ayyad's rakish smirk and smiled in response. Dr. Fahad's fist of courage crumpling up faxes of fatwas returned to my memory, and Faris's gallant sadness and clumsy generosities touched me once again. In my mind's eye, I could see the warmth and elegance of Maha, her enormous bravery unique to those under life-long oppression, that dazzled alongside the quiet pathos and courage of Reem's silent loyalty beside me in this special moment.

I gave thanks for the humility and trust of my nameless, countless patients to whom I could never speak and prayed I might one day have a fraction of the dignity of Haneefa the Meccan maid who had memorized the Quran. As I sat and stared at the Ka'aba, Samha and Sabha, the Arabian horses who had kept my solitudes at bay, nuzzled my heart, injecting me with warmth. The tearful compassion of Hesham the bereaved father, the innocent death of his son whom I never knew, the wit and warmth of Fatima the hopeful divorcée, the defiance and courage of Manaal in the face of leering Muttawa, the simple kindness of Nadir the surgeon… the images were dissolving into one another.

The Kingdom of Strangers was disappearing. Instead, this country had opened its private sanctuaries to me, imbibing me inward until I was compelled to drink from its mysteries and finally unlock the secrets of Islam, which had eluded me until now. A journey that had begun as excluding and withholding and rejecting, had become inclusive and embracing and accepting. I had been improved, uplifted, and strengthened by my time among the Kingdom-dwellers. I was leaving them, altered as a woman, as a physician, and above all as a Muslim.

I thought and saw this and much more as I gazed upon the Ka'aba, wishing I would be allowed to return once more. At last, we had to leave, and with a final farewell as if to a beloved, I reluctantly tore myself away. Even with my back turned I could feel the Ka'aba breathing, beating, living. The compulsion to return was enormous, but this visit had reached its end. I left with head high, heart full, and hopes raised.

Completing our rituals, Reem suggested we eat. Buying a shwarma from a street vendor, we picnicked just outside the mosque, completing the last morsels of food just before the sounding of cannon that marked the beginning of the fast. Reem and I had shared an especially auspicious Umrah on this, the eve of Ramadan. We felt fortunate, privileged, and enormously blessed. Returning to the car, we raced away on the smooth, Cadillac glide. The sky was lightening. The flat roads carried us back to Jeddah and finally to the airport. After a very long hug that said more than any words ever could, I left Reem and returned to Riyadh. It was time to go.

Shipping containers packed, a small army of Filipino men arrived to take my things away. A Sudanese veterinarian came to retrieve Souhaa and ship her overseas to my next home. The apartment was quiet. All farewells had been said. I gazed out at the illuminated tennis courts, once my first view of a barren world that had gone on to yield such enormous fruit. I pulled on my French suit and quickly disguised it under my dying abbayah. I called Imran a final time, confirming I was ready.

"But I wish I had got to see Imad tonight," I mentioned plaintively.

"Call him, Qanta. Just dial the number. He can't call you anyway because you don't have a mobile. Maybe he is back from his meeting?" I looked at my watch. It was three hours before take-off.

"OK, let me try him." Dialing the familiar number, I waited for the phone to switch into voicemail.

"Allo?" Instead came Imad's voice.

"It's me. I didn't think you were around," I began.

"I am just about to take off from Jeddah, heading to Riyadh."

"Oh, what time do you get in?"

"One a.m."

"And I take off at two a.m. Let's meet at King Khalid," I found myself saying, suddenly excited.

"Yes, Qanta, let's do that. I'll be there. I'll look for you and we can talk until take-off. I have to go now." And with that he hung up. Filled with excitement at the prospect of a final romantic farewell at the airport, I ordered my ride out of the compound, my ride to my next life.

Arriving at the marble airport, I felt elated. Yes, I was sad to leave the exoticism behind. I wondered when I would smell the hybrid of heat and dust again, when I would hear the casual staccato Najdi Arabic again, when I would scurry around in an abbayah once more, when I would drink mint tea on a veranda behind high walls, or when I would ride horses who understood Arabic under the same starry skies that had bewitched Lawrence almost a hundred years earlier. Yes, I wondered when I would next have tickets to my Maker in my pocket. But I knew I would be back. I knew next time, no longer a stranger, I would be welcome.

Tonight I moved easily and without fear. But Imad was nowhere to be seen. I waited for what seemed too long, until finally I had to go through passport control. I searched the airport from the elevated departure area but couldn't spy the lone Saudi in khakis anywhere. I found myself heavy with disappointment. Hours later, connecting in London, I would learn in an email that he too had been searching for me.

I boarded the plane and settled into my seat. Like other women in the cabin, I tore off my abbayah and unceremoniously bundled it up in the overhead bin. Eventually, hours and continents later, I landed at Kennedy. I gathered my items, preparing to step out in the beloved city that was my cultural home. I decided to leave the abbayah in the cabin. I would never wear it again.

As I stepped over the raised threshold, the PA rang out with an announcement.

"The lady in seat 32A has forgotten her abbayah. Please return for it. We have it here for you."

Straightening the sleeves on my navy jacket, I glanced furtively around to see if anyone could tell the offender was me. After an imperceptible pause, I placed a stockinged, high-heeled foot outside of the cabin onto the gangway. The announcer was still appealing for the abbayah-wearer as I strode away. I couldn't help laughing out loud.

I was finally free.

RUGGED GLORY

Jane had just woken up from major surgery when the alarms rang out announcing a disaster. In the next hours, the same men who had chastised my sadness at 9/11 attended the 178 injured who presented to the National Guard Hospital in difficult, numbing hours. In the same ICU, they too were humbled, broken, and bowed by the terror. I didn't need to say anything. We all remembered. They finally felt the sadness too.

It was Mu'ayyad who had to identify the remains of his friends, including the son of the governor of Riyadh, killed in the May 2003 bombings perpetrated in Riyadh. He told me himself, in wheezy paragraphs interrupted by long drags on his Dunhills as we talked while he commuted home in his massive Benz. Now and again he stopped, placating a worsening smoker's cough. Mu'ayaad's voice descended to a croaky whisper as he described unzipping the

body bags and searching for the fragments of his childhood friendships within. Immediately after, he floored his monster sedan,
rushing to operate on some of the worst eye injuries and burns he
had seen in his storied career. Most of the patients were expatriates; many had been Americans. In true form, he worked without
respite for days, and I knew in this Mu'ayyad was bowed in a way
he couldn't have prepared for. I believe he now begins to understand the power of hate and through that knowledge he finally
attenuates his own hates. On the crackling speakerphone I could
hear a new vulnerability in his voice, one which is familiar to those
of us who have experienced New York, London, Bali, or Madrid.

On my most recent trip later in the decade, I stayed in a five-
star hotel, checked in under my own female name. I ate alone at
the Globe at the apex of the al-Faisaliyah Tower. The cityscape
unfurled below, flat save for the Mumlaqa, reminding me of a
misplaced Vegas. I stared into the glittering Saudi night and found
myself thinking of the elusive Prince al-Waleed. Doubtless he was
traveling these same skies, flown in private jets by the first Saudi
female pilot, Captain Hanadi Hindi.

Later, waiting to descend, an elevator door opened. A Saudi man
stepped aside for me to enter. I found myself transiently immobile
until I realized he was waiting for me. We shared the slim-line lift
until we reached our respective floors. There was no acrimony, no
contempt, only courtesy. During the same visit, when I entered a
lobby, another Saudi man held open the door, another first for me
in Riyadh. I began to find as a woman perhaps I wasn't as invisible
as I had felt years earlier.

Some days afterward, returning from Mecca in business class
on a Sunday morning, a Saudi passenger retrieved me a pillow.
Soon I found myself tucking his card into my handbag. The
charming man worked in Riyadh to uncover money laundering
cells, one of the millions of Saudis "on our side." He loved America,

having just moved from Boston. We connected, as Muslims, as American migrants, as people.

Unquestionably, Riyadh increasingly feels more relaxed than it did in the years immediately leading up to 9/11. Some of this is due to the increasing access to advanced communication, the new monarch, and the maturation of an intellectual elite that is gracefully pushing the envelope. Something unspoken is slowly easing. People are more confident, hopeful, and progressive. Voices are growing stronger, Mutawaeen perhaps weaker, women emboldened. Now and again, the old ways resurface in the shape of gang rapes and lashings, but instead it is Saudi citizens who call at once for human rights, not only the international watchdogs. Blogging in Arabic and English is burgeoning, unthinkable in the years I had lived there, inviting the opportunity for a collective, public introspection.

Today my friends continue their work inside the Kingdom and often carry their contributions with them to the wider world. We see the Saudi flag displayed at medical conferences in the United States. International collaboration is increasing, academic publications growing, clinical services expanding. Most importantly to me, the Holocaust denier now collaborates with a Jewish academic, his small mind finally widened by the generous experience of a patient American.

Of my Saudi love, all that remain are memories and fragments. Imad and I were never reunited after our foiled meeting at King Khalid International. He is now the father of two and in these intervening years has made a successful marriage of his endogamous betrothal. I feel both proud and poignant as I watch him enter the pressured role of Saudi fatherhood. He has melded happiness of a kind for himself in his country, still disguising his conflicts in a rebellion of Boss and Brioni.

Ghadah is already defending her PhD thesis. She made the local papers in England, where reporters wrote about (and photographed) the beautiful, married Saudi woman who was commuting from Riyadh to study among them. Back in Riyadh, she unfurls the tattered cutting for me to read as we sip coffee in her baroque living room. Her face is beaming with a rare pride and she giggles at her wondrous surgeon-husband who manages the children in Riyadh while she studies for two weeks out of every three, five thousand miles away. Cardiac surgery is less aging, he jokes, than playing Mr. Mom. The wide-eyed girls admire their mother even more. She has grown their world in the realization of her dreams.

And Ghadah is also a local force for feminism. The last time I saw her she had built her new house, which was scattered with her busy life amid the Lalique and Versace and Daum. She hosts lunch parties every weekend for her circle of young Saudi marrieds for whom she has become something of a figurehead. Even now she remains the most beautiful woman I know. It is heartening to know they have each other to exchange ideas, discuss politics, and even watch the national obsession—soccer.

Today Dr. Fahad advises the Monarch. He cultivates honey from his own hives and serves it to his guests for breakfast. I can confirm it is delicious. He also raises a beloved granddaughter, Lulu, who at three already has more motorized vehicles than her grandfather. At home he teaches her to swim. She is a brave paddler and an able tricyclist. She will grow into a feisty, enchanting woman, witty like her charming grandfather, but will certainly drive herself in her own car to more opportunity than her mother's generation could ever know.

Zubaidah is, like me, unmarried. This month she completed her Hajj. Zubaidah didn't wait to meet her Maker until after marriage. She moves at her own speed and her life is not arrested by a late marriage. She remains the consummate Muslim and a softly spoken, highly fragrant feminist. I miss her enormously.

Fatima remains a divorcée but still hopeful for love. Faris sends me pictures of his new wife. They smile into the sunlight, squinting atop a hill in Beirut. For the first time in years he looks really happy, and his marriage was to be extremely timely. A few months later his new bride would nurse him after a catastrophic illness. I spoke to her in my fractured Arabic until finally the nurse held the receiver for Faris. For a few sad minutes, I listened to his fluent English replaced by a dysphasic struggle to conquer speech made woolly with disease. Weakened, he is making a slow recovery and he worries to meet the responsibilities of his four unmarried children in this lifetime.

Reem never operated again, instead delivering three daughters. She bought her own house where she lives with her husband and her in-laws. When we talk of medicine she is wistful. I don't believe she will ever return to vascular surgery. I hope she is fulfilled even if her talents are not. She keeps her own counsel, but we both know she squandered her dreams. It makes us both sad.

And what of the Gloria Steinem? Only this morning Maha emailed me with details of the end of the ban on women's driving in the Kingdom. The day is nearing and who, we wondered at once, would teach all the women to drive? Often I imagine I would like nothing better than to drive myself right up to the House of God. Perhaps one day I will, and maybe Maha hopes for the same herself. She continues to be a force for change. Like all women who do this work everywhere in the world, she is not always popular and she is oftentimes alone, but I carry her in my thoughts always, as I know will each reader.

And so the stories continue. Perhaps the storyteller failed to meet her task with justice. No matter how deeply I connect, the Saudis remain enigmatic, their surface a brilliant veneer refractory to insight. And yet I have to admit, I still count the dichotomies: angry divorcées who dream of becoming second wives; conflicted

Saudi men who cannot forsake the expectations of powerful matri-archs; womanhood that is both oppressed and liberated by veiling; Saudi men who are feminists and Saudi grandmothers who prop-agate female suppression; and the women… the women!

It is the women who really opened the door to this society for me. Women who confided, women who guided, women who competed, women who disdained, women whom I attempted to heal and who in turn would heal me, women who were illiterate yet had memorized the Quran, women who could repair aneurysms but could not make a three-point turn, women who were objects of affection from even within their closeted veils.

It is these same women who hold the keys to change, through their daughters and their sons but most of all through themselves. It is the voices of these mothers, wives, sisters, aunts, and daugh-ters that we crave and their voices that narrow men fear. It is women's voices that are becoming audible, women's actions that are becoming visible, and through their actions, Saudi women who are daily becoming more powerful. Nothing is as fierce or imbued with goodness as the oppressed who have overcome their cowardly oppressor. It is these small women, scurrying around in their abbayahs, who will seize their justice from the jaws of extremists and wrest their new place beyond the gender apartheid which is still the Kingdom. The gender apartheid committed in the name of Islam is already dying, rasping its last, soured breaths.

And the other corners of silent observation that somehow speak volumes resound even now. The inscrutable prejudices that are dearly held in the face of rational logic; a firmly held, deep suspicion and simultaneous admiration of the West; a religious attachment to Americana and to the accoutrements of the Bedouin, whether a Dior ghutra or a Bedouin in a Detroit SUV; a rigid Islamic theocracy that cannot suppress the true beauty in Islam no matter how weighty the suffocation. Most touching:

the enormous resilience and tenderness that persists in the most unexpected places.

The Kingdom's ability to both infuriate and humble me at once is what I hold dearest, for it was that which I so needed until I could finally see what I had always possessed: a place in Islam no matter how displaced I had become. Inside the Kingdom there was and there remains a beauty in her harshness that stays with me even now. No amount of petrodollars or paneling or polish can conceal its rugged glory. It is for this that I thank the Kingdom, for this that I thank the Stranger I was once within it, and for this that I thank those of the Kingdom Dwellers who made me, and still make me, welcome.

Charleston, South Carolina, United States
January 29, 2008

ENDNOTES

[1] While Saudis never call themselves Wahabis, I use the term in the Western sense to identify the extremely orthodox, rigid, and regressive face of Islam. Wahabi implies a follower of Wahabiism and is a widely used term which can encompass several meanings. Wahabiism refers to the 18th century polemical teachings of Abdul Wahab (which were published in 1730 in his sole work Kitab-Ul-Tawhid, which translates as the Book of Monotheism). Abdul Wahab was a self-appointed Islamic "reformer" advocating a regressive version of Islam. Abdul Wahab denounced any interpretation or innovation as un-Islamic which is counter to the mainstream Muslims of many sects, instead promoting archaic rigidity which has been carried to a ridiculous extreme.

While the term Wahabiism is one first ascribed to the region by Western diplomacy in the 19th Century (first appearing in

1803), it has today become inextricably linked in Western literature to radical manifestations of enforced and compulsive indoctrination deemed by some elements to be Islam.

Saudis never call themselves Wahabis and never introduced themselves as such to me during my six years of living in or traveling to the Kingdom. In fact, they actually find the term offensive because the implication of following Abdul Wahab is suggested and worship of any intermediary between man and God is anathema to Muslims.

Famously one senior prince, Salman bin Abdul Aziz, the Governor of Riyadh, contemptuously referred in a 1998 speech to outside commentators as "those who call us Wahabi," implying a fundamental misunderstanding of Saudi Islam. Rather, Saudi Muslims are more likely to refer to themselves as Salfists or Salfiyuun which means followers of the Salafi, the original disciples of the Prophet Muhammad (PBUH), or Muwahhiddun, which means unitarian.

Throughout this book I chose to use Wahabi in the Western sense to identify the extremely orthodox and rigid regressive face of Islam which is a significant element of Kingdom life; and while not representative of *all* Saudis (perhaps even not representative of *most* Saudis), it is a reasonable lay-term to ascribe to much of the state sanctioned, legislated clerical policing of all religion in the Kingdom.

Readers are directed to more academic references for deeper insights listed in the bibliography, particularly to Pascal Ménoret's excellent *The Saudi Enigma*, for further clarification.

[2] *Feminism and Islam, Legal and Literary Perspectives* by Mai Yamani. In "Chapter 12: Some Observations on Women in Saudi Arabia," page 279 (263-281).

[3] Ibid.

4 *The Saudi Enigma* by Pascal Ménoret. In "Chapter 7: The Appearance of Women," page 183. Also *Changed Identities: The Challenge of the New Generation in Saudi Arabia* by Mai Yamani. Page 106.

5 *A Modern History of the Islamic World* by Reinhard Schulze. In "Chapter 5: 'Ascendancy of Islamic Ideologies 1973-89' The Crisis of Mecca," pages 226-229.

6 Ibid.

7 Sullivan, Kevin. "Saudi Youth Use Cellphone Savvy to Outwit the Sentries of Romance." *Washington Post Foreign Service*. August 6, 2006. Accessed February 24, 2008, at washington-post.com.

8 Shalhoub, Lulwa. "Women-Only Hospitals: Who Will Rule the Roost, Idealists or Pragmatists?" *Arab News*. February 1, 2008.

9 *Journal of Palliative Medicine 2006* Volume 9 Number 6 Hedayat, K, 1282-1291.

10 *Guests of God: Pilgrimage and Politics in the Islamic World* by Robert R Bianchi.

11 Ibid.

12 Ibid.

13 *Feminism and Islam, Legal and Literary Perspectives* by Mai Yamani. In "Chapter 12: Some Observations on Women in Saudi Arabia," page 279 (263-281).

14 *The Two Faces of Islam: Saudi Fundamentalism and Its Role in Terrorism* by Stephen Schwartz. In "Chapter 1: Snow in the Desert," Page 10.

15 *Pyramids and Nightclubs: A Travel Ethnography of Arab and Western Imaginations of Egypt, from King Tut and a colony of Atlantis to Rumors of Sex Orgies, Urban Legends about a Marauding Prince and Blond Belly Dancers* by L.L. Wynn.

16 Sardar, Ziauddin. "Islam: Enter a new, improved Saudi philanthropist." *The New Statesman*. July 24, 2006.

17 *The Saudi Enigma* by Pascal Ménoret. In "Chapter 3: Genesis and Structure of the Modern State."

18. *A Modern History of the Islamic World* by Reinhard Schulze.

19 al-Sanea, Rajaa. "My Saudi Valentine." *New York Times*. February 13, 2008.

20 Zawawi, Susan. "Red is Banned till Fri." *The Saudi Gazette*. February 11, 2008. Accessed February 24, 2008, at http://www.saudigazette.com.sa/index.php?option=com_content&task=view&id=46708&Itemid=1.

21 Qusti, Raid. "Coffee with Colleague Lands Woman in Trouble" *Arab News*. February 15, 2008. Accessed February 24, 2008, at http://www.arabnews.com.

22 Labi, Nadya. "Kingdom in the Closet." *The Atlantic Monthly*. May 2007.

23 *The Great Theft, Wrestling Islam from the Extremists*, by Khaled Abou El Fadl.

24 "Abusing the Concept of Blood Money." *Arab News*. November 30, 2007. Accessed February 24, 2008, at http://www.arabnews.com/services/email/email.asp?artid=104141&d=30&m=11&y=2007&hl=Abusing%20the%20Concept%20of%20Blood%20Money.

25 *The Saudi Enigma* by Pascal Ménoret. In "Chapter 3: Genesis and Structure of the Modern State."

26 *The Saudi Enigma* by Pascal Ménoret. In "Chapter 7: The Appearance of Women," pages 173-189.

27 http://www.islam-watch.org/AdrianMorgan/Women-Under-Islam2.htm.

28 *Feminism and Islam*, by Mai Yamani. In "Chapter 12: Women in Saudi Arabia," pages 263-281.

29 Kandela, Peter. "Egypt's Trade in Hymen Repair." *The Lancet*. 1996:347(9015):1615. Also Patterson-Brown, Sara. "Commentary: Education about the Hymen is Needed." *British Medical Journal*. 1998:316:461.

[30] ABC News "Saudi Arabia, Land of Shadowy Contrasts, A Rare Inside Look at Saudi Arabia," by Barbara Walters. March 29, 2002.

[31] Vuilliamy, Ed. "Breaking the Silence." *The Guardian*. October 5, 2005. Also Dr. Maha al-Muneef's Speech: "Gender Health from Violence to HIV: Women are Breaking the Silence" June 26, 2006, in Vienna, Austria.

[32] Vuilliamy, Ed. "Breaking the Silence." *The Guardian*. October 5, 2005.

[33] Qusti, Raid. "Cases of Child Abuse on the Rise." *Arab News*. July 19, 2006.

[34] *Pyramids and Nightclubs: A Travel Ethnography of Arab and Western Imaginations of Egypt, from King Tut and a Colony of Atlantis to Rumors of Sex Orgies, Urban Legends about a Marauding Prince and Blond Belly Dancers* by L.L. Wynn.

BIBLIOGRAPHY

Bailey, David A. and Tawadros, Gilane, eds. 2003. *Veil: Veiling Representation and Contemporary Art*. London: Institution of International Visual Arts.

Bianchi, Robert R. 2004. *Guests of God: Pilgrimage and Politics in the Islamic World*. Oxford: Oxford University Press.

El Fadl, Khaled Abou. 2005. *The Great Theft: Wrestling Islam from the Extremists*. San Francisco: Harper San Francisco.

Labi, Nadya. May 2007. "Kingdom in the Closet." *The Atlantic Monthly*.

Ménoret, Pascal. 2005. *The Saudi Enigma*. Beruit, Lebanon: World Book Publishing.

Schulze, Reinhard. 2000. *A Modern History of the Islamic World*. London: I.B Tauris and Co. Ltd.

Schwartz, Stephen. 2002. *The Two Faces of Islam*. New York: Doubleday.

Wynn, L.L. 2007. *Pyramids and Nightclubs*. Austin: University of Texas Press.

READING GROUP GUIDE

Saudi Arabia has been described as a schizophrenic state. What are the complexities of the society you can identify that are revealed in this book? Would you agree with this description?

Virginity has a medicolegal value in Islam, leading some women to seek hymen reconstruction out of desperation. Is such an intense value of chastity an alternate form of oppression?

While male supremacy is state legislated in the Kingdom, there are certain situations in which men are oppressed as well as women. What are the tools of this male oppression and how effective are they?

What might be some goals in terms of Saudi-U.S. relations? How can Saudi Arabia and the United States better understand each other?

The author repeatedly reminds readers of the compassion of the Islam religion. Can a mandated Islamic Theocracy truly be Islamic?

While some women reject or resent the veils they are forced to wear and customs they are forced to obey, others wholeheartedly embrace them. Why do you think they do this?

With so much social pressure to conform, it is no wonder so many do so. There are several people Qanta meets in Saudi Arabia who refuse to conform at enormous personal risk. What do you think gives them the courage to defy the rules and mores of their own government and society?

Have you ever personally encountered an injustice that horrified you, but you were afraid to speak out about it fearing of some kind of reprisal? If you had the courage to speak out about the injustice, what gave you that courage?

What do you think of the way Qanta prepared for this journey? Would you prepare differently? Do you think it would have dulled the shock if she had known more about the traditions, culture, and politics of Saudi Arabia before she left? Why or why not?

Early on in the book, Qanta wonders at the behavior of the boy struggling to make sure his mother's veil is kept on during her surgery, "Didn't he know God was Merciful, tolerant, and understanding and would never quibble over the wearing of a veil in such circumstances, or I doubted, any circumstances?" There are many examples throughout scriptures of all denominations of Gods acting in ways that cannot be described as merciful, tolerant, or understanding, and there are many people who don't feel this way about God. How do you think peoples' and cultures' ideas about Gods' personalities are shaped?

When Qanta boards the plane for Saudi Arabia, the pilot prays in Arabic, which strikes her as a noteworthy and soothing ritual. Does the United States have any rituals that might strike an outsider as odd, but may be soothing to Americans?

The author writes, "No central air, when it would be over 120°F in the summer? I wondered of the furnace of summer ahead." The author faces many challenges, both physical and mental, in this trip. Do you think the kinds of challenges faced by someone moving to a landscape and a culture entirely different than their own are something that we have the strength for throughout our lives? Or that it is something that we can only throw ourselves into with the energy and strength of youth?

On a daily basis, are there things you would rather not do in order to fit into society and not cause a fuss? Do you think these simple acts are as oppressive as those experienced by Saudi women?

In Saudi Arabia, it is very difficult to get to know your husband or wife before you are married. Not nearly as many people in the United States or countless other countries would make such a large commitment having never spent more than a few hours at a time with the other person. However, some Saudi marriages are successful, and very happy. How do you think so many Saudis can make these types of marriages work?

Some Saudis are so exasperated by the confinements of their home, that they choose to leave Saudi Arabia, even though all of their family and friends continue to reside in the Kingdom. What kind of personality do you think it would take to make such a dramatic step? Are you surprised more people don't do this, given the dramatic restrictions of life in Saudi Arabia?

The law in Saudi Arabia is remarkably harsh. Beheadings, lashings, and other brutal treatments are not uncommon outcomes of criminal trials. In contrast to most other countries, why do you think Saudi Arabia continues to adhere to these customs and traditions?

Qanta encounters many people with very literal interpretations of the Quran. What do you think about literal interpretations of religious texts? Do you feel it is possible to be faithful, while not following or believing in every tenet of your faith?

The Mutawaeen (the religious police) are a constant, and often terrifying, presence in this book. What do you think could motivate someone to so violently guard his faith?

The author has a very unique experience on 9/11 in Saudi Arabia. Why do you think so many Muslims expressed approval about 9/11? Was it just the brainwashing of their society, or was their reaction due to some deeper reasons?

The author has an amazing religious experience at Mecca. Have you ever gone on a religious pilgrimage, or encountered a deep symbol of a particular faith? What effect did that have on you?

ACKNOWLEDGMENTS

I HAVE BEEN READING BOOKS ALL my life but never until now understood how much work is required in the shape of truly inspired encouragement cosseting the author. All I had to do as a writer was "show up," whether in the Kingdom or at the laptop. For everyone else, this was the proverbial blood, sweat, and tears. For these selfless optimists and hope-mongerers, for these generous soulful supporters, for these sages ripe with wisdom, for these workers of magic and wordsmiths, for each of you, I offer my deepest gratitude. Without you, there would be no here.

For Wendy Lipkind, my dear, dear literary agent; from the first meeting you ensnared me, we were truly "bookends." It was in those stylish moments encapsulated in your smoky, sultry, so-good voice that I knew I was embarking on a new journey which will remain with me long after these words are forgotten. Your kindnesses unleashed the river within the writer, and (once un-dammed) its subsequent careful containment has fueled the turbulent adventure into the high-walled gorges of my memories. Thank you for the patient phone calls, the compassion, and all the cold dinners you endured during my monologues. Thank you, Wendy, for your goodness, for your grace, and, most of all, for your late mother's handbag to ward off my demons!

For Hillel Black, my chief literary editor at Sourcebooks, the kindest, most gracious, so generous Word-Meister, I have no words which could convey the gratitude I feel. Your voice is pure New York, your quips take no prisoners, but, for sure, in the meticulous resections of my flabby first offerings, I have to say, the surgery, "Dr." Black, if rather bloody, was a success. A writer couldn't ask for more than an editor of such honesty and God-given horse-sense. But it is the tinkering archeology of resurrecting memories into language at which you truly excel. I most treasure our private discoveries which you salvaged into the most surprising paragraphs. Thank you, Hillel, for your wisdom and substance. Above all, thank you for your boundless, wondrous curiosity.

Dominique Raccah at Sourcebooks, the pint-sized pistol of publishing, I thank most for the opportunity and the belief at a time when I lacked both. You heard the outcast concealed within and broadcast her voice. From the moment you spoke, in your raw, passionate, plain-speaking voice, I knew my book was home. What an amazing company you have created, where on my first visit every single employee stood up to greet me, shake my hand, and speak about my then book-in-utero. The enthusiasm and passion which infuses Sourcebooks from restroom to stockroom to boardroom, comes from the force within you. Thank you for breathing life into this book.

Also at Sourcebooks I thank Sarah Riley, Heather Moore, Tony Viardo, Christiaan Simmons, and Whitney Lehman. Thank you so much, each of you, for being the first encouraging contacts beyond my world of words. You gave the dream its first mantles of reality. On a chilly October day in Naperville it was the warmth and energy of your belief which made the book begin to feel real. Your spirits transformed mine, and in those short friendly moments I grew from a doctor fiddling around with stories into a writer with a readership. Thank you for then, thank you for now, and thank you for all that is to come.

To Ted Carmichael at Sourcebooks, for all your patient emails and edits, for your polite queries and tireless corrections, I thank you most. For the referencing and the footnotes, thank you, and please can you show me how to do that when we next meet? That you could read both my innumerable comments and Hillel's anguished writing straight from a nineteenth century prescription pad was truly heroic. What can I say, but "Holy Christ," Ted, thank you!

And to the unflappable Stephen O'Rear: enormous thanks for the meticulous, fastidious, and tireless reviewing, advice, and dedicated commitment to the production of this book. You handled my last-minute, strained, extremely under-the-wire insertions with poise and aplomb. If production editor doesn't work out, consider neurosurgery! Thank you, Stephen, more than ever on this, the final day of writing.

And last, but never least, to the beginning.

To my teacher, Miss Connolly (or "Bernadette," since I turned thirty). It began when you lent me *The Borrowers Afloat*. I was six, perhaps seven, when I decided to write a story inspired by that book. A generation ago, you carefully boxed the penciled, childish essay in your English attic. I still glimpse the memory of that story: longer than I was tall, lined paper pasted to purple backing which matched my velvet headband, the whole suspended high on the school notice board, all of it perched there by someone with long arms. I think it may have been you. It was with those brass drawing pins, you turned a small girl into a gap-toothed winner, a writer into someone who was read.

Thank you Bernadette for the first letters I learned. Thank you for the first books I read. Above all, thank you for the first invitation to write. You are my first agent, editor, publisher, and reader. You, my teacher, are my hero, I mean, "heroine," as you will surely correct, in your red-inked flourish.

ABOUT THE AUTHOR

TRAINED IN NEW YORK CITY, Dr. Ahmed is a board certified pulmonologist and sleep specialist. She is currently appointed an Assistant Professor of Medicine at the Medical University of South Carolina at Charleston, where she lives and practices.